Latinos and the Liberal City

POLITICS AND CULTURE IN MODERN AMERICA

Series Editors:
Margot Canaday, Glenda Gilmore, Matthew Lassiter, Stephen Pitti, Thomas J. Sugrue

Volumes in the series narrate and analyze political and social change in the
broadest dimensions from 1865 to the present, including ideas about the ways
people have sought and wielded power in the public sphere and the language
and institutions of politics at all levels—local, national, and transnational. The
series is motivated by a desire to reverse the fragmentation of modern U.S. history
and to encourage synthetic perspectives on social movements and the state, on
gender, race, and labor, and on intellectual history and popular culture.

CONTENTS

ABBREVIATIONS

AASF	Archives of the Archdiocese of San Francisco
ACWU	Alaska Cannery Workers Union
AFL	American Federation of Labor
ANMA	Asociación Nacional Mexico Americana
ASFBS	Archives of the San Francisco Board of Supervisors
BACABI	Bay Area Committee Against the Briggs Initiative
BAGL	Bay Area Gay Liberation
BANC	Bancroft Library, University of California, Berkeley
BAR	*Bay Area Reporter*
BART	Bay Area Rapid Transit
CALA	Centro Activista Latino Americano
CAP	Community Action Program
CBPOD	California Ballot Propositions Online Database
CCSS	Catholic Council for the Spanish Speaking
CCU	Council for Civic Unity
CDA	city demonstration agency
CIO	Congress of Industrial Organizations
CPWU	Cannery and Preserve Workers Union
CSO	Community Service Organization
CSS	Catholic Social Service
CUAP	Citizens United Against Poverty
CWU	Cannery Workers Union
El Congreso	Congress of Spanish Speaking Peoples
ED	*El Democrata*
EM	*El Mundo*
EOC	Economic Opportunity Council
ET	*El Tecolote*
FEP	fair employment practices
FEPC	Fair Employment Practices Commission

FRP	Family Rehabilitation Program
GALA	Gay Latino Alliance
GLBTHS	Gay, Lesbian, Bisexual, and Transgender Historical Society of Northern California
GMCC	Greater Mission Citizens Council
HA	*Hispano América*
HRSG	Housing Rights Study Group
HUD	U.S. Department of Housing and Urban Development
IHRC	Immigration History Research Center, University of Minnesota, Minneapolis
IISF	International Institute of San Francisco
ILA	International Longshoremen's Association
ILGWU	International Ladies' Garment Workers Union
ILWU	International Longshoremen's and Warehousemen's Union
LaC	*La Crónica*
LAPV	Lesbians Against Police Violence
LARC	Labor Archives and Research Center, San Francisco State University
LaREAL	La Raza En Acción Local
LAT	*Los Angeles Times*
LATA	Latin American Teachers Association
LC	*Labor Clarion*
LGA	Lesbian and Gay Action
LH	*Labor Herald*
LO	*Lucha Obrera*
LSDC	Los Siete Defense Committee
LULAC	League of United Latin American Citizens
MAC	Mission Anti-Displacement Coalition
MACAB	Mission Area Community Action Board
MACAP	Mission Area Community Action Program
MAOC	Mission Area Organization Committee
MAPA	Mexican American Political Association
MCO	Mission Coalition Organization
MCOR	Mission Council on Redevelopment
MCS	Marine Cooks and Stewards Union
MDC	Mission Defense Committee
MDRC	Mission District Renewal Commission
MFC	Movimiento Familiar Cristiano

MFP	Maritime Federation of the Pacific
MMA	Mission Merchants Association
MMNC	Mission Model Neighborhood Corporation
MNC	Mission Neighborhood Centers
MPC	Mission Planning Council
MWIU	Marine Workers International Union
NAACP	National Association for the Advancement of Colored People
NARA	National Archives and Records Administration
NIRA	National Industrial Recovery Act
NNM	*New Nueva Mission*
NYT	*New York Times*
OBECA	Organization for Business, Education and Community Advancement
PAC	political action committee
PAT	Parents and Taxpayers
PHA	Public Housing Authority
PRWO	Puerto Rican Women's Organization
RM	*La Razón Mestiza*
RMPT	Responsible Merchants, Property Owners and Tenants
SCSU	Special Collections, Stanford University
SFAH	San Franciscans for Affordable Housing
SFBPD	San Francisco Ballot Propositions Database
SFC	*San Francisco Chronicle*
SFCFEPO	San Francisco Committee for a Fair Employment Practices Ordinance
SFCIO	San Francisco Congress of Industrial Organizations
SFCOPE	San Francisco Committee on Political Education
SFCSRA	San Francisco Committee to Stop the Redevelopment Agency
SFDE	San Franciscans for District Elections
SFE	*San Francisco Examiner*
SFFL	San Francisco Fairness League
SFHC	San Francisco Housing Coalition
SFILGWU	San Francisco Joint ILGWU Board
SFLC	San Francisco Labor Council
SFP	*San Francisco Progress*
SFPL	San Francisco Public Library
SFPWD	San Francisco Public Welfare Department

SFRA	San Francisco Redevelopment Agency
SFSHP	San Franciscans for Sensible Housing Policy
SPUR	San Francisco Planning and Urban Renewal Association
SSCF	Spanish Speaking Citizens Foundation
SSU	Ship Scalers Union
SWOC	Steel Workers Organizing Committee
TUUL	Trade Union Unity League
TWW	*The Waterfront Worker*
UCAPAWA	United Cannery, Agricultural, Packing, and Allied Workers of America
UFW	United Furniture Workers of America
ULAA	United Latin Americans of America
WW	*Western Worker*

Latinos, Liberalism, Latinidad

Richard Camplís, Pete Garcia, and their friends in San Francisco's Ship Scalers Union struck out on a radical course in October 1940: they refrained from endorsing Franklin D. Roosevelt's bid for a third term as president. The six-year-old organization represented men who cleaned and conditioned ships on city wharves, and many of its members were Latinos. Scalers' moxie, their immersion in waterfront activism, and New Deal labor legislation coalesced in the mid-1930s and contributed to the union's growth. In 1936, the scalers had joined the left-liberal coalition that kept Roosevelt in the White House; they now chose to withhold their support. Camplís and his colleagues had by no means turned away from the New Deal or lost admiration for the sitting president. Instead, they feared that some in the liberal establishment were retreating from the government agenda or selectively choosing which segments of the working class deserved federal protection. The men's ire in 1940 specifically stemmed from the managerial machinations at American President Lines, which had recently come under state control. Scalers found it appalling that "a Company which [was] over 90% government owned, and headed by an appointed representative of President Roosevelt, [sought] to violate the Wagner Act" by refusing to engage in collective bargaining and pursuing "court injunctions against [their] bona-fide picket lines."[1] The decision to abstain from endorsing FDR became, at first glance, a means to protest and garner public attention. Below the surface, though, it conveyed at least two other political messages. Scalers made clear they were not blind, uncritical devotees of the Democratic Party. These unskilled, marginal, and nonwhite workers expected the same treatment—and rights—as their skilled, better-known, and white counterparts.

Thirty-eight years later, Rosario Anaya and Roberto Lemus stood before allied crowds, one at San Francisco State University and another at the city's Civic Center, and proclaimed the rights of all people to labor and exercise their vocations in workplaces free of harassment, irrespective of sexual identity. Sharing the stage with such political luminaries as Willie Brown and Harvey Milk, the two education professionals denounced the Briggs Initiative, a statewide proposition aiming to ban gay educators from public schools. Neither Anaya nor Lemus belonged to the Gay Latino Alliance or any other gay rights organizations. Anaya directed a language and vocational school serving Latino adults and sat on the city's school board. Lemus spoke for the Latin American Teachers Association, one of the groups sponsoring the human justice rally at the Civic Center. Alongside local and statewide teachers' unions, Lemus and his colleagues warned that the initiative would harm all educators. Its passage would legalize discrimination, punish school workers who discussed homosexuality in positive terms, and set a precedent for circumventing union rights. Anaya echoed many of Lemus's sentiments. She emphasized that "guaranteeing a healthy educational environment" could and should be done without reverting to prejudice. Going further, Anaya cast opposition to the measure as a matter of human rights. The state and its institutions had a responsibility to promote humanity and well-being, she implied, rather than impose moral codes built on bigotry and exclusion.[2]

Occurring at the temporal poles of what historians have identified as the "New Deal order" and America's "liberal universe," these two vignettes illuminate unexplored, and perhaps surprising, layers of Latino political history.[3] The scalers lived in the West's quintessential metropolis and formed part of an urban industrial workforce. Their triumphs and losses, decades of uninterrupted action, and connections to the city's progressive labor movement distinguished them from the rural proletariat of the mid-twentieth century. Yet with few exceptions, urban Latino laborers in California have escaped the purview of historians, who have overwhelmingly focused on, or are at least knowledgeable about, agricultural workers.[4] The linkage between California farm labor and Latinos—specifically ethnic Mexicans—is strong. Scholars and history enthusiasts alike are sometimes astonished to learn that San Francisco's Latinos toiled in varied arenas except agricultural fields. From a different perspective, educational activism among Latinos has steadily captured attention. Historians have done well to address questions of segregation, curricular reform, and bilingual education.[5] The par-

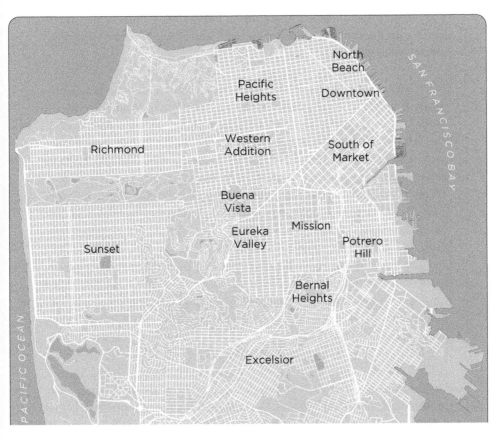

Map 1. Selected neighborhoods of San Francisco. Design by Michael Webster.
Courtesy of San Francisco Planning Department.

ticipation of Lemus, Anaya, and their colleagues in the anti–Briggs Initiative campaign demonstrated how they—as educators and citizens—were not consumed only with issues immediately classified as Latino causes. Gay-identified Latinos of course grasped the proposition's stakes and organized against it. Their work and heterosexual Latinos' support exposed nuanced and flexible meditations on rights, morality, and coalition building, which historians have not yet analyzed. Together, these two sketches reveal Latino politics as more intricate and less predictable than we currently appreciate.

Both stories make another thing clear: Latinos have preoccupied themselves with the workings, possibilities, and limitations of American liberalism for quite some time.

In the early twenty-first century, journalists, pundits, and social scientists regularly weigh in on the potency of Latinos' liberal orientations, their loyalty to the Democratic Party, and the significance of their electoral participation. The "Latino vote" has become a mantra in the media, and its invocation is particularly common during presidential election cycles. "Latinos are more likely than other Americans to say they're liberal," reported an online publication in 2012, relying on poll findings released by the Pew Research Center. Analysts at that think tank later compared data from 2012 and 2016 and found that party affiliation among Latino registered voters remained relatively unchanged. Approximately two-thirds of those surveyed, 70 percent and 64 percent, respectively, identified with or leaned toward the Democratic Party. This identification or inclination did not necessarily translate into a wholesale embrace of Democratic policies or candidates, however, a fact acknowledged by researchers and commentators alike. How many Latinos would actually vote in the forthcoming election, Pew experts noted in October 2016, remained to be seen. Many months earlier, Roberto Suro, a public policy professor writing for the *New York Times*, had reproached Latinos' "lackadaisical approach to civic engagement" as evidenced by lower voter turnout than whites and African Americans. "Whatever happened to Latino political power?" Suro wondered. Brooding over an aspiration yet to be realized, he suggested that the influence that ultimately matters had to be displayed on the national stage.[6]

These present-day discussions of Latinos in the political arena are informative and thought provoking. Presidential elections obviously have significant repercussions. A healthy and inclusive democracy demands that Latinos and all citizens be motivated and allowed to vote. Recent surveys and reflections on Latino political life should also inspire us to scrutinize the deeper historical production of political subjectivities and the process of civic participation. Determining why Latinos vote, or not, necessitates a probing of dispositions, conditions, institutions, and movements that have inspired or hindered electoral participation—past and present. That undertaking is best accomplished by considering local contexts and dynamics, which have tended to color the kinds of civic life people see as possible and their connections to regional and national polities. Attending to political potential at the national level, including its prospects and roadblocks, should transpire alongside analyses of how clout is—and has been—acquired, exerted, and lost locally. At the same time, it behooves us to approach Latino political action expansively, across a wide ideological spectrum, while uncovering its historical roots; the pursuit of power and representation, after all, has been carried out in manifold ways for specific goals and been dependent on historical exigencies.

Contemporary deliberations on Latinos as liberals or as liberal leaning raise a number of fundamental questions: How and why did this orientation take hold? What has this political inclination meant exactly and how has it unfolded over time? If current projections hold true, Latinos' political proclivities will prove critical for the future of liberal—or perhaps conservative—America. Such prognostications should not preclude investigations of Latinos' past roles in grappling with liberal worldviews and agendas—not as a theoretical enterprise per se but as political practice grounded in lived experience. Demographic forecasts, in fact, make historical inquiry more imperative. Ascertaining why Latinos gravitated to American liberalism, how they challenged and reformulated it, and what demands and concessions they have made along the way exposes the potency and malleability of this ideology in Latino life while illuminating its endurance.

A liberal city par excellence, San Francisco offers an optimal setting for a historical investigation of Latino political life. Its ethnoracial profile has belied the white-black binary since its founding, and the city has housed a motley Latino population since the Gold Rush era. By the early twentieth century, residents of Latin American ancestry traced their heritage to nations including Mexico, Puerto Rico, Nicaragua, El Salvador, Chile, and Peru.[7] Politically, San Francisco's dynamic history of organizing, civic action, and dissent has marked it as a progressive metropolis. This legacy of activism has seminal roots in the Big Strike of 1934: a maritime work stoppage that morphed into a general strike and transformed the citizenry's relationship to the polity.[8] The ramifications of this political saga proved particularly critical for workers, immigrants, and nonwhites. Though standing at the intersection of these social categories, Latinos' involvement in the 1934 uprising has rarely been considered. The significance of the Big Strike has itself become eclipsed by scholarly attention to, and popular fascination with, the 1960s counterculture and the city's sexual revolution.[9] What many students, tourists, and the general public today identify as liberal about San Francisco (its celebration of

cultural nonconformity and sexual diversity) owes much to the ascendancy
of multiculturalism and the tempering of an older tenet of liberalism, what
legal scholar Reuel Schiller calls "economic egalitarianism," dominant for
some decades after the Big Strike.[10] Notably, whether approached from the
1930s or the 1960s, Latinos remain relegated to the sidelines of San Francisco's political history. We are thus left with a portrait of a population residing
in one of this country's most liberal metropolises yet insulated from, unin-
volved in, and unconcerned with its political affairs.

Latinos and the Liberal City challenges this scholarly and popular perception by placing Latinos at the center of the story. Bounded by the labor up-
heavals of the 1930s and the cultural battles of the 1970s, it elucidates how and
why Latinos became politically engaged and how their civic energies evolved
and diversified over time. It attends to the workings of Latino political action
in response to the quotidian conditions of their American lives—in contrast
to a preoccupation with the affairs of the Latin American nations that shaped
their historical and cultural identities. In some critical ways, the inquiry parallels recent scholarship in U.S. Latino/a history, especially historian Lorrin
Thomas's analysis of Puerto Ricans' political identities and aspirations in
twentieth-century New York City. It departs from the bulk of historical research on Latinos by unraveling how a heterogeneous population—of diverse
national origins—emerged as political subjects and crystallized into a political
community. Anthropologist Steven Gregory's treatment of community is particularly useful here. The concept is best conceived analytically, Gregory explains, as "a power-laden field of social relations whose meanings, structures,
and frontiers are continually produced, contested, and reworked in relation to
a complex range of sociopolitical attachments and antagonisms."[11] To identify
Latinos as a political community, then, demands a recognition that their efforts were not marked by invariability, absence of conflict, or uniformity of
thought and approach. The array of political work covered in this study
evinced just the opposite: change and adaptation, discord, and a multiplicity
of interests, strategies, and philosophies.

At its core, this book excavates the ambitions and struggles that propelled
Latinos to immerse themselves in public deliberations about power, rights,
representation, and policymaking. Spanning five decades and ranging from
formal interaction with the state to communal disputes involving sexuality,
its thematic scope is broad. It brings together unionization efforts; civil rights
organizing; electoral politics; mobilizations during the Great Society; and
feminist, gay, and lesbian activism. Essentially an analysis of Latino political

life, the account aligns with a scholarly tradition that historians Meg Jacobs and Julian Zelizer classify as sociocultural political history. This approach acknowledges the importance of non-elite groups and the grassroots in shaping government policy, electoral outcomes, social movements, and other facets of the polity and civic life. Latinos and other ordinary people in San Francisco did just that by participating in campaigns, initiatives, and debates concerning labor and civil rights; poverty and economic opportunity; urban renewal and gentrification; and gender relations, sex education, and homosexuality. In so doing, they embroiled themselves in the many "hard fought contests" that unfolded in the city.[12]

This study makes clear that San Francisco's public sphere nurtured Latinos' political subjectivities and that their politicization contributed to the vibrancy of local political culture. It is at once a history of Latinos and the city itself—as a social terrain of political possibilities, experimentation, and strife. As much of the discussion in ensuing chapters will show, Latinos' ambitions and mobilizations regularly materialized in collaboration or friction with coworkers, neighbors, politicians, and other authorities. Latinos were neither disconnected from the public sphere nor from other San Franciscans.

The city's topography notwithstanding, San Francisco has exhibited and experienced its share of unique characteristics and developments. It certainly is not representative of other U.S. cities; it has not been an anomalous place in urban America either. Historians Robert W. Cherny and William Issel have recently challenged us to interrogate exceptional and mythical narratives about San Francisco. Its actual history, asserts Issel, has been "complicated and closer to the American mainstream."[13] The task taken up here is to consider how layers of distinctiveness interfaced with and fit within broader trends and the course of American political history—while assigning Latinos an active role in sustaining and challenging the liberal contours of this metropolis.

Latinos and the Liberal City advances this central argument: though Latino political life has long been marked by diversity and contestation, it consistently involved and reckoned with the ideological denominators of liberalism and latinidad. American liberalism as understood in the twentieth century refers to a philosophy broadly sustained by principles of activist government, social reform, freedom, and progress.[14] Latinos evinced an ongoing engagement with liberalism from the Great Depression era to the late postwar period, one that generated multiple perspectives on state action, race, and culture. The contention here is not that all Latinos became liberals or identified as such. Rather, their political subjectivities in the twentieth-century city cannot be understood or extricated from attention to liberal ideas, policies, and undertakings. This engagement with liberalism contributed to the construction—and eventually the fissures—of latinidad, an ideology emphasizing unity, commonality, and affinity among Latinos.[15] Largely nourished by the liberal promise of the early postwar years, latinidad met challenges in the late 1960s and 1970s—begot in part by the shortcomings of liberalism itself. Stumbling blocks did not mean the framework became irrelevant or disposable. In fact, some reformulations of latinidad proceeded alongside expanded understandings of liberalism—furthering the linkage between the two credos.

Liberalism as a political ideology has fundamentally influenced currents in U.S. politics, the state's functions, and conceptions of citizenship since the New Deal era. Scholars studying varied regions, epochs, and communities have been careful to tease out its multiple meanings, contradictions, and "protean character." As historian Gary Gerstle reminds us, "Liberalism in twentieth-century America has emerged as a variable, somewhat tractable, political philosophy." Its versatility exhibited itself in deliberations and policies involving government interference in economic affairs, the range of state-sponsored social welfare, ways to balance individual freedoms vis-à-vis group rights, and the course of social relations in a multicultural nation. Liberalism's capaciousness was not preordained, automatic, or undisputed, which makes it imperative to track the detours and contexts shaping its "shifting definitions."[16]

Historical studies of American politics and Latino life have yet to comprehensively account for Latinos' preoccupations with liberalism.[17] This book takes up this task while braiding the politicization of Latinos into the mainstream of American life. By moving from the 1930s onward and situating Latinos within the New Deal coalition, the analysis departs from assumptions that Latinos were latecomers to the liberal project or merely one community whose identity politics provoked the dissolution of that foundational electoral alliance in the 1960s.[18] Applying liberalism as an interpretive thread makes it possible to map and comprehend the continuities, alterations, and disruptions in Latino political life; in effect, it serves as connective tissue across historical eras. This design offers a dynamic means to discern Latinos' diverse aspirations and priorities, their varied articulations of citizenship, and their evolving sense of rights.

In San Francisco, Latinos wrestled with at least four variants of liberalism. In the 1930s, they began a protracted investment with New Deal liberalism, which centered on the regulation of capitalism and the expansion and protection of labor rights.[19] Labor unions transformed working-class Latinos into political actors as New Deal legislation emanated from Washington; the Ship Scalers Union and its counterparts would function as the most prominent sites of Latino activism and agency for at least two decades. Through multiple layers of political work, Latinos became connected to and supportive of a liberal vision of the state: an activist government that endorsed workers' rights, promoted economic security, and held the potential to advance equality and opportunity for all Americans.

As Latinos expanded drives for economic stability and fairness, they set out to outlaw racial discrimination. Historians generally agree that the New Deal state prioritized class-based questions over racial matters. Latinos and other nonwhite workers rarely made a neat distinction between economic and racial inequities; many envisioned and called for a governmental attack on racial injustice before politicians and policymakers did so. But civil rights liberalism, with its emphasis on racial equality and equal opportunity, would not become ascendant until the 1940s and 1950s.[20] Local governments took the lead in translating this variant of liberalism into policy after World War II. They typically did so in response to grassroots advocacy and agitation.

In 1957, San Francisco became the first major city in California to pass a fair employment practices (FEP) ordinance. A local civil rights coalition had been pushing for it for more than a decade. Latinos formed part of that alliance and were regularly drawn into it by their unions. While conventional narratives of postwar civil rights efforts cast Latinos as building on African American activism and embarking on campaigns for racial justice from the 1960s forward, *Latinos and the Liberal City* demonstrates otherwise. Latino San Franciscans had mobilized for civil rights alongside African Americans, Asian Americans, and white allies for some time. Any discussion of political piggybacking must consider how some Latinos living in the 1960s and after likely found inspiration in the activities of their ethnoracial predecessors, who had clung to the tenets of civil rights liberalism decades earlier.

Latinos' engagement with liberalism was neither monolithic nor static. Their course of political action exhibited manifold, evolving, and sometimes opposing visions for tackling the challenges in urban life. Some Latinos embraced liberalism, or least some of its strands. Others interrogated the ideology or rejected it altogether.

In the 1950s, as the labor movement experienced mounting obstacles, civic-minded Latinos—largely middle class and presenting themselves as patriotic and respectable—started to draft an ethnic-based agenda centered on greater access to social services, an enhancement of family life, and cultural assimilation. Exhibiting great faith in liberalism, they identified government authorities as partners in their work and soon lobbied for state aid, which they argued would boost Latinos' socioeconomic standing. Working-class residents gradually joined them at mid-century and especially in the 1960s, when they gravitated to Great Society liberalism—a variant stressing increased commitment to social welfare and governmental assistance to low-income and minority communities.[21] As the War on Poverty got under way, the liberal state came to legitimize the existence of a Latino community—regularly referred to as the Spanish-speaking population—in need of governmental assistance akin to African Americans.

Neither the promise nor the workings of liberalism went unchallenged. By the late 1960s, a younger generation of Latinos—radicalized by the antiwar and Third World liberation movements—chastised those who supported, or entangled themselves with, the American state. Latino radicals involved in various youth organizations believed that the government itself was an apparatus of economic inequality and racial oppression. Resembling the trajectory of African Americans in such cities as Philadelphia, Latinos who expressed "optimism [in] mid-century American liberalism" now met a protest movement against it.[22]

Communal disagreement over the merits and shortcomings of Great Society liberalism proceeded as Latinos confronted the cultural politics of gender, family, and sexuality. Living in a city where the sexual revolution occurred with great force led Latinos to multiple positions. Some affirmed a culturally conservative ethos or simply observed with fascination. Others promoted cultural liberalism or at least backed portions of a culturally liberal project from a distance. Those who sided with cultural conservatism emphasized traditional and fixed notions of male authority, female dependence, heterosexuality, and religious morality. Feminists, gay men, and lesbians upended this worldview. They politicized women's inequality, reproductive issues, sex education, and homosexuality and advocated cultural liberalism, a variant championing gender equity, sexual freedom, and respect for cultural difference.[23] Drawing on liberal ideas of equality, freedom, and opportunity, their approaches underscored openness and flexibility regarding gender roles, sexual identity, and sexual autonomy. Adherents of traditional culture and morality often ignored or derided feminist aims and calls for sexual liberation. But they by no means represented all non–feminist identified or heterosexual Latinos.

A gamut of perspectives on gender and sexuality became most evident when "intimate matters" intersected with public policy.[24] Latinos' long-standing support for civil rights liberalism could and did temper some culturally conservative outlooks. *Latinos and the Liberal City* at once shows that not all Latinos were culturally conservative and that those who were sometimes accommodated to a larger liberal project built on notions of equity, freedom, and nondiscrimination. By and large, a culturally liberal ethos did not propel Latinos to retreat from liberalism as a whole, even if they frowned upon some of its strands or proved unwilling to reconsider some contours of latinidad.

Latinidad as a political credo, like liberalism, demands some elaboration. Social scientists and cultural studies scholars have spent much time reflecting on the term's meaning, usefulness, and pitfalls. It has been variously defined as a pan-ethnic identity or consciousness, the sociohistorical process through which that identity is constructed, and its mobilization vis-à-vis social movements.[25] *Latinos and the Liberal City* relies on all these scholarly treatments; it primarily approaches latinidad as an ideology: a set of ideas deployed for political purposes, in certain moments or epochs, and never quite settled or permanently actualized. Political scientist Cristina Beltrán explains that "the political logic of *Latinidad*" rests on underscoring Latino unity.[26] Indeed, unity together with commonality and affinity have functioned as its most salient tenets. The unification of Latinos has been considered possible owing to shared cultural characteristics and deemed imperative because of their socioeconomic parallelism. Oft-cited elements of commonality include linguistic ties, religion, devotion to family, and geographic origins in Latin America. Latinos' affinity—their connection or resemblance—is and has been thought to develop from processes and experiences of racialization, cultural chauvinism, economic inequity, and political marginalization. Together, commonality and affinity theoretically present the building blocks for solidarity. Achieving that unity in practice—on the ground—has often proven difficult and ephemeral for myriad reasons, including Latinos' varying attachments to liberalism.

Historians have devoted little attention to latinidad. Their investigations of Latino life have typically focused on individual ethnic or national origin communities (e.g., Mexican Americans/Chicanos, Puerto Ricans).[27] Part of the logic undergirding these scholarly approaches has been simple: few U.S. localities housed Latinos of multiple national origins until the late twentieth century. San Francisco, as *Latinos and the Liberal City* makes manifest, was one of them, making it possible to historicize the rationale, utility, and fragmentation of a pan-ethnic creed.

Latinidad was neither predestined nor imposed from outside Latinos' own social world. Vestiges of a proto-latinidad surfaced fleetingly in the third quarter of the nineteenth century; these did not crystallize into a political outlook in part because of population decline and expulsion from San Francisco. In the early twentieth-century city, Latinos once again encountered preliminary, albeit more sustained, invocations of latinidad. The Spanish-language press operated as the key institution engrossed in political education and community defense at this time. In the 1920s, journalists began to lay the foundations of latinidad by linking Latinos' cultural and historical ties with their material conditions and political interests locally. It was a nascent undertaking, and gained little traction in the 1930s and 1940s. Discussions and recognition of parallel lived experiences still occurred within the ranks of the labor movement, even though these did not orient Latinos to a pan-ethnic framework. Latinidad's import was by no means a foregone conclusion in 1945 or 1950. Yet some of its components—commonality and affinity—had circulated in varying degrees by the time the ideology acquired prominence at mid-century.

The political force of latinidad, starting in the early 1960s, depended on a confluence of factors. Population growth and continued diversification proved to be just one of them; after all, the city's Latinos had been ethnically heterogeneous for some time. Latinidad flourished at this particular moment as a result of postwar constraints on class-based analyses to explain social relations, decreased levels of unionization, an upswing in ethnic-based organizing, and the evolution of liberalism itself. At mid-century, burgeoning governmental attention to the plight of racial minorities encouraged Latinos' identification as a people with shared cultural characteristics and collective socioeconomic interests. Activists, community leaders, and politicians all turned to latinidad, which allowed them to represent—and attempt to mobilize—Latinos as one community, a political constituency, and an ethnic bloc.

Its gravity was not instantaneous, wholesale, or uncontested. The promotion of latinidad spawned discord by the late 1960s. Some activists and organizations questioned its logic and the usefulness of prioritizing Latinos' plight over that of other residents who faced similar life challenges. They therefore worked to deemphasize the specificity of Latino interests in favor of class-based agendas. Others sought to redefine some cultural contours of latinidad, especially those involving gender relations and sexual life. Feminists, gay men, and lesbians embraced the project of unity and claimed a place in the Latino community. Yet they insisted that Latino solidarity should not be predicated on male authority and heterosexuality. These activist cohorts offered but two alternatives to the architecture of latinidad and its interplay with liberalism. These two ideologies, as this book demonstrates, produced bonds *and* ruptures among Latinos as they deliberated on the parameters of state intervention, the primacy of ethnoracial alliance, and the cultural ties that bound them.

This book applies the term *Latino* in four ways. At a descriptive level, it serves as a broad, shorthand way to label and refer to residents of Latin American descent and Spanish-speaking heritage. The heterogeneity of San Francisco's Latino population demands a blanket term in a study of this size; it would be narratively taxing to spell out "Mexicans, Puerto Ricans, Nicaraguans, Salvadorans, Chileans, and Peruvians," as one example, in every third or fourth sentence. This does not mean individual ethnic identities or national origins are inconsequential; their deployment and relevance are discussed whenever these proved meaningful. In our present day, *Latino* has acquired the sociopolitical currency and, to some extent, equivalency that labels like Spanish American, Latin, Latin American, or the Spanish Speaking had in earlier epochs. It is therefore used synonymously with terms that are now outmoded or employed less frequently.

Latino and its precursors did not operate simply as markers of ethnicity; they were also racial categories. Historian Mae M. Ngai has shown how Asian- and Mexican-origin peoples' ethnic and racial categorization became intertwined in the early twentieth century, in contrast to populations of European descent who experienced a decoupling of ethnicity from race.[28] The terms *Mexican* and *Chinese* specifically, and *Latin American* and *Asian* more broadly, thus came to function as ethnoracial markers. Treating *Latino* as an ethnoracial category makes it possible to track Latinos' standing in the racial order and how that location molded their lived experiences and, in turn, their political activism. Lastly, this academic enterprise takes some cues from literary scholar Raúl Coronado who applies *Latino* in anticipation of its future use. His recent analysis of nineteenth-century Latino writing and print culture relies on the term to approach a literary and intellectual culture with a "non-national specificity."[29] This orientation is useful for a study of political efforts and visions organized around lived experiences in San Francisco rather than national attachments, Latin American political projects, or longings for a homeland left behind.

Latinos is linguistically gendered and an imperfect way to classify a population composed of women, men, and individuals who may have identified otherwise. In recent years, scholars in Latino/a Studies, especially those in literary and cultural studies, have taken up such terms as *Latino/a, Latin@,* and *Latinx* to gesture toward gender inclusivity and fluidity. This book acknowledges the significance of gender in everyday life and political culture. Those sections addressing specific gendered experiences will differentiate between Latinas and Latino men. The bulk of archival sources consulted for this work did not identify transgender or gender-variant persons; the limitations presented by the archives and the research method should by no means lead us to conclude that these individuals were nonexistent in Latino life.

The generic *Latinos* will be employed when discussing the population and community as a whole. Three reasons undergird this decision. While it might be ideal to use "Latinas, Latinos, and potentially gender-variant individuals" throughout this discussion, doing so in every other sentence would prove verbose and draining for the reader. Labels such as *Latino/a, Latin@,* or *Latinx* do not quite work for this historical project. In contrast to *Latino,* these recent terms and categories had no circulation during the period covered here. Above all, historical protagonists generally understood that gendered terms did not automatically mean exclusion or nonrecognition. *Los latinoamericanos* literally translates to Latin Americans, and most women assumed it included them. *La colonia latinoamericana* referred to the local Latin American community, which was not composed exclusively of women. And *el público latino* of the early twentieth century exhibited great diversity across multiple layers of social existence, including gender. That Latino public is the subject of the first chapter.

====

El Público Latino

Community Life
in the Early Twentieth Century

Twenty-four-year-old Abraham Valle and his younger sisters, Mary and Soledad, bade farewell to their mother and to León, Nicaragua, their birthplace, in late March 1924. That month, they boarded the SS *Venezuela* at the port of Corinto and embarked on a fifteen-day voyage to California. Abraham had returned to León months earlier and spent time helping his sisters with travel preparations. In San Francisco, he toiled as a metal polisher, which meant he either cleaned ships stationed at the waterfront or burnished silverware at a local restaurant. Nineteen-year-old Mary was a dressmaker in León and would likely find employment in the city's garment industry. She paid for her own passage and head tax while Abraham took care of his and fourteen-year-old Soledad's. On their arrival, the Valle siblings reunited with their other brother, Ernesto, and began to plan their new lives together. They all "intend[ed] to remain" in the country on a permanent basis, become citizens, and settle in San Francisco.[1]

Some ten years before the Valle siblings' journey, and two months after the opening of the Panama Canal in August 1914, San Francisco's Spanish-language newspaper made a striking projection. *La Crónica* predicted "thousands of Central and South American emigrants [would] come" to California in search of work and opportunity once "the Panama Canal reache[d] its full traffic."[2] This forecast acknowledged that the operation of the waterway would involve more than an expansion of American economic might and geostrategic authority in the hemisphere.[3] Indeed, as U.S. capital investment and military power intensified in Central America, residents of the region began to trek northward to the United States. Just as *La Crónica* had foreseen, increased water traffic along the isthmus and the western coast of Mexico facilitated travel to California, and many Latinos staked out a future in San Francisco.

Latino migration to the city rose steadily in the early twentieth century. The foreign-born population of Latin American descent grew from approximately two thousand persons in 1910 to almost thirteen thousand by 1930.[4] A new life, or at least a temporary sojourn, in San Francisco made sense as it was the epicenter of commerce, manufacturing, and transportation on the Pacific coast.[5] Latinos sought economic prosperity and political stability, not unlike their counterparts who went to Los Angeles, Chicago, and New York City.[6] Their diverse national origins resulted in the creation of a distinct and motley Latino social world, unmatched by any other locality at the time. Settlement house staff at the International Institute recognized this heterogeneity by the early 1920s. While congressional leaders in Washington debated the future of immigration from Europe and Asia, local social workers reported growing contact with migrants from the Western Hemisphere, including Mexico, Puerto Rico, and El Salvador. The presence of these new residents and their children—together with subsequent generations of "Latino immigrants"—held important ramifications for the twentieth-century metropolis, demographically and politically.[7]

Latino San Franciscans created, accessed, and traversed a fertile terrain of sociocultural spaces and institutions. This landscape abounded with social clubs and mutual aid societies, which were typically organized around national origin and ethnic ties. Some of these communal institutions had been in existence since the nineteenth century. In contrast, Latino political life—as marked by attention to power, rights, and policymaking—proved limited and ephemeral.

Recent experiences of migration, marginal ties to the city's political establishment, and a constricting public sphere during the late 1910s and 1920s worked in tandem to impede the cultivation of vigorous and ongoing activism. As most Latinos had recently arrived, their principal focus lay in managing a new environment rather than engaging in political activity. The small fraction of Latinos within the general population, in contrast to Italians, meant they had negligible attention from and connections to the local political establishment or non-Latino political institutions.[8] San Francisco's political arena actually became less open to immigrants—and the working class in general—during and after the World War I era, when Latinos entered the city in greater numbers. The country's involvement in the war generated intense patriotism, xenophobia, and widespread calls for immigration restriction. And the Bolshevik triumph in Russia produced dismay over labor unions' activities, resulting in the twentieth century's first Red Scare once the war ended.[9] These conditions collectively fueled the divergence between Latinos' sociocultural and political lives.

This is not to say that political action was nonexistent. Some Latinos participated in short-lived experiments with unionization in the early 1900s and 1910s. Mutual aid societies occasionally involved themselves in advocacy work. Above all, the Spanish-language press functioned as the key institution engaged in political education and community defense. *La Crónica* (1914–1917) and its successor, *Hispano América* (1917–1934)—the two leading immigrant newspapers—informed Latinos about local and international affairs, rallied them to vote, and critiqued their everyday perils and inequities. Branding themselves as independent and nonpartisan, editors' political sympathies were consistently clear: they were pro-immigrant, espoused racial justice, and sought "the betterment of the working classes."[10]

The Spanish-language press also played a pivotal role in identifying key layers of latinidad. While references to unity and a common destiny among Latinos dated back to the nineteenth century, the ideology of solidarity and affinity circulated with more prominence as the population grew and diversified. Journalists underscored their commitment to champion readers' wellbeing. They simultaneously stressed the ties, concerns, and predicaments linking Latinos together. As newspapers informed and exposed their audiences to the social world around them, they educated patrons on their shared bonds and interests as Latinos.

Nineteenth-Century Roots

For a half-century before it became a *pueblo* (town) in 1835, San Francisco housed Spanish-speaking peoples and Costanoan/Ohlone, Miwok, and Patwin Indians.[11] The inhabitants of the Misión de San Francisco de Asís and its adjacent presidio, both established in 1776, included Spanish missionaries, Spanish and Mexican military personnel, Mexican laborers, and members of various Native communities.[12] They composed a population of approximately six hundred persons by the early 1830s, when the Mexican Congress decreed the breakup and secularization of mission lands. In 1835, the governor of

Alta California began issuing land grants to military officials and other individuals with ties to the provincial government. These land grantees and their
families formed a gentry deeply identified as Californios, by tracing or claiming a lineage to Spanish colonists and differentiating themselves from Mexican laborers and Indians. Californio men presided over the community and
elected their first *alcalde* (mayor) that same year; this official governed the
village of Dolores, the vast land area previously comprising the mission.[13]

Californios forged economic ties with Anglo-American and European
immigrants who laid the foundations for a commercial village named Yerba
Buena. Also established in 1835, with support from the Mexican government, Yerba Buena developed modestly over the next decade and remained
"inferior in population [and authority] to the village of Dolores."[14] The number and political influence of Anglos grew rapidly after the American military occupation in July 1846, a consequence of the U.S.-Mexico War.[15] In
1847, the town's first census identified more than half of its 459 residents as
Americans, 32 as persons of Spanish or Mexican descent, 34 as Indians, and
the rest as other "foreigners." This enumeration only accounted for Californios and Mexicans living in Yerba Buena and "did not include the village of
Dolores," thereby undercounting the presence of Latinos in the territory that
came to be known as San Francisco.[16]

The Latino population multiplied and diversified during the Gold Rush
era as immigrants from Latin America joined thousands of domestic and
international migrants in search of fortune. During the first six months of
1849 alone, "nearly ten thousand [gold seekers] came by sea, and landed at
San Francisco . . . [These] arrivals were principally from Chili [*sic*], Mexico,
and other countries on the Pacific coasts of America." Thousands more arrived in Northern California in the early 1850s.[17] Most migrants disem-
barked in or passed through San Francisco en route to the gold fields and
the mines. Many returned to the city as a result of antagonism and violence
experienced in gold country or in search of work during the winter months,
a practice that proved common for gold seekers irrespective of their place of
origin. Some Latinos eventually opted for permanent settlement in a setting
transformed from "makeshift town" to "instant city" within a decade.[18] By
the mid-1850s, some three thousand persons belonging to the "Spanish
races" resided in San Francisco. Contemporary observers estimated that
one-half of these were Mexicans, "one-third Chilians," and "the remaining
sixth consist[ed] of Peruvians and natives of Old Spain, and other parts of
Spanish America."[19]

On the eve of the Civil War, Latinos shared a "non-American" status with other peoples who entered the city at mid-century, including immigrants from Ireland, France, and China. Latinos' location as outsiders within the social order was not exclusively predicated on a standing as recent immigrants. It was heavily informed by their non-Anglo, Latin heritage. Most Spanish-speaking people living in Dolores and Yerba Buena before the U.S.-Mexico War, in fact, became "foreigners in their native land."[20] Vestiges of anti-Mexican sentiment promulgated by Anglos during the armed conflict of the 1840s and Latinos' reluctance "to identify with [the United States]" worked in tandem to create a climate of hostility, harassment, unequal protection under the law, and few job opportunities. As newspapers like *El Eco del Pacífico* noted in the late 1850s, the "Spanish race" found itself besieged by countless "injustices, abuses, and outrages."[21]

Latinos pursued multiple strategies in response to unfavorable conditions during the latter part of the nineteenth century. Elite Californio families turned to the legal system and intermarriage (a practice that primarily involved Californio daughters and Anglo men) in their attempts to retain land and their economic position. In contrast, the landless and recent arrivals considered various routes in their quest for survival. Some headed to central or southern California, hoping for better economic prospects and more welcoming surroundings. Others deemed it best to return to Latin America. And some chose to stay in San Francisco, scrape by as best they could, and seek support from other Spanish-speaking residents.

Latino Immigrants in the Early Twentieth Century

Economic transformation and political upheaval in Latin America and the Caribbean, induced in great part by U.S. capitalist and imperialist designs, reignited migration northward in the first three decades of the new century. San Francisco's Spanish-speaking population—including Spaniards and U.S.-born Latinos—grew at least tenfold during this period, numbering almost twenty thousand by the mid-1930s.[22] Government authorities and politicians paid little attention to Latinos at this time, focusing instead on the larger number of immigrants from Southern Europe and Asia. Coverage in Spanish-language newspapers and accounts from social workers nevertheless confirmed their increasing presence. In 1916, for example, a feature article in *La Crónica* acknowledged the labors and contributions of "new emigrants who plant[ed] roots in these lands . . . Spaniards, Mexicans, Central Americans, and Italians."[23]

Mexicans formed the single largest group of Latinos entering San Francisco. Driven by poverty, land dislocation, and the political instability produced by the Mexican Revolution (1910–1920), they formed part of the mass exodus of approximately one million people who migrated to the United States between 1900 and 1930.[24] "Mexican laborers," explained a reporter in 1915, "have come to this country in search of better life prospects, seduced by great promises of powerful companies, [and] also pushed by the fear of suffering grave harm unleashed by the revolution."[25] Living conditions in Mexico began to deteriorate in the late nineteenth century, when president-dictator Porfirio Díaz expanded his national project of modernization and economic progress. Díaz's regime supported the expansion of mining and railroad industries—largely controlled by American investors—and backed the consolidation of *haciendas* (estates) intent on voluminous agricultural production. These developments impelled the appropriation of communal lands; furthered peonage and destitution among the peasantry; and fomented popular discontent, rebellion, and eventually revolution.[26]

Laborers, refugees of all political factions, and persons from middle-class and landowning backgrounds came to the city during the revolutionary years.[27] Most migrants hailed from Mexico's western-central provinces, which experienced a great deal of economic devastation and political unrest. Residents of towns and villages caught in the torrents of turmoil, as experienced by those in Michoacán and Jalisco, regularly headed north seeking jobs and security.[28] Access to transportation networks made their movement feasible. People living near port cities (e.g., San Blás, Nayarit, and Mazatlán, Sinaloa) sometimes boarded ships bound for San Francisco. Others relied on railroads traversing central and western Mexico, which transported them to the U.S.-Mexico border and then to localities across the West and Midwest.[29] Many laborers actually arrived in San Francisco after working for the railroads or in seasonal agriculture in central or southern California. A feature story in the *San Francisco Examiner* described this phenomenon in 1923. "The Mexicans who are building and keeping in repair the railroads," relayed the writer, "come in at El Paso and move out all over the West, sometimes in large gangs, sometimes in isolated groups."[30] The account stressed that Mexicans' "nomad[ic]" lives, especially their engagement in farm labor, made it difficult to accurately determine their numerical presence in the city. The quantitative challenge notwithstanding, two qualitative developments were definitely clear: The

Mexican-origin population had grown since the turn of the century, and the newcomers and their children now outnumbered the descendants of Californios and nineteenth-century migrants.

Like their Mexican counterparts, Puerto Rican laborers opted to migrate in response to declining livelihoods on the island. Increased concentration of land, economic insecurity, and political conflict became key features of life in Puerto Rico following the U.S. occupation and annexation in 1898. Under American colonial rule, Puerto Ricans experienced the extensive acquisition of land by American sugar companies, heightened proletarianization, a dearth of political autonomy, and violent repression of any opposition to U.S. domination.[31] These multiple factors created the distress propelling the early twentieth-century "Porto Rican exodus," as demonstrated by thousands who began to "flee" the island beginning in 1900.[32]

Puerto Rican migrants did not set out to establish themselves in San Francisco. Instead, the city was to serve as a transportation transfer point for contract laborers bound for the sugar plantations in Hawaii. Numerous accounts from the early 1900s discussed the initial voyage to New York or New Orleans by steamer, then westward via train, and subsequently by ship from San Francisco to Hawaii. Once in the Pacific islands, Puerto Ricans found their new lives to be challenging, marked by labor exploitation and cultural alienation.[33] As *La Correspondencia*, a Puerto Rico–based newspaper, recounted some decades later: "Our brothers found themselves in a strange land, without knowing its language and customs . . . [and] mistreated by their employers." These conditions led many to migrate again, once their contracts expired or whenever they determined it was necessary "to find better ways of making ends meet."[34]

Return travel to the continental United States led Puerto Ricans directly to San Francisco, where they encountered a more copious economic landscape as well as an existing Spanish-speaking population. Some laborers came after short-lived experiences in Hawaii; others migrated once they learned a "Puerto Rican colony" had been established, a noticeable development by the early 1910s. Most Puerto Ricans living in the city by the 1920s had participated in these migratory trajectories.[35] They were joined by some individuals who left Puerto Rico during and after World War I, as part of a larger wave of emigration from the island.[36] In 1918, *Hispano América* informed its readers about the "50,000 workers from Puerto Rico" who "would be brought" to the United States to work for the railroads and in farms. Most were not bound for San Francisco, but some eventually made their way to the city after working in areas in the Southwest. The arrival of Puerto Rican migrants, albeit not in the scale of Mexicans, would continue into the early 1930s.[37]

San Francisco also became one of the earliest destinations for Central Americans settling in the United States.[38] People with roots in Nicaragua, El Salvador, and Guatemala arrived in small numbers during the early 1900s and intensified their migration by the 1920s. The International Institute acknowledged this trend and increasingly noted how Salvadorans and Nicaraguans stood behind Mexicans as the most numerous immigrants from Latin America.[39] Central Americans' decisions to leave the isthmus occurred against the backdrop of analogous transformations befalling Mexico and Puerto Rico. They, too, witnessed their governments' emphases on economic modernization, the collusion between local elites and North American businesses committed to a capitalist vision of progress, and mass impoverishment. The cultivation of coffee and bananas as export crops augmented the breakup of communal lands, the exploitation of labor, and the solidification of oligarchies with robust ties to corporate and political leaders in the United States. Dissatisfaction with this socioeconomic situation generated popular mobilization and political discord, which led the U.S. government to continuously monitor the region and turn to military intervention to protect American economic and geopolitical interests.[40]

Central Americans moved to San Francisco because the city was entangled in some of these economic and geostrategic developments. The large-scale production of coffee, for example, connected Central American elites with North American capitalists, especially those in areas that processed and sold the product in U.S. and European markets. In the early twentieth century, landowners and merchants cemented economic relationships with San Francisco–based coffee companies and other businesses; these ties encouraged and facilitated travel and migration. The Panama Canal's operation, on the other hand, expanded the city's preeminence in trade and commerce while presenting Central American laborers with opportunities to work for shipping lines or to simply board ships en route to San Francisco.[41] In 1921, *Centro América*—a boosterish publication promoting investment in the isthmus—reported that growing numbers of young Central Americans came to the "Golden City . . . expecting to find work plentiful."[42] Accessible transportation and a nonquota immigration policy for people from the Western Hemisphere—though entrance requirements included a head tax and a literacy test—allowed the Valle siblings, introduced in this chapter's opening vignette, to migrate with relative ease. Laborers like them were soon joined by "political emigrants" who critiqued the workings of capitalism and U.S. imperialism. In the late 1920s and early 1930s, some union activists, journalists, and intellectuals from Nicaragua and El Salvador opted to migrate when faced with persecution for their political work.[43] San Francisco became a logical choice given their knowledge that other Central Americans had already made the city their home.

Race in the Golden City

Latinos' phenotypic diversity, national origins, and cultural heritage informed their "anomalous position" in the racial order.[44] Though "white by law," their lived experience demonstrated that this legal framework did not correspond with everyday realities. The legal system and the state's bureaucratic apparatus (e.g., the census bureau) classified Latinos as white. Yet they regularly encountered discrimination and marginalization based on commonplace, societal assumptions of them as nonwhite. Historians and legal scholars have noted that this paradox produced limited privileges and vast inequities for Mexican Americans and Puerto Ricans.[45] Chileans, Peruvians, and Central Americans met parallel contradictions in San Francisco. Latinos thus muddled through a terrain in which they were legally white yet socially "colored" owing to phenotype, their Latinness, and the residual effects of Anglo-American colonization.[46]

A host of racial ideologies had been forged in the cauldrons of conquest, war, nationalism, economic competition, and U.S. empire building. Nineteenth-century Anglo Americans created and reproduced multiple racial logics to cast people of Latin American descent as inferior, backward, and degraded. They relied on Latinos' physical appearance, blood lineage, religion, and social conditions as the bases for racialist thought. Journalists, lawyers, doctors, and politicians variously described the "Spanish race" and "Hispano-Americans" as "partly pure, partly crossed with red blood," "swarthy [in] complexion," ignorant, and dirty. The "admixture of Indian blood" with Castilian and "Moorish blood," in particular, served as the entry point to mark Latinos as racially flawed, impure, and nonwhite.[47] These appraisals intersected with, and came to rationalize, biased notions about Latinos' work ethic, intelligence, and morality. Anglo Americans pointed to Californios' partial development of their lands and limited engagement with a market economy as evidence of deficient enterprise, slothfulness, and a disregard for progress and civilization. They concomitantly equated Mexican and Chilean immigrants' toil in "low and servile occupations" with feeble mental capacities and a lack of ambition. On the moral front, some Latinas' engagement in sex work came to be interpreted as signs of their "vile" and "shameful" character and of their communities' propensity for sexual excess.[48] All products of mid-nineteenth-century circumstances and assessments, vestiges and modified versions of these perspectives retained much currency in the new century.

Social commentators writing in the early twentieth century regularly called attention to Latinos' racial mixture, variation of skin tones, and cultural shortcomings, and used these attributes to define this non-Anglo population before general audiences. By describing Latinos' manifold physiognomies, observers ascertained their subjects' murky, indeterminate, and nonwhite location in the racial order. A 1907 exposé of Little Mexico, an enclave within the city, concluded that its inhabitants were "colored" and "dark." A contemporaneous account involving Puerto Rican residents identified them as "black, white, and intermediate."[49] Commentators concurrently reproduced longstanding assumptions regarding Latinos' deficiencies in development and inadequate work ethic. The era's civilizational ideology, in fact, intensified the belief that the world's peoples ranked along a continuum of mental, physical, and cultural advancement. Some pundits relied on personal observations to characterize Mexicans as people of "childlike simplicity;" others turned to anthropological data to position Puerto Ricans as "lowest in the scale of civilization."[50] Such states of being supposedly explained these groups' lack of initiative, low intelligence, and pursuit of pleasure over productivity. The judgments essentially cast Latinos as unmotivated, torpid, and immature. San Franciscans who read these accounts coupled them with their own impressions of what Latinos were and where they stood in the social hierarchy.

Immigration authorities, too, preoccupied themselves with color and race. In the 1910s, officials in San Francisco described Central Americans' complexion as ranging from fair and light to brown and dark. Their racial classification was simply Spanish American.[51] The extrication of color from race grew out of the era's common association of race with national origin. Thomas Guglielmo's recent study of Italian immigrants richly unraveled this color-race distinction. He explains that this group's color was considered white, whereas their race was either Southern Italian or Northern Italian.[52] Immigrants from Latin America encountered a related process of categorization, though they found themselves positioned along a spectrum of color. This continuum indicated that Latinos did not and would not fit neatly into the country's color binary. And it confirmed that *Spanish American* was not immediately synonymous with *white*.

Beyond official processes of labeling, some San Franciscans labored to distinguish Spanish Americans both from Anglo Americans and other "Latin races." The city's Latin races included Italians, the French, the Portuguese, Spaniards, and Latin Americans. A linguistic family tree, Catholicism, and comparable temperaments supposedly linked these peoples together. Yet commentators made sure to point out their differences. In 1907, the *San Francisco Call* introduced readers to the city's "real Spanish colony"—made up of people from provinces like Galicia and Catalonia—and contrasted them with local Latin Americans. The feature writer identified slovenliness, indolence, and poverty as characteristics unique to Spanish Americans; she stressed that Spanish immigrants were "neither untidy nor lazy nor poor nor illiterate."[53] By and large, Latinos did not regard themselves in such negative terms; they certainly did not interpret poverty as a result of laziness. Most celebrated being Spanish American or Latin American, as subsequent pages will show. The biases generated by these labels—operating as racial markers—nevertheless had material consequences. Latinos would grapple with their ramifications at interpersonal and institutional levels, as they navigated relationships and challenges with neighbors, government authorities, and employers.

Living in San Francisco

Early twentieth-century San Francisco offered Latinos an urban milieu marked by population density, cultural heterogeneity, and economic diversity. The city had long held the largest concentration of people in the West and did so until 1920, when Los Angeles outstripped it of that distinction. Its residents were predominantly white, but a substantial minority of Asian-origin peoples and a smaller community of African Americans lived there too. Immigrants from Europe, Asia, and Latin America, along with their U.S.-born children, collectively made up more than half of the city's population throughout the century's early decades.[54] This demographic composition made San Francisco look more like Chicago and New York than Denver or Los Angeles. The parallel with New York also manifested itself in an economic topography characterized by a vigorous financial sector, intensive

commerce, low-scale manufacturing, and a host of waterfront-related industries. While New York operated as the paramount entry point of ideas, goods,
and people in the East, San Francisco served a comparable role in the West.

San Francisco's port molded key sectors of its economy and various layers
of social life, including settlement patterns and neighborhood composition.
Latinos tended to dwell in working-class neighborhoods close to the waterfront, especially North Beach (see Map 1). Since the mid-nineteenth century,
North Beach had served as a principal place of residence for Latin American
immigrants and other newly arrived denizens. The district contained board-
inghouses, general stores, and other businesses catering to, and sometimes
owned by, Latinos. In the mid-1860s, the vicinity near the intersection of
Broadway, Montgomery (present-day Columbus Avenue), and Dupont
(present-day Grant Avenue) included establishments such as Gertrudís Mo-
lina's Hermosillo (restaurant), Jose Alcayaga's La Unión (general store), and
Charles Castera's hair salon, which offered clients "everything concerning the
art of hair styling."[55] The area also had numerous hotels and houses offering
food and lodging to Spanish-speaking clients. In 1875, the Archdiocese of
San Francisco established Our Lady of Guadalupe Church, on Broadway just
west of Mason, to specifically serve Spanish-speaking parishioners. Latino
residential concentration near the church and at the foot of Telegraph Hill led
observers to dub these district zones as Little Mexico and Little Chile, respectively.[56] These residential, commercial, and religious factors positioned North
Beach as the principal area in which to settle as more Latinos entered the city
after 1900.

Like most neighborhoods at the turn of the last century, North Beach was
not ethnically homogeneous. Latinos shared the district with Italians, Spaniards, the Portuguese, and Filipinos. The intermingling of Romance languages,
Catholicism, and a festive public culture produced the area's identification as
the city's Latin Quarter. Italians predominated owing to their massive wave of
immigration at the time, but certain blocks held a significant concentration
of Latinos. In the 1910s, the flats along Mason, Taylor, and Jones Streets presented prime housing choices for them, in part because these were located
within walking distance to Guadalupe Church. D. Villanon, a barber, his
wife, and four children resided on Mason Street and "all [went] to church
pretty regularly." Fellow parishioner Noel E., a tobacconist by trade, and his
family lived nearby on Jones Street but only attended church services when
they could.[57] Public observance of faith aside, Latinos generally found housing throughout the district and accessed a more expansive commercial sector

than their nineteenth-century predecessors. While grocery stores and restaurants proliferated, they also patronized specialty shops, such as Juan Puerta's Librería Hispano-Americana (bookstore), Ricardo Rojas's jewelry store, and J. Y. Billones's photography studio, among others. Non-Latino merchants, especially Italian and Chinese ones, recognized Latinos as consumers, advertised their goods and services in the Spanish-language press, and emphasized that their personnel spoke Spanish. North Beach may have been viewed as the Italian enclave by outsiders, but its residents and those in adjacent Chinatown knew Latin Americans also dwelled there and formed part of the "distrito Latino."[58]

North Beach as the anchor of Latino residential and commercial life did not preclude settlement in other neighborhoods, albeit in less concentrated and discernible form. The Mission District—the area encompassing the old village of Dolores—once again began to draw Latinos after the earthquake and fire of 1906. Californios and Mexicans had greatly diminished in number following the land disputes and dispossession of the mid-late 1800s. After the disasters in 1906, many Latinos turned to the Mission and set up "camp at the site that is now Mission Dolores Park."[59] They joined thousands of Irish, Italians, and others who fled the northeastern neighborhoods, including North Beach, destroyed by the catastrophic events. This process of intracity movement transformed the Mission into a solidly working-class and overwhelmingly Irish enclave, though its Latino presence would continue to grow in ensuing decades.[60]

In the mid-late 1910s and 1920s, increased immigration combined with high density in North Beach propelled Latinos to seek housing in such areas as the Mission. Some new migrants settled there immediately on arriving in the city, often joining relatives who already resided in the district. The experiences of Maria Ocequeda and Maria López exemplified this phenomenon. Ocequeda, a housekeeper, left Mazatlán in 1916 to reunite with her husband who lived on Elizabeth Street, just west of Castro. López, a dressmaker, arrived four years later from Acapulco, to join her sister residing at 149 Caledonia Street, an alley block near Valencia and 16th Streets.[61] The vicinity around 16th and Valencia, in fact, showed initial signs of Latino-owned businesses. As early as 1914, M. Ramirez ran a millinery shop at 3170 16th Street, just west of Valencia. A few blocks east, Rosendo López operated a laundry on Alabama Street.[62] New businesses would continue to open in the 1920s and early 1930s as the Mission attracted more and more Latinos.

At least three other districts became sites of Latino settlement before the

Great Depression: Pacific Heights, the Western Addition, and South of Market. Approximately one mile west of North Beach, Pacific Heights symbolized wealth and privilege; it was one of two upper-class enclaves in the city. Latinos who resided there tended to be businesspeople, members of Central America's coffee oligarchy, and consular officials. Eduardo Estrada, a merchant and consulate representative, for example, lived at 2825 Gough Street with his wife, two children, and female servants. The Estradas arrived in 1916 and were considered one of "the finest Guatemalan families" in San Francisco. Other households like theirs took up dwelling along the prestigious stretches of Clay, Franklin, and California Streets.[63]

South of Pacific Heights, the Western Addition typified the city's middle-class district of this era. Populated by merchants and professionals, its ethnic tenor was heavily German and Jewish.[64] But the area also housed a compact community of African Americans and the city's Japantown. African Americans and Japanese Americans settled near the Geary Boulevard corridor, west and east of Fillmore, respectively. Some Latinos did as well, a decision driven in part by the greater number of homes that had been divided into apartment units. In the early 1920s, Emilia Taboada, a piano teacher from El Salvador taught "classes [from her] residence [at] 1453 Buchanan Street, near O'Farrell."[65] Designer Maria Elizondo and her two siblings, who had moved from Mazatlán in 1918, lived a few blocks away on Laguna Street, south of Pine. Others established themselves around Alamo Square and Buena Vista Park. Sisters and dressmakers Sara and Virginia Cárdenas arrived from Colima, Mexico, in 1920 and settled in with their cousin at 876 Grove Street, east of Fillmore. And mechanic Arturo Butter left Usulután, El Salvador, in 1927 to join his cousin on Shrader Street, two blocks south of Haight.[66] The presence of mechanics, dressmakers, designers, and teachers revealed that Latinos in the Western Addition had both middle- and working-class standing. While the district's white population was largely middle class, Latinos living there—like African Americans—had more varied class backgrounds.

In contrast to the Western Addition, San Franciscans in South of Market—abutting the Embarcadero's southern part—were overwhelmingly working class or members of the working poor. A significant percentage of its residents worked as sailors or longshoremen and in other waterfront-related occupations. Ethnically, it was largely Irish, Italian, and Scandinavian.[67] The proximity to jobs and availability of cheap housing led Latinos and Filipinos there beginning in the 1920s. Sebastian Rivera, a tailor from Nicaragua, and his wife, Berta, spent some time living with a relative on 3rd Street, near Harrison,

Figure 1. Maria Segrove (right), a resident of the Western Addition, and two female friends socializing at Golden Gate Park, 1925. Courtesy of Shades of San Francisco, San Francisco History Center, San Francisco Public Library.

in early 1924. A few blocks south, Ernesto and Rafaela Marquez dwelled on 6th Street, between Harrison and Bryant. The couple from Mexico regarded their place in South of Market as "home."[68] They were not alone. In fact, South of Market, like the Western Addition and the Mission, would draw more Latinos in the decades that followed.

As Latinos adjusted to a new, urban environment, they sought out spaces for social interaction and connection. Like other early twentieth-century cities, San Francisco offered a rich and abundant arena of commercialized leisure, one replete with saloons, dance halls, nickelodeons, theaters, and other establishments.[69] Latinos could access these sites of sociability and amusement, unlike the Chinese who were overwhelmingly barred from doing so because of vehement racial animus.[70] But for Latinos, it was a conditional entrée and participation in mainstream (i.e., white) leisure spaces as they sometimes encountered challenges owing to color or national origin. In the late 1910s, some bar patrons explained how certain saloons in North Beach only welcomed them and treated them well if they called themselves Spanish. Identifying as Spanish marked them as European and white, or at least off-white, while Mexican or Guatemalan denoted racial indeterminacy or simply nonwhiteness. The experiences of conditional access bore some resemblance to the restrictions faced by African Americans, who could also enter mainstream establishments but on whites' terms.[71] White biases must have served as an incentive to seek out and create social venues and spaces specifically for Latinos.

There existed other salient motives for doing so: a desire to congregate with persons of similar ethnic backgrounds, to mingle with other Spanish speakers, and to consume culturally specific entertainment led them to Latino-oriented spaces. Latinos frequented bars, theaters, restaurants offering live music, and other sites of diversion catering to them. A network of social clubs offered opportunities to socialize and engage in revelry as well. Social clubs held intimate gatherings in private homes and staged larger festivities in hotel ballrooms and event halls. Throughout the mid- to late 1910s and 1920s, Club Alegría and Club Primavera, among others, organized weekly get-togethers, dances, costume balls, and fancy fiestas.[72]

Beyond their function as conduits for merriment, social clubs served ethnic, edificatory, and class-specific objectives. Most clubs' raison d'être revolved around the celebration and veneration of cultural heritage. This orientation manifested itself along regional (e.g., Club Hidalgo), national (e.g., Club Peru, Club Portorriqueño), and hemispheric (e.g., Club Social

Latino Americano) axes. Such a panoply of social organizations revealed that ethnic pride and camaraderie could, and did, occur at multiple levels. Other groups drew on ethnic ties to fashion socially and morally acceptable forms of recreation. El Club Juventud y Reforma, founded in 1916, included the Spanish words for *youth* and *reform* in its name to signal its mission. Like other Progressive-era initiatives focused on young people in urban settings, it sought to provide alternatives to an expansive realm of commercialized, undisciplined, and unsupervised leisure.[73] Backing for the effort likely came from adults concerned with morality and class standing. Some social organizations explicitly underscored their role in cementing economic and class-based relationships. "Distinguished elements of the Central American colony," explained a reporter in early 1921, had recently established a club to foster sociability and inspire mutuality among "select groups." In the ensuing years, El Club Social Centro Americano brought together businesspeople, landowners, and government officials in the spirit of cultural commonality and shared economic interests.[74]

Fellowship and cultural festivities could also be found in faith-based settings. Religious societies offered Catholic Latinos a blend of social and moral support; by 1910, parishioners at Guadalupe Church could choose from at least four socioreligious collectives. The groups made it possible to gather together in less formal settings and obtain ongoing spiritual sustenance. Some societies emphasized prayer and devotion to a particular saint (e.g., Las Hijas de Maria, or the Daughters of Mary); others engaged in discussions about the relationship between moral development and everyday life. Participants concurrently promoted cultural traditions by coordinating saints' feast days, Christmas celebrations, and Holy Week events. And they informally oversaw the workings of their church, sometimes calling on the ecclesiastical hierarchy to consider the laity's wishes and interests when assigning new priests to the parish.[75]

If religious societies addressed spiritual and parish-centered affairs, mutual aid societies concerned themselves with the secular world. Mutual aid associations extended multiple forms of social and material support (e.g., assistance with medical costs and funeral services) to members who paid weekly or monthly dues. Latinos' commitment to mutual aid dated back to the mid-nineteenth century, when in 1860 they founded the Spanish American Mutual Benevolent Society. Its three-year lifespan was followed by the establishment of the Mexican Benevolent Society (1868–1875), which worked to "assist sick and indigent Mexicans." A new incarnation of the Spanish Mutual Benevolent

Society emerged two years later in 1877. It rededicated itself to benevolence and mutual assistance, claimed about two hundred members, and had an impressive twenty-eight-year existence.[76]

Latinos built on this mutual-aid tradition in the twentieth century. Their numerical growth and diversification generated a host of new associations. In contrast to an earlier era, Latinos now had access to a more expansive institutional field. Some of the most prominent organizations included La Sociedad Peruana de Auxilios Mutuos (founded in 1908), La Sociedad Española de Beneficencia Mutua (reestablished in 1914), La Alianza de Auxilios Mutuos (founded in 1921), and La Liga Portorriqueña (founded in 1922). All pledged mutual assistance among their members, emphasized fraternity, and staged cultural events to raise funds for and to publicize their work.[77] As their names suggested, specific ethnic or national origin bonds typically brought people into the organizations' fold. A common cultural background often fostered a sense of camaraderie, familiarity, patriotism, and connectedness. Still, Latino heterogeneity propelled some groups toward inclusivity and affinity across ethnic or national identification. The Peruvian Society, for one, regularly invited the entire "Hispanic-American colony" to its festivities and "all Latin Americans [were] welcome as members."[78]

An awareness of commonality and reciprocity occasionally led mutual aid societies into the realm of advocacy and civic action. As some groups saw it, a commitment to mutuality demanded attention to societal concerns and injustices faced by their members or comrades. La Liga Portorriqueña did exactly this in summer 1924, when it launched a fundraising campaign and legal defense of a young man accused of murder. Earlier that year, while aboard a ship headed to San Francisco, Primitivo Rodríguez experienced incessant taunting and physical bullying from a coworker, for petty reasons and specifically for speaking Spanish. The situation turned bloody when the co-worker decided to "strike him without mercy," leading Rodríguez to fight back, grab an ax, and kill his attacker. La Liga took up the case and explained that the episode revealed the harassment and biases often faced by Puerto Ricans. Joined by the Puerto Rican Club, the organizations asserted that Rodríguez had acted in self-defense, distributed "propaganda in favor of the cause," and raised funds to pay for legal counsel.[79] Rodríguez's eventual acquittal came to represent a victory for the accused, his lawyers, and the community backing him. The campaign behind the triumph at once affirmed the importance and the benefits of mutuality and goodwill.

Material benevolence at times radiated from religious and social circles concerned with the misery and hunger of the least fortunate community members.[80] Offerings of charity proved common during the holiday season or at special public events. One such occasion occurred in early December 1914 when La Liga de la Raza Ibero-Americana hosted a community meeting and dinner at Guadalupe Church. Merchants and professionals had founded this religious-oriented society earlier that year, intent on raising funds for a monument honoring Queen Isabella (1451–1504) at the 1915 Panama-Pacific International Exposition, the world's fair commemorating the Panama Canal's completion. The organization now invited all members of "our race" to join them in celebrating the society's work. Its leaders emphasized "there [would] be meat and bread for all compatriots who came, without notions of country, without resources, and without protection except from heaven."[81] Here, religious devotion merged with panethnic pride to provide nourishment for the needy, at least temporarily.

Periodic manifestations of beneficence emanated from social clubs too. The groups sometimes used the proceeds from cultural events to assist the poor, as exemplified by the activities of El Club Azteca de Señoras. Founded in 1912 and composed of well-to-do women of Mexican heritage, this club held "dances for charity" and used the revenue to buy Christmas gifts, candy, and ice cream for poor Mexican families and orphan children.[82] Seasonal regularity, an altruistic orientation, and sympathy for residents in need marked efforts like these. Yet class standing and economic interests blinded most club members to the structural constraints faced by the poor and the working class. More specifically, their impulse to alleviate suffering did not include attention to the economic inequities and predicaments created by capitalism.

Class and Labor Before 1929

Class standing circumscribed much of Latinos' lived experiences. To be sure, they sometimes interacted across class lines in church, commercial spaces, and at cultural events. Monetary resources and occupational status nevertheless informed housing choices, social ties, access to medical care, and overall financial security. Class identities likely shaped their political outlooks in countries of origin and the United States as well.

Upper-class Latinos shared a similar profile: They belonged to a small elite whose members sought to increase business ventures and expand their fortunes or to retreat from the political turmoil in Latin America. Central

American coffee planters and ranchers, along with their families, entered the city with regularity during the mid- to late 1910s. San Francisco also witnessed the arrival of a cluster of *hacendados* (large landowners) from Mexico in the 1920s. They found themselves "bereft of their estates and property" following the revolution.[83] Business and social connections in the city—as well as financial investments—allowed these well-to-do families to maintain an affluent lifestyle and continue to set themselves apart from the middle and working classes.

The Latino middle class exhibited occupational variation and played a key role in local Latino economic development. It included accountants, dentists, doctors, journalists, lawyers, and teachers. Spanish-language publications regularly ran professional advertisements from such individuals as Carlos Leiva and Manuel Urrea, doctors from El Salvador and Mexico, respectively.[84] Professionals like these joined merchants—who owned restaurants, drugstores, flower shops, and other small businesses—in creating the contours of a market niche organized around ethnic lines. Unlike upper-class Latinos who typically lived off the wealth and investment generated by land and products in Latin America, their middle-class counterparts made a living by selling their expertise, services, and goods in the United States. Their principal consumer base was the city's Latino population, which was largely working class.

The ranks of the working class proved considerably diverse in terms of national origin and occupational standing. Working-class households usually depended on the monetary contributions of both men and women, and Latinas participated actively in wage labor. Some Latino men held skilled jobs, such as carpenters, bricklayers, barbers, and bakers. Most found unskilled employment in restaurants, hotels, and canneries and along the waterfront. The only skilled occupation commonly available to women involved garment production. In fact, some companies consistently circulated employment ads in search of dressmakers, which surely influenced the migration decisions of Latinas who possessed this craft.[85] Women also labored as waitresses, domestic servants, tortilla makers, nannies, and "dancing girls" at nightspots. The latter were joined by singers and musicians who performed at Latino restaurants, entertainment venues, and cultural events.[86] Together, this cross-section of Latinos formed a motley working class with an embryonic awareness of common fortunes and collective interests.

The city's labor movement did little to cultivate a working-class political consciousness among them. Disconnection and marginality generally char-

acterized Latinos' relationship to labor unions before the 1930s. While organized labor made some gains and acquired political authority during the
Progressive era, Latinos did not benefit from these developments. Unions'
prioritization of skilled workers, racial discrimination, and an overall nonrecognition of Latinos—owing in part to their low numbers—collectively inhibited their immersion in the labor movement. Historians Michael Kazin
and Albert Broussard have underscored the centrality of racism in impeding
Asian and African American unionization at this time.[87] Though Latinos
were not ideologically targeted for exclusion, their experiences were rarely
ones of inclusion and equity. In 1915, *La Crónica* reported that "workers
from Latin American nations" did not benefit from the same "salaries, treatment, and job assignments" as "Americans."[88] These circumstances resulted
from obstacles in accessing higher-paying, skilled jobs and from racial
animus—often functioning interdependently—which served to block their
admission into most unions. Tellingly, even skilled Latino workers found
themselves relegated to segregated locals. Such was the case of Local 95 of the
International Brotherhood of Carpenters, a Latin local composed of Italian,
French, Spanish, and Latino craftsmen. Its existence notwithstanding, this
union's membership was low and it did not become a significant force in the
labor movement or in Latino life.[89]

Unskilled laborers in the Ship Scalers Union (SSU) did embark on sustained organizing efforts during these years. This union brought together
men who cleaned and conditioned ships while stationed at the waterfront;
most of them were Italians, Spaniards, and Latinos. Scalers' interest in establishing a union occurred amid a period of growing unionization in the early
1900s, a product of recent labor victories by the teamsters and waterfront
unions as well as some openness from City Hall.[90] In December 1909, Arthur
Puga and Jose Martinez wrote to the San Francisco Labor Council (SFLC),
the city's branch of the American Federation of Labor (AFL), and informed
officials about ongoing efforts to unionize. The men proceeded to ask the
council for assistance and underscored how scalers "[were] ready to be organized." Within weeks, the union received its charter from the AFL, became
an SFLC affiliate, and disseminated copies of the AFL constitution to its
members, including "one hundred . . . in Spanish."[91]

The SSU led the way in directly and forcefully engaging Latinos in political action. It did so by rallying its members at practical and ideological levels:
by directing them to halt their labors, picket, and claim a set of rights as
workers. The union staged numerous strikes in the early 1910s, ones in which

laborers demanded higher wages and shorter workdays. In March 1910, the union struck for $2.50 per day and against employers' preferences for contractors when distributing jobs. A reliance on labor contractors, members explained, resulted in lower wages (the contractors usually kept a portion of a worker's earnings) and allowed employers to avoid negotiations with their union. As Humberto Costa and J. Calvo noted five weeks into the strike, "We have kept a most hard and bitter fight against the combination of the Steam Ship Companies and the contractors." Their goals remained largely unrealized in 1910, but the union struck again two years later and added the eight-hour workday to their demands. Jose Castillo underscored the "main issue" propelling the June 1912 strike against the American Hawaiian Steam Ship Company and the Oceanic Steam Ship Company. He and his comrades believed "that nobody should go to work on either Company, unless we were granted the eight hours." A centerpiece of the labor movement nationwide, the SSU took up the eight-hour day campaign with gusto and couched it under the language of rights. Its members identified eight hours as "a fair thing," as a feature of work life they were entitled to and that employers had to honor.[92] Though employers disagreed, the perspectives and actions placed the SSU at the vanguard of organizations instilling a sense of economic justice among Latinos and directing them to push for workers' rights.

Scalers' activism revealed that "the gospel of unionism," to borrow Shelton Stromquist's apt phrase, reached some in the Latino working class before World War I.[93] Their victories remained slim. Though they occasionally succeeded in persuading a company to meet some demands, most employers used various ploys to circumvent and thwart union efforts. Bosses' tactics ranged from hiring out-of-work sailors and firemen, relying on strikebreakers, and using intimidation to force union members to "leave town." All these "freezing out methods," as J. Calvo called them, formed part of the repertoire against organized labor nationwide. Employers' opposition greatly hindered a union's survival, especially a small one composed of previously unorganized and marginal workers like the scalers.[94] The SSU concurrently grappled with organizational troubles, including tensions between Italian- and Spanish-speaking factions and limited aid from the labor council. In 1911, Frank Morrison, AFL secretary, contacted SFLC officials and discussed the possibility of employing "some man who speaks [the scalers'] language." While some SSU members spoke English, Morrison acknowledged that linguistic barriers made it difficult to obtain support from the infrastructure available to city unions. These challenges alongside employer hostility produced a fragile and vulnerable existence for the scalers. Continuous obstacles harmed and discouraged them, leading many to look for employment elsewhere or leave the union altogether. A record of few gains and an ongoing "exodus" of members made the union defunct by 1914.[95] Still, the SSU set a precedent and left an imprint for another generation who would resuscitate the union twenty years later.

A spirit of unionism and an emergent class consciousness emanated from other locations, especially from other waterfront unions and workers' collectives. Jobs in the shipyards and port workshops became more common for Mexicans and other Latin Americans in the mid-1910s, a product of heightened production and transportation during World War I. Latinos toiling there encountered the activities of the Riggers and Stevedores Union in some form or another, and some joined it.[96] In fall 1919, amid a nationwide, postwar strike wave, this organization led a major protest that halted the operation of San Francisco's port and crippled many sectors of economic life. All longshoremen and shipyard workers in the city—including "Mexicans and other Spanish-speaking laborers"—participated in the work stoppages and demanded higher wages and better working conditions. Even a group of Mexican strikebreakers brought in from Stockton left their jobs once they met the wrath of strikers and understood the gravity of the situation.[97]

The mood of labor solidarity and cooperation inspired the creation of at least two worker-oriented collectives during the postwar years. Unlike existing social clubs and mutual aid societies, these new outfits directly connected ethnicity and working-class status. In early 1919, a group of laborers called attention to the "utmost necessity" of bringing together *los trabajadores de la raza* (Latin American workers). La Confederación Benefica Hispano-Americana "would work for: unity, culture, peoplehood, language, progress, protection, and noble ideals," explained Angel Gomez, its spokesman. Other ethnicity-centered groups, of course, shared similar objectives. But the emphases on progress and protection took on particular significance in the context of labor unrest and backlash against radicalism.[98] Progress may well have meant a desire for improved socioeconomic conditions through a different relationship between capital and labor. The stress on protection possibly grew out of concerns regarding governmental repression and the deportation of labor activists, socialists, and foreign radicals. La Confederación's political orientation probably resulted in its short existence. A more permanent worker-oriented mutual aid society emerged in 1921 and named itself La

Alianza de Auxilios Mutuos. Proud of its working-class members and orientation, it coordinated standard mutual aid and cultural activities spanning the 1920s. Extant evidence does not reveal La Alianza engaged in political action or advocacy work during this decade, a decision potentially colored by the demise of its predecessor. Still, some laborers who had found appeal in La Confederacion's original call likely gravitated toward La Alianza, where they could ruminate further on their commonalities as working-class Latinos.[99]

The Spanish-Language Press, Political Education, and the Foundations of Latinidad

In the 1910s and 1920s, community defense, political education, and the promotion of latinidad most often originated from the Spanish-language press. Editors, columnists, and guest writers at *La Crónica* and *Hispano América* labored as purveyors of information as well as champions of Latinos' welfare. They charged themselves with speaking—and looking out—for their ethnic kin; after all, Latinos lacked a comparable institutional vehicle with wide reach and a capacity to represent the community as a whole. In April 1914, weeks after *La Crónica*'s emergence, a commentator praised the "warriors" who founded this outlet of "action and development," which pledged to fight "on behalf of the race." The newspaper eventually branded itself "*[el] defensor de la raza*" (the guardian of the people) after changing its name to *Hispano América* in 1918.[100] In tandem, this sense of purpose and identity solidified journalists' drive to advocate for improvements in Latinos' life conditions. They did so while advising their public on how to avoid or address troubles with employers, governmental authorities, and their neighbors. As more Latinos settled in the city, Spanish-language newspapers augmented their attention to the structural forces shaping, and often limiting, their readers' daily lives.

Work life and labor exploitation loomed large in newspapers' community defense agenda. In its advocate role, the Spanish-language press informed and warned Latinos about the pitfalls in the labor market. It also attempted to persuade employers to increase wages and improve working conditions. The approach was not inconsequential, yet it hinged on cautious, amiable, and passive forms of defense. Journalists typically proposed solutions at the individual level, vis-à-vis workers' and employers' own personal decisions. Being pro-worker, quite notably, did not mean that newspaper editors backed the labor movement. They neither encouraged workers to challenge unfavorable conditions through mass protest nor motivated them to consider unionization as the means to confront inequity and hardship.

Hispano América's attention to the plight of Alaska cannery workers exemplified the character of journalistic advocacy and defense. These itinerant laborers journeyed northward during the spring and summer months to clean, can, and pack salmon. Long comprised of Chinese and Filipino workers, this mobile labor force was joined by Mexicans, Spaniards, and South Americans during and after the war. For Latinos with limited skills or who had recently arrived in the country, a seasonal job presented a better alternative to unemployment. Toiling in Alaska canneries proved arduous: long hours, harsh work environments, and separation from family and friends for up to six months demanded a great deal of physical and emotional fortitude. Laborers recounted experiences of malnutrition, loss of wages while ill, fourteen-hour days, and unremunerated overtime pay. Their misfortunes garnered media attention by the late 1910s and journalists increasingly exposed the hazards, cruelty, "wage fraud," and overall "hell" met by Latinos who went to Alaska.[101]

News reporters combined education, condemnation, and persuasion in their advocacy work. Raising awareness about human suffering in the canneries, *Hispano América* reproached contractors, bosses, and employers for their chicanery, avarice, and callousness. Public denunciation occurred alongside efforts—coordinated with the Mexican consulate—to press the packinghouses for an amelioration of working conditions. In meetings with editors and consular officials, company owners deflected blame to contractors and promised to address the problems. Diplomacy proved ineffectual. So did the newspaper's subsequent strategy to dissuade Latinos from laboring in Alaska. "It is preferable to earn a living where workers are treated humanely," avowed Julio Arce in 1919. "Workers of the Hispanic race," the editor exhorted, "Do Not Go to Alaska."[102] The appeal may have persuaded some, but economic necessity proved more powerful for others. Hundreds of Latinos continued to travel to the canneries year after year, thereby exposing themselves to the perils and "torture" there. The newspaper's team, for its part, hoped ongoing coverage and persuasion would succor the community at large and would eventually deter all Latinos from trekking to Alaska.[103]

A resolve to protect the Latino working class overlapped with an enterprise of political education. Community advocates on one hand, newspapers operated as a civic tutors and counselors on the other. *La Crónica* and

Hispano América both encouraged Latinos to concern themselves with policy matters and steered them toward the polity. Their editors consistently promoted formal political engagement by urging those residents who could vote to do so. They simultaneously endeavored to mold political allegiances and outlooks by endorsing candidates and backing legislative programs deemed beneficial for Latinos. In fall 1914, *La Crónica* praised California governor Hiram Johnson's track record, stressing his administration's dedication to "the people," and advised Latino voters to reelect him. "We won't grow tired of reminding all Spanish-speakers who have the franchise in the United States," its correspondents averred. "Vote for Johnson!"[104] The endorsement affirmed the governor's progressive agenda—one that included minimum-wage laws and a state commission that investigated immigrants' working and living conditions—as it foreshadowed the central function of Latino institutions in promoting an activist government. Support for increased governmental authority locally prompted *Hispano América* to favor San Francisco mayor James Rolph in 1919, 1923, and 1927. First elected in 1911, Rolph presided over public infrastructure projects—including the municipal railway's construction and upgrades in water supply—praised by the Spanish-language press. "Rolph must be reelected," explained Arce in 1923, because he had spearheaded "improvements in San Francisco over the past decade" and "his highly progressive spirit [was] the best guarantee for prosperity and well-being of the community."[105] Good fortune, of course, proved relative and elusive in the 1920s—as the Alaska cannery workers could attest—and depended on much more than an experienced mayor. Arce and his contemporaries nevertheless relied on notions of progress and reform to proceed with political tutelage and direct Latinos to the voting booth.

The quest for communal well-being was real, not just rhetorical. Journalists often grounded their endorsements in a desire to enhance the welfare of all San Franciscans. With that in mind, they monitored policy proposals under consideration, made them intelligible—by presenting the issues in plain Spanish and free of legislative jargon—and informed voters about the benefits or potential harm. In 1920, *Hispano América* beckoned Latinos to "Vote YES" on proposals to increase funding for the University of California (Proposition 12), to raise salaries for firefighters, and to allow citizens to confirm mayoral appointments to the board of education. It concurrently urged voters to reject initiatives that aimed to overturn mandatory vaccinations in public schools, to deny foreigners the right to own land (Proposition 1), and to exact a poll tax from foreign-born citizens. These recommendations exposed three foundational perspectives undergirding political education. First, the Spanish-language press instilled an appreciation for state involvement in the provision of social welfare and conveyed the importance of a social contract among the citizenry. The endorsement of Proposition 12 specifically legitimized raising taxes to bolster public education. Other recommendations signaled the gravity of protecting civil rights and opposing all attempts to codify unequal treatment based on race and national origin. Proposition 1 did not technically apply to most Latinos as it targeted "aliens ineligible for citizenship," the era's juridical euphemism for Asian immigrants. But the newspaper cast all forms of discrimination against foreigners as abhorrent and asked Latino voters to see Asians' plight as connected to their own. Third, the electoral advice impelled Latinos to value the commonweal and to recognize that communal well-being should apply to everyone. All San Franciscans had a civic obligation, the newspaper intimated, to prioritize the "good of the collective" over "individualistic interests."[106]

The Latino collective itself stood at the core of the newspapers' raison d'être. Advocacy work and political education proved critical in identifying communal concerns, shared interests, and a common standing in the city. At the same time, newspapers discussed Latinos' cultural connections and began to encourage readers to see themselves as one community. The undertaking paralleled a long-established practice, in other epochs and contexts, of using print culture to construct identities and imagine communities.[107] It was an incipient enterprise at this time—one that would unfold over the decades to come. Newspapers certainly did not seek to erase or downplay the histories or cultural backgrounds of individual Latino groups. But they acknowledged a set of ties and experiences that bound Latinos together and the possibility of marshaling those bonds into collective action.

Early twentieth-century deliberations on unity and fraternity proceeded along constitutional and functionalist tracks. This is to say, commentators considered both the sources and usefulness of alliance and kinship. Some saw Spain's past splendor, California's Spanish heritage, Catholicism, and language as adhesives holding together the "great Spanish-American family." Members of this cultural clan had to take up an "enterprise of unification," noted one writer, and collectively generate awareness about their contributions to San Francisco's and California's development; in the process, they would bring honor and prestige to their community.[108] Promotional and class inflected, the proponents of this framework celebrated Spanish colonization, longed for positive recognition from San Francisco elites, and sought to topple the negative and racist assumptions about Spanish-speaking residents. Other commentators proved less absorbed with Spanishness and instead identified Latin America as the source of Latinos' affinity. They considered the historical record and the predicaments faced by modern Latin America (e.g., U.S. imperial ventures, domination of industries and natural resources by European and North American elites) as the principal determinants of commonality and comradeship. Latin American nations and their peoples "confront[ed] identical problems, similar dangers, and the same difficulties," noted Julio Arce in 1918. They therefore had to extend mutual assistance to one another, promote economic development from within the region, and collaborate in bucking the tide of U.S. imperialism. Iterations of this perspective would circulate and expand as U.S. intervention in Latin America intensified in the 1920s.[109]

Exponents of this Latin America–centered paradigm stressed two other bases of connectedness: the Spanish language and race. Latinos' solidarity stemmed from linguistic ties and an ongoing struggle for the "ideals of our race and our homelands," averred Miguel Ruelas, who became *Hispano América*'s editor in 1927. The multiple definitions of race—whether understood as a particular group of people, a synonym for national origin, a category of social standing, or phenotypic descriptor—all cast the Spanish-speaking population as different: not Anglo American, foreign, and overwhelmingly nonwhite. Though the concept of *la raza* generally connoted peoplehood and pride among Latin Americans, their race vis-à-vis the United States marked them as distinct, suspect, and inferior. This paradox thus presented another crucial layer of similitude. The brotherhood of Mexicans and Central Americans, explained another journalist, sprang from cultural closeness as well as "geography, race, and the misfortune" engendered by Spanish conquest and U.S. imperialism.[110] By emphasizing cultural kinship, history, and race, *Hispano América*'s staff formulated a genealogical connection among people of Latin American descent. These linkages combined with contemporary economic quandaries and experiences of imperialism supposedly made it possible and necessary for Latin American nations to mount a unified response to common challenges. If unity and cooperation were feasible and desirable in Latin America, the same would be said for Latinos living in the United States.

Reflections and encouragement of Latino confederation and fellowship did not emerge exclusively from the Spanish-language press. Mutual aid societies, social clubs, and other collectives engaged in the endeavor as well, even if less didactically. The Spanish Mutual Benevolent Society's resurgence in the mid-1910s, according to one observer, signaled a "fraternal awakening" among Spanish-speaking San Franciscans. Society leaders aspired to integrate all members of the "Hispanic family" and cultivate rapport among them. As they saw it, adjusting to—and prospering in—a new environment would be more easily accomplished through mutual dependence and cooperation instead of separation. Other groups relied on social interaction though dinners, dances, and special events to foster communion among city residents who traced their heritage to "fraternal nations in blood, language, and beliefs."[111] Annual observances of Latin American nations' independence from Spain, el Día de la Raza (marking Columbus's arrival in the New World), and Holy Week reminded Latinos of their historical and cultural linkages. While these events became conduits for celebration and commemoration, some San Franciscans began to weigh the possibility of translating cultural bonds into political action. As discussed earlier, La Confederación Benefica Hispano-Americana animated working-class Latinos to mobilize for enhanced conditions on the job and beyond. Four years after that collective's emergence, in 1923, a group of merchants and professionals founded a political club known as the Spanish-American Club for Rolph. It echoed *Hispano America*'s endorsement of James Rolph and rallied "Hispanic Americans who had the right to vote" to reelect him.[112] The club's existence, not unlike La Confederación's, proved short-lived. But these fleeting experiments, and possibly others like them, pointed to a budding practice of relying on cultural connections as the bases for political organizing. Notably, as journalists discussed a shared past and present in Latin America, small clusters of Latino residents and activists began to ponder an interrelated present and future in San Francisco. Their contemplations on unity, commonality, and kinship— dependent on history, culture, present-day predicaments, and race— essentially functioned as the ideological building blocks of latinidad.

By the end of the 1920s, Latino San Franciscans had built, resided in, and moved through a vibrant communal landscape. This *mundo hispano-americano* (Hispanic-American world) boasted remarkable diversity— demographically and institutionally—and encompassed an extensive array of social clubs, religious groups, and mutual aid societies. Some of these organizations offered camaraderie, gaiety, and diversion; others extended vital forms of spiritual and material support. Latinos' political life, in marked contrast, exhibited less richness, vigor, and permanence. Fleeting unionization efforts and short-lived forays into the civic arena nevertheless attested to the potential benefits of collective political action. The Spanish-language press certainly did its part to advocate on behalf of Latinos and orient them toward the formal polity. Journalists' judicious, passive, and top-down enterprise eventually met change. In the 1930s and 1940s, the revived Ship Scalers Union, a collective of Alaska cannery workers, and other labor organizations ushered in an era of robust political engagement from the bottom up. Though its social and cultural dynamism remained constant, the Latino world underwent dramatic metamorphosis amid economic depression and war. Latinos now developed and matured as political actors, and did so as proud members of the city's labor movement.

CHAPTER 2

La Lucha Obrera

Mass Action and Inclusion
in the Progressive Labor Movement

At 1:00 a.m., on 08 May 1934, Adrian Duhagon, Edward Camacho, and some six hundred Mexican, Puerto Rican, and Filipino cannery workers defied their leaders' recommendations and "marched in squads" to the San Francisco waterfront. They planned to establish a picket line and protest packing companies' employment of nonunionized workers bound for the fish canneries in Alaska. Their efforts specifically aimed "to stop the *Delaroff*, loaded with scabs, from sailing" and to continue their push for recognition of the Alaska Cannery Workers Union (ACWU). Officials from the SFLC opposed such tactics and underscored the policies set by the AFL, which dissuaded workers from challenging the city's antipicketing ordinance and encouraged negotiation with employers. Yet the rank and file believed it imperative to use direct action to effect concrete and significant changes in their work lives. Local police authorities responded to unionists' resolve by emphasizing their duty to protect employers and the public, while "attempting to terrorize the workers." Officers attacked, beat, chased, and opened fire at the picketers. Workers retaliated by taunting the police, running away, resuming their picketing, and throwing bricks at their opponents. The skirmish lasted for more than two hours until the crowd finally dispersed, leaving an unreported number of wounded and prompting the arrest of at least three individuals.[1] Back at their union hall, the cannery workers vowed to resume and expand their struggle for labor rights, a pledge they strove to actualize in the subsequent months of 1934 and over the ensuing decade.

Alaska cannery workers' determination evidenced a newfound politicization among Latinos and other working-class San Franciscans in the 1930s. The militancy described in the incident above formed part of a nationwide constellation of "pitched battles in the streets," as one historian has put it, between "fledging unions" and armed forces in the service of capital. Workers' vigorous activism became the response to their frustrations with economic dislocation produced by the Great Depression, resentment at employers' actions, and the promise of the New Deal.[2] Their political awareness and mobilization was a product of a high tide of unionization during this decade. Locally, the rate of union membership doubled between 1933 and 1940 alone.[3] In joining unions, the city's ethnically heterogeneous working class began to envision and to demand altered social experiences and arrangements, first in the workplace and then in society at large.

Triggered by a climate of insecurity and violence along the waterfront, the maritime and general strikes of 1934 epitomized foundational episodes in the history of modern San Francisco and in the history of Latino politics. The general strike signaled citywide support for labor's cause and made clear that governmental authorities could no longer ignore workers' struggles.[4] For Latinos, the mobilizations of 1934 presaged the centrality and vitality of labor organizing in their daily lives. Unionization transformed them into political actors and labor unions became their most prominent sites of activism at this time. To be sure, Latinos participated in other organizations before and during this decade, including mutual aid societies, social clubs, and hometown associations. But these bodies functioned primarily as social and cultural entities, not political ones.

Latinos' pursuit of rights, power, recognition, and representation emanated—first and foremost—within their unions. They did not join labor organizations with this aspiration per se; the quest became a by-product of their immersion in labor's orbit at a time of seismic change. Like millions of other working people, the Latino proletariat found much appeal in the labor movement during the 1930s. Urban workers' impulse and ability to unionize, however, was not uniform. Recent scholarship about Depression-era Chicago and New York suggests that few Latinos joined unions there, either because of disinterest or ongoing exclusionary policies.[5] In contrast, Latino San Franciscans encountered budding inclusion and benefited from incorporation into a citywide crusade for labor rights. The organizations that pulled them into their ambit typically espoused rank-and-file control of union affairs; direct action; and participation regardless of skill, race, national origin, and other characteristics that had previously made it difficult for nonwhite workers to unionize. Many laborers therefore came to favor a militant ethos and championed mass mobilization to secure workers' rights and protections.

Latino unionists embraced a laborite agenda that encompassed a commitment to civil rights and one that became the basis for affinity with American liberalism. The struggle for labor rights was in and of itself a crusade for civil rights. Duhagon and fellow Alaska cannery workers, for example, coveted freedom to speak up and protest without harassment, sought equity and democracy in the workplace, and wanted to be treated with dignity. Their quest for economic fairness and security, like African American tobacco workers and Mexican American metal workers elsewhere, went hand in hand with an attack on racial discrimination.[6] Working-class Latinos notably stood at the vanguard of efforts for racial equality long before their middle-class and professional counterparts established a local civil rights organization. Through union-centered political work, they also became connected to and supportive of a liberal vision of the state. Latinos' engagement with New Deal liberalism has received limited attention from historians; it is nevertheless evident that many historical actors began to see the liberal state as an ally and apparatus to yield socioeconomic change. In 1930s San Francisco, they backed an activist government that endorsed workers' rights, promoted economic security, and held the potential to advance equality and opportunity for all.

La Colonia Latinoamericana Circa 1932

In mid-1932, two years before residents felt the energy and convulsion produced by the Big Strike, "the Latin American colony" experienced the social flurry that accompanied its summer and fall festivities. Social clubs and mutual aid societies led the way, coordinating national holiday celebrations, Día de la Raza commemorations, and Halloween parties. In July, the long-standing Sociedad Peruana de Auxilios Mutuos held its annual dinner to mark Peru's independence. Two months later, El Club Azteca de Señoras orchestrated an impressive lineup of events to observe Mexicans' *fiestas patrias* (national holidays). In October, the Club Social Puerta de Oro, popular among Central Americans, organized a Halloween dance replete with prizes for best costume. All these celebrations offered temporary respite from the economic crisis, reminding residents of the simple pleasures to be found in music and dance and assuring them that some facets of life remained the same. Most important, the events confirmed the persistence of community amid a climate of unprecedented distress.[7]

The era's economic catastrophe spawned manifold burdens, including job loss, reduced working hours, family strife, and repatriation. While small clusters of Latinos continued to lead middle- and upper-class lives, as discussed in Chapter 1, the population was overwhelmingly found in the working class. Latinos often toiled together in canneries, garment shops, and furniture factories and on the waterfront; they typically held semiskilled or unskilled positions offering low wages and little protection against unemployment. For many, mutual aid societies became the principal recourse to offset their precariousness; the organizations helped with covering rent, medical care, and other living expenses. Historian Stephen Pitti has emphasized that these institutions "peaked in importance" during the Depression precisely because they provided safeguards against complete instability.[8] Dependent on members' dues, mutual aid societies also organized cultural events to raise funds and boost their institutional coffers. Neighborliness and cultural bonds surely prompted some Latinos to assist their ethnic brethren stricken with misfortune. But the Depression created a charity conundrum: the need for assistance increased while the public had less to give. Cultural affinities alone simply could not shield residents from the economic maelstrom.

Concrete and long-term sustenance ultimately depended on employment. Mutual aid societies, social service agencies, and the Spanish-language press all agreed that reduced working hours and the lack of jobs created perilous livelihoods. Staff at the International Institute sometimes attempted to procure employment for their clients. Successful job placements proved limited, materialized on a case-by-case basis, and typically involved domestic service.[9] Public employment relief, on the other hand, did not become a viable recourse for most Latinos. In 1931, city voters approved a $2.5 million bond measure for infrastructure improvement through public employment. "The City employs hundreds of men to assist them," reported *Hispano América* when the program took effect. Yet many Latinos found it difficult to access these jobs owing to municipal residency requirements, lack of citizenship, and racial animus. The convergence of unemployment, exclusion from relief programs, and antagonism against immigrants led to a steady "exodus of foreigners" from the city. Observers acknowledged that Depression conditions at once curtailed immigration and pushed established residents to return to their countries of origin.[10]

Ethnic Mexicans, in particular, found themselves at the center of a repatriation movement unfolding nationwide. Approximately half a million Mexican-origin residents—immigrants and their U.S.-born children—left the country as a result of voluntary and involuntary back-to-Mexico drives. San Francisco authorities do not appear to have coordinated official repatriation efforts on par with their counterparts in Los Angeles.[11] A smaller ethnic Mexican population and the municipality's more efficacious response to unemployment accounted for some of this difference. Thousands of ethnic Mexicans still left the city and surrounding Bay Area localities.[12] The Ventura family was among them: the couple arrived in the city in 1919 and raised and schooled their children here. As they prepared to leave, they told social workers, "'[Our] children will come back to make a success where we have failed.'" Although the Venturas interpreted their situation as a product of individual shortcomings, their predicament actually resulted from inequities and circumstances well beyond the confines of their households. Economic insecurity, exclusion from relief programs, encouragement from the Mexican government, and fear of deportation coalesced and induced them to "share the long trek back to Mexico" with others like themselves.[13]

An atmosphere of uncertainty and repatriation alongside an emphasis on self-help did little to orient Latinos toward the local or national polity. But they were not entirely disconnected from political affairs and certainly not from politicians. In September 1930, Mayor James Rolph attended a Mexican holiday celebration, a decision that involved more than respect for residents' cultural heritage. The mayor came to garner support for his gubernatorial run. Months later, *Hispano América* hailed Rolph's victory, reporting that "good citizens" of Hispanic American descent esteemed him and gave him their votes. Noticeably, editors fell silent on the mayor's policy record and campaign platform. Pointing out that Rolph's "official labors were not [theirs] to judge," they suggested that tradition and appreciation were enough to send him to Sacramento.[14]

Policy matters received some consideration during the 1932 presidential election, but the Latino public generally did not devote extensive attention to the contest. Social clubs and mutual aid societies carried on with their usual activities, while the press detailed political developments in Latin America with much more frequency. A largely immigrant population and the prospect of repatriation translated into nominal investment in the U.S. polity. But some Latinos who were U.S. citizens and *Hispano América*—still the dominant vehicle of political education—encouraged residents to back Herbert Hoover. Newspapermen maintained that the incumbent president had taken positive measures to address the economic crisis, such as approving federal bonds for building the San Francisco–Oakland Bay Bridge. "There [was] no doubt," they said, that Hoover "[would] be reelected." Their confidence signaled either ignorance of or indifference to the tide of resentment against Hoover and the national electorate's desire for new leadership. Once election results came in, the publication admitted that Franklin D. Roosevelt's presidency would "bring a complete change to the country's domestic and foreign policies."[15] This projection contained more accuracy. As would soon become evident, the Roosevelt administration and the New Deal agenda recast the federal government's role in the economy and the state's relationship to the citizenry, including Latinos.

¡*Huelga!*: The Maritime and General Strikes of 1934

Soon after Roosevelt's first hundred days in office, news correspondents apprised their Spanish-speaking readers of the president's plan for economic relief and recovery. Their discussion surveyed key initiatives of the early New Deal, including the Federal Emergency Relief Administration, but did not weigh on whether Latinos would actually benefit from the measures. Journalists tellingly identified the National Industrial Recovery Act (NIRA) as FDR's most "transcendental" venture. The experiment of centralized industrial planning certainly surpassed any previous economic effort undertaken by the federal government during peacetime. In practice, the NIRA spawned controversy as well as inspiration.[16] The act's Section 7(a) recognized workers' legal right to join unions and to engage in collective bargaining. It thus emboldened the working class to see the labor movement and the New Deal as instruments that could transform their daily existence.

Thousands of San Franciscans first encountered the promise of Section 7(a) on the waterfront. Workers who toiled on the city's wharves had engaged in vigorous mobilizations during the 1910s, but employer onslaught, governmental insouciance, red-baiting, and laborers' internal divisions quelled most organizing by the early 1920s. The economic downturn of the 1930s triggered the reemergence of maritime activism. Increased misery and vulnerability sparked organic discussions about collective action and a reconstitution of worker-controlled organizations to counter company unions. This awareness expanded as waterfront laborers interacted with Communist organizers from the Marine Workers International Union (MWIU). Founded in New York in 1930, the MWIU functioned as an industrial organization for seamen, longshoremen, and other maritime workers. MWIU organizers applauded and backed the efforts of politically savvy rank-and-filers who produced the *Waterfront Worker* beginning in early 1933. A powerful tool of political education, the bulletin consistently emphasized the gravity of establishing a union "built by US, the stevedores, right here on the docks."[17] The NIRA's passage in June 1933 legitimized their desires. Within weeks, dockworkers revived their local chapter of the International Longshoremen's Association (ILA).

Some Latino men labored as stevedores, but their presence proved more substantial in two other maritime sectors: Alaska cannery work and ship cleaning and conditioning. The Alaska canning industry depended on immigrant labor as most native-born, white workers shunned the seasonal, arduous, and low-paid nature of the work. Three years into the Depression, the Alaska Packers Association continued to recruit Latinos by running employment ads in *Hispano América*. Directing its attention to unemployed men, the company touted "excellent treatment, sustenance, and sanitary conditions, aboard the ships and in the canneries."[18] Most laborers thought otherwise. Cannery conditions had changed little since the early 1900s. Workers' outlooks and expectations, however, had indeed shifted.

By 1933, Alaska cannery men—exploited and unorganized for generations—found themselves eager to build a labor union. Longtime "Alaskenses" Duhagon, Camacho, and Jose Inclan began organizing the ACWU in April. These men had engaged in cannery work for years: Inclan and Camacho had both done so for at least a decade. Duhagon and his colleagues recruited members outside labor contractors' headquarters and in the waterfront's general vicinity. Some five hundred men heeded their call to organize by the year's end. Their organization was a multiracial entity from its inception, a characteristic shared with agricultural unions in California. Most members were Latinos and Filipinos, though some Japanese, Chinese, and white workers joined them as well.[19] Like the state's farmworkers and the city's longshoremen, the Alaska cannery men also received assistance from Communist organizers, especially ones from the Trade Union Unity League (TUUL). The TUUL sought to establish Communist-led industrial unions that would operate autonomously from the AFL.[20] While workers welcomed outside support, TUUL operatives did not control their organization. The ACWU actually dashed Communists' hopes by affiliating with the AFL in early 1934, a decision akin to longshoremen's return to the ILA (also an AFL affiliate).

With this strategic move, the workers assumed the labor establishment would offer protection and stability. The Communist-led *Lucha Obrera* noted that Alaska workers "opted" for this alliance by "determining that only the AFL [could] get them out of 'a jam.'" Reporters then warned workers about the AFL's cautious operations, "dirty tricks," divisive tactics, and complicity with capitalist interests.[21] The rank and file would themselves assess the AFL's modus operandi once they became embroiled in the maritime strike.

Before the maritime struggle engulfed them, the cannery men experienced a formidable victory. The triumph involved a class-action suit stemming from their resolve to fight the abuses and extortion practiced by labor contractors. In fall 1933, hundreds of union members met with officials from the State Labor Commission and filed sworn complaints against an agency managed by Emile Mayer. The grievances prompted state authorities to investigate and then bring charges against the labor contractors for "conspiracy to violate the state peonage law." At the trial, men like Miguel Valdez recounted an array of offenses and maltreatment, including being forced to buy unnecessary clothing and other gear, paying inordinate prices for these items, and often "starving in Alaska." Others discussed how they departed for the canneries already indebted to Mayer's agency, being "held in servitude until they worked out their bills," and returning to San Francisco with little money to show for three to six months' work. In March 1934, the jury found the defendants guilty and issued sentences ranging from six months to two years at the state penitentiary. The conviction consoled the workers and galvanized them to augment their crusade against workplace malfeasance.[22]

This experience impressed critical lessons about unionization and state authority on the cannery men. In less than a year, they witnessed how a unified front could proactively redress their horrid working conditions. Collective action eclipsed labor contractors' intimidation tactics, which had traditionally kept individual protestors in silence and submission. It made laborers realize that if they could challenge labor contractors, they could also confront the packing companies. "The workers are determined to clinch their victory by organizing stronger," noted an observer, "for this season's [forthcoming] struggles."[23] Responses from the Labor Commission and the district attorney concurrently exposed the cannery men to the state's positive and beneficial role. In an earlier era, some individuals occasionally approached foreign consulates for intercession. Now, union members turned to U.S. authorities for assistance and protection. Unionization essentially began to reorient workers' relationships to one another and to the state. But governmental interference was not confined to benevolent action. The violence during the maritime upheaval, four months after their legal victory, would keenly remind cannery workers of the state's repressive power.

The cannery men's push for justice had much support from other marginalized workers, especially the ship scalers. Men who cleaned and conditioned ships shared much in common with those who traveled to Alaska: they held the grimiest and least desirable jobs on the waterfront. Most were Latinos and African Americans, though some Asians and whites also engaged in scaling work during the Depression. The scalers had unionized for a few years in the early 1910s but then remained unorganized for two decades. In early May 1934, Jacinto Penalver, Armando Ruiz, and hundreds of others responded to the unionization drive spearheaded by MWIU organizers and joined the new Ship Scalers Union. The organization's resurrection occurred precisely as the longshoremen considered a Pacific coast–wide strike. The scalers' first mobilization, in fact, entailed joining the united front of all waterfront workers.[24]

Fifteen hundred city longshoremen and their counterparts from Seattle to San Diego walked off their jobs on 09 May 1934, launching a maritime strike that paralyzed the shipping industry for three months. Strike action had loomed for months as workers, ILA officials, employer representatives, and government officials jockeyed to reach an agreement between the longshoremen and shipowners.[25] While the ILA and AFL hierarchy endorsed compromise and arbitration, the rank and file clung to their aims: $1.00 per hour wage, $1.50 per hour overtime, a thirty-hour work week, union recognition, a union-controlled hiring hall, a closed shop, and a coast-wide agreement covering all stevedores of the Pacific. The ILA Strike Committee, led by Harry Bridges, underscored the dockworkers' desire to fully actualize the New Deal promise. "The strike is not called in defiance of the government," read a committee statement. "It is called to get all the things the government itself has advocated."[26]

Waterfront workers from all occupational and racial backgrounds enmeshed themselves in the maritime strike. "The seamen and the scalers," reported *Lucha Obrera*, "demonstrated their solidarity by declaring themselves on strike as soon as the longshoremen declared [theirs]." ACWU members backed the stevedores within days as well, although AFL officials attempted to prevent them from doing so by "rais[ing] the red scare."[27] The influence of MWIU organizers dismayed the labor establishment, and employers immediately cast the strike as a Communist plot. Red-baiting had long been used to delegitimize radical unions and to generate dissension among the rank and file. In the 1930s, however, many in the working class saw capitalism, not communism, as a menacing force. The "red issue" therefore did not have the potency to "split the workers." Neither did racism. The longshoremen, allied waterfront unions, and other sympathetic organizations insisted that workers' unity could not be compromised by cultivating antagonism along color lines.[28]

Workers' culture, comparable agendas, and political strategy informed the scalers' and cannery men's involvement. Waterfront workers traversed a common physical terrain with spaces and opportunities to disseminate information, share laughs, and commiserate about employment woes. MWIU organizers, too, played a role in stimulating affinity among the port's labor force. After all, they preached the gospel of industrial unionism instead of craft-based organizing, and hoped to bring the longshoremen, seamen, scalers, and cannery workers into the MWIU. The prospect of industry-wide settlements must have been particularly appealing to smaller unions, whose demands also included higher wages, union recognition, and the closed shop. And aligning with the longshoremen held strategic value. The stevedores were the largest and most powerful segment of the waterfront proletariat. In joining the strike, the cannery men and scalers solidified their political relationships with dockworkers and amassed indispensable allies.

In unison, "all workers connected with the marine industry" succeeded in shutting down San Francisco's port.[29] The waterfront quickly metamorphosed from center of economic activity to industrial battlefield. The most infamous confrontation occurred on Thursday, 05 July 1934, after shipping companies attempted to resume business operations by turning to nonunionized workers. Strikers contested the move by sneering at strikebreakers, blocking vehicles transporting goods from the docks to the warehouses, and pelting them with stones, bricks, and any debris in their path. Their actions met with the wrath of some seven hundred police officers, who used clubs, pistols, and tear gas to quash the resistance. By the day's end, two workers lay dead, hundreds faced injuries, and hundreds of others headed to jail. The "state of tumult [and] riot" prompted Governor Frank Merriam to send five thousand California militiamen to San Francisco.[30] Military occupation had three immediate objectives: to prevent more violence, to enable employers to proceed with their affairs, and to break strikers' defiant spirit. While this situation presented a tremendous setback, it did not destroy the unionists' crusade.

Outrage and support from all city unions and the public at large amplified the momentum for a general strike. Weeks before Bloody Thursday, the

ILA local had surmised that citywide action could exert more pressure on employers. *Lucha Obrera* likewise apprised its Spanish-speaking readers of this possibility and underscored the importance of continued solidarity with the longshoremen.[31] On 16 July, working people and their allies began a four-day general strike that froze all commercial and industrial activities, effectively bringing San Francisco to a standstill. En masse, the city's proletariat condemned employers' intransigence while censuring the excessive use of police power and military occupation. San Franciscans essentially defied industrial might and defended unions' right to exist and make claims on employers. "The immediate cause of the general strike," explained historian Ira B. Cross in 1935, "was the presence of the militia. . . . The fundamental cause, however, was the fear that the remnants of trade unionism in San Francisco might be destroyed."[32] An impressive display of public support together with concerns about the city's economic life propelled shipowners to resume negotiations and led the SFLC to declare the strike's end on 19 July. Ten days later, the rank and file accepted an agreement, brokered by the National Longshoreman's Board, which incorporated their key demands and established a jointly operated hiring hall. The eighty-three-day maritime strike, sustained by the stamina and dedication of "thousands of anonymous workers," was over.[33]

Immersion in this insurgency proved to be a seminal experience for working-class Latinos, especially those engaged in scaling and Alaska cannery work. Though they did not hold positions on strike committees or partake in arbitration proceedings, rank-and-file involvement concretized the rigors and promise of unionization, and furthered Latinos' incorporation into the city's labor movement. A union's size, workers' skills, and cultural backgrounds proved inconsequential at this time. What mattered most was the willingness to stand alongside other workers and make the sacrifices necessary to support the strikes. By committing themselves to this cause, nascent unionists learned and confirmed—viscerally and tangibly—that alterations to workers' status and lives hinged on struggle and collective mobilization.

Latinos now discerned the magnitude of direct action in effecting change, and they amassed indispensable allies along the way. Shortly after the strikes ended, the SSU became an ILA local; it then affiliated with the International Longshoremen's and Warehousemen's Union following the ILWU's formation in 1937. ACWU members would retain strong ties to waterfront workers but eventually joined the United Cannery, Agricultural, Packing, and Allied Workers of America (UCAPAWA). These locals and their respective industrial

Figure 2. Ship Scalers Union on strike, 1936. Courtesy of International
Longshore and Warehouse Union (ILWU) Library and Archive.

associations would forcefully orient Latinos and other racial minorities toward
a progressive agenda emphasizing economic security and civil rights. Participation in the 1934 strikes taught these union members that political action
could not be a passive, top-down, or insular undertaking. Instead, an effective
and comprehensive political practice had to be sustained by grassroots organizing, vigorous protest, and solidarity. Other unionists would soon share this
perspective too. The militant spirit of unionism forged on the waterfront,
however, positioned the scalers and Alaska cannery workers at the forefront of
this venture long after the maritime uprising.

Lucha Obrera, 1934–1937

Mary Sandoval's labors exemplified Latinos' enlistment in *la lucha obrera*—the
workers' struggle—at mid-decade. A stenographer by trade, she likely had fa-

milial ties to maritime laborers because the 1934 waterfront contest spurred her to action. Sandoval immersed herself in demonstrations and even produced a broadside for the picket lines. Her allegiance to labor's cause, her vocation, and her bilingual proficiency led to a position as the SSU's secretary-treasurer in summer 1934, an appointment she held for a decade.[34] Managing the scalers' institutional affairs did not prevent her from engaging in other efforts. In 1936, Sandoval began organizing Latinas and other women who toiled in city canneries. She eventually served on California's Congress of Industrial Organizations (CIO) Minorities Committee, which bolstered the CIO's agenda on racial equality and fair employment. Deeply committed to *la lucha obrera*, her trajectory encompassed key layers of Latino political life in this period: a strengthening of existing labor organizations, the formation of new unions, and a direct linkage between unionization and civil rights.

Union recognition and survival remained key preoccupations for the scalers and Alaska cannery workers after the maritime upheaval. While the longshoremen and sailors secured significant gains, smaller unions remained vulnerable. Numbers certainly circumscribed how much pressure workers could exert on employers, but this was only one reason for precariousness. Laborers in Alaska learned that seasonal work and distant job sites made it difficult to keep AFL officials and employers accountable. The scalers confronted a different but related conundrum. The AFL-controlled labor council regularly questioned the SSU's jurisdiction, allowing employers to stall on union recognition. Unskilled, minority workers thus found themselves grappling with antagonism from employers and apathy from the mainstream labor establishment.

Disconnection defined much of the relationship between AFL officials and cannery men. This situation was a by-product of two factors. First, ACWU members, like the longshoremen, exhibited a more rebellious ethos and often disagreed with AFL representatives' moderate stances. Second, the AFL's dedication to cannery workers was tepid at best. This negligence formed part of what Glenna Matthews has identified as "the AFL's historic willingness to ignore" food-processing workers.[35] Despite formal affiliation with the AFL, the ACWU received little assistance from the labor council when it attempted to secure a labor contract. Cannery men sought union recognition, an extortion-free workplace, and a minimum wage based on the approved salmon code.[36] Employers rebuffed the demands while AFL leaders sat back and recommended patience. The rank and file instead chose the streets and the picket line, as recounted in this chapter's opening vignette.

The maritime strike energized ACWU members, yet their organization floundered once the waterfront upheaval ended. In September 1934, one witness reported on persistent exploitation in the canneries, employers' preference for scabs, and AFL representatives' "theft and deceit." Laborers resented union officials who made great promises, collected fees, and then abandoned them to fend for themselves. This state of affairs highlighted unionists' estrangement from the AFL, which crushed their spirits and elicited questions about the usefulness of unionization. To counter the malaise, *Lucha Obrera* urged them to extricate themselves from the AFL and establish a separate union "controlled by the grassroots." This vision did not come to pass, at least not immediately. Instead, the ACWU disbanded by early 1935.[37]

The ship scalers fared slightly better. Their union obtained an ILA charter after the Big Strike ended, effectively establishing a formal bond with the longshoremen. This development did not generate validation from the AFL or ease the process of union recognition. In September 1934, union president Penalver and secretary Sandoval contacted the SFLC and applied for admission into the AFL. Their objectives were simple: to garner more allies and to procure backing when bargaining with employers. (AFL affiliation could of course yield little change as the cannery men found out.) What appeared to be a straightforward request, however, landed the scalers in a bureaucratic quagmire. For three months, AFL administrators deliberated over who had the jurisdiction to organize laborers who scaled boilers and cleaned up ship plates. The bureaucratic matter was not a trivial one: it essentially interrogated the SSU's authority to mobilize and represent the scalers. Penalver and Sandoval soon learned that the International Brotherhood of Boilermakers, Iron Ship Builders, and Helpers of America claimed and intended to enforce their purview over scaling work, a plan backed by the AFL.[38] The SSU thus found itself without AFL affiliation and in conflict with a more established union as it pressed shipowners to recognize their organization. In the short and long terms, jurisdictional rivalries spawned strife among workers and enabled employers to exploit these divisions during negotiations.

Nascent unions confronted yet another obstacle: the discharge and blacklisting of militant organizers. The ACWU met this challenge early on. Inclan and Duhagon, who spearheaded the union's creation, were denied employment during the 1934 season. Employers' agents offered no reason for their actions, but unionists regarded the move as a form of political discrimination against those "who have been active in organizing this union."[39] It was a logical conclusion given industrialists' long-standing custom of targeting assertive labor activists, which hindered individual livelihoods and dissuaded others from vigorous activism. The ACWU expected that the NIRA would protect them from this biased practice. It did not. Little by little, they learned Section 7(a) neither compelled employers to bargain with workers nor shielded laborers from arbitrary dismissal and intimidation.

Persecution of radical activists continued even after the passage of the National Labor Relations Act (also known as the Wagner Act) in July 1935. In the wake of the Supreme Court's abrogation of the NIRA, the 1935 law cemented the New Deal covenant with labor by guaranteeing industrial workers the right to unionize and to engage in collective bargaining. It also outlawed unfair labor practices such as blacklisting. But government policy did not translate into immediate employer acquiescence. As the scalers discovered that summer, their bosses would not honor these new rights unless workers fought for them. The SSU struck in August, challenging shipowners' continued reliance on labor contractors and adherence to the open shop. While a few employers acceded to scalers' demands, most opposed doing so. Tensions escalated as a couple of "reactionary" members—seen as agitators paid off by labor contractors—questioned the strike's aims and wreaked havoc at union meetings. In September, a melee sent ten scalers to the hospital and a dozen into police custody; four men faced charges of assault with intent to murder. The SSU responded by mounting a robust campaign to defend its members and the union.[40]

Unionists construed the murder charges against Archie Brown, Julio Canales, and two others as an effort to "disrupt and smash" their organization. They regarded the men's prosecution as a machination engineered by shipowners seeking to tarnish the SSU's reputation and to stymie its strength. "The people and interests we work for," scalers explained, wanted to "discredit the union" and "stop [its] progressiveness and militancy."[41] Their perspective fit within a body of political thought shared by other waterfront laborers, who also denounced union-busting schemes, red-baiting, and other tactics to curb workers' rights. Like-mindedness and the fraternity forged during the Big Strike now proved essential. The *Waterfront Worker* rallied all maritime laborers to stand with the SSU and exert public pressure to exonerate the accused men. Longshoremen and others did so: they attended street protests, packed court proceedings, and eventually participated in a scaler-led work stoppage.[42]

"Men have a right to organize—a right to be heard—a right to strike— and a right to be free from boss and employer inspired riots," affirmed the scalers in mid-December 1935. One week into their colleagues' trial, their declaration conveyed two unequivocal stances. Unionists made clear their ordeal involved a concerted attack on their rights as workers, and they decreed they would not relinquish union principles and government-sanctioned guarantees, vowing to fight to preserve them. Their pivotal offensive consisted of a complete work stoppage along the waterfront, an industry-wide action endorsed by the longshoremen's local, the Sailors Union, and the Maritime Federation of the Pacific (MFP).[43] A labor moratorium had been under discussion for weeks; days before Christmas, all members of the city's seafaring and shoreside unions ceased working for thirty minutes. Protesting the frame-up, they issued a message of collective outrage and solidarity; they also signaled the potential of future dissent if the jury issued a guilty verdict.[44]

An acquittal days before the new year neutralized the prospect of heightened waterfront unrest. The men's exoneration owed much to the defense team led by labor attorney Leo Gallagher. Scalers' mobilization and backing from maritime allies proved vital as well. One supporter actually identified "mass pressure and protest action" as the key factors behind the exculpation, even though unionists could not quantitatively assess how their grassroots campaign influenced the jury's decision. Still, the clamor during and since the Big Strike must have reminded jurors that waterfront laborers would not accept a conviction quietly; the recent work stoppage confirmed that "working class indignation" would have consequences for employers and the city at large.[45] Workers had much at stake after all: the case threatened the lives of four innocent men and the continuation of progressive unionism.

Waterfront unions of the 1930s were almost exclusively male domains, yet some, such as the SSU, depended on the managerial and clerical work performed by women. Sandoval knew the SSU well, and the union's success with Latino men inspired her to turn attention to Latinas. In late 1936, she employed her expertise and began organizing women who canned fish, fruit, and vegetables in the city. A dozen cannery women, including Julia Jimenez and Nellie Alba, swiftly embraced Sandoval's message of unionization. They became charter members of the Cannery and Preserve Workers Union (CPWU) and affiliated with the AFL. By April 1937, five months into Sandoval's organizational campaign, five hundred employees of city canneries—women and men, Latinos and non-Latinos—had joined the union.[46]

The CPWU celebrated its first triumph in June 1937. That month, the IXL Workman Packing Company became the first cannery closed shop in the state. The company hired ethnic Mexicans and other Latinos to can tamales, enchiladas, and chili. Earlier that spring, workers struck and demanded union recognition, a closed shop, a union hiring hall, and a forty-hour week.[47] The company's acceptance of these terms emboldened those in other city canneries to mount or continue strike action. Significantly, the IXL strike and negotiation occurred at the height of the state's infamous cannery struggles and predated the well-documented California Sanitary Canning Company (Cal San) strike in Los Angeles two years later.[48] An early victory in San Francisco suggested that cannery workers here benefited, at least temporarily, from an environment more receptive to unionization and from strong ties to ILA activists.

With Stockton as its epicenter, the cannery crisis embodied the deepening jurisdictional strife between the AFL and the CIO. Leaders from the California State Federation of Labor conducted an "all-out assault" on radical cannery unions—ones advocating local autonomy, rank-and-file leadership, and a militant spirit—beginning in April 1937. San Franciscans were not immune. Two weeks after the IXL settlement, the AFL declared the CPWU's ongoing strikes illegal. State federation secretary Edward Vandeleur reinforced this decision by authorizing the teamsters to break the strikes and then invalidated the union's charter.[49] Recently unionized cannery workers weathered these AFL-sponsored raids throughout the summer, which intensified after the CPWU affiliated with the CIO. Organizer Pauline Gordon urged her comrades to stave off the "campaign of slander and terror," vowing that the AFL would not take over their union. Her projection held true in the short term. But by 1940, while almost all city canneries had been unionized, most fell under AFL jurisdiction.[50] The early cannery experiment with progressive unionism lost much ground, and city canneries did not become powerful centers of rank-and-file activism. For Latinos specifically, this meant that cannery work in San Francisco, unlike Los Angeles, did not function as a critical arena for ongoing politicization.

San Franciscans who toiled in Alaska canneries followed a different trajectory. The ACWU, defunct for a year, resurfaced in March 1936. A unionist ethos had certainly not waned among many rank and filers. Assistance and encouragement from the scalers further propelled their union's rebirth. Scaler organizer George Woolf was actually working with Alaska canners on a full-time basis by early 1937. Woolf possibly left the SSU to cement the ACWU's reorganization; the union's admission into the MFP formalized cannery men's ties to the scalers and longshoremen. Backing from the MFP and weeks of picketing during a strike in spring 1936 forced the Alaska Packers Association to capitulate to unionists' demands. That year's canning season was unlike any other that cannery men had ever experienced: they worked in a closed shop, and their union now claimed jurisdiction over Alaska canneries.[51]

The enhanced work lives of cannery men like Guillermo Lopez and Samuel Garcia revealed the immense change generated by unionization and union recognition. Concrete gains for these men and their counterparts were astounding. Wages increased by 100 percent, and workers now spent eight hours on the job in contrast to eleven to fourteen hours a day without a union contract. The ACWU eliminated the contractor system and set up a hiring hall, key accomplishments as labor contractors had excelled at tormenting and dividing the laborers. Working and living conditions altered dramatically too: hot- and cold-water showers, fresh meat, and adherence to sanitation standards in the canneries boosted workers' health and safety. Employers also agreed to provide medical care and transport ill or injured laborers back to San Francisco, where the union procured treatment for them. "After generations of the worst exploitation known," concluded the *Western Worker* in September 1937, "the Alaska cannery workers have forged head."[52]

The ACWU and the SSU underwent other pivotal changes that fall: they annexed their locals to UCAPAWA and the ILWU, respectively, and joined the CIO. In October, Pete Garcia and Sandoval informed MFP officials of the scalers' decision and a new name: Ship Scalers and Painters Union, ILWU Local 2.[53] The CIO's tenets of industrial unionism, organizing the unorganized, and inclusion regardless of skill, race, and national origin emphatically resonated with the scalers and cannery men. Most were unskilled, minority workers who had long experienced the AFL's neglect, indifference, and resistance to their militancy. The visions promoted by UCAPAWA and the ILWU (both founded in 1937), in contrast, included an openness to radicalism and an emphasis on grassroots democracy. Cannery men's and scalers' institutional decisions in the autumn of 1937 in effect fortified their commitment to the progressive labor movement.[54]

Progressive advocates of the late 1930s pushed for an amplification of proactive government power and unionization. Communists, socialists, and liberals could all be counted as such; united in the Popular Front, they supported the New Deal's continuation and expansion. The AFL establishment, in contrast, had strong reservations about augmenting the state's involvement in economic affairs.[55] Most craft unions' deference to tradition and privilege—

Figure 3. Alaska Cannery Workers Union marching in Labor Day parade, late 1930s. *Labor Herald* Photograph Collection. Courtesy of Labor Archives and Research Center, San Francisco State University.

together with AFL officials' assailment of unions considered subversive or impertinent—perpetuated a laborite culture that was conservative and exclusionary. The CIO's outlook ruptured the AFL's worldview by insisting on more state action and mobilizing workers who had been barred from, or chastised by, the AFL. Latino workers—men and women—responded to and benefited from the CIO's organizational drives in 1937 and subsequent years. They thus became part of what Harry Bridges, now ILWU president, identified as the city's "progressive labor forces."[56]

Edelmiro Huertas, Amelia Rivera, and Raymond Montes were but three of hundreds of Latinos who gravitated to emergent CIO unions. They joined the United Furniture Workers of America (UFW) Local 262, the Textile Workers Union Locals 71 and 158, and the Steel Workers Organizing Committee (SWOC) Local 1684. Some skilled workers in industries targeted by these locals had previously accessed craft unions (e.g., the Upholsterers International Union), but organizing strategy and political ideology led them to the CIO. "Seven hundred S.F. furniture workers join CIO," related the *Labor Herald* in November 1937, because they had established an industrial union and "not been allowed representation in the A.F. of L." Local AFL leaders saw the decision differently. Earlier that year, they accused CIO organizers of dividing the labor movement and using "disruptive tactics" to coax can production workers into SWOC.[57] The denunciation made evident that increased unionization of minority and female laborers would occur alongside an intensification of the AFL-CIO divide.

One AFL affiliate retained its preeminence in unionizing Latinas: the Dressmakers Union Local 101 of the International Ladies' Garment Workers Union (ILGWU). The garment industry had long relied on immigrant women and their daughters, on both the East and West Coasts.[58] Latinas entered the city's apparel industry as early as the 1910s—making everything from dresses to lingerie—and manufacturers regularly recruited them for this line of work. Yet unlike New York's Jewish and Italian women, who had organized earlier in the century, San Francisco's dressmakers did not do so until the mid-1930s. In February 1934, Rose Pesotta, coordinator of the Los Angeles dressmakers' strike the previous fall, came north "to inaugurate an organization campaign among local dressmakers."[59] Pesotta laid the groundwork for many months, but it was her successor, Jennie Matyas, who spearheaded the organizing drives throughout the decade. Matyas became the ILGWU's organizer and educational director in late 1934 and quickly learned that "a tremendous number [of dressmakers] were Spanish-speaking, Mexican, Costa Rican, all south of the border."[60]

Latinas' decisions to join the Dressmakers Union as early as 1934 confirmed one indispensable fact: they embraced the spirit of unionism and became labor activists at the same time as men. Carmen Covarubias and Beatrice Lopez were among the many Spanish-surnamed women who enrolled in Local 101 during its formative years.[61] Immigrant and U.S.-born Latinas typically worked alongside women who shared a similar cultural or linguistic heritage. Though the union brought Italians, Russians, and Anglos into its fold as well, individual shops exhibited considerable segmentation along ethnic lines.

In fall 1935, Aida Hogan and most of her coworkers—overwhelmingly bilingual and ethnic Mexicans—at the Maloof Corporation left their sewing machines behind and set up a picket line on Market and 2nd Streets. Their action defied their employer and the company union. The garment company had recently instituted a thirty-seven-hour work week, but bosses refused to bargain over wages and other grievances. Growing frustrations spurred Hogan and her colleagues to contact Jennie Matyas. They did not turn to the ILGWU organizer for a lesson on oppression; their quotidian experiences on the job, and some familiarity with other labor struggles in the city, taught them that company practices were unjust. The dressmakers expected Matyas to offer guidance and for the ILGWU "to back them up in a fight."[62] Matyas advised them to persuade company union members to collaborate, while she attempted to confer with company managers. Neither strategy succeeded. The employer preferred retribution: outspoken women began to lose their jobs. It was at this moment that the dressmakers struck.

Insurgent dressmakers exhibited tenacity and a willingness to take risks in exchange for enhanced work lives protected by a union contract. For many weeks beginning in November, they picketed outside the shop's premises, urged their compliant colleagues to side with them, and aroused the sympathies of downtown shoppers. One of their messiest and most memorable actions included using ripe persimmons—obtained from a nearby fruit stand—as weapons to fend off police interference. Arrested on at least three occasions, Hogan and other "zig-zag girls" consistently returned to the picket line because they "were fighting for their jobs." Fellow workers who initially crossed the picket line took more notice as the strike wore on, gradually "lost courage about going to work," and eventually stopped doing so. Without a labor force as the holiday season approached, the company finally agreed to enter into a contract. The newest members of Local 101 rejoiced and fully understood that the win had only been possible through struggle and perseverance.[63]

Civil Liberties and Civil Rights

A charge regularly levied against the dressmakers involved their breach of San Francisco's long-standing antipicketing ordinance. Employers relied on the law to curtail public protests, police authorities enforced it at will, and it remained in effect even after the passage of the Wagner Act. Some industrial leaders simply evaded the federal legislation; others argued that workers could legally and technically go on strike without picketing. Workers ardently disagreed. Most believed that the statute "shackled labor" and abrogated the rights promised by Congress and Roosevelt's administration.[64] Energized by a pro-labor climate in Washington and the ascendancy of union power locally, unionists across the political spectrum mobilized to repeal the antipicketing law.

The scalers signed on to the repeal campaign quite early. In September 1936, Sandoval apprised the SFLC of the SSU's decision "to take action towards getting the law revoked." They had no doubt the "vicious" ordinance was anti-labor: its existence debilitated unions' strength and crippled workers' right to strike. Unionists' analysis—a product of the mid-1930s that would have been impossible when the ordinance first went into effect—turned the issue of legal infraction on its head. While employers insisted that picketing violated local law, workers retorted that the ordinance infringed on their federally recognized rights. The SSU accordingly set out to invalidate the policy by demanding that elected officials revoke it. Its members urged direct action to bring collective claims before elected officials and propel representative government to address their demands. Schooled in public protest, the scalers recommended "mass picket lines and pressure upon City supervisors." Their plan fit within the democratic process, even though industrialists and other critics alleged that such demonstrations laid the groundwork for anarchy.[65]

Labor's political moxie bore initial success. In November, the supervisors agreed to consider a repeal proposal: they drafted a proposition and placed it before voters in March 1937. Unionists now set out to augment public support for their cause. For months, they staged rallies, distributed leaflets in their neighborhoods, and urged fellow citizens to approve the proposition. Their efforts paid off: 53 percent of voters agreed to annul the ordinance by approving Proposition 19. "The will of the people of San Francisco," proclaimed the SSU, had been "expressed in their vote."[66]

Scalers quickly found out the contest was not over. On the ground, police authorities proceeded as if the ordinance remained in place. In April, while on strike alongside Works Progress Administration workers, SSU members confronted city police who "[came] waylaying our pickets with clubs and smashing up the picket lines at every corner." They interpreted this development as an evasion of the recent plebiscite and an attempt to nullify the citizenry's wishes.[67] It was a prescient forecast. Beginning that spring, the local Chamber of Commerce and the city's Industrial Association initiated efforts to restore the antipicketing law. Business leaders, industrialists, and allies built their case by raising the banners of order and progress. They contended that the practice endangered the public by fomenting violence and disorder, and imperiling the city's economy and overall prosperity. The argument worked: antipicketing forces garnered enough signatures to put an initiative before voters in November. "Prevent picketing," explained Proposition 8 (1937) supporters, and "let San Francisco have peace, maintenance of law and order, [and] security for all its citizens."[68]

Now on the defensive, the labor movement denounced Proposition 8 by branding it as perilous to all San Franciscans because it suppressed their constitutional rights. Unionists knew the measure targeted them first and foremost. But focusing on civil liberties enabled them to define it as an attack on everyone's constitutional guarantees. They impugned the proposal as repressive and inimical to the country's foundational credos, including the freedom of speech, assembly, and the press. Hundreds of civic clubs, religious congregations, and immigrant groups came to share this sentiment and signed on to fight the antipicketing law.[69] Alianza Hispano-Americana and Sociedad Peruana de Auxilios Mutuos were but two ethnic organizations that did so. Latinos in mutual aid societies had grown increasingly tied to the labor movement by this time. Messages of solidarity embedded in mutual aid work aligned well with the unionist spirit, a connection made simple as more Latinos became union members. In tandem, unions and ethnic organizations impelled Latinos who were citizens to the voting booth. In so doing, they joined the popular front that eventually rejected Proposition 8.

For San Franciscans in CIO unions, especially the members of ILWU and UCAPAWA locals, protecting civil liberties often proceeded alongside a commitment to civil rights. The scalers and Alaska cannery men, like the longshoremen, espoused a philosophy of unity grounded in inclusion, equality, and opportunity. These sentiments had circulated among maritime laborers even before the 1934 strikes. In October 1933, the *Waterfront Worker* had linked victory in labor's struggle with absolute unity. The publication affirmed that workers' triumph depended on stamping out "race hatred" and other divisive practices.[70] Such formulations became part of waterfront workers' ideological heritage and explained the prominent roles their unions would have in antidiscrimination campaigns. In 1937, the ILWU's constitutional preamble incorporated a pledge to eradicate racial and religious discrimination. UCAPAWA took an even more comprehensive position on integration. Its 1938 constitution identified the union as one "which unites all workers in our industry on an industrial and democratic basis, regardless of age, sex, nationality, race, creed, color, or political and religious beliefs."[71] These international unions' reverence for local autonomy, however, meant that the implementation of nondiscrimination policies exhibited some regional variation. In San Francisco, ILWU and UCAPAWA locals took the lead in championing a civil rights agenda.

The ACWU advanced one of the most formidable programs of unity and nondiscrimination. A multiracial labor force and employers' record of divisive tactics by "setting race against race, nationality against nationality" spurred the union to confront these divisions directly and proactively.[72] Its unity

program proceeded along several fronts. The union celebrated its heterogeneous character and took pride in being a multiracial organization. Cannery
men emphasized that they did not tolerate bigotry or segregation: they
worked in mixed crews, and membership was open to all. "The cannery men
not only talk no discrimination," reported the *Western Worker*, "but what is
better still, they practice it."[73]

ACWU members further agreed that leaders should reflect the organization's diversity. They incorporated this vision into their governing structure
and specified that the executive committee's composition hinged on race: the
union would apportion seats based on aggregates from each ethnoracial
group. In 1937, Latinos held the most positions on the policymaking board;
seven of nineteen seats went to them. This "quota" system was pragmatic and
visionary. Ensuring that members from all backgrounds gained experience in
managing union affairs, the arrangement diffused power and safeguarded
against a concentration of authority by one group. In using race as the decisive factor for purposes of representation—instead of age, religion, or marital
status—the ACWU acknowledged the weight of racial and cultural identities.[74] Rather than attempting to unify members by ignoring or downplaying
race, the union created a mechanism to make certain all unionists saw themselves as decision makers. It was a novel and constructive approach for cultivating progressive race relations.

Cannery men Pedro Gutierrez and Milton Olguín understood both class
and race shaped laborers' lives and that the struggles for economic fairness
and racial equity could not be disconnected from each other. In December
1939, they traveled to Los Angeles to participate in the second convention of
the Congress of Spanish Speaking Peoples (El Congreso), one of the earliest
Latino civil rights conferences in the country. The ACWU elected these men
to represent its six hundred Spanish-speaking members, who made up almost 50 percent of the union.[75] In so doing, the San Francisco-based unionists interfaced with other activists who endeavored "to elevate [Latinos']
economic, political, educational, and cultural conditions."[76]

Shepherded into existence by Luisa Moreno, a national organizer for
UCAPAWA, El Congreso devised an ambitious blueprint for civil rights and
political action. Its analyses of social relations contained arresting insight,
pointing out how the workings of discrimination were multidimensional
and intersectional. "Racial distinctions against the Spanish speaking people," delegates explained, begot wage differentials, employment discrimination, educational segregation, and exclusion from housing. Their exposition

went further: low economic status itself engendered racial prejudice. Here, El Congreso put forth a community-based explanation of how the apparatus of racism reproduced itself and overlapped with class inequity. Assembly members recognized that racism intensified material disparities; the products of economic marginalization subsequently sustained ideas about racial inferiority and became the basis for exclusion. Confronting these challenges, they concluded, required education, advocacy, electoral participation, and grassroots mobilization. These political efforts had to proceed alongside an expanded New Deal agenda, including increases in appropriations for the Works Progress Administration, a stronger Wagner Act, and federal legislation that would tackle unequal treatment in all arenas of public life. As the decade came to an end, El Congreso made clear its representatives embraced New Deal liberalism and regarded the labor movement as "the most basic agency" to continue assisting Latinos in their pursuit of rights and opportunities.[77]

The Alaska cannery men could not have agreed more. After all, their union, the Ship Scalers Union, the Dressmakers Union, and other labor organizations had succeeded in mobilizing and politicizing Latinos in unprecedented ways. Union members and their families increasingly committed themselves to a political agenda emanating from a grassroots base and grounded in *la lucha obrera*. Driven by a spirit of solidarity, galvanized into action by the 1934 strikes, and emboldened by the New Deal, working-class Latinos joined their peers in pressing for rights, recognition, equity, and justice, and often did so despite great obstacles.

Whether they toiled on the waterfront or in the garment industry, the process and experience of unionization transformed Latinos' social reality and their consciousness as workers and citizens. Employment covered by a union contract afforded higher wages, a measure of economic security, and enhanced working conditions, all of which benefited workers and their families. These material gains represented the products of political struggle. Latinos and other working-class San Franciscans had come to understand that considerable improvements in their economic circumstances demanded sacrifice, solidarity, and rank-and-file action. They also recognized that union power rested, in large part, on the preservation of labor rights and protections, which the city's proletariat claimed and fought to safeguard. With the liberal state as their ally, Latinos and their comrades in CIO unions and some AFL affiliates found themselves in a vastly different position than they had been in before the 1934 strikes. Becoming union men and union women in effect meant that Latinos had become political actors.

CHAPTER 3

"Big Jobs to Do"

Economic Security, Electoral Politics, and Civil Rights Liberalism

Regino Gonzalez and his family greeted the 1940s in a rental home in the Excelsior District, along Bayshore Boulevard, where they eked out a living built around a household economy. Born in Puerto Rico, Regino and his wife, Cristina, arrived in San Francisco in the early 1910s and raised six children in California. The Gonzalezes relied on the unpaid domestic labors of Cristina and younger children as well as multiple incomes earned at a furniture factory. Regino, oldest son, Paul, nephew Rafael, and daughter Grace worked as a finisher, upholsterers, and a panel maker, respectively. Furniture making was literally a family affair.[1]

The union representing Gonzalez and his kinfolk—the UFW Local 262—expanded its base at mid-century and tenaciously exercised its political brawn. A wartime ethos of harmonious labor relations translated into no-strike pledges and employer acquiescence to upgrade union agreements. In October 1942, the UFW's negotiations with the Simmons Bed Company afforded workers the most robust contract to date. Gains included a $2 per week bonus, a 2 percent Christmas bonus, and increased vacation time. Adhering to its cornerstone of industrial unionism, the union also pursued wage parity and demanded a "guaranteed $1 an hour rate" irrespective of job skill.[2] This climate of mutual concession, however, broke down once the war ended. In February 1946, the UFW found itself back on the picket line. Following various months of negotiations, Edelmiro Huertas and Rogelio Herrera joined some seven hundred fellow Simmons Company workers and struck for higher wages. The 1 percent increase as offered by management, unionists insisted, was not "a decent offer" and did not signal an auspicious postwar future.[3]

While economic prosperity governed unions' ambitions, working-class Latinos increasingly reckoned their labor organizations could also assist them beyond the workplace. Huertas and other unionists who belonged to the Puerto Rican Club confirmed such aspirations in 1946. That year, the three-decades-old social club, now based in the Excelsior District, encountered a tide of hostility and harassment, prompting group leaders to ask the San Francisco CIO (SFCIO) Council for guidance and support. This council functioned as the coordinating body of all local unions affiliated with the Congress of Industrial Organizations. Turning to the council proved logical as the club drew many members from CIO unions, including the locals representing longshoremen, warehousemen, scalers, and furniture workers.

The Puerto Rican Club's troubles became apparent that summer when its events, especially its dances, generated consternation and antipathy among district residents and police authorities alike. Neighbors complained about the noise produced by live entertainment and the "rowdyism" from crowds attending the club's festivities. Police authorities' official response followed the standard protocol for handling such matters: they asked the club to be mindful of neighbors' concerns and to lessen the music's volume. Acknowledging the liveliness of their festivities, club leaders stressed that their dances occurred on Saturday nights and ended by midnight. In addition, they underscored the club's policies of only selling beer, prohibiting all forms of disorderly conduct, and monitoring "the premises so as to keep out undesirable" guests. These assurances and policies did not appear to be enough, at least not for the police department.[4]

Police authorities soon made known their views about Puerto Ricans: they saw them as troublesome, unwelcome, and nonwhite. Standard protocol gave way to increased surveillance, verbal aggravation, and intimidation. Police officers routinely attended and patrolled the dances, nagged club leaders about noise levels and crowd control, and sometimes commented on a desire to halt the events altogether. On one occasion, a sergeant purportedly told a club officer, "This is a residential district and it is not supposed to be open to Niggers and Pachucos."[5] The term *pachuco* gained prominence in 1940s California as a referent for Mexican Americans involved in or suspected of participating in youth gang activities.[6] Applying this label alongside the racist epithet used for African Americans at once referenced Puerto Ricans' multiracial composition and pointed to their racial unintelligibility.

Law enforcement agents maneuvered their misrecognition by positioning Puerto Ricans as both black and Mexican or at least comparable to those other racialized populations.

The SFCIO Council's executive officers confirmed what club leaders probably surmised: the predicament did not stem from noise but from race. Enlisted in the unions most committed to ending racial discrimination, the club's members likely understood that their problems revolved around tensions over fair housing, concerns over Puerto Ricans' suitability as neighbors, and police harassment of racial minorities. The quandary led the council to ask the mayor and chief of police to intervene in the matter. "[We] appeal to you to put a stop to the improper behaviour of the police," wrote Paul Schnur, the body's secretary. The labor alliance concurrently urged city leaders to "prevent the city administration from lending its weight to . . . a species of persecution based upon racial considerations."[7]

Though surviving evidence does not reveal if city officials attended to the situation, the case exposed pivotal layers of Latinos' life circumstances at mid-century. Increased migration during the war years and the postwar decades led some Latinos to neighborhoods with a long-standing Latino presence; others turned to new areas of settlement because of shrinking housing options in such districts as North Beach, density concerns, and a penchant for more pastoral spaces. But if employers availed themselves of Latinos as laborers, some San Franciscans did not accept them as neighbors and social equals. The phenomenon was not specific to the city, and Latinos faced analogous conditions in other urban centers at the time.[8] This is not to say that inequity and bias were absent from the employment arena. Eradicating racial inequality in the workplace, in fact, stood at the center of civil rights organizing throughout the 1940s and 1950s. Such activity formed part of the unions' agendas—especially the CIO affiliates—for economic stability and civic advancement. During these decades, the labor movement remained the pivotal force urging an enhancement of San Franciscans' quality of life. Latino unionists who belonged to the Puerto Rican Club and other such organizations recognized this fact; they therefore turned to their unions to shore up their rights as workers and citizens.

Deeply immersed in labor's sphere, Latinos' political praxis in the mid-twentieth century exhibited continuity, amplification, and disruption. The unionization impulse broadened, and the pursuit of economic security guided the programs of experienced and nascent unionists alike. Seasoned organizations, such as the Ship Scalers Union, and budding outfits, such as the Tortilla Makers Union, pressed for higher wages, overtime pay, holiday and vacation leaves, and hazard-free work settings.[9] Union members also set out to reinforce their New Deal protections and to defend the inviolability of the closed shop in times of armed conflict and cold war. They did so through direct action and heightened attention to both electoral and legislative processes. Latinos had occasionally engaged with the formal political arena in decades past; their unions now regularly rallied them to vote, to back pro-labor candidates, and to push for public policy initiatives of keen concern to them.

The decade-long campaign to pass a fair employment practices (FEP) statute epitomized labor unions' fusion of grassroots organizing and policy work. Partnering with other racial minorities and white allies, Latinos embraced and championed civil rights liberalism. Proponents of this "racial paradigm," as one historian has called it, consistently urged political and business leaders to actualize the tenets of equal opportunity, colorblindness, and equal protection of the law.[10] San Francisco's enactment of an FEP ordinance in 1957 codified this vision into law and testified to an upswing in local government's assurance of equality. The ascendancy of civil rights liberalism, however, occurred as the labor movement increasingly found itself on the defensive. Jurisdictional raids and anticommunist attacks on progressive unions that welcomed Latinos and other racial minorities accelerated during the early postwar years. And by the end of the 1950s, organized labor confronted a statewide movement aiming to invalidate the closed shop and institute right-to-work policies. Latino unionists and their comrades fought strenuously against these assaults. In so doing, they weathered a mixed political climate, navigating gains and losses, progress and morass.

Migration and Neighborhood Transition at Mid-Century

Born in Walsenburg, Colorado, just fifty miles north of the New Mexico border, seventeen-year-old Bertha Castro headed to San Francisco in late 1942. Her sister Anna had arrived earlier and held a job at Reliance Trailer and Truck Company, which manufactured industrial tractors used heavily by waterfront companies. Bertha first worked as a salesgirl and then a waitress; by February 1943, she had procured a position as an assembler/helper at Reliance. Both siblings also became members of the Automotive Machinist Union Local 1305 of the International Association of Machinists.[11] Their trajectory was not an exceptional one. Finding wartime work and joining the ranks of organized labor proved to be a common experience for many Latinos who entered the city in the 1940s.

A booming labor market, workforce shortages, and the economic might of defense industries across the Bay Area spurred a new wave of Latino migration during the war years and the decade that followed. An expanded economy marked by soaring business activity and increased levels of employment in manufacturing, construction, and transportation (sectors that all grew by 50 percent or more) triggered what some scholars have labeled as the second gold rush to Northern California.[12] Thousands of domestic and international migrants came to the region to better their economic standing. San Francisco's overall population rose by more than 20 percent in ten years alone, from approximately 634,535 residents in 1940 to roughly 775,360 city dwellers by 1950. The number of Latinos almost doubled during this decade, from more than 14,000 in 1940 to approximately 24,000 by 1950.[13] Though still a small part of the general population, Latinos' cumulative growth foreshadowed a demographic trend in motion: their numbers would double again by 1960 and once more by 1970.

Ethnic Mexicans remained the most numerous Latino subgroup in the 1940s. Numbers alone obscured a heterogeneity marked by distinctions in residential history, birthplace, generation, and citizenship. In 1940, census enumerators determined that approximately half of the city's Mexican-origin residents had been born in the United States. This figure only accounted for native-born Mexican Americans with at least one immigrant parent.[14] Other U.S.-born residents who clung to their cultural heritage included those "descendants of the original inhabitants of California, Texas, and New Mexico."[15] In fact, domestic migrants like the Castro sisters from Colorado regularly left various southwestern localities in search of work opportunities in San Francisco. They were joined by immigrants who entered directly from Mexico. Still others first spent time as farm laborers or railroad workers—sometimes participating in a contract labor effort known as the Bracero program— before arriving in the city.[16]

Marked diversification among ethnic Mexicans coincided with a steady inflow of Central Americans. The 1940s actually became a transitional decade of outmigration from the isthmus, as well as the demographic configuration of the city's overall Latino population. By the decade's end, Central American immigrants began to outnumber Mexican immigrants.[17] While the city presented one of many settlement options for Mexican nationals, Central

Americans remained overwhelmingly concentrated in San Francisco. A quest for better economic opportunities coupled with social ties to individuals who had arrived in decades past inspired more and more Nicaraguans and Salvadorans to migrate. Some migrants learned about jobs from family and friends; others did so by coming into contact with labor agents—especially ones representing shipyard companies—who "recruited workers from Nicaragua and El Salvador."[18] Julio Andrade formed part of this movement. Decades later, he recalled that many in 1940s El Salvador "wanted to come to work painting ships in San Francisco." Doing so led many of them into the ranks of organized labor. By 1944, the SSU acknowledged the presence of Central Americans and identified them as one of the minority groups it represented.[19]

Work opportunities likewise inspired more Puerto Ricans to set their sights on San Francisco. Some migrants now came directly from the island; others first worked in California agriculture or served in the armed forces before taking up residence in the metropolis.[20] Ismael Sandoval Adorno first journeyed from Puerto Rico in the mid-1940s, picked fruit in Fresno for a few seasons, and eventually deduced that year-round, urban employment would be more advantageous. He then brought his siblings, uncle, and other relatives once he had established himself in the city. Elba Montes and her parents experienced a similar trajectory. They moved to San Francisco in 1949, but their settlement process was facilitated by kin who had left the island years earlier. Montes, Sandoval, and their relatives were but two families who formed part of the Puerto Rican diaspora living by the Golden Gate. Though the city did not become a major destination during the postwar migration years, it retained the most sizable Puerto Rican community on the West Coast until 1970.[21]

Population growth amplified Latinos' concentration in central-city areas, especially the Western Addition, Buena Vista (present-day Haight-Ashbury), the Mission, and South of Market. Still a predominantly working-class population, Latinos typically gravitated to these districts because they offered cheap housing and proximity to factories, garment shops, and the waterfront. Leticia Guerrero and Julia Melendez were among the many Latinas who joined the Dressmakers Union in the 1940s and called Buena Vista home. A popular account from this era simultaneously revealed that most Central Americans were workers and resided in the Western Addition.[22] Considerable numbers of blue-collar individuals and families also lived in Potrero Hill, Bernal Heights, Bayview, and the Outer Mission. Some of their middle-class counterparts lived in these various neighborhoods too; others procured housing in the Richmond and Sunset districts, which were solidly middle class and overwhelmingly white. Latinos did not encounter impenetrable racial barriers in the housing market, yet accessing white neighborhoods often hinged on having lighter skin, claiming a Spanish identity, and speaking English.[23] Although the exclusion differed from that experienced by African Americans—in degree and in kind—most Latinos found themselves living in multiracial areas deemed unappealing and blighted as the postwar era wore on.

By 1950, the prewar preeminence of North Beach as a hub of Latino settlement had been eclipsed by the Western Addition, Buena Vista, and the Mission.[24] A congested rental market and soaring density gradually made North Beach a less viable and attractive option. The surge in residential dispersion coincided with a heightened diffusion of sociocultural and commercial life. Restaurants, food marts, bookstores, home furnishings shops, and other businesses catering to Latinos steadily dotted the Western Addition and especially the Mission. Nightspots and theaters featuring Spanish-language films enriched leisure life in these districts as well.[25] Social service institutions, too, served as grounds for recreational activities. Beginning in the late 1940s, the Canon Kip Community Center in South of Market organized dances, picnics, and sporting activities for adolescents. The center concurrently sponsored a youth council and teen newspaper, with Tony Fernandez, Josie Sigala, and other young Latinos as contributing writers. On the sacred front, while Guadalupe Church retained historical and communal prominence, Latino Catholics who did not live in North Beach now sought out other parishes. St. Joseph's Church in South of Market along with St. Charles Borromeo and St. Peter's in the Mission had sizable Spanish-speaking congregations by the mid-1950s; parishioners there attended masses, *novenas*, and religious fiestas.[26] All these budding fields of fellowship and conviviality indicated that the districts hemmed around downtown offered more than just housing: they sustained and diversified Latinos' social and communal existence.

Power and Resilience in the Early to Mid-1940s

One aspect of everyday life remained constant amid population growth and neighborhood transition: political consciousness and action continued to be chiefly cultivated within the labor movement. Three years before the country entered the war, a cadre of middle-class Latinos led by attorney Louis Vásquez and newspaper publisher Nick Di Matteo formed a Spanish-American Democratic Club. They sought "to unite all the Spanish and Latin-American voters of the State in a political club."[27] The group's reach and activities proved extremely limited. Political mobilization built exclusively around ethnic identity and disconnected from labor did not attract many followers at this time. Some Latinos probably did not regard ethnicity alone as a force for unity or activism; others may have considered labor organizing as more directly relevant to their lives or simply may have been unaware of Vasquez's and Di Matteo's effort. Di Matteo's *El Imparcial* actually ceased publication in 1938, and city residents would not see the publication of a stand-alone, Spanish-language newspaper until 1948. Working-class Latinos instead obtained news and political education through the labor press, including the Spanish-language version of the ILGWU's *Justice* and Spanish-language inserts in the ILWU's *Dispatcher*.

Maritime laborers and garment workers began the new decade with gusto to shore up their gains, rights, and leverage. In spring 1940, warehousemen, cannery workers, scalers, and knitwear workers all found themselves on the picket line, in arbitration, or in jurisdictional disputes. Bread-and-butter issues regularly propelled them to action as employers attempted to trim union contracts. While warehousemen like John Gomez struck for increased wages and vacation time, Philip Cano and his cannery brothers sought contract renewal free of wage cuts. The ACWU and eleven other unions engaged in seasonal fishing expeditions expected to maintain or boost past agreements. Neither weeks of governmental mediation nor employers' claims of soaring operational costs weakened unionists' resolve. The San Francisco salmon packers eventually opted to abandon the season instead of yielding to workers' demands. This outcome had critical economic implications for thousands of seasonal laborers and their families. Men such as Cano could nevertheless find political and affective succor in knowing that their determination and unanimity of purpose, though tested, had not been broken.[28]

Proletarian fearlessness and a veneration of unionism remained ascendant despite spiraling and sometimes unexpected obstacles. Cognizant of employers' attempts to minimize workers' clout, unionists consistently affirmed the sanctity of the closed shop and the indispensability of workplace solidarity. The "courage and stamina" of Latinas and their workmates in the Knitgoods Workers Union, ILGWU Local 191, presented a case in point. In late 1939, 250 women began an extended challenge to adverse conditions and "abuses" at the Gantner and Mattern plant, where they made sportswear and swimsuits. Toiling under an expired contract, the company's rejection of cost-of-living adjustments and an all-inclusive vacation clause bred resentment. Unionists concurrently complained about managers' issuance of pink slips and the use of "coercion and intimidation" to speed up production. Tensions escalated in October when janitors at this same plant went on strike and the knitgoods workers—adhering to union principles—refused to cross the custodians' picket line. Their secondary strike spawned an unforeseen conundrum: Gantner executives asserted their prerogative over job reinstatement once the janitors' dispute ended. Months of stalled negotiations and the firm's unwillingness to reemploy 80 workers—a decision the union defined as a lockout—then impelled Local 191 to launch its own strike in March 1940.[29]

For the next fifteen months, knitgoods workers staged an offensive that won them allies and sympathizers near and far, even though Gantner's position remained unchanged. Unionists charged the company with circumventing the process of collective bargaining; discriminating against union members; and supplanting older, well-paid laborers with nonunionized, cheaper ones. Bosses offered a simple justification for denying employment to individuals "left out": those workers supposedly had poor rates of productivity. The dispute eventually came before the National Labor Relations Board, which dismissed the union's grievances in January 1941 and emboldened the business to proceed with operations as it saw fit.[30] Still, strikers did not back down. They persisted with their pickets as the ILGWU instituted a nationwide boycott of Gantner products; other unions also mounted secondary boycotts and refused to handle "hot cargo" (i.e., goods produced at a struck site). Incessant pickets, property damage, decreased profits, store closures, and a "vilified" reputation did not move Gantner to reconsider negotiation. By mid-1941, most strikers began to accept their loss and look for new jobs elsewhere. The outcome delivered a painful reminder that "great fervor" and resilience did not always generate triumph.[31]

The knitgoods workers' strike converged with the scalers' seven-month campaign to quell encroachment on their syndical turf. In March 1940, president Pete Garcia excoriated AFL-backed machinations to organize a rival union, one that would "wreck the conditions the [scalers] have fought so hard to get" by accepting lower wages and "no closed shop and hiring hall."[32] Matters turned more perilous months later when the Sailors Union began pressing some shipping companies to offer scaling jobs to unemployed seafarers. Construing the situation as a threat to their livelihood and their union's bailiwick, Garcia and his comrades set up a picket line in October and called on other ILWU locals for support. Denying any wrongdoing, representatives for the American President Lines instead accused the sailors of strong-arm methods and identified the scalers as "employees of certain contractors" lacking a collective bargaining agreement with the company itself. ILWU officials rebutted: they circulated an existing agreement and chided the firm for colluding with the sailors' organization. "Designating land workers as standby sailors," Harry Bridges communicated, allowed the shipping line to "evade federal [labor] laws" and practice "subterfuge," effectively benefiting the company's pockets at the scalers' expense. Bridges went further and raised the specter of secondary strikes and boycotts of hot cargo by reminding the Waterfront Employers Association that longshoremen would observe the scalers' picket line.[33]

As deliberations unfolded, shoreside tensions escalated, and the scalers fended off sailors' attempts to break up their picket line. The showdown—filled with indignation, insults, and incessant scuffles—led some workers to seek medical assistance while others found themselves in police custody. Scalers' protests and the ILWU's intervention nevertheless bore fruit. Within weeks, the SSU had "forced the American President Lines to agree . . . that a contract covering their work ought to be negotiated with their union."[34] Employers' volte-face befittingly provoked boasting and cheering. The celebration masked what some scalers may have suspected and feared: intractable employers and jurisdictional troubles would consume their energies many times again.

Broader reflections on the state of citywide labor relations likely influenced the scalers' fortunes. Rising antagonism between capital and labor received considerable attention in the public sphere, and city dailies devoted much coverage to the tense situation in workplaces around town. In April 1940, the *San Francisco Chronicle* reported on the Maritime Federation of the Pacific's "warning that waterfront peace [would be] impossible if employers insist[ed] on 'chiseling' unions out of gains already established."[35] The scalers' troubles began around this time, and their dispute presented one of multiple cases marked by doubtful labor-management amity. Domestic harmony came to acquire paramount significance—ideologically, materially, and strategically—once the United States formally entered World War II in December 1941. As the nation and its industries converted to wartime production, unions began to proclaim "Unity for Victory."[36] Translating these declarations into practice depended on easing the AFL-CIO divide and nurturing friendly relations between workers and their employers.

American unionists comprised a vast "volunteer army of production sol-
diers," blazoned the *Labor Herald* in March 1942. Harry Bridges, as ILWU
president and California CIO director, could not have agreed more. That
month, he urged labor leaders to "concentrate all their energies on speeding
up production for war." John Acosta, Richard Camplís, and other Latinos
who sat on the local CIO council or presided over their unions gave heed and
moved to embrace Bridges's message. The directive positioned working people as agents, or "instruments," of freedom, democracy, and resistance to to-
talitarianism.[37] Pragmatically, blueprints for victory attended to global and
local concerns. The furniture workers' win-the-war program, for instance,
emphasized the speedy conversion to wartime production, the formation of
labor-management committees to oversee industrial output and work rules,
and the stabilization of wages to offset the upsurge in costs of living. Their
sweat and "sinew," unionists foresaw, would buttress the nation, its armed
forces, its economy, and their households.[38]

Patriotism and practical expectations aside, the fulfillment of labor-
management cooperation was neither automatic nor straightforward. Agreement and accommodation proceeded expeditiously in some industries while
discord and complications stalled the process in others. Rapprochement
often depended on economic calculations and openness to wartime adapta-
tions. Employers and laborers with stakes in the Alaska salmon industry presented a case in point: they proved amenable to conciliation given the costs
incurred from the work season's cancellation in 1940 and the thorny negotiations a year later. In June 1942, Stephen Glumaz and Pete Gutierrez rejoiced
with their union brothers after securing wage increases and a boost in overtime pay. The two men sat on a joint negotiating committee responsible for
brokering a Pacific coast–wide contract that standardized pay and work conditions for Alaska-bound men from San Francisco, Portland, and Seattle.
Unionists in other industries celebrated salary upgrades as well. San Franciscans in the Textile Workers Union Local 71—composed of women and men
who made potato sacks, tents, and other such goods—reached a compromise
with their bosses in October 1942. Frank Garcia, John Ortega, and others on
the bargaining committee accepted "5 cents an hour pay raises" and back pay
for some five hundred workers in three plants; they saw this as a preferable
alternative to protracted arbitration from the War Labor Board, which could
have prescribed a similar or less favorable settlement.[39]

In contrast, steelworkers at the American Can Company plant—where they
manufactured everything from motor-oil cans to ammunition containers—

consistently declined to lower their demands and eventually turned to the War Labor Board after negotiations broke down. Gladys Lara, Alfred Padilla, and hundreds of others in the Steel Workers Organizing Committee Local 1684 sought wage increments, "equal pay to women doing men's work," and participation in an "industry council to plan production."[40] Their strategies, including work shutdowns and appeals for intercession from the War Production Board, did not sway the company. American Can leaders' aversion to a labor-management committee illustrated how this model of cooperation had much more buy-in from unionists and government officials. The road to unity, as the steelworkers learned, could be a rough one, even in wartime.

The labor movement faced other obstacles during the war years, which unions met with grassroots mobilization and electoral participation. The parameters of free speech and the scope of labor solidarity, in particular, came under more scrutiny from employers, policymakers, and the public at large. In June 1941, the California legislature enacted a statute outlawing secondary boycotts as well as unionists' practice of refusing to handle hot cargo. Overriding a gubernatorial veto and backed by agricultural growers and industrialists, most state legislators defended the act as economically sound and in the public's interest. The law would prevent the loss of revenue for individuals, businesses, and the state, they argued, while curbing "interference with the production of goods and equipment for national defense."[41] Union leaders, the rank and file, and their supporters dissented loudly: they viewed the legislation as an infringement on civil liberties and a constriction of labor's power. Assemblyman Thomas Maloney from San Francisco opposed the measure because it stripped a worker's "right to strike to help another employee" and curtailed freedoms of speech and assembly. More than thirty thousand union men and women petitioned Maloney and his colleagues to protect these rights during the bill's consideration; they then pledged to overturn the statute through a referendum. By September, the "union labor forces of California," admonished the *Los Angeles Times*, had "made good on their threat to block the anti-hot cargo act." The collection of more than two hundred thousand signatures indeed halted the law's implementation, making it possible to place the issue directly before voters the following year.[42]

Throughout 1942, AFL and CIO unionists alike devoted great energy to public education, fundraising, and get-out-the-vote drives, especially as the fight over hot cargo intensified during the summer and fall months. Prominent labor leaders built their case by arming themselves with nationalism and the language of freedom. They cast the law as un-American, autocratic, and "a veritable slave bill," one that "would compel employees to work against their will." Patriotism was of course a malleable tool. The rhetoric of national unity and industrial peace, the emphasis on wartime production, and concerns about material scarcity had grown more potent since the legislature's original action. In November 1942, approximately 55 percent of California voters upheld the state's ban on hot cargo and secondary boycotts for the remainder of the war.[43]

San Franciscans could take some comfort in knowing they bucked the statewide trend: a majority of those who voted opted to invalidate the law.[44] Even so, the setback brought two essential points to the fore. It reminded union members that labor rights were not immutable, and pushed them to recognize the need to expand their vigilance and strategies to confront further obstacles. Future success, some labor activists noted, required a reorientation of grassroots action and a more relatable rendering of their agenda. "We're not going to stop mobilizing . . . through the union apparatus," explained the SFCIO Political Action Committee (PAC) in 1943. "But experience has shown that *this is not enough*." The newly created branch of the local CIO prescribed a far-reaching operation built on precinct work. Ace de Losada, Barbara Santos, and all others engaged with this committee accordingly set out to widen their outreach activities, strengthen political ties with neighbors, and convince nonunionists that "their interests and ours are the same." De Losada and Santos were not the only Latino unionists who did so. Dozens of them traversed their neighborhoods during election campaigns—canvassing residents, establishing common ground, and imploring citizens to vote.[45]

In turning to precinct work, Pearl Gonzales, Anacleto Varoz, and others embraced three facts of mid-century political life. They understood activism had to take place within and beyond their unions and that amassing allies required ongoing education and rapport building. Gonzales and her peers also knew that upending any future detriment to working people demanded robust engagement with the electoral process. These realities took on particular significance during the 1944 presidential campaign. Organized labor intended to keep Roosevelt in the White House and devoted a good portion of its political energies to do so. "[We] have two big jobs to do," stressed the SSU that fall. Alongside their paid labors, union members rang doorbells and encouraged neighbors to back the Roosevelt-Truman ticket. Like other CIO unionists, the scalers identified Roosevelt as the leader who would broker peace, permit the labor movement to flourish, and ensure postwar security. A vote for FDR, as union officers John Acosta and Mary Sandoval explained it, would amount to victory in war and prosperity for the nation, as well as the advancement of workers' rights and interests.[46]

Latinos' engagement with the Democratic Party before the 1960s has received rather limited scholarly attention, though they turned to the Democratic Party apparatus long before the Viva Kennedy clubs and the War on Poverty.[47] In San Francisco, the SSU and its partners solidly nurtured connection and allegiance to Democratic leaders and agendas by the 1940s. "*Se les suplica se registren* (We beseech you to register)," read a bilingual piece in the *Dispatcher*, "to reelect President Franklin D. Roosevelt."[48] Appeals like these and immersion in the "Roosevelt camp" extended well beyond the ILWU and presidential elections. The campaign work of furniture workers Edelmiro Huertas, Elvira Silva, and others in UFW 262 confirmed as much. In 1944, they crisscrossed their precincts, distributed campaign literature, and urged neighbors to send Franck Havenner back to Congress. A staunch progressive, Havenner had lost his congressional seat in 1940; the "Roosevelt candidate" now regained it by promising a postwar future marked by harmony and abundance.[49] The votes and outreach efforts of Latino unionists contributed to Havenner's win, and they did so again two years later. By 1946, subcommittees of Spanish-speaking and Chinese voters, among others, sprouted within the SFCIO PAC. The development affirmed the value and utility of summoning ethnic ties for electoral purposes. A year later, as Havenner set his sights on the mayor's office, his campaign team recognized Latinos as a budding political bloc. "*Mire la obra de Havenner* (Look at the Havenner Record)," instructed a 1947 pamphlet, as it extolled the politician's commitment to the working class, racial minorities, and the well-being of all San Franciscans.[50] Union members were of course already well acquainted with the politician. But in what represented one of the earliest formal overtures by a mayoral candidate, Havenner underscored his awareness of Latinos' linguistic heritage and civic interests. The production and dissemination of bilingual materials made evident that the candidate wanted all Latinos to see him as their next mayor.

Fair Play, Equal Opportunity, Civic Unity

Latinos, other people of color, and white residents committed to fulfilling the nation's civic creed consistently identified "fair play," equal opportunity, and inclusion as part and parcel of prosperity. Throughout the 1940s and 1950s, they undertook a crusade to eradicate inequities and exclusionary practices based on race, color, national origin, and religion. This civic venture developed and flourished—forcefully although not exclusively—in the labor movement, especially within the CIO. In postwar California, the CIO and the West Coast branch of the National Association for the Advancement of Colored People (NAACP-WC) spearheaded the statewide FEP drive.[51] Local civil rights activism fed into this regional effort and, notably, drew a heterogeneous cast of participants from the start. Many CIO unions and a few AFL locals advancing a civil rights agenda were, after all, multiracial entities. Studies of mid-century San Francisco have nevertheless tended to overlook Latino and Asian American involvement in the quest for racial equality. The absence or minimal role of institutional advocates akin to the NAACP explains some of this oversight. Yet the historical record reveals that Latinos were not disconnected or peripheral to civil rights work. Their sensibilities and organizing just happened to materialize most vigorously and extensively within their unions.

The ethos of equality and tolerance propagated by the ILWU and UCAPAWA in the 1930s permeated other CIO locals by the 1940s. Wartime mobilization, worker protest, and President Roosevelt's Executive Order 8802 (1941)—barring discrimination in war production industries—impelled more labor unions to adopt forceful stances on inclusion and equal access to jobs. Some unionists sustained their position by making a utilitarian correlation. As the furniture workers stressed, maximum wartime output depended on the employment and unity of all laborers irrespective of background. Casting discrimination as an impediment to manpower essentially offered a pragmatic strategy to push for civil rights. The Union of Marine Cooks and Stewards (MCS), which had lagged behind other CIO maritime unions on matters of equity, likewise seized on the "productionist rhetoric" and soon emerged as a fearless proponent of racial justice. Other unionists built a more explicit connection between wartime rhetoric, inclusion, and American ideals. Steel workers in SWOC 1684 branded racial exclusion and discrimination as inimical to the country's civic creed and pledged to abrogate such practices. The "fight for democracy" abroad, they posited, had to be accompanied with a democratization of the American workplace and society at large.[52]

Local unions' civil rights efforts intersected with the work of the California CIO's Minorities Committee, established in 1943. Frank Lopez of UFW 262 and Mary Sandoval sat on this statewide body from its formation. The committee offered technical assistance to CIO locals as they ironed out their "minorities programs;" it also devoted much energy to critical analysis, advocacy, and the formulation of legislative proposals with sharp attention to race. Amid world war, Lopez, Sandoval, and their colleagues engrossed themselves in the ideological process of welding integration and opportunity into the win-the-war platform. "The establishment of the Four Freedoms for all nations, minority groups and colonial people," relayed their task force, "require[d] an end to abuses" motivated by racial hatred and intolerance. Committee members translated this vision into a docket of activities and public policy proposals calling for justice and equality.[53]

In August 1943, the Minorities Committee invited over six hundred representatives from unions—both CIO and AFL locals—and civic groups to San Francisco for a regional conference on racial and national unity. Attendees considered a myriad of issues and resolved to press for the abolition of poll taxes, hiring teachers and police officers from minority groups, a liberalization of immigration laws for the Chinese, and the continuation and expansion of the Fair Employment Practices Commission (FEPC), among other measures. Civil rights advocates understood that the workings of California's multiple color lines required attacks on many fronts; many likewise acknowledged that legislative change would be unlikely to materialize without education and public pressure. The Minorities Committee accordingly recommended political action and mobilization to "educate out, legislate out, blast out, and banish [discrimination] from American life."[54]

Gatherings like the 1943 unity conference connected progressive unionists with individuals and citizen groups that regarded "walls of prejudice" as corrosive to everyday stability and harmony.[55] If population growth and wartime dislocations compromised social relations, these same factors compelled numerous organizations to take strong stands against bigotry and hatred. The Bay Area Council Against Discrimination pulled in leaders and activists from the local NAACP, the San Francisco League of Women Voters, the International Institute, and other community-minded institutions, and acceded that "tolerant" San Francisco was not without its share of racial troubles. Its antidote for discord and acrimony was simple: like other mid-twentieth-century liberals, the league's participants believed that the democratic creed would flourish and materialize through education, persuasion, and interracial interaction. Its successor, the Council for Civic Unity (CCU), would propagate this outlook during the postwar era.[56]

San Franciscans of middle-class and professional standing generally constituted the CCU's membership, while their working-class counterparts

Figure 4. Mary Sandoval, Joe Mendez, and Gwen Kircher of the Ship Scalers
Union, and Revels Cayton of the California CIO Minorities Committee,
1943 (left to right). Courtesy of ILWU Library and Archive.

continued to mobilize for civil rights through their unions. City residents in
these networks shared the goals of equality and fairness; differences in tone
and strategies, however, would eventually influence their alliances and the
evolution of civil rights organizing in a Cold War context. Latinos did not
hold leadership positions in the CCU or its predecessor. Social workers, lawyers, and other professionals backed the CCU's efforts as interested citizens
or staffers of the council's institutional partners. Attorney Louis Vásquez and
caseworker Tomás Garcia fit such profiles: Vásquez had a track record of civic
engagement and Garcia ran a youth program at the International Institute.
Some working-class Latinos probably learned about the CCU through the
SFCIO Council or their unions but did not participate in the CCU's day-to-
day activities. Still, working- and middle-class citizens involved in civil rights
work crossed paths at high-profile events and collaborated with one another
in the immediate post–World War II years.

In early March 1946, San Francisco's civil rights brigade converged at a public meeting to promote and push for a statewide measure prohibiting discrimination in employment. Members and allies of the SFCIO Council, the CCU, the San Francisco NAACP, the Warehousemen's Union, the SSU, and the ACWU collectively hailed FEP as a hallmark of Americans' unity. A number of progressive and multiracial AFL locals—such as the Cooks Union Local 44 and the Miscellaneous Employees Union Local 110 (representing dishwashers, kitchen porters, and restaurant custodians)—joined them as well.[57] Community assemblies such as these had transpired since early 1945, when Assemblyman Augustus Hawkins (D-Los Angeles) introduced a proposal to codify FEP into law and set up a California FEPC to monitor its implementation. Civil rights advocates praised and mobilized forcefully behind Hawkins's plan. But the bill encountered consistent opposition in Sacramento and did not move out of committee in either summer 1945 or winter 1946.[58]

The labor and civic forces of equality did not back down: they "found another way to act" by turning to a citizen-led initiative. The California CIO and the Statewide Committee for a California FEPC, which counted Luisa Moreno and Louis Vásquez on its planning boards, coordinated an effort to bring the issue directly before voters in November 1946. These umbrella organizations underscored that success hinged on "putting on the heaviest pressure" and mounting large-scale educational campaigns at the local level.[59] San Franciscans who gathered at the civic center in March 1946 enthusiastically answered the call. In subsequent months, unionists involved in the SFCIO's PAC prepared mass mailings, distributed leaflets on street corners, and urged residents to back FEP by voting for Proposition 11. The largest number of precinct workers came from ILWU locals and the MCS, whose members also made monetary contributions to the PAC. Such actions affirmed unionists' devotion to the democratic process, street-level mobilization, and civil rights.[60]

Californians who backed Proposition 11 stressed that the measure advanced American democracy. The labor market, they explained, should complement the polity and be structured around parity of access and participation. Their opponents thought otherwise and branded the initiative as biased, dangerous, counterproductive, and un-American. The artfully named Committee for Tolerance, based in Southern California but with statewide reach, maligned the proposition as unfair and menacing. It construed the measure as an infringement on employers' rights to make decisions about their private enterprises and disadvantageous for laborers—naturalized as white—who might be replaced by minority candidates. The California Chamber of Commerce and the Farm Bureau Federation, representing agribusiness across the state, agreed and emphasized that a law mandating integration would spawn friction between workers, leading to turmoil, violence, and decreased productivity.

The "No on 11" forces interlaced their economic rationalizations with teachings about social relations and excessive government power. Tolerance could only be achieved through education and free will, they insisted, not by compulsory legislation or "any attempt to force social regulations by law." Their analysis effectively foreclosed the educational potential presented by a diverse workplace and instead assailed integration as a by-product of "governmental coercion." And to fully discredit the advocates of racial liberalism, the opposition turned to red-baiting and excoriated the FEP plan as "a pet of both the CIO-PAC and the Communists." Proposition 11 embodied a "communistic plan," claimed the Committee for Tolerance and other critics, because it would authorize undue and oppressive governmental action while generating discord and instability in daily life. The multilayered critique succeeded: two out of three voters in November 1946 embraced an illiberal view of tolerance and cast suspicion on state action to democratize the workplace.[61]

Samuel Valadez, Antonio Montoya, and Reinaldo Viquez, while dejected, did not construe the proposition's defeat as the deathblow to the FEP crusade. These MCS members remained convinced that their democratic and integrated work environments should not be the exception but the rule. Thousands in the SFCIO's orbit shared this sentiment. Unionists' continued organizing and, in particular, the CCU's activities (e.g., meetings with city power brokers, presentations before official bodies) found receptive ears at decade's end. In October 1949, the Mayor's Committee on Human Relations— created a year earlier and composed of varied representatives from civil society—released a report and policy proposal urging the San Francisco Board of Supervisors to pass a municipal FEP ordinance. The committee had considered the issue for many months; heard the perspectives from labor, business, and minority groups; and reviewed research data presented by the CCU. It concluded, as one member put it, "If we as Americans believe that discrimination is morally wrong then we certainly have a moral right to legislate against it."[62] Local legislators would have to be swayed by more than moral certitude. They accordingly embarked on a protracted consideration of FEP, which lasted until spring 1951.

San Francisco's supervisors had to weigh whether the city they had identified, back in 1948, as "outstanding for amity and good relations among her
various racial, religious, and ethnic groups" should stamp out employment
discrimination through legislative channels. Valadez, Montoya, and Viquez
certainly hoped their elected officials would do so. In January 1950, these
leaders from the Asociación Latina Hispana Americana wrote the supervisors and implored them to pass an FEP ordinance. This association, an affiliate of the Asociación Nacional Mexico Americana (ANMA), attracted many
members from left-leaning labor unions such as the MCS. Valadez and his
colleagues drew on their lived experience to counter views of prejudice as an
illusion. "We are convinced that discrimination does exist here," they noted.
"And we can find no connection between a person's skin coloring or national
origin and *that* person's ability."[63]

Latinos across the city shared a parallel sentiment and expressed their
views in multiple ways. Some chose to contact the supervisors directly. "To
stop prejudice, discrimination, et al. is the ideal before us," communicated
E. M. in a letter to the board. Simply identifying as "a Mexican," this resident
clamored for public redress and reminded the supervisors that they "[were]
the controlling factor" in mitigating inequity. Others made such views known
by signing petitions circulated by unions, civic groups, and mutual aid societies. That hundreds of Latinos endorsed the FEP measure by listing their
union affiliation alongside their names revealed the enduring interdepen-
dence between unionization and political identity as the 1950s began.[64] Many
scalers, warehouse workers, longshoremen, dishwashers, cooks, and stewards
appealed not only through written petitions but also through public protests
outside City Hall. Doing so fit squarely within an established tradition of direct action. Their detractors quickly seized on the Cold War atmosphere to
censure confrontational tactics and to marginalize unionists' pursuit of FEP.

Resistance to a nondiscrimination ordinance proceeded from constituencies who revived and amplified the critiques levied against Proposition 11.
San Franciscans in business organizations, homeowner associations, and
neighborhood improvement clubs—whose membership and property interests sometimes overlapped—consistently reminded the supervisors that city
voters rejected the 1946 initiative "by a majority of better than two to one."
Economic power brokers, such as Almon Roth and Erwin Easton, believed
that an FEP mandate would at once override the 1946 popular vote—thereby
undermining the democratic process—and unduly encroach upon "the prerogatives of management." Roth presided over the San Francisco Employers

Council while Easton spoke for downtown interests organized under the North Central Improvement Association. Their perspectives typified much of the anti-FEP sentiment and became boilerplates within entrepreneurial circles. Adamantly opposed to state action, they instead praised and favored educational drives, employers' voluntary action, and managerial goodwill. "We feel that the solution to the problem is one of education, rather than legislation," related C. F. De Lano of the Golden Gate Restaurant Association. Many foes of FEP went further and claimed that discrimination had gradually declined. "Compared to other cities," maintained Roth, the metropolis "is eminently fair to its minority groups and exceptionally free from racial prejudice and discrimination." In this light, San Francisco's distinctiveness and openness—promotional if conjectural—together with employer benevolence made state interference dispensable. This line of reasoning then interlocked with charges of governmental overreach. FEP critics characterized their rivals as ill-informed citizens who could not substantiate "alleged discrimination" and failed to grasp the dangers posed by governmental intrusion into private economic affairs.[65]

As the Cold War reached its apogee, anti-FEP forces had potent ideological armor at their disposal: they maligned FEP proponents as belonging to Communist and subversive groups that stoked antagonism and created havoc in their tolerant and fair city. Antonio Montoya and Jose Correa saw nothing destructive or disloyal about forcefully pressing for civil rights and collaborating with hundreds of other FEP advocates in militant, left-wing groups. "*El deber es de nosotros* (It is our duty)," Montoya reminded fellow Latino unionists in the MCS, "to combat discrimination with all possible force." Also a regional organizer for ANMA—an advocacy organization working to secure labor and civil rights for ethnic Mexicans—he underscored the imperative of collaborating with other minority groups and demanding full equality for all.[66] Fellow radical Correa could not agree more. He belonged to the Warehousemen's Union (ILWU 6), beckoned residents to the Independent Progressive Party, and served as executive vice chair of the San Francisco Committee for a Fair Employment Practices Ordinance (SFCFEPO). This leftist coalition brought together church groups, civil rights organizations (e.g., the city's chapters of the Civil Rights Congress and ANMA), and labor unions expelled from the CIO on charges of being Communist-controlled, among them the MCS and ILWU locals.[67]

The SFCFEPO relied on political lobbying, advocacy, and direct action to press for the enactment of a compulsory FEP law. Correa and his partners delivered passionate testimony at public hearings and reminded their city supervisors about citizens' future electoral decision-making. In so doing, they evinced an adherence to the democratic process and confidence in their political muscle. "FEPC will inevertably [sic] become an election issure [sic]," forecast Reverend R. L. Turner, SFCFEPO chairman, "and you would as a public official win for yourself many friends . . . [by] voting to pass this Needed compolsory [sic] ordinance."[68] But having their voices fully heard, some committee members argued, required action outside the legislative chambers and beyond the ballot box. A January 1950 demonstration outside City Hall became emblematic of this orientation. San Franciscans who joined the mass protest that month set out to vocalize their support for FEP, publicize how employers benefited from the status quo, and compel legislators to pass the ordinance. Although local Communist cadres coordinated the event, many picketers had ties to groups in the SFCFEPO. Most participants were probably fellow travelers or independent leftists who drew on a radical tradition of direct action and confrontational politics. Yet such activists as Montoya, Correa, and their political kin all found themselves branded as Communists and, concomitantly, unpatriotic, rebellious, and menacing.[69]

Denunciations of radicalism flowed from the business sector, government officials, and pro-FEP civic bodies stressing national allegiance, political moderation, and public decorum. The CCU and the city's NAACP branch, which had previously collaborated with ILWU locals and others drawn to street protest, now gravitated toward the San Francisco Citizens Committee for Equal Employment Opportunity—composed of ethnic organizations, mainline religious bodies, and AFL and CIO locals. This committee emerged in 1949 and identified itself as "the only organization authorized to speak for the overwhelming majority of citizens and groups interested in eliminating job discrimination." Determined to steer the FEP drive, the liberal network refuted business groups' views while condemning the tone and "leftist side shows" of radical supporters.[70] Prominent spokesmen, including Edward Howden from the CCU and Richard Dettering of the Citizens Committee, depicted the employers' voluntary plan as well intentioned yet slow to yield change; a full-scale attack on discrimination, they insisted, rested on a policy directive and its enforcement by a municipal FEPC. Howden, Dettering, and their allies concurrently upended employers' tendency to equate advocacy of FEP with communism. They subsumed their brand of civil rights liberalism under Cold War consensus and posited that state protection of civil rights could and should be used to fight communism. Distancing themselves from "political extremists," they criticized protest activities that antagonized elected officials and the general public, while arguing that an FEP ordinance would actually weaken Communist sympathies by "depriving [militants] of a prime source of grievance and agitation." Nondiscrimination legislation, according to liberal supporters, would silence radicals at home and project a positive image of the United States abroad. Enacting the FEP measure "[will] demonstrate to the peoples of the [world] that our democracy works for all the people," relayed the Citizens Committee in 1951.[71]

Committee partners, such as the United Latin Americans of America (ULAA), built their case for FEP precisely by exalting America's civic creed and cloaking themselves with patriotism. ULAA epitomized a new kind of civic society available to Latinos—one engaged with the polity but directed by middle-class individuals who emphasized the bonds of ethnicity over class. Its members pledged loyalty to the United States, expressed optimism in the American promise, and undertook civic action that was respectable and nonconfrontational. Their political orientation and connection to the dominant civic bodies positioned ULAA as the ambassador of "Americans of Latin American extraction" in City Hall. In 1951, Manuel Maldonado, one of the society's leaders, explained to the Board of Supervisors that "employment on an equal efficiency basis" would allow Latinos "to take their rightful place in the community." Inclusion and opportunity, in ULAA's estimation, would "instill greater faith [among] all Americans . . . in this great democracy of ours."[72]

Neither liberal-moderate appeals nor radical-leftist exhortations persuaded a majority of supervisors to add FEP to the municipal code. In 1950, seven out of eleven supervisors voted against the proposal; they concluded that employers' voluntary measures together with potential action in Sacramento made a local ordinance extraneous. Some among them also thought FEP proponents failed to offer concrete evidence of discrimination to warrant "the police power necessary for such a law." Downplaying experiential accounts and requesting more empirical data, these legislators instead praised and encouraged further independent efforts from employers. An observer from the judicial branch interpreted the board's 1950 decision as one that sent FEP "into the never-never land of 'more study' and vague voluntary agreements."[73] Almon Roth and his allies begged to differ. In 1951, when city supervisors took up the issue again, employer groups lauded the voluntary plan as extensive, popular, and effective. Roth went further, claiming that San Francisco's discrimination record paled in comparison to New York's—a city with an FEPC in place—and continuing to depict the proposal as a Communist initiative. These stances essentially condensed FEP into a futile scheme designed by sinister forces. Six supervisors sided with some or all of these perspectives and rejected the measure for a second time in sixteen months.[74] In these early Cold War years, employers' prerogative, their private convictions, and anticommunism neatly coalesced to trump state action and the codification of fair employment.

Security or Depression: Labor in the 1950s

Two weeks after the impassioned deliberations over FEP, in June 1951, the *Dispatcher* bemoaned the final vote and liberal organizations' efforts to exclude and silence radical activists. The Citizens Committee for Equal Employment Opportunity and its partners, according to the ILWU newspaper, offered their perspectives alongside "considerable redbaiting... and indicated they didn't think anyone else should be allowed to speak."[75] Now outside the CIO, leftist unionists faced off with former allies who set out to impede radicals' participation in civic life. The situation had looked remarkably different just four years earlier, when the SFCIO Council adopted resolutions proscribing the Taft-Hartley Act and President Harry Truman's Loyalty Program. In mid-May 1947, thousands of CIO members and their friends assembled at the civic center and denounced the legislation that "would rob American trade unions of their freedoms" and "repress labor."[76] Yet, by 1950, the escalation of anticommunist hysteria combined with dissension and repression within the CIO apparatus had eroded the once robust partnership of liberals and radicals.

The Cold War climate undermined the fortunes and gravitas of those unions that had figured prominently in Latino political life since the 1930s, in San Francisco and elsewhere.[77] Notably, though, leftist political recession did not exhibit a single trajectory, and the process unfolded in a multitude of ways. The Alaska cannery workers confronted one of the earliest and most extreme episodes of decline. Their union had undergone a series of institutional challenges since the mid-1940s, when it amalgamated with Seattle's Cannery Workers and Farm Laborers Union Local 7. By late 1947, as Local 7 and other UCAPAWA affiliates found themselves "forced to fight for [their] life" amid attacks on radical unions, the San Francisco branch dissolved.[78] Without a local body to represent them, the city's cannery men were left with two options: join the rival AFL union or find jobs elsewhere. Their long-established friends and collaborators, the scalers, fared better. The SSU survived well after the postwar era and benefited from the unity and protection of the ILWU. It was a precarious existence as jurisdictional raids intensified throughout the 1950s. Scalers' presence and legitimacy in public affairs beyond their workplace, moreover, plummeted. Though they kept their union alive during the Cold War, the scalers could not abrogate their marginalization within the larger polity. Former allies such as the furniture workers struck a liberal course by accepting the Cold War consensus and remaining in the CIO. Their accommodation technically offered economic stability and room for public engagement sanctioned by governmental authorities. Yet UFW Local 262 and other CIO unions increasingly functioned as political auxiliaries to mainstream citizen organizations that now commanded the civic agenda, including FEP. Additionally, furniture workers' economic prospects gradually shrank as their employers migrated to the suburbs; their local ceased operations in San Francisco by the early 1970s. Irrespective of their political leanings, then, most labor organizations that had spearheaded Latino unionization in the 1930s and 1940s met constriction during the Cold War era.

Garment workers' unions notably sidestepped this downward trend. The Dressmakers Union and the General Garment Workers Union Local 352 (formed in the early 1940s) continued to attract members, often Latinas, during the postwar years. Industry leaders themselves acknowledged the prominence of Latin American workers at their plants. In 1951, Walter Haas Jr. of Levi Strauss & Company revealed that 30 percent of employees there were Central Americans. Relatives Elena and Libia Arana were among them: they began making casual wear at Levi Strauss in the mid-1940s. The women then transitioned to high-end women's apparel at the Lilli Ann Company in the early 1950s. Work histories such as theirs were common among garment workers, especially when they sought advancement or experienced layoffs. The change of workplace, of course, did not alter their union membership and unions' obligations to them.[79]

Garment workers consistently relied on their unions to enhance their work lives. The ILGWU locals owed much of their durability to an emphasis on simple unionism and leaders' anticommunist leanings. Political moderation by no means equated with inaction on inequity or wrongdoing. In 1951, Soledad Selva, Aida Jarquín, and other machine operators at the Morris Goldman Company filed complaints involving pay rates that did not conform to their level of experience and work classification. Months of arbitration between union officials and employer representatives eventually resulted in wage adjustments. These women's experience was not unique: faulty remuneration proved to be a frequent grievance brought before ILGWU officials. Garment workers concurrently asked union leaders to mitigate on-the-job perils. Frances Moreno, for example, sought protection from harassment. In 1954, the fourteen-year veteran of Morris Goldman informed ILGWU leaders of some troubles with a male coworker who "bothers and insoltes [*sic*] me in every way." Moreno identified the man in question but did not elaborate on the cause of aggravation; it may well have involved an affront to her know-how and authority (given her seniority), unwanted sexual advances, or retaliation for rejecting those overtures. She definitely wanted her local to intervene and vowed to keep "coming to the union" if the situation did not improve. In asking union officials to correct another employee's misconduct and pursuing redress for an employer's infraction, these workers confirmed abiding faith in and reliance on labor unions to ensure their well-being.[80]

Individual cases of protest did not forestall collective mobilization to tackle shared grievances. Navigating the Cold War current of course demanded prudence and calculation. Strike action often functioned as a last recourse, and locals had to obtain authorization from the local board overseeing all ILGWU unions and the San Francisco Labor Council (SFLC). Political restraint and institutional hierarchy notwithstanding, the Dressmakers Union struck on numerous occasions in the 1950s. In January 1952, after months of negotiation and "fruitless conferences" with the Sidley Corporation, Local 101 members lost patience and walked off the job. A similar scenario ensued in July 1956. This time, an impasse over demands for a 20 percent increase in wages, two-week vacations, two additional holidays, and severance pay convinced dressmakers that a strike was indispensable.[81] Jessie Gonzales and Mary Meza surely played decisive roles in rallying and assisting their colleagues. Both women immersed themselves in union affairs, sought positions in the local's executive board in 1956, and may have sat on the negotiations committee.[82] Gonzales and Meza must have also been keenly aware of a newfound predicament: some garment shops had started operating outside the city. Though employers grudgingly compromised on wages and some fringe benefits, they resisted contract clauses that impeded them from "reducing the normal or customary volume of work in San Francisco."[83] Dressmakers and others who held manufacturing jobs, in effect, began to witness the incipient stages of deindustrialization. This process would become more acute in the coming years, even though unionists did not treat it as a foregone conclusion. As the decade wore on, Gonzales, Meza, and their coworkers pressed on with a repertoire of negotiation and mobilization to protect their union jobs and the benefits that came with them.

Hotel kitchen assistants Willie Bolaños and Enrique Osorio, too, understood that union membership was paramount to economic stability. The men worked at the Hotel Panama, one of many inns within the downtown core, and belonged to the Miscellaneous Employees Union Local 110. Within the AFL orbit, Local 110 and the ILGWU locals had long held the distinction of organizing sizable numbers of Latinos. In January 1954, Bolaños, Osorio, and others accepted a transfer to another hotel and, by doing so, evaded crossing a sister union's picket line. Room clerks in the Hotel and Club Service Workers Union Local 283 went on strike that month; the kitchen assistants' relocation circumvented the prohibition of sympathy strikes mandated by the Taft-Hartley Act.[84] The move—literal and political—betrayed how these Local 110 members clutched to the tenets of labor solidarity and reverence for the closed shop, and translated them from theory into practice.

As the 1950s progressed, more AFL unions began to welcome minority workers. The process benefited Latinos and the labor movement as a whole: it improved workers' economic standing while furthering their loyalty to a labor-centered agenda. The void created by radical organizations' floundering, the ascendancy of fair employment as a dominant principle within the mainstream labor movement, and the AFL-CIO merger in 1955 all facilitated this openness. To be sure, it was a gradual and uneven development. Latinos found it easiest to join unions representing unskilled workers or those with nondiscrimination clauses. Both the Hod Carriers, Building, and Common Laborers Union Local 36 and the Teamsters Local 85 drew clusters of Latinos throughout the 1950s. Admission into craft unions, especially the building trades, remained more difficult. The skill and language requirements for employment, the tie-in between apprenticeships and job opportunities, and a culture of brotherhood pivoting around white privilege and ethnic bonds all presented roadblocks for minority workers. Still, it was not an impossible feat: Claude Alarid (plumber), Joe Torres (carpenter), Louis Hernandez (electrician), and a handful of others managed to break into their respective craft unions. In a parallel development, some Latinos in professional occupations entered white-collar unions. Educators Ena Aguirre, Luisa Ezquerro, and David Sánchez Jr. enlisted in the American Federation of Teachers Local 61 in the late 1950s.[85] This varied, albeit lopsided field of unionization proved essential in fortifying Latinos' political sensibilities as the decade neared its end.

In 1957, fair employment practices reemerged as a priority for San Franciscans championing civil rights. ULAA and other civic groups now gravitated toward the reconstituted San Francisco Committee for Equal Job Opportunity, the citizens' alliance leading the FEP drive. The SFLC concurrently set up its own Committee for a San Francisco FEPC, with representatives from twenty-eight local AFL-CIO unions charged with public education and building rank-and-file support for the proposed ordinance.[86] Few Latinos served as union officers and delegates at this time; labor's perspectives circulating in the public sphere typically originated from SFLC functionaries who were white. Conveying Latinos' interest in FEP essentially fell to ULAA. Its spokesperson, attorney Louis Garcia, appeared before the supervisors early that year, noting, "I can safely say that the sentiment of the Spanish-speaking community of San Francisco overwhelmingly endorses the proposed FEP ordinance." He then delineated ULAA's position by invoking American civic principles, reflecting on moral values, and identifying nondiscrimination as a prerequisite for progress.[87] Garcia's testimony echoed other proponents' statements; still, parallel contributions did not diminish the exigencies of collaboration and representation. ULAA, after all, functioned as the preeminent Latino civic body of the late 1950s. Garcia's remarks ensured that ULAA's investment in FEP entered the public record and that Latinos were recognized as stakeholders in this decisive civil rights campaign.

The 1957 "civic controversy over FEP legislation" initially mirrored and then diverged from the contest six years earlier.[88] Proponents and critics reprised an enduring set of ideological postures and arguments—pitting democratic ideals and legislative redress against employers' liberty and voluntary action. Red-baiting, tellingly, figured less prominently in these debates. The decline and silencing of radical groups made the discursive portrayal of FEP as either a defense against Communist agitation or a Communist scheme less compelling. Street demonstrations, confrontational exchanges, and other forms of direct action waned as well. Advocates and foes alike relied on methodical and measured lobbying efforts with little grassroots mobilization. Elected officials responded by exhibiting more willingness to pass the ordinance. Politicians' personal evolution on the matter, the existence of similar ordinances in other major cities, and concrete data confirming the range of discrimination occasioned this readiness in City Hall.[89]

In late May, the San Francisco Board of Supervisors' preliminary approval emboldened civil rights advocates, embittered downtown businessmen, and spawned an experiment in civic bargaining. Finding themselves on the defensive, FEP opponents threatened to sponsor a referendum if the pending bill became law. The move made proponents uneasy for two reasons: a plebiscite would prolong their work, and city voters could well repeal the mandate from City Hall, a fear informed by past repudiation of Proposition 11. Lawmakers addressed these frustrations and anxieties by delaying final action and encouraging negotiation. Accommodation became an efficacious and diplomatic alternative to the quandary, and rival groups expeditiously acceded. The compromise plan retained key pieces from earlier proposals: it prohibited racial discrimination in hiring and created a Commission of Equal Employment Opportunity. Tasked solely with investigation and mediation, this new body lacked "punitive authority" and could not sue an employer or union for violation of the law. Fines for an infraction could not exceed three months of pay for the job in question, and all commission proceedings remained secret unless the city attorney undertook legal action. These concessions departed heavily from the robust regulatory mechanism and stringent penalties once envisioned by champions of FEP. The measure's "turbulent history" and its uncertain future, however, convinced liberals in mid-1957 that a weak ordinance, unanimously approved by the supervisors in July, was preferable to nothing at all.[90]

Employment, civil rights, and the public's will converged again in 1958 as California voters considered a "right to work" initiative under Proposition 18. Engineered by the Citizens Committee for Democracy in Labor Unions—an outfit of dissident union members and anti-labor forces—the proposal made it unlawful to deny or curtail employment based on membership or nonmembership in a labor organization. It invalidated the union shop by affixing the "principle of voluntary unionism" to the state constitution.[91] Supporters insisted that the amendment would open job opportunities, protect workers' individual rights, and guarantee their freedom of association. The San Francisco Chamber of Commerce and other probusiness entities hailed the initiative as a way to guarantee "greater democracy in labor union elections and [make] union officers more responsible to the wishes of union members."[92] City labor circles, in marked contrast, found the proposition troubling and did not regard it as a mechanism to invigorate their organizations. They identified the proposal as an anti-labor plan intended to erode unions' power, divide working people, and restore employers' unrestrained authority over employees. Echoing arguments made by organized labor elsewhere, the SFLC charged that right-to-work arrangements would destroy labor unions, stamp out collective bargaining, and nullify the job security obtained through a union contract. The labor establishment simultaneously capsized proponents' discussions about rights and freedoms, stressing that the proposition would only elevate managerial prerogatives and shackle workers to the "whims of the boss." A plurality of the rank and file concurred.[93]

Individual unions and civic groups pulled Latinos, including the Alarid family, into the "No on 18" fray. Claude belonged to the Plumbers and Pipefitters Union Local 38; Ruth was active in ULAA; both volunteered with the Latin American Committee for Defense of Our Jobs. This ethnic-centered collective, sponsored by the SFLC's Committee on Political Education, connected unionists with civic advocates, and they jointly spurred Latinos to vote against the initiative. Signaling the maturation of an alliance nourished by a shared investment in unionization and civil rights, the Latin American Committee determined that Proposition 18 threatened job security and "sustain[ed] discrimination." Its members told residents what its passage would "really mean": reduced salaries, a loss of union benefits, and fewer job opportunities for racial minorities. This prognosis stemmed from fears of the open shop and knowledge that many pro-18 backers opposed FEP legislation. With an eye to political numismatics, activists cast the destruction of union jobs and resistance to nondiscrimination as two sides of an employer-minted coin. Pecuniary alarm bred social anxieties as well, especially concerns about familial stability. Relying on the era's potent imagery and ideology of the nuclear family and a male breadwinner, the Latin American Committee cast Proposition 18 as inimical to domestic cohesion and male authority. "Do not destroy your household's union," the group told Latinos. "Protect your family's security." The warning surely persuaded family-oriented Latinos, even if their household arrangements did not conform to societal ideals. Still, some may not have been swayed by elaborate or allegorical arguments. Proposition challengers had one basic message for them: the measure did not guarantee or create jobs for anyone.[94]

Latinos in and outside the Latin American Committee advanced the tradition of grassroots campaign work and political education first expanded by their counterparts in the early 1940s. The 1958 election season found electrical workers Louis Hernandez and Robert Parra disseminating the "unpleasant facts" about the right-to-work proposal in their neighborhoods, street corners, transportation hubs, and other public areas. They were but two

SEGURIDAD
O
DEPRESION?

NO DESTRUYA LA UNION DE SU HOGAR ......
PROTEJA LA SEGURIDAD DE SU FAMILIA ....

No se deje engañar por el egoismo de algunos políticos y patrones. La Iniciativa de Relaciones entre Patrones y Empleados (Proposicion No. 18), tiene por objeto redúcir los salarios y destrúir las Organizaciones de Trabajo.

**ESTA INICIATIVA NO GARAN-
TIZA A NADIE NINGUN DE-
RECHO Y MUCHISIMO MENOS
NINGUN TRABAJO!**

La Proposicion No. 18 real- mente quiere decir:

- Ninguna seguridad en el empleo
- Salarios más bajos
- Reduccion en el nivel de vivir
- Pérdida de todos sus beneficios mas importante de su Union
- Eliminacion de los planes de salud, beneficencia y pensiones

La Proposicion No. 18 **destruye totalmente la seguridad en el trabajo** y apoya la discriminacion entre nuestro pueblo trabajador.

VOTE "NO" EN PROP. No. 18

COMITE LATINO-AMERICANO PARA LA DEFENSA DE NUESTROS TRABAJOS

Figure 5. Comite Latino-Americano para la Defensa de Nuestros Trabajos, "*Seguridad ó Depresión* (Security or Depression)?" flyer, 1958. California Federation of Labor Collection. Courtesy of Labor Archives and Research Center.

Latinos who took up canvassing, distributed leaflets, and reminded Spanish-speaking residents that their "first vote should be NO on Proposition 18." Precinct work complemented voter registration efforts. Long before the election, the SFLC sponsored training for union members and civic activists, including ones from ULAA, to become deputized registrars; this volunteer corps then undertook an aggressive registration drive during the spring and summer months.[95] These overlapping efforts from the bottom up doubtlessly influenced the electoral results. Approximately 70 percent of city voters rejected the proposition, which was also "beaten by a wide margin" across the state.[96] Between the euphoria and relief, the Alarids and their friends must have felt proud for having done their part to preserve labor rights.

Efforts to defeat Proposition 18 pulled together the dominant strands of Latinos' political agenda at mid-century: the pursuit of economic security, the drive for civil rights, and an engagement with the electoral process. Union members and civic activists who enlisted in the "most bitterly fought" contest of 1958 understood the link between the closed shop, material prosperity, and fair employment practices, and they translated this connection—linguistically and conceptually—to their relatives and neighbors.[97] From one vantage point, activism in the late 1950s resembled the challenge to the statewide prohibition of hot cargo during World War II and the 1946 mobilizations to enact FEP via Proposition 11. But much had changed since the early to mid-1940s. The Cold War ethos altered political life even in San Francisco, stifling the messages, tone, and activities of radical organizations. Notably, as the Ship Scalers Union and its counterparts confronted repression, civic associations enlarged and legitimized their involvement in the polity by stressing respectability, loyalty, and patriotism. The United Latin Americans of America especially endeavored to rally Latinos by expanding a model of civic action that accentuated ethnic concerns as it sidestepped class struggle. To be sure, economic questions did not disappear and ULAA members regularly collaborated with the labor establishment—as exemplified by the Latin American Committee's work in 1958. Latinos would remain active in labor unions in years to come. The ascendancy and risk-free nature of ethnic-based organizing, however, meant that large-scale considerations of economic opportunity, electoral power, and state obligations to citizens' welfare would overwhelmingly emanate from groups akin to ULAA.

CHAPTER 4

"Taking Latin Americans into Account"

Civic Action, the State, and the Promotion of Latinidad

In April 1962, Ruth Alarid sat down with a survey team studying the Spanish-speaking community in the Mission District. The civic activist and ULAA veteran lived in the district's southwestern end, near Noe and Valley Streets, and now presided over the local chapter of the Mexican American Political Association (MAPA). Field researchers from the Mission Neighborhood Centers (MNC) wanted to meet "leaders of the Latin American colony," learn about organizations like hers, and discuss their agency's interest in having more Latinos access their social services. Alarid offered a brief history of MAPA and discussed its focus on increasing electoral participation and acquainting members with policy issues, candidates, and political platforms. She then expressed a conviction that all community organizations should work toward improving the district's physical appearance. Alarid did not comment on the connection between ethnic political mobilization and social service provision. It would soon become evident that MAPA and other Latino-focused organizations had their own ideas about delivering social services to their ethnic kin, while simultaneously treating the Mission as their geopolitical base.[1]

Alarid's conversation with the MNC team transpired as two postwar processes matured: social analyses of nonwhite residents living in central-city areas and the work of Latino political groups defined by ethnic identification amplified in the early 1960s. Both developments had begun to unfold at least a decade earlier. A noticeable concentration of ethnoracial minorities in neighborhoods near the downtown core prompted social welfare professionals to evaluate these populations' life conditions and problems. Concurrently, an interest in civic engagement, apprehension about the everyday challenges and representation of minority residents, and the limitations placed on class-based activism propelled the expansion of ethnic-oriented political action. Brushing against each other in the 1950s, these trends fully intersected as the War on Poverty began in the mid-1960s. MAPA and like-minded organizations flourished during the era of convergence, promoting an ethnic consciousness and underscoring Latinos' needs and predicaments. Ethnic leaders then rallied their constituencies to press the state for resources, services, and attention. In so doing, Latinos politicized the planning and provision of social services and pushed for greater recognition—as community stakeholders, citizens, and a distinct minority.

Two years into the War on Poverty, in October 1966, community representatives at an annual Latin American leadership conference applauded the upsurge in "attention to the pressing problems of the fast growing Spanish-speaking population."[2] Herman Gallegos delivered the opening address and reviewed the reasons behind communal strides over the preceding decade. He had returned to San Francisco in 1960, following years of activism in San Jose and San Bernardino, and devoted much energy to the Community Service Organization (CSO), MAPA, and the Catholic Council for the Spanish Speaking (CCSS), among others. He credited these institutions for mounting strong civic action programs and fomenting Latinos' "political determination" to jointly tackle life hurdles and strive for advancement. Latino unionists, of course, had known about the significance of collective action for decades. Tellingly, Gallegos left labor unions out of the equation for prosperity, a testament to the primacy of ethnicity-driven organizing by this time. Politicians and government authorities, for their part, had taken notice of ethnic institutions' goals and activities, especially their voter registration drives and Latinos' growing electoral strength. Leaving the question of patronage to inference, Gallegos identified the assistance and policy reforms backed by Governor Edmund G. "Pat" Brown (e.g., old-age pensions for non-citizens and a statewide FEP law in 1959) as other sources of communal betterment. He concluded by reminding his colleagues that Latinos "[had] progressed because since 1960 we have enjoyed the interest and assistance of a responsive Federal administration."[3] Beneath this assertion lay the correlation between ethnic political mobilization and social service delivery: the funds and services to wage the War on Poverty typified the capstone of and reward for ethnic-based activism and loyalty to the Democratic Party. Most conference attendees knew this as they rose to welcome U.S. Senator Robert F. Kennedy (D-NY) to the stage.

As Gallegos's observations attest, ethnicity undergirded much of Latino political efforts over the course of the 1950s and 1960s. This development had its origins in ethnic-based civic activism, as exemplified by ULAA's work, and culminated with the successes and challenges spawned by the War on Poverty. Advancing a political agenda organized around ethnoracial ties—at once an ambition and a process—came to be supported by the latinization of the Mission, an increased identification of this district as a Latino barrio, and the proliferation of organizations concerned with the Latino condition as the 1960s began. In this period, ethnic institutions consistently invoked and nurtured latinidad by promoting Latino unity and affinity; leaders simultaneously represented Latinos as one community and constituency before politicians and public bodies. The liberal state, in turn, legitimized the existence of a Spanish-speaking population in need of governmental attention and assistance akin to African Americans. Latinos' ethnic-based political work blossomed, reaching its high tide, as the War on Poverty materialized: liberalism and latinidad now interlocked in ways they had never done before.

Ethnic-Based Civic Work and Political Action

A decade and a half before they saluted Senator Kennedy, leaders from local Latin American groups welcomed an iconic figure from closer to home. In October 1949, they lauded Edward Roybal's arrival in San Francisco. Roybal had recently become the first Mexican American to sit on the Los Angeles City Council since the 1880s. His election inspired pride in the man, his ethnic community, and the grassroots movement that put him in office. Roybal's victory depended heavily on the voter registration and get-out-the-vote drives spearheaded by the CSO. Originating in 1947, the CSO soon became the preeminent civic association of Mexican Americans and other Latinos in postwar California; new chapters gradually formed across the state throughout the 1950s. This civic ethos at the local level coincided with renewed efforts to establish "a state-wide organization to promote the interests of Californians of Latin-American ancestry." Roybal's itinerary in San Francisco included sessions with this state-organizing body, local organizations, and officers from the California Democratic Central Committee. Conversations with the trailblazing political figure impressed three pivotal messages as the 1940s closed: tangible change demanded civic activism; efforts for community improvement had to transpire locally and regionally; and the Democratic Party had some interest in backing this undertaking.[4]

Alfred Espinor, Julius Castelan, Louis Vásquez, and others in ULAA received these messages enthusiastically—and resolved to expand their civic work in San Francisco. Established around 1948, their civic society initially functioned as a social club: it organized picnics, dances, and other leisure events. ULAA's orientation began to shift in mid-1949 as its leaders strengthened their connections with the California Federation for Civic Unity—based in the city—and learned more about Roybal's triumph and the CSO. The group found much commonality with the League of United Latin American Citizens (LULAC), headquartered in Texas, but ULAA does not appear to have operated as a LULAC chapter.[5] Both organizations shared an ideological orientation and programmatic aims, including emphases on cultural assimilation, patriotism, respectability, educational advancement, and electoral participation. ULAA consistently emphasized its dedication to "better living by better citizenship."[6] Its members assumed that this process of betterment hinged on exalting America's civic creed, pledging allegiance to the United States as the anticommunism crusade escalated, and opting for improved lives through naturalization. They concurrently prescribed active and ongoing participation in civic life to enhance one's individual and communal existence.

With its gaze on citizen action, ULAA built relationships with civic and municipal authorities, surveyed the activities of other ethnic institutions, and connected with Mexican American political circles beyond city limits. Most members shared a middle-class, professional status and hailed from Mexican American backgrounds. Attorneys, journalists, social workers, doctors, and engineers gravitated to the organization. Working-class Latinos were less involved in ULAA, particularly during its early years. Some did not turn to it because they remained active in their unions; others refrained from doing so owing to time constraints, disinterest, or distaste for the group's formal and didactic style. Individuals trained in law, social work, and other professions, in contrast, generally felt more comfortable in forums filled with lectures and discussions of social research. It was in settings like these that ULAA members sketched out civic action plans and weighed the ways "to improve the conditions of Hispanic-Americans." [7]

Hispanic American and *Latin American* as categories of social difference easily and regularly stood for ethnic Mexicans throughout California but not in San Francisco. The preponderance of Mexican-origin persons in the state offered a basic explanation for the custom. Some middle-class Mexican Americans also adopted *Latin American* as a means to diminish the pejorative connotations attached to *Mexican*. ULAA sometimes adhered to this practice both for demographic and strategic reasons. Yet leaders such as Vásquez well knew that local Latinos were not all ethnically Mexican. His newspaper, *El Democrata*, regularly commented on the varied composition of the city's "Latin American conglomerate." As early as 1949, ULAA members called for the creation of a social agency for Latino youth who traced their "origins [to] all the Americas." In San Francisco, then, *Latin American* was not a simple and exclusive synonym for *Mexican*.[8] ULAA's inconsistent application of the term nevertheless suggests one possible reason for the limited involvement of Puerto Ricans, Central Americans, and other Latinos in that organization. Of course, some non-Mexican-origin Latinos may have preferred to join other ethnic associations or none at all.

ULAA's attention to multiple issues, its local and regional connections, and immersion in civic life solidified its position as Latinos' institutional representative of the early postwar era. The society identified as a "political-social group" by 1951 and continuously stressed its commitment to a "movement" set on asserting Latinos' "civic rights." The pursuit of rights and recognition unfolded in multiple ways. As early as 1949, ULAA called upon social welfare agencies "to develop their programs by taking Latin Americans into account."[9] Bilingual and culturally appropriate services, its leaders believed, would ensure that Latinos accessed and received the assistance they needed. In making these recommendations, the association began to draft a social service agenda that would be reproduced and expanded by other Latino institutions in years to come. ULAA concurrently advised Latinos to broaden their participation in public life—by involving themselves in civic affairs, registering to vote, and engaging with the electoral process. Advocacy efforts multiplied as the group enlisted in campaigns to eradicate racial discrimination and to protect labor rights. As discussed in Chapter 3, ULAA formed part of the liberal civil rights coalition pressing for FEP legislation. Its members sometimes allied with the mainstream labor movement of the mid- to late 1950s, as evidenced by the efforts to defeat the "right-to-work" proposition in 1958.

Early on in its transition from social club to communal advocate, ULAA organized civic conferences for residents and public authorities interested in enhancing Latinos' welfare. These events exposed key layers of its social service vision, attracted institutional allies, and revealed some unexpected limitations. Civic advocates and social welfare experts gathered at a July 1949 conference on Latin American adolescents' well-being, for example, considered ways to promote youth development and to strengthen child-parent relationships. Their focus fit within a larger societal effort, locally and nationally, to counter youth alienation and delinquency. It also aligned with ULAA's overall mission. As Manuel Maldonado explained in 1951, "We are vitally interested in the future of our youth and encourage them to strive for higher education."[10] Perspectives such as these surely guided some conversations at the 1949 gathering. Conference participants stressed the imperative of appointing more teachers, social workers, and other civil servants who understood Latinos' needs, "idiosyncrasies," and cultural differences. They also agreed on the importance of augmenting parental involvement in children's educational and recreational lives, while encouraging adults to familiarize themselves with the resources available at public and private agencies. Notably, at this time, ULAA made a case for culturally sensitive staff and programming within established, non-ethnic-specific institutions. Representatives from the San Francisco Department of Education and the California Youth Authority, among others, applauded these goals; their responsiveness signaled both interest in and legitimization of ULAA's work.

Common ground between public authorities and community leaders notwithstanding, ULAA's civic forums materialized with limited involvement from Latinos at large. Vásquez and his contemporaries hoped Latino residents would attend the events, where they could deliberate on communal problems and their potential solutions. It was on this front that ULAA met some stumbling blocks: the public it aspired to arouse proved only mildly receptive to these undertakings. "Only a very small group of Latin Americans attended these important conferences," lamented *El Democrata* days after the July 1949 gathering. Its editors, both active in ULAA, interpreted the low turnout as indicative of Latinos' "inexplicable apathy to take part in activities that were not exclusively social or related to leisure." Though this assessment may have applied to some residents, it was shortsighted and incomplete. It wholly ignored the era's labor activism and failed to consider that some Latinos may have felt uneasy in classroom-style lectures and round-table deliberations with experts. The media report nonetheless disclosed a disconnection, albeit inadvertently, between ULAA and the Latino public it represented. And it impressed some points for further reflection. Journalists piercingly told readers "Latin Americans [would] not be taken into account" unless they became more visible and active in civic life. Addressed to Latinos en masse, the conclusion surely prompted ULAA to review its strategies and efforts to reach the constituency it spoke for.[11]

Comprehensive recognition as a community with shared interests and concerns, ethnic leaders deduced, depended on a stronger public presence— at civic forums and at the ballot box. To be sure, some public bodies (e.g., the Department of Education) and local politicians (e.g., Supervisor George Christopher) had already taken notice of ULAA and may have inferred the sociopolitical ramifications of Latino population growth. The association aspired to widen this field of governmental recognition by drawing more Latinos into its orbit. Its members expected that numerical brawn would translate into full and ongoing consideration of their agenda. Set on increasing their outreach, they turned to those circles with a record of organizing Latinos but which, paradoxically, had been overlooked by editors from *El Democrata*. ULAA's deepening relationship with the mainstream labor movement of the 1950s hence involved a desire to amass more allies and augment its organizational reach. The partnership simultaneously bolstered the pro-labor network and fostered Latino connections across activist spheres.

Civic advocates and union members did more than support the same causes (e.g., FEP legislation, opposition to the "right-to-work" initiative). They undertook joint voter registration drives and set out to elect public servants attentive to Latinos' multiple aspirations—whether these emerged from their identification as working people, an ethnic constituency on the rise, or both. Politicians such as Edward Roybal made the alignment of class-based concerns and ethnic ambitions emphatically simple. In early 1954, the Los Angeles councilman set his eyes on the lieutenant governor's office and joined a slate endorsed by the California Democratic Council. Roybal's candidacy aroused Latino voters; he was the most prominent Spanish-speaking political figure of mid-1950s California, one who championed FEP, labor protections, and state-sponsored social welfare. His platform included a public works proposal to curb rising unemployment, allocation of state funds for emergency hospital care, and appeals to temper McCarthyist hysteria.[12] ULAA activists eagerly enrolled in the Northern California Campaign Committee to Elect Ed Roybal, with Ruth Alarid serving as local coordinator and Louis Vásquez, Joaquin Garay, and others acting as sponsors. They disseminated the campaign message widely and targeted such outfits as the Dressmakers Union, which continued to organize Latinas. Roybal himself thanked ILGWU members for "[their] support of my campaign and particularly [their] contribution of $100.00 to my campaign fund."[13] Though he did not win, the campaign presented Latinos with yet another catalyst to expand their electoral base, fortify the nexus between civic activism and labor organizing, and further orient them toward the Democratic Party.

Republicans envied Democrats' "virtual control" of the Latino electorate. A survey conducted in 1956 revealed that 80 percent of more than 150,000 registered voters of Latin American descent living in San Francisco and Alameda Counties (encompassing Oakland and its suburbs) identified as Democrats and planned to back Adlai Stevenson's bid for the U.S. presidency. Alarmed by this situation, Latinos involved in Republican circles organized the Northern California Latin Americans for Eisenhower. Continued peace and prosperity, they explained, depended on keeping the incumbent president in the White House. At the same time, these "Latins for Ike" viewed their campaign work as a stepping-stone to bring more Latinos into the Republican Party. Their efforts did not gain much traction. Preliminary evidence based on voting patterns in districts with a noticeable Latino presence suggests greater support for Stevenson.[14] Not surprisingly, and in what had become conventional practice, Latinos received electoral cues from labor unions and political clubs such as the Spanish and Latin American Democrats. This push-pull movement into Democratic ranks would remain ascendant for the rest of the decade.

Latino leaders held onto a conviction that civic engagement coupled with electoral participation would generate political recognition and attendant resources. Still, some worried about politicians' neglect and complacency in taking Latino votes and organizational endorsements for granted. Determined to "make [their ethnic community] heard and felt, understood and respected at every level of government," ULAA officers traveled to Fresno in April 1960 and took part in founding MAPA. This association's emergence signaled the culmination of a decade-long drive to establish an "instrument of [ethnic] organization" in California.[15] It ushered in a new chapter in electoral mobilization and political education. MAPA expressly set out to secure the election of Mexican Americans and their political allies to public office. A Mexican American foundation did not necessarily exclude other Latinos. As Julius Castelan relayed to city journalists, MAPA intended to push for "the economic and civic betterment of Americans of Mexican descent and all other Spanish speaking Americans." All Latinos who were U.S. citizens, in fact, could be members and hold office in the association.[16] Statewide efforts would be complemented by local chapters' activities in communities with a high concentration of Latinos. San Francisco's MAPA members needed little time to define the geographic center for their work: the Mission District. The area surrounding the cradle of Spanish colonial society now became the principal site for Latinos to demand recognition as an ethnic community deserving political representation and governmental resources.

The Latinization of the Mission

"The Spanish came first—and last," stressed David Braaten in his multipart feature story on the postwar Mission published in 1962. "The latest settlers— the Spanish-speaking," he continued, "bring the Mission District's immigration full circle as it was the Spanish who discovered the area in the first place."[17] Sticking with the standard practice of treating *Spanish* and *Latin American* synonymously, the journalist's account aligned with a contemporary interest in mapping the demographic evolution of central-city neighborhoods. Latinos' steady settlement in the Mission, as previous chapters have noted, dated back to earlier decades. Marked population growth and concentration in the Inner Mission—the district's core region generally bounded by the Central Freeway on the north to Army Street (now Cesar Chavez Street) on the south and Church Street on the west to Potrero Avenue on the east— occurred during the postwar era. Latinos' presence here grew from 5,531 (11 percent of the total Inner Mission population) in 1950 to 11,625 (23 percent) in 1960, and then climbed to 23,183 (45 percent) by 1970.[18] These numbers elicited manifold responses within and beyond the district. Braaten's reports exposed and reproduced popular impressions about a Latino "invasion" in the making. Social welfare experts weighed the ramifications of neighborhood change and population shifts on the district's socioeconomic stability. Civic advocates such as Ruth Alarid, for their part, coupled attention on residents' everyday needs with a vision to augment Latinos' political advantage in what many increasingly saw as their neighborhood.[19]

Alarid's discussion with community researchers, which opened this chapter, took place just weeks before Braaten published his report and formed part of a "social planning" initiative undertaken by the MNC. Since the late 1950s, the MNC spent much time examining life conditions and community problems in what it called the Greater Mission, an area encompassing the city's southeastern quadrant—roughly south of Market Street and east of Twin Peaks. Agency directors expressed particular concern about how a "blighted" landscape—viewed both in environmental and human terms—spelled a future as a slum. Population growth and the arrival of more minority groups, they explained, exacerbated physical dilapidation and bred social decay (e.g., overcrowding, intergroup tensions, and street crime). The MNC did not single out Latinos as the residents exclusively responsible for the district's state of flux. But others eventually did so. By the mid-1960s, officials from the Economic Opportunity Council (EOC), the administrative body overseeing the local War on Poverty, placed Latinos at the center of a demographic transformation unraveling in a precarious socioeconomic terrain. "For ten years now, the Mission merchants have watched the change from an Anglo community to almost completely a Spanish-American one," noted EOC staffers in 1965. "Latin Americans are here by the thousands. . . . This is at best a modest neighborhood, well on its way to becoming a slum."[20]

Latino residential concentration in the Mission was the by-product of broader developments unfolding during the postwar period. First, paralleling a course evident in other cities, many white residents took advantage of government-backed loans and abandoned older, densely populated areas such as the Mission. Western districts (e.g., the Sunset and the Richmond) and the burgeoning suburbs promised newer residences, more open space, a secure financial investment, familial stability, and racial homogeneity.[21] The housing left behind became one alternative for persons displaced by urban renewal in the Western Addition and South of Market. In its 1959 study, the MNC noted how the city's redevelopment projects caused some African Americans, Filipinos, and Latinos to move to the Mission. Most profoundly, whites' outmigration coincided with the latest "Latin American influx" to San Francisco. Thousands of immigrants from the Western Hemisphere poured into the metropolis during the 1950s and 1960s.[22] As an example, some 2,500 adult immigrants from Mexico and Central America entered the city from 1958 to 1960 alone, including 834 persons from El Salvador, 783 from Nicaragua, and 655 from Mexico. Twenty-year-old Roger Ortega was among them; he left Nicaragua in 1958 and joined an uncle who had arrived years earlier. Ortega explained that "a state of [economic] depression" and an atmosphere of political discontent led him and others "to get away." Similar factors informed the decisions of most Latino migrants. The pursuit of economic improvement, political instability and repression in their countries of origin, and the prospect of family reunification all functioned as catalysts for migration.[23] Largely working class or lower middle class, they sought out cheap and available housing in areas with an existing Spanish-speaking population. The Mission offered all this and more. Ortega and his contemporaries found the district appealing because they could live near other Latinos, access familiar goods and services (e.g., imported produce, Spanish-language films), and enjoy a warmer climate in a typically cold and foggy San Francisco.[24]

Postwar migration together with human reproduction fueled Latino population growth in San Francisco and the Mission. A 1962 consumer survey identified them as an "important special market" owing to their linguistic ties and because their numerical presence had almost doubled between 1950 and 1960. Market researchers concurrently predicted that the Latino population would "continue to grow at approximately this rate for the next twenty years."[25] Their assessment could not have been more precise. Citywide, the number of Latino residents increased from roughly 24,000 in 1950 to more than 51,500 by 1960. This figure doubled again and approached 102,000 by 1970. Immigration only accounted for a fraction of this growth. In 1960, two out of three Latinos had been born in the United States, a ratio that appears to have remained constant throughout the decade.[26] Many of these U.S.-born children and their immigrant parents became an integral part of the Mission's demographic transformation. By 1970, the Inner Mission housed almost 25 percent of all city Latinos. Approximately half of the total Latino population lived within the Greater Mission, including Bernal Heights, Potrero Hill, Noe Valley, and the Outer Mission. Residents and contemporary observers, of course, did not need official figures to corroborate what they witnessed firsthand. "Most [Latinos] either live or shop or find their entertainment and friends in the Mission," concluded a features writer in 1967.[27] In effect, commentators, social workers, and policy makers all concurred that the Mission had undergone a process of latinization.

Social Action and Latinidad in the Early 1960s

Civically and politically minded Latinos zeroed in on population growth and the Mission's latinization in particular to boost their drive for more social services and political representation. In the early 1960s, activists turned to a host of organizations that drew on the legacy left behind by ULAA. At the forefront of civic activism in the 1950s, ULAA disbanded around 1960 as some members focused their energies on MAPA and others reoriented their priorities. "Social action groups in the Latin-American community" never-theless flourished as the new decade began. A concept with much currency in social work settings, "social action" became an ideological and organizational bridge from 1950s civic work to mid-1960s community action. The approach retained an emphasis on advocacy and engagement with the polity; it also opened the door for grassroots organizing.[28] Latinos' attraction to social ac-tion grew as they learned about Mexican American activism in other Califor-nia localities, witnessed African American civil rights organizing locally and nationally, and joined networks supportive of the paradigm. Notably, while Latinos lived in many city neighborhoods, residential concentration and marked visibility in the Mission meant that the bulk of their social activism took place in and radiated from the district.

Social action burgeoned alongside mounting efforts to promote latini-dad. Bolstering a sense of unity and affinity became imperative in light of in-terlocking and pressing issues. Latinos' soaring population coincided with the reproduction and magnification of ethnic heterogeneity. One aspect of their multiformity proved particularly striking: Central Americans, still overwhelmingly Nicaraguans and Salvadorans, now outnumbered ethnic Mexicans. In a 1962 report on outreach to Latinos, officials from the Arch-diocese of San Francisco identified Central Americans as the city's "dominant Latin group." Residents, journalists, and government authorities made simi-lar observations during these years.[29] Commentators and social workers con-currently acknowledged that patriotism and diffusion by national origin resulted in a "lack of cohesiveness" and cooperation in tackling common problems. Others pointed out that Latinos of non-Mexican descent equated "attempt[s] to organize the Spanish speaking community" as ones geared toward ethnic Mexicans.[30] More suggestive than conclusive, ULAA's weak re-cord of engaging non-Mexican Latinos and a limited number of leaders who were not Mexican Americans likely shaped this impression. Activists drawn to social action now deemed it critical to pull Latinos of all backgrounds into their sphere. Regularly relying on language and religion as cultural adhesives, they set out to animate an awareness of parallel experiences and fortunes—economically and politically—irrespective of national origins and ethnic par-ticularities. Doing so would ensure that Latino organizations represented the hopes and struggles of a collective, while projecting a cohesive community before non-Latino authorities.

Latinos embarked on a new phase of associational life when husband-and-wife team William and Mary Salazar, brothers Herman and Elmer Gallegos, and some two dozen others established a local chapter of the Community Service Organization in August 1961. San Francisco's CSO filled a void left behind by ULAA's demise, drew on the successes of more than thirty chapters across the state, and paved the way for community action at mid-decade. Applauding its emergence, one clergyman characterized the CSO as an instrument "for Latins to take part in community organization and civic responsibility."[31] Billing itself as a nonpolitical and nonsectarian group, much of the CSO's work revolved around political matters and liberal concerns. Electoral engagement, policy analysis, and attention to the distribution of government resources regularly headlined its agenda. In 1963, Elmer Gallegos urged all CSO members and friends to contact Sacramento legislators and express support for increased state assistance to economically disadvantaged youth. Gallegos and his colleagues clearly viewed citizen advocacy as a means to influence the allocation of public monies. In this instance, they sought funds to offer services "needed in the Mission District for our students."[32] The prospective beneficiaries were young Latinos, irrespective of individual or familial identification by ethnic subgroup. High school teacher Luisa Ezquerro understood this service priority well. A Latina of Nicaraguan descent, she became involved in the CSO in the early 1960s. She was not the only Central American who did so. Organization leaders employed various strategies (e.g., community conferences, house meetings, on-the-job introductions) to grow the membership and recruit Latinos of all backgrounds to the group. In this way, San Francisco's CSO functioned as a Latino organization, one with a Mexican American foundation but with an orientation to enhance the life conditions of a motley Spanish-speaking community.[33]

A cluster of CSO members simultaneously joined and helped build another communal body in 1962: the Catholic Council for the Spanish Speaking. A product of the archdiocese's efforts to augment its influence over Latinos, the CCSS brought together lay people, local priests, and representatives from secular groups interested in mitigating "Latin problems" and "identifying the Church with the cause of the Latin American."[34] The council's initial work ranged from encouraging residents to attend mass regularly and promoting religious instruction to proposing more church services and spiritual guidance in Spanish, including the appointment of more Spanish-speaking clergy. It soon coupled sacred matters with attention to secular concerns. "Eas[ing] the integration of the Spanish Speaking into society," explained CCSS leaders, required simultaneous consideration of "the needs of body and soul." This premise led them to mount small-scale service proj-

Figure 6. Eduardo López (standing on far left) and supporters of the Catholic Council for the Spanish Speaking, 1963. *TCV* Photograph Collection, Archives of the Archdiocese of San Francisco. Courtesy of the *Catholic Voice* (Oakland, CA).

ects in 1963, including English classes in five parishes and a summer enrichment program for teenagers at risk of quitting school. Experiments such as these affirmed the need to expand these very services. They also exposed a basic reality: neither the CCSS nor the Church alone could tackle and ameliorate the gamut of Latinos' educational and economic challenges. Leaders Eduardo López and Carmen Solis soon acknowledged that "dealing with [the] social problems of Spanish-speaking residents" required involvement from the public sector. The two-year-old, faith-based CCSS now began to morph into an advocacy organization championing governmental assistance to enhance Latino lives.[35]

Faith, social services, and invocations for state aid circulated within Protestant milieus as well. In the Mission, Reverend Roger Granados and others involved in the Presbyterian Inner-City Project, an initiative backed by the United Presbyterian Church of the USA, took the lead in shoring up the well-being of congregants at four churches. Latino Protestants of multiple traditions and denominations accessed these spaces with varying degrees; they especially flocked to the Good Shepherd–El Buen Pastor headed by Joseph Mesa and Granados. There, some obtained job placement advice and others enrolled in English-language classes. The parallels between these supportive services and ones undertaken by the CCSS were not lost on their leaders. Participants in these religious networks affirmed that tackling the "range of problems endured by the Spanish-speaking poor" took precedence over the Catholic-Protestant divide. Their rapport rose as the decade advanced, and they soon called on state authorities to assist them in expanding their service programs.[36]

In June 1964, ten community leaders, all of them men, met at Granados's home and formed a collaborative temporarily known as Centro Activista Latino Americano (CALA). "Destined to look after the interests of Latin American residents," it drew representatives from the CCSS, the CSO, and Protestant congregations from the Mission. Mutual aspirations to elevate Latinos' educational and economic standing brought them together.[37]

Philosophically, CALA's organizers identified two concepts as fundamental for their community's development: citizen action and latinidad. Their activist call did not present a radical departure from previous iterations made by ULAA or the CSO. It remained rooted in a quest to engage residents in efforts for individual and communal betterment. Yet it took on more political valence and urgency as the War on Poverty began and as apprehensions over urban unrest expanded. "It is truly necessary and timely to promote an intelligent evolution," read CALA's founding statement, "not a grand revolution." Interweaving religious virtue with liberal tenets of progress and reform, its framers hoped their vision would be accomplished by "faithful endurance [but] not with violence." The men simultaneously exalted the imperatives of latinidad. Advancement and success, according to Granados and his colleagues, required cooperation sustained by an understanding of parallel circumstances, challenges, and fortunes. They cast Latinos' "lack of unity" as the cause for the "ineffectiveness of isolated efforts" and "shameful rivalries" that proved counterproductive. Their organization set out to upend this state of affairs and impelled residents to work toward communal well-being without distinctions of national origin, class, political orientation, or religion. "Constructing a strong wall of solidarity," CALA organizers believed, presented the optimal means for generating change.[38]

CALA's founders were not alone in linking service, activism, and latinidad. Two months after that organization's emergence, a separate group of "Spanish ancestry" created the Spanish Speaking Citizens Foundation (SSCF).

Its architects included former ULAA activists, MAPA devotees, and members of the Spanish-American Committee, another group intent on mobilizing Latino voters. Some foundation boosters were attorneys, doctors, journalists, and civil servants; others came from distinctly working-class backgrounds. Lawrence Palacios headed the Laundry Workers Union and served as the SSCF's first president; Abel Gonzales, who led the Construction and General Laborers Union Local 261, also played a prominent role in the SSCF. Foundation leaders identified their institutional mission as one oriented toward "raising the economic, education and social level of Spanish speaking groups."[39]

The SSCF's raison d'être did not necessarily distinguish it from CALA. Neither did its reliance on latinidad. "It is [our] aim, principle and ideal," proclaimed the SSCF, "to cultivate feelings of security, friendship and unity amongst the Spanish speaking throughout the city of San Francisco." Foundation members believed goodwill and common cause among Latinos would yield pragmatic and political benefits. Echoing CALA's vision, the SSCF approached latinidad as a means to increase the coordination and breadth of social services. Its leaders surmised that tackling a myriad of social problems would be best accomplished if Latinos "organize[d] and unite[d] under one banner." In contrast to CALA, the SSCF communicated the link between latinidad and governmental assistance more explicitly. A cohesive ethnic community—with shared interests and numerically noticeable—held the potential to garner sustained attention from federal, state, and local authorities. Palacios, Gonzales, and their colleagues reckoned that the state would concern itself more with Latinos' plight if they presented "a stronger and united voice before governmental agencies." The promise of latinidad lay here: it could be channeled to augment social services, government assistance, and recognition as a unified political community.[40]

War on Poverty, War of Representation

Promoting latinidad proved particularly valuable and consequential as the War on Poverty got under way. In the months between President Lyndon B. Johnson's declaration to combat poverty and the passage of the Economic Opportunity Act of 1964—the policy apparatus sustaining the federal initiative—Latino leaders participated in numerous discussions about poverty and its attendant ills.[41] Meetings and forums with public officials and social welfare authorities offered opportunities to present a Latino community with similar needs and challenges irrespective of national origins. Once Congress authorized public monies, Latino power brokers engaged in local planning efforts and rallied Latinos as an ethnoracial bloc—one that deserved representation and assistance comparable with other minority communities.

The anti-poverty crusade animated the proposition of a Latino collective with shared burdens and aspirations unlike any governmental initiative launched before it. By the mid-1960s, community spokesmen, such as Herman Gallegos and Eduardo López, routinely appeared before public bodies and explained Latinos' concerns and their socioeconomic plight. In spring 1964, Latino leaders took part in meetings sponsored by the California State Social Welfare Board, which sought information about San Francisco's "poverty-prone" populations. Official figures designated 50 percent of the city's Spanish-surname families as economically disadvantaged, with one quarter of these living at or below the federal poverty level. Community representatives identified job upgrading and better housing as the basic prerequisites for improving the lives of poor—and overwhelmingly nonwhite—San Franciscans. Gallegos, López, and their counterparts concurrently underscored that Latinos, like African Americans, typically accessed social services at underfunded community institutions because they found government agencies inaccessible, burdensome, and lacking in cultural competency. Given this situation, ethnic leaders called for an expansion of community-based programs that inner-city residents would experience as welcoming and familiar. Their recommendation departed from one made by ULAA back in the 1950s, when that civic association simply prescribed the placement of culturally competent personnel at existing public agencies. The 1960s orientation greatly aligned with the logic of War on Poverty efforts, especially the Community Action Program (CAP), making it quite easy to advocate for services and programs offered for and by Latinos.[42]

A hallmark of the War on Poverty, the CAP introduced a novel approach for tackling socioeconomic adversity. Of all the programs created under the Economic Opportunity Act, the CAP presented the most innovation—and eventually the most controversy—because it awarded federal funds to local communities to mount their own anti-poverty projects. Federal administrators touted it as a "daring and original" experiment, one that demanded "community responsibility, empathy and basic democracy."[43] Indeed, civic duty and compassion coalesced into a strategy emphasizing poor people's direct involvement in the anti-poverty campaign. Broadening notions of influence and expertise, federal authorities reasoned that the poor themselves had to seek solutions to their socioeconomic plight. The logic resulted from a convergence of three ideological currents within governmental circles: a long-standing valorization of self-help, a desire to placate growing disquietude in inner cities, and genuine commitment to expanding citizen engagement. Some congressional leaders stressed that the crusade's success hinged on the participation of the poor. "Unless [the poor] react to their poverty," explained Adam Clayton Powell (D-New York), chairman of the House Subcommittee on the War on Poverty, "unless they have a major part in improving their station: it will be impossible to bring about this miracle we have undertaken."[44]

The CAP's directive of "maximum feasible participation" energized the poor in urban and rural communities alike. At the same time, the scope of citizen participation produced much dissension and disillusion as poor people, their leaders, and local politicians grappled with its parameters and implications. San Franciscans invested in the CAP met a contentious and prolonged struggle over representation, decision-making, and resources; their experience was a particularly intense variant of a national phenomenon.[45]

San Francisco's mayor, John F. Shelley, had not foreseen conflict when his office created the EOC and appointed all fifty members to the council in late 1964. The EOC had the "responsibility of developing and implementing a plan of action to break the cycle of poverty" as mandated by federal legislation.[46] Its initial accomplishments included designating four poverty target areas (i.e., Chinatown, the Western Addition, the Mission, and Hunters Point), compiling research data about the city's poor, and supervising the work of contact committees in each target area. Local residents' roles and contributions during this early stage appeared marginal and imprecise, especially in policymaking and program development. This state of affairs led community advocates to interrogate the mayor's version of citizen participation. Charging that City Hall's approach circumvented the CAP's philosophical underpinnings, they gradually rallied their base behind an alternative drawn from the bottom up.

In February 1965, Latinos learned about the emergence of Citizens United Against Poverty (CUAP), a coalition of civic, religious, and civil rights groups spearheading a drive to obtain decision-making power in the local CAP. African Americans led the way, and their grassroots organizations sustained the alliance. Yet individuals such as Leandro "Lee" Soto followed

CUAP's activities closely and apprised Latinos of its significance. Soto participated in the CCSS and MAPA and wrote for the *Sun-Reporter*, the city's African American newspaper, whose publisher backed CUAP. He was but one Latino figure with ties to African Americans' activist network, and he labored to link the concerns shared by both minority communities. Individuals like him deduced that building interracial partnerships could be mutually advantageous. On this occasion, Latinos leaned on and benefited from African Americans' initiative. Expanding CUAP's legitimacy soon required support from other communities. Making a comprehensive case for its vision of citizen participation—one that would guide a citywide program—depended on drawing Asian Americans, Latinos, and white allies into its campaign. CUAP managed to do so within three months of its formation.[47]

CUAP's unrest revolved around Mayor Shelley's "apparent power grab" of the anti-poverty program, which contained weak mechanisms for full participation by the poor. True citizen participation, advocates explained, depended on equipping the poor with voting power on the EOC. "Since the poor people are not receiving adequate appointments to the economic opportunity council," explained CUAP's leaders, "they are not going to have any say in how the program is being handled let alone what it is doing."[48] The coalition equated meaningful participation with direct influence over the CAP and pushed for grassroots control of the EOC. It specifically demanded that eight of thirteen members on the council's executive committee be elected by residents from the target areas. Months of intense meetings, rallies, and accusations in the press led the mayor to express conditional support for CUAP's proposal, if he could select the neighborhoods' candidates. Shelley's position quickly turned into political fodder—further proof that his office indeed sought to control the CAP.

The standoff evinced a protracted struggle over elected officials' authority, citizen participation, and public funds. Shelley insisted that his office and mayoral appointees had to manage the CAP because the venture relied on federal and local monies. Residents' involvement, according to the mayor, should not translate into a revocation of executive oversight or a reduction of mayoral accountability before other public bodies. "A power play and politics are being thrown into it and we are not going to get anywhere that way," noted Shelley in May 1965. "They want the City to pay, but they don't want The City to do anything about it." The citizens' group certainly sought to acquire power; the mayor expected to preserve his.[49]

CUAP by no means rejected mayoral input or the presence of mayoral appointees on the EOC. Its backers instead condemned Shelley's determination to "prevent the people from controlling" the CAP. Adding fuel to the fire, the mayor questioned coalition leaders' intentions and labeled them a "self-anointed group" that did not truly speak for the poor and other minority populations.[50] Yet poor residents proved receptive to CUAP's agenda, and the group amassed more followers and allies by disseminating its message across all target areas. By late August 1965, representatives from a host of organizations, including MAPA, the SSCF, and the Puerto Rican Political Association, arrived in City Hall and aligned themselves with CUAP's plan. Overwhelming support for neighborhood control and city leaders' interest in ensuring that the conflict did not "flare up into disturbances"—a tangible concern given the Watts uprising in Los Angeles that very month—persuaded Shelley to yield. As the mayor put it, "There seems to be a very strong feeling that control of the program should be with those who are involved in it."[51]

While Latinos only played supporting roles in the citywide struggle to control the CAP, they took center stage in the Mission's arena of anti-poverty politicking. District leaders began competing for authority and sway over the target area's residents even before Washington had fully authorized the War on Poverty. In what was not a coincidental development, CALA and the SSCF both emerged as the anti-poverty legislation moved through Congress. Latino advocates who had long called for governmental assistance surely grasped the stakes: public funds, social service provision, and political recognition. They also found themselves wrestling over which political networks had stronger connections to the Mission's poor and could therefore best represent their interests. In August 1964, Eduardo López and Roger Granados, both involved in CALA, attended an SSCF meeting and raised questions about the foundation's agenda. The men advised SSCF leaders to consult with existing organizations, spend more time in the Mission, and "observe the services now being tendered to the people." CALA leaders implicitly positioned themselves as community insiders tasked with vetting plans crafted by outsiders and asked to review the foundation's constitution. Felipe Marquez, Louis Garcia, and other SSCF members found the approach frustrating and felt slighted by the insinuation of intrusion. They downplayed the suggestion of interloping and cast CALA's leaders as obstructionists to the cause of Latino progress. López's and Granados's attitude, according to Marquez, exemplified "the deterrent factor in efforts to help" Latinos.[52]

These frictions belied a core element driving latinidad: the pursuit of unity. The roadblocks to solidarity and harmony, quite notably, did not arise from divisions over national origins (e.g., Puerto Ricans versus Nicaraguans) or cultural distinctions (e.g., Spanish language variation, culinary preferences). Ethnocultural particularities have often offered scholars and commentators a facile explanation for discord among Latinos. Yet these were not the arresting sources of conflict during San Francisco's War on Poverty.

Three other factors proved more salient in fomenting the schism between CALA, the SSCF, and their respective allies. First, Latinos in these organizations disagreed over who had more direct and ongoing contact with Mission residents. They specifically sparred over their records of community service, a point used to weigh their connections to the grassroots. Jess Hernandez, chairman of the CSO, identified "the intrusion of an organization that purports to speak" for Latinos as a key political crisis confronting them. Aligned with CALA, CSO leaders regarded the SSCF as a body "trying to usurp the effective work of many years by recognized Spanish-speaking groups."[53] Such a perspective drew on recent circumstances but ignored a longer history of community-oriented efforts and activities beyond the Mission. In the early 1960s, the CSO, the CCSS, and other faith-based groups definitely led the way in civic work. Still, some SSCF members had participated in ULAA or labor unions, or both, in previous decades. The generational divide itself bred contention. Louis Vásquez, Ruth Alarid, Edelmiro Huertas, and others in the SSCF could point to a long-standing commitment to improving Latinos' life conditions. They faced off with a new cadre of activists and leaders, including Granados, López, and Herman Gallegos, whose local advocacy began in the early 1960s and now formed the vanguard of social action and service provision.

Generational standing and organizational approaches concurrently informed understandings of state-sponsored social welfare. The professedly nonpolitical CSO and its faith-based partners proceeded from an outlook equating government assistance with public duty and social conscience. When their leaders advocated before state authorities, they did so as informants and supplicants, not as lobbyists.[54] Political maneuvering and the marshaling of electoral power, in contrast, guided the work of San Franciscans associated with the SSCF. Latinos immersed in MAPA, the Puerto Rican Political Association, and labor unions understood that government responsiveness often flowed from electoral mobilization and political loyalties. Herein lay another ideological fault line faced by Latinos. While some regarded the War on Poverty as emblematic of governmental goodwill, others saw the operation as a by-product of political patronage. Gallegos implied as much by commenting on the disconnection between the CSO and MAPA in December 1964. Addressing MAPA's executive board, he noted, "In the past our two organizations have not always agreed on the methods we would seek to bring about our participation in the 'Great Society.'"[55]

Latinos' differences escalated and then abated as CUAP's campaign unraveled. Three months before CUAP's emergence in early 1965, Granados and his allies assembled a committee to strategize about the Mission's war on poverty. Staffers for the original EOC expected district committees would gather residents' concerns and offer suggestions to the citywide council. Granados and other faith-based leaders knew the anti-poverty initiative promised more. They found much appeal in designing their own self-help program and building "grass roots strength" among the poor.[56] A synchronous emphasis on organizing poor people led Granados's secular synod—convened as the Mission Area Organization Committee (MAOC) in March 1965—to partner with CUAP. MAOC popularized CUAP's vision in the Mission, drafted an action agenda, and set priorities for initial service programs.

MAOC's activities vexed Latinos in the SSCF, who challenged the committee's transparency and inclusion. Branding it as an "undemocratic and self-appointed group," Lawrence Palacios and his comrades claimed that MAOC did not fully involve the poor and excluded everyone outside Granados's milieu.[57] This affront curiously reproduced Mayor Shelley's charges against CUAP—allegations intended to delegitimize the opposition—and evidenced a deep distrust and acrimony between organizational factions. MAOC weathered the SSCF's indictment by pointing to the participation of and support from religious congregations, the CCSS, the CSO, non-Latino civic groups, and unaffiliated residents. Gallegos, Mary Salazar, and others in the CSO's anti-poverty committee, for example, immersed themselves in MAOC's work, and the civic association as a whole expressed full confidence in Granados's work.

The CSO instead identified Mayor Shelley's recalcitrance as the major impediment before them. An absence of neighborhood control over the CAP, its members explained, would translate into "non-benefit from the War on Poverty." The SSCF found common cause with this position. Its leaders believed that the intent of Congress could only be accomplished through "proper representation of the poor."[58] Ideological congruity on this issue alongside grassroots interest in the cause led Latinos into the citywide front calling for the actualization of CUAP's plan. The showdown with Mayor Shelley essentially managed to mitigate tensions, at least temporarily, in the Mission. Like their contemporaries in New York City, San Francisco's Latinos experienced "unity [from] their discontent" with City Hall.[59] The question of who best represented the poor remained unsettled; they nevertheless concurred on designing a CAP controlled at the grassroots.

The War on Poverty on the Ground

Neighborhood control advocates' victory in August 1965 spawned a reconstructed EOC, autonomy for the target areas, and direct opportunities for poor people to influence anti-poverty efforts. Elected representatives from the city's poverty areas would now form the majority on the EOC and its executive committee. The council's key functions became two: offering technical assistance and conducting final reviews of programmatic proposals before forwarding them to Washington. Anti-poverty plans and decisions now flowed upward from target areas to the EOC. "All programs that require action by the Council or its official agents," read the new EOC's bylaws, "must originate in the Area Boards or receive prior written approval by the Area Boards." This model actualized CUAP's and MAOC's bottom-up philosophy and resulted in the creation of four (later five) relatively independent CAPs in the city. In the Mission, policymaking and program administration emanated from the Mission Area Community Action Board (MACAB), also elected by district residents. MACAB's work and structure would theoretically allay the SSCF's criticisms of MAOC, which coordinated the transition process.[60]

The builders of MACAB underscored that board membership should not be based on race or organizational affiliation. Pragmatism and political calculus guided this orientation: the district's ethnoracial diversity and "conflicting pressures" would make it difficult to assign seats to every ethnic or community group in the district. Seats on MACAB instead depended on low-income status, district residence, and parity across the Mission's subareas, including Bernal Heights and Potrero Hill. As the only target area board with explicitly low-income criteria, this arrangement would allow the poor to directly approve and oversee all projects created under the Mission Area Community Action Program (MACAP). It also presented an opportunity to design a poor people's program addressing the socioeconomic disparities and challenges confronting the Mission's heterogeneous population.[61]

Racial politics, organizational influence, and latinidad remained prominent. Some Latinos, especially those affiliated with the SSCF, insisted on representing the Mission on the EOC, sitting on MACAB, and directing MACAP. Their ethnic kin would most benefit from the War on Poverty, they deduced, if Latinos had influence over policymaking and program development. Part of their assessment stemmed from a desire to counter public and private agencies' long-standing neglect of their cultural and linguistic needs. Latinos sought more access to "social resources," explained Herman Gallegos in January 1966, and the "public power" (i.e., political influence) increasingly available to African Americans. Months earlier, Lawrence Palacios presented a less abstract proposition by stressing that voting for Spanish-surnamed representatives would result in jobs, services, and other advantages for Latinos. Invoking latinidad, his foundation told its *amigos latinos* that "adequate representation" and "full recognition" were only possible through their unity, which the SSCF consistently affirmed as their source of strength.[62]

Many Latinos treated MACAP as a terrain from which to offer services, advocate on behalf of coethnics, and nurture political affinities. Non-Latino Missionites took heed. Drawn to a similar ethnic strategy or concerned about Latino predominance, or both, district poverty warriors found themselves bargaining over staffing and programmatic priorities. Outside observers remarked how Missionites' ethnoracial "identifications tended to be much more significant than low-income status," making it difficult to mount one overarching poor people's program. To be sure, some practical considerations fed this situation. The district's linguistic and cultural diversity demanded that some efforts focus on specific population needs. But program development involved more than just cultural sensitivity. Ethnic-specific projects translated into employment opportunities, services, and a client base that could press for ongoing state assistance in exchange for electoral allegiance. Social scientists have noted that many "activities funded by the [Great Society] programs recalled those of the old political machine" by relying on community-based leaders and workers "to dispense the new federal patronage."[63] Some historical actors were well aware of these dynamics. Alex Zermeño and his contemporaries understood their "purpose in the Mission" as twofold: to build community institutions and to cement a Latino political bloc. Active in Oakland's CSO and MAPA chapters, Zermeño served as MACAP's first director; his appointment signaled rapprochement across Latino factions. Tensions between the CSO and MAPA-SSCF had begun to thaw as more advocates accepted that government assistance depended on a blend of nonpartisan advocacy, voter registration and mobilization, and political endorsements. The anti-poverty program offered them "an opportunity not only to fund needed services in the community," observed Mike Miller, a white community organizer, "but also an opportunity to build a base of Latino power in the city."[64]

Yet MACAP could not operate exclusively for Latinos: it had to serve and involve the poverty area's heterogeneous population. Its policymaking board attempted to balance low-income needs, ethnic interests, and cultural considerations by establishing a multiservice center—offering job counseling, medical screenings, and other forms of assistance—and projects targeting specific populations. Community Action for the Urbanized American Indian, for example, aided Native peoples while coping with relocation and adjusting to city life. Many of these Missionites had left their reservations in the 1950s; an enhanced social support network promised to orient them toward services, expand "community self-awareness," and lay the groundwork for integration into larger society. Monolingual, Spanish-speaking residents' basic integration depended on English-language acquisition. They experienced varied social and economic constraints (e.g., communication impasses with their children's teachers, unemployment and underemployment) because they lacked rudimentary English; staff at the Mission English Language Center set out to upend the situation. Job training and placement were, of course, essential as well. The Potrero Hill Manpower and Employment Research Project focused its attention on African Americans and strove to procure jobs for them. Its coordinators acknowledged, "Ideally, a community action program should be comprehensive in its employment efforts." Yet, like other service-oriented ventures, locally and nationally, the project could only tackle the symptoms of poverty (e.g., lack of job preparedness), not the structural forces producing it (e.g., deindustrialization).[65]

Poor residents benefited from these service-oriented efforts as clients, sometimes as employees, but rarely as managers or directors. While the poor routinely offered input about their needs, they remained marginal in creating and managing service projects. Most undertakings actually originated from groups or leaders with some established community presence. Poor people generally lacked the expertise necessary to compile social scientific data, write grant proposals, and prepare budgets. Additionally, the rush to submit proposals to federal authorities deterred MACAB from developing adequate channels for technical assistance. This situation revealed an important gap in the process of citizen participation. Pragmatic considerations together with MACAB's maneuvering of ethnic agendas impeded the creation of service programs designed organically by the poor.

Grassroots organizing presented vastly different opportunities for engaging poor Missionites. Direct action work concretized the philosophy of citizen participation in ways that service provision could not. There was, of course, an interrelationship between service and action strategies. The former prioritized the dispensation of immediate assistance to mitigate pressing problems; the latter encouraged residents' mobilization to alter the workings of service delivery. Waging a war on poverty, many MACAB members underscored, required more than the provision of social services. They believed that the crusade should assist the poor in becoming agents—not merely recipients—of reform. "The most conclusive evidence" of citizen involvement, board members noted, would "be the establishment and development of 'permanent' neighborhood groups which [could] educate and motivate low-income residents" to confront the socioeconomic obstacles before them. Here, they affirmed and expanded the congressional principle undergirding anti-poverty efforts: maximum feasible participation hinged on community organizing.[66]

Under the rubric of "community organization," poverty warriors set out to animate, canvass, and mobilize district residents. They wanted Latinos and their neighbors to "exercise [their] residential and citizen rights," as Zermeño put it, and encouraged this by educating and rallying them at the grassroots level. In tackling neighborhood problems, proposing solutions, and recognizing the potential to effect change, Missionites would tangibly "experience the rights and privileges of community citizenship."[67] Block clubs, tenant councils, and other small groups became the vehicles to carry out this endeavor; these collectives relied on the labors of twenty-five community organizers, all employed by MACAP. Elba Montes, a twenty-five-year-old single mother with a partial secondary education, was among them. "We went into the community and started meetings with individuals, people within blocks," she recounted. "We brought people to talk about . . . problems in the Mission. . . . [We then asked] well, what is it that you want to do about it?"[68] Basic quality-of-life concerns guided the work of Movimiento Latino, Bernal Heights Action for Progress, and other collectives assembled by Montes and her counterparts. They pressed for improved rental housing, the installation of traffic signs at heavily traversed intersections, and more bilingual teachers at area schools, among other proposals. At house gatherings, street demonstrations, press conferences, and meetings with public officials, many Missionites came to understand they had to "organize to help [themselves]."[69]

Housing concerns spawned some of the most intense organizing drives. Mission residents consistently expressed dissatisfaction with conditions at public housing sites, the need for rent control, and their fear of redevelopment. Mounting anxieties over an urban renewal proposal, in fact, propelled the creation of the Mission Council on Redevelopment (MCOR), with great assistance from MACAP. As Chapter 5 will show, many nascent groups drawn to direct action joined MCOR and demanded control over the redevelopment process. The district-wide mobilization to upend the San Francisco Redevelopment Agency's plans unfolded as smaller campaigns targeted the local Public Housing Authority (PHA). In summer 1966, tenants at Valencia Gardens, most of whom were Native Americans and Latinos, staged demonstrations and pressured PHA officials to improve fumigation services, reopen a recreation center, and revise burdensome regulations and fees. African Americans at the Carolina Projects took things further and organized a rent strike some months later.[70] The Potrero Hill Actions Committee demanded that public housing residents sit on the city's housing commission, which oversaw the PHA's work. Casting the PHA as "the biggest slumlord in town," committee members underscored that tenants should have direct say over the agency's activities because political appointees had "little knowledge of things and conditions at these houses."[71] Activists drew strength from their understanding of citizen participation and their efforts epitomized the workings of community organization: residents came together and proposed solutions to basic problems making it difficult to lead decent lives.

The most tangible and collective form of citizen participation, grassroots organizing called into question the CAP's purpose and parameters. Street demonstrations, rent strikes, and other forms of direct action as layers of government-funded anti-poverty work generated ire and controversy, in and beyond San Francisco. Elected officials, "agencies whose deficiencies [were] being pointed out," and some taxpayers decried the usage of public funds for political action. The Redevelopment Agency, for example, charged that MACAP's involvement in the redevelopment struggle placed anti-poverty staff in a biased role that betrayed their public mandate. Other municipal entities expressed related critiques. They believed that the city's CAPs and their poverty warriors stood on perilous ground: at once linking residents to public services yet instigating them to protest the practices of government agencies. Grassroots organizers generally saw a correlation, not a contradiction, between direct action and service delivery. They rapidly "learned that [their] organizing [was] not always welcomed."[72]

The citywide EOC attempted to allay mounting criticism by increasing its oversight of target areas' work and limiting the scope of community organization. These decisions complicated matters further. MACAB and its counterparts expected to maintain their autonomy and assumed their representatives on the EOC would side with them. Neighborhood control of the council, however, was quite slim, and not all poverty area representatives thought alike or voted as a bloc. By 1967, a majority of EOC members chose to increase allocations for service-based activities even as area boards requested more funds for community organization. Some target area leaders and staff responded by accusing the central administration of disloyalty, either for compromising too much or for aligning with mayoral appointees opposed to community organizing. Neighborhood control advocates also grew resentful of the EOC's bureaucratic orientation; they had envisioned that the citywide body would "be close to people and free of red tape." Tensions escalated over many months, resulting in countless confrontations, staff turnover, and public scorn. The political infighting and controversies over grassroots organizing led many observers to conclude that the anti-poverty program had to be revamped or ended altogether.[73]

Washington first opted for amendments. Congressional representatives and administrators at the Office of Economic Opportunity had followed the enthusiasm, frustration, and discord generated by the CAP in San Francisco and across the country. Communities invested in the program met comparable promise, predicaments, and, ultimately, destinies.[74] Municipal and regional leaders often identified community control as the CAP's root problem because the process bypassed the traditional federal-local arrangement for managing government assistance. The CAP challenged "established political structures," as historian Michael Katz has written, by allowing the citizenry to access public monies directly and use some funds to criticize governmental authorities. Federal administrators initially supported communal autonomy and "tolerated" grassroots organizing but growing turmoil soon produced a shift in federal policy.[75] In 1967, Congress amended the Economic Opportunity Act and equipped local governments with greater jurisdiction and responsibility for the CAP. The new regulations made San Francisco's EOC chiefly accountable to City Hall and pushed the council to augment its supervision of the target areas.[76] Many leaders and activists in the Mission, including Zermeño and Montes, responded to diminished influence, disillusionment, and exhaustion by ending their formal work with MACAP. While service-oriented activities continued, monies for community organizing dried up further. The development was not entirely surprising. "[We] predicted that if we became very active in community organization and threatening [to] the political structure of San Francisco and everybody else," recalled Zermeño, "the government would cut us off."[77]

Challenges and limitations notwithstanding, the War on Poverty presented Latinos with a watershed in ethnic recognition, citizen participation, and grassroots mobilization. The long-standing exhortation to take "Latin Americans into account," made since the late 1940s, bore some concrete successes by the mid-1960s. Some leaders and activists viewed their influence and the benefits from the government initiative as compensation for—and the crystallization of—a political strategy sustained by ethnicity. The SSCF hailed its "ethnic oriented approach" as both the key for tackling the problems confronting Latinos and "the secret [for] relating to, involving and motivating the Spanish surname people."[78] Numerous projects and activities supported by public funds confirmed this assessment. Still, the anti-poverty crusade offered more than an experiment in consolidating an ethnic bloc. The philosophy of citizen participation energized low-income San Franciscans and inspired them to become stakeholders in the Great Society. This democratic axiom and the concomitant pursuit of community control would color Latino political life even after the CAP's restructuring. Making a coordinated, robust case for citizen participation and authority would depend on ongoing action from the bottom up. A renewal of Latino grassroots organizing, in fact, became one of MACAP's greatest accomplishments. The seminal experiments with mass mobilization during the 1960s and early 1970s, as we will see, drew on the visions and energies of leaders, activists, and residents who had been poverty warriors.[79]

Anti-poverty efforts allowed Latinos to advance an ethnic agenda first drafted in the early postwar years and to revive some grassroots traditions from the 1930s and 1940s. Along the way, they met two challenges that MACAP could not reconcile. The interplay between service delivery and direct action would continue to raise questions and generate discord. Other Great Society initiatives soon sparked and magnified tensions over social service priorities, the allocation and management of government funds, and the scope of community organizing. At the same time, the logic of latinidad remained appealing yet conflict ridden. Ongoing aspirations to augment Latino political power and growing cultural nationalism made this objective imperative for some. Others insisted that the Mission's diverse makeup demanded a program for social change that did not give primacy to one eth-noracial constituency. As they transitioned from a war on poverty to building a model city, Latinos and their neighbors once again grappled with their terms of engagement with the liberal state. And Latinos remained divided over the key source of solidarity: class standing or latinidad.

CHAPTER 5

"The Color of Citizen Participation"

Community Control and the Contest
over Great Society Liberalism

Some one thousand residents gathered at the Marshall Elementary School grounds, near 16th and Mission Streets, on the crisp Saturday morning of 17 May 1969. An arresting sense of purpose and a spirit of solidarity had brought them to this site, in the heart of the district and three blocks east of the mission established by the Spanish empire two centuries earlier. On this day, Latinos and their neighbors rallied and prepared to march toward the Civic Center—"to display their unity" and make their wishes known before City Hall. Accompanied by a mariachi band, they proceeded north along Mission Street to Van Ness Avenue; they crossed Market Street and then advanced east, along Grove Street, to the city's public square. Their banners and signs relayed messages of institutional might, communal fortitude, and the force of latinidad. Placards heralding "Viva MCO" underscored the Mission Coalition Organization's ascendancy; signs professing "Brown Power" affirmed ethnoracial pride and Latinos' ongoing quest for greater political influence.[1]

Marchers shared a seemingly simple yet administratively complex goal: to obtain community control of the Model Cities program. A hallmark of the Great Society, Model Cities offered federal funds for community development efforts in metropolitan areas.[2] The experiment typified the federal government's attempts to ameliorate various symptoms of the urban crisis crippling inner-city neighborhoods, including lack of job training, housing deterioration, and limited educational opportunities.[3] Many district activists and leaders themselves advocated for increased governmental assistance, yet insisted on the community's authority to design and direct its own undertaking for socioeconomic improvement. Ideologically, the credo of community control served to foment a grassroots movement and to define the community's relationship to the liberal state. Missionites' procession and open-air convention that spring day—if marked by a "fiesta-like atmosphere" infused with balloons and music—was, above all, a manifestation of political vision and resolve.[4]

Missionites' demonstration in May 1969 occurred at the pinnacle of postwar Latino politicization. Marches and rallies like these—along with town hall meetings, walkouts, and other forms of collective action—resumed prominence and regularity in Latino life from the mid-1960s forward. Latinos had consistently engaged in public protest and mass mobilization during the 1930s and 1940s, but the magnitude of these activities ebbed during the early postwar period. By the mid-1960s, a new generation of Latinos reinvigorated the community organizing tradition. They found inspiration in the dynamism of the African American civil rights movement, the civic orientation nurtured by Latino institutions established earlier that decade, and the philosophical underpinnings of the War on Poverty's CAP. Notably, some of the most impressive activism from the mid-1960s to the early 1970s—the core of the Latino social movement era—involved questions of state power, the nature of government assistance, and the scope of citizen participation. The organizing drives and communal strife concerning Model Cities fit within this trajectory.[5]

In this period, the proposed implementation of two federal initiatives, urban renewal and Model Cities, engendered myriad visions, conflicts, and mobilizations among Missionites. Analogous policy directives undergirded these governmental undertakings, both of which targeted the Mission and its residents during the apogee of the Great Society. The Mission had undergone a substantial process of latinization during the postwar years, yet it remained racially and ethnically heterogeneous. Latinos composed approximately 25 percent of the district's population in 1960 and, by 1970, grew to 45 percent of its inhabitants.[6] Their neighbors included other racial minorities—African Americans, Native Americans, Filipinos, and American Samoans—and a substantial number of white ethnics, primarily Irish and Italian Americans. And though the Mission had a working-class tenor and government authorities classified it as a low-income area, it was also home to middle-class individuals and households. This social diversity informed racial dynamics, class interests, and popular reactions to governmental designs for socioeconomic progress.

The campaigns Missionites launched in response to an urban renewal proposal and the Model Cities program embodied grassroots contests over Great Society liberalism. Their outlooks and activism evinced profound struggles concerning the promise, character, and necessity of state-sponsored social welfare, and especially government assistance to poor and minority communities. One historian has argued that "all conflicts over liberalism occurred at the local level."[7] The political developments in the Mission fell decidedly in line with this historical pattern. Activists and residents battled extensively and vociferously over the nature of government involvement in their district. In doing so, they marshaled manifold visions regarding the process of citizen participation, the workings of community control, and the primacy of latinidad.

In the mid-1960s, Latinos joined a low-income, minority coalition known as the Mission Council on Redevelopment and forged a politically sophisticated campaign that actually embraced urban renewal—if carried out on their own terms. Inspired by the tenets of citizen participation and community control promulgated during the War on Poverty, they proved willing to support urban renewal if the city granted them official, decision-making power over the project. Middle-class groups with a white conservative base embarked on a separate course and unequivocally opposed the city's plan. They believed redevelopment formed part of a government agenda that stood against their economic interests and did not benefit them. An inclusion of white conservatives is essential here because these residents criticized their less prosperous and nonwhite neighbors for supporting and benefiting from Great Society liberalism.

The political visions circulating at mid-decade flourished, multiplied, and influenced the course of Missionites' activism in the late 1960s and early 1970s. This dynamic was evident in the collaboration and friction within the Mission Coalition Organization (MCO)—the institutional descendant of MCOR—as its members weighed the opportunities and limitations posed by Model Cities. Publicly driven by the pursuit of community control, MCO activists confronted divisions over political strategy and latinidad. Latinos committed to ethnic-based organizing supported Model Cities—if allowed to manage its direction—and treated the effort as a mechanism to expand social services for Latinos. Some of their allies, both Latinos and non-Latinos, had reservations about the logic of community control and found the premise of latinidad to be limiting. Instead, they espoused a class-based, populist framework to guide grassroots organizing and service delivery.

The MCO concurrently met dissension from the right and the far left. White conservatives revived their derision of the Great Society and now applied racist and anticommunist attacks against MCO supporters. At the same time, a younger generation of Latinos—radicalized by the antiwar and Third World liberation movements—chastised the MCO for its support of and entanglement with the American state. Latino radicals from various youth organizations believed that the government itself was an apparatus of economic inequality and racial oppression. Taken together, the promulgation of these multifaceted political ideologies demonstrated that Latinos and their neighbors did not share a unified faith in liberalism or in the preeminence of latinidad.

Urban Renewal and the Mission Council on Redevelopment

In late June 1966, four hundred Missionites crowded into the auditorium at Horace Mann Junior High School to express "concern for their future" in the district. Tenants, homeowners, and small merchants turned up at this town hall meeting to share their sentiments and suspicions about a proposed urban renewal project. Attendees underscored they did not want their community to suffer a fate similar to that of the Western Addition and South of Market, where redevelopment resulted in displacement, destruction of housing, and disruption to local business life. Representatives from the San Francisco Redevelopment Agency (SFRA), the Department of City Planning, and Mayor John Shelley's office attempted to allay people's fears; they "stressed every effort [would] be made to keep most of them in the district."[8] Such vows were not enough for residents, who demanded more from public authorities. Some committed themselves to obtaining formal guarantees that the city would fulfill its promises, while others pledged to block the city's plan in its entirety. The meeting that evening confirmed citizens' determination to impede the established course of state-sponsored urban transformation.

For the next six months, Missionites undertook a protracted "fight against redevelopment" that evidenced a surprising, flexible, and variegated field of political action.[9] Latinos and other residents in MCOR condemned the city's record of urban renewal yet acknowledged the need for state assistance to communities facing socioeconomic constraints. They chose to back redevelopment if allowed to control the program and thereby upend it from an apparatus of removal to an engine of communal progress and survival. Latinos and their allies in effect demanded a concrete voice in the urban planning process and, like thousands of others involved in community action, "insisted on being heard."[10] Middle-class organizations with an overwhelmingly white constituency coordinated separate organizing drives and diagnosed urban renewal as a malignant form of government power. Citizens involved in these groups contended that the initiative endangered their economic investments and would expel the middle class from the city. They regarded redevelopment as a direct threat to their property and a manifestation of liberal governments' misappropriation of their taxes—an assumption that linked them to other white conservatives in California and the nation.[11]

Popular mobilization and citizens' opposition ultimately led to the circumvention of community devastation, an atypical outcome in the city and the nation. Redevelopment usually resulted in the corporate reconstruction of central-city areas and the evisceration of poor and minority neighborhoods through demolition and removal.[12] The common fate of citizens touched by urban renewal, by and large, was one marked by loss of homes, social dislocation, and political defeat.[13] Missionites' encounter with urban renewal diverged from this traditional trajectory. In the short term, their crusade against redevelopment instead resulted in triumph and endurance, not disappointment and deracination.

The Impetus for Renewal and Initial Community Responses

Latinos and others in the Mission entered the renewal fray some fifteen years after San Francisco initiated its renewal experiments. Since the early postwar years, cities across the country used this federal-local initiative to stimulate commercial redevelopment and halt the expansion of housing slums. Business leaders and city planners sought to deter urban decay in central cities by reenergizing business life and reducing the migration of capital, jobs, and white residents to the suburbs. Often touting their efforts as a public good, the attack against urban blight typically produced advantages for the downtown business sector and disadvantages for residents of central-city neighborhoods. Scholars have explained how urban renewal assisted in securing San Francisco's role as the hub of finance, insurance, and real estate industries on the West Coast. Early renewal projects—carried out in proximity to the financial district—transformed the built environment and became sites of convention centers, office buildings, and luxury housing. In the early 1960s, approximately four thousand African American families found themselves displaced as a consequence of the Western Addition A-1 project, where more than a hundred acres came to house a trade center, a cathedral, new office space, and high-rise apartments.[14] Experiences like these galvanized Missionites into action once they learned their district had been designated for renewal.

The Mission's postwar future had not always been tied to urban renewal. The SFRA did not include it in its 1950s classification of areas suitable for redevelopment, which typically meant planning, demolition, and clearance by public authorities and rebuilding by private enterprise. But in 1963, the San Francisco Board of Supervisors passed a resolution urging planning bodies to devote their "highest priority" to Mission renewal planning.[15] City leaders issued their mandate as they finalized blueprints for the construction of the Bay Area Rapid Transit (BART) system. The commuter rail network would include two stations in the Mission, and numerous studies linked it to the neighborhood's future. Urban planners spearheading the Mission District Urban Design Study forecast that subway construction would propel economic growth, including heightened land values, business development, new office space, and increased tourism to Mission Dolores. The study also predicted BART would produce great changes, and perhaps dislocation, for existing residents and businesses. The SFRA relied on these projections to insist that civic duty demanded urban renewal. Its team professed that public authorities needed to mediate the progressive and unfettered course of economic transformation in a setting besieged by increasing blight (e.g., decrepit housing, inadequate street lighting). In May 1966, the agency approved a resolution and application to begin surveys and planning within sixty-one blocks of the Inner Mission.[16]

A commitment to neighborhood enhancement and citizen participation, redevelopment officials stressed, guided their efforts. They identified improved housing stock, new schools and parks, and overall district beautification as the project's foreseeable benefits. The SFRA also promoted citizen participation as a means to learn residents' needs and desires. This was a necessary and strategic position. Federal guidelines stipulated that urban renewal should prove beneficial to existing communities and that public bodies obtain neighborhood buy-in for their initiatives. "Existing property owners and tenants will be encouraged to organize," agency staff explained, "[and] to participate in the rebuilding program."[17] The nature of citizen participation, however, became a key source of debate as some constituencies pointed out its limitations and others questioned its premises.

Missionites who regarded urban renewal as an instrument of economic promise and social stability initially backed the SFRA's proposal. Endorsements from the Mission District Renewal Commission (MDRC) and the Greater Mission Citizens Council (GMCC) corroborated the SFRA's claims of citizen support. These organizations spoke for individuals and groups—most of whom were white—with long-standing ties to the district. The MDRC's membership included realtors, bankers, and merchants; they generally reproduced the SFRA's economic rationale for renewal under the guise of concerned and active citizens. With a downtown office, the organization had profound ties to the city's political and economic establishments; its board of directors included presidents from the San Francisco Life Insurance Company, Golden Gate National Bank, and other institutions with an extended reach beyond the district.[18] In contrast, the GMCC had firm roots in the Mission and originally welcomed the plan on civic grounds, as an opportunity for community improvement. Founded in 1960 and sponsored by the Mission Neighborhood Centers, the GMCC drew residents involved in home-owner associations, civic pride clubs, and some church-affiliated groups. Missionites in these circles had grown increasingly worried about population changes and the district's prospect of becoming a slum. Notably, few Latinos and other racial minorities participated in such discussions because they lacked connection to these organizations and their associational lives took them elsewhere.

Driven by civic-mindedness, the GMCC kept abreast of Missionites' social realities and preoccupations. Its members first endorsed the renewal agenda after preliminary meetings with the SFRA in April 1966. They did so earnestly yet conditionally: they expected a "proscription [sic] of concrete citizen participation" and assurances that all existing residents and businesses would remain in the district. Redevelopment officials wove a broad version of community involvement into their application but ignored the council's position on displacement. The formal proposal actually included dislocation estimates, which led the GMCC to criticize the SFRA for failing to reveal this information before obtaining its support. Questioning SFRA's transparency, the GMCC reevaluated its endorsement and now requested safeguards against the relocation problems met by residents in other neighborhoods. A resolution passed in late June 1966 called on the SFRA to build new, low-rent housing for all potential displacees; locate it in the Mission; and complete it before demolition of older structures began. It further stipulated that home-owners would receive assistance in finding comparable residences "as an out-right exchange without cost."[19] In outlining these expectations, the GMCC joined a growing chorus of Missionites demanding tangible governmental protections—ones that would shield all residents from the disruptions spawned by redevelopment.

Latinos and the Low-Income, Minority Coalition

Two weeks before the GMCC issued its June resolution, an ad hoc committee representing Latinos, other minority groups, and low-income residents came together to discuss the "burning local issue[s]" of redevelopment and the prospect of displacement. It drew leaders from the CSO; the CCSS; the American Indian Center, a social service organization for Native Americans; the Mission Area Community Action Board; and the Mission Tenants Union, a group promoting tenant rights and protections. Activists and ministers drawn to Saul Alinsky–style community organizing joined them as well. This model of grassroots politics emphasized mass mobilization and pressure tac-tics to effect changes in the lives of poor and disenfranchised people. They collectively determined that redevelopment presented grave troubles for mi-nority and low-income residents. And they pledged to organize Missionites to stop urban renewal from unfolding as it had in other neighborhoods.[20]

Community leaders outlined guiding principles that led to the creation of MCOR, founded on 24 June 1966. With Herman Gallegos and Reverend Jerry Pence as their chairmen, all who joined this alliance of neighborhood organizations agreed that human needs should be prioritized before altera-tions to the physical environment took place. Gallegos was a prominent fig-ure in the CSO and the CCSS; Pence had ties to the Presbyterian Inner-City Project, a faith-based initiative focused on social justice and the search for solutions to urban problems. "Physical planning must come after, and de-pend on social planning," the men consistently affirmed, "people before buildings."[21] Leaders and activists also reformulated the concept of citizen participation. They believed true citizen participation had to incorporate the perspectives and influence of minority and low-income peoples. Ideologi-cally and procedurally, this meant citizens' input combined with actual decision-making power. They deemed it imperative for a communal body to bring together diverse constituencies and function as the community's emissary before the SFRA and City Hall—a role MCOR energetically assumed.

As the institutional voice for low-income and minority Missionites, MCOR quickly positioned itself as a pivotal force in the contest over redevelopment. The coalition appealed to people from multiple class backgrounds and to whites committed to equality and opportunity. Some sixty-five organizations sent representatives to its foundational gathering, including religious congregations, civic bodies such as the GMCC, and a host of nascent groups funded by War on Poverty monies. Politically moderate organizations (e.g., the CCSS and MAPA) emphasized consultation and negotiation with the SFRA and City Hall. The Mission Tenants Union and radicalized Protestant congregations promoted grassroots mobilization and direct action to hold public authorities accountable to district residents. MCOR's success came to depend on both strategies: after all, an inclusive and comprehensive response had to accommodate both deliberation and protest.[22]

A majority of MCOR members shared a key point of departure: urban renewal as practiced to date had produced much damage in low-income and minority communities. The SFRA's plans, according to many activists, spelled profits for developers and their friends at the expense of established residents. "The real purpose of redevelopment is to increase land values," detailed an MCOR report, "in order to expand the tax base, and to provide more money for the city to run its government." Here, the council placed urban renewal squarely within the agenda of San Francisco's progrowth urban regime, led by monied interests and their supporters in City Hall.[23] MCOR's leaders further deduced that the BART-induced economic growth referenced in the renewal application actually depended on displacing existing residents. "If low income units and small businessmen remain," posited Pence and Gallegos, "property values will not go up because high renters do not want to live near poor property. Only when [an] area is radically cleared and new development begun, do values go up."[24] Their analysis inverted the logic of urban renewal: the initiative would not assist Missionites in confronting the economic transformations generated by BART. Instead, redevelopment would propel and escalate BART-related changes. Urban renewal stood to benefit BART and harm Missionites unless residents themselves controlled the SFRA's plans. Failure to do so left residents' future—one that would likely include clearance and displacement—in that agency's hands.

MCOR and its partners acknowledged the desirability of efforts to improve the physical infrastructure of urban neighborhoods. They agreed that poor housing and such environmental problems as inadequate street lighting affected Missionites' quality of life. Many residents concurred. They regularly expressed a desire for better housing, refurbished schools, and more play-grounds in letters to elected officials. Manuel Cirilo wrote it "[was] difficult to find good and cheap housing" while Antonio Morales pointed out the need to repair "the condition of the older houses." Others, including Maria Lucero and Andres and Lucy Torres, longed for more parks and recreational spaces.[25] All these aspirations aligned well with the SFRA's official aims. Yet San Fran-ciscans in other renewal areas had experienced how redevelopment typically proceeded: new housing and amenities materialized following expulsion from their communities. MCOR activists set out to apprise Cirilo and his neighbors of that record and mobilize them behind an alternative.

Whether through block clubs, church groups, or civic associations, many Missionites energetically joined MCOR and formed its rank and file. Grass-roots organizers hired by MACAP proved particularly crucial in rallying residents. The district's poverty warriors had backed MCOR's creation and MACAP's thirty Spanish-speaking organizers, including Elba Montes, now took the lead in educating Latinos about redevelopment. In mid- to late June 1966, Montes and her colleagues contacted thousands of residents and steered them to the community assembly at the middle school discussed ear-lier. Organizers told residents "they could lose their homes or be moved out of the area" if elected officials approved the application.[26] The prospect of dis-placement alarmed residents and spurred them to action. They attended town hall meetings, demonstrations, and public hearings at City Hall; there, they made their sentiments known and displayed grassroots support for MCOR's agenda.

On 29 June 1966, council members appeared before a committee of city supervisors and presented a nuanced and surprising position: they backed the renewal proposal "provided that, and only if" a set of conditions materialized. Eduardo López, the CCSS president, spoke for MCOR and qualified the stance by delineating the council's understanding of citizen participation. "Residents must be given the indispensable means to be effective participants of a self-development program for themselves and their community," López asserted forcefully.[27] He then clarified how MCOR's vision departed from the SFRA's. Agency officials traditionally made intermittent presentations to community groups, asked for input, and proceeded with their proposals, even if a com-munity challenged their plans. MCOR sought a different path: it demanded ongoing, direct involvement in planning as well as decision-making power.

Figure 7. Elba Montes Tuttle, center, late 1960s. Spence Limbocker
MCO Photograph Collection. Courtesy of Spence Limbocker.

Under this arrangement, Mission citizens—represented by MCOR—would
drive the renewal process by shaping and revising it, not merely hearing
about or reacting to it.

Echoing the perspectives expanded during the planning for the anti-
poverty crusade, López and his allies linked citizen participation with neighborhood control. Full and meaningful participation, they explained, hinged
on having a formal and equal voice in the renewal process—a voice with concrete power recognized by City Hall. If Missionites directly influenced the
course of redevelopment, they themselves would control their district's future. MCOR expected to review and alter the SFRA's work on a regular basis,
negotiate with the agency as needed, and cosign all agreements made between the SFRA and the federal government.[28] This last condition was the
boldest one. Designating the council as an equal partner in the district's redevelopment would have monumental ramifications. Cosignatory power left
room open for veto power, which came to epitomize neighborhood control.
MCOR essentially sought the authority to block the renewal effort if the
SFRA undertook activities that ignored the community's wishes. Veto power
would serve as the ultimate protection against a powerful SFRA with a record

of displacement and disregard for low-income, minority communities. If re-development genuinely involved community improvement and citizen participation, MCOR members reasoned, then neighborhood residents should fully control its direction. With neighborhood control, they would ensure the renewal plan benefited them, not "drive them out of the district."[29]

Property, Taxation, and the Middle-Class Response

MCOR's openness to community-driven redevelopment fit within a liberal worldview that promoted state action to ameliorate socioeconomic inequities. Council leaders and activists believed that the government had a "social and moral obligation" to improve life prospects for racial minorities and the poor. Their perspective revealed a faith in Great Society liberalism, the mid-1960s variant of American liberalism championing racial equality, governmental assistance to low-income and minority communities, and the expansion of social welfare.[30] Not everyone in the Mission or in San Francisco, however, embraced this political orientation. If members of the low-income, minority coalition welcomed government assistance, albeit with an emphasis on community control, some middle-class, white organizations mobilized to curtail it.

White conservatives grounded their opposition and critiques in denunciations of an expanding state apparatus. Strongly identified as middle class, they regarded urban renewal as a governmental initiative antithetical to their interests and a direct threat to their property. Most were owners of homes and small businesses, and they gravitated to organizations espousing what some historians have called antiliberalism and antistatism. These political outlooks promoted a vision of society marked by fiscal conservatism, a resistance to social welfare programs, and a reproach of Democratic administrations' resolve to expand opportunities for racial minorities and the poor (at the local and national levels).[31]

Few Latinos joined these conservative circles. As an example, they numbered less than 10 among the 105 most active members of the San Francisco Committee to Stop the Redevelopment Agency (SFCSRA). Latinos' minimal participation in such groups could be explained in at least three ways. First, many found the racial sentiments of middle-class groups off-putting. Some conservative leaders equated the "concentration of Spanish speaking people" with the district's stigma as a ghetto; in so doing, they suggested that Latinos bore blame for the Mission's decline.[32] Additionally, some Latino business owners embraced the SFRA's proposal because they determined it would assist them in coping with the competition and speculation generated by BART. "The only way for the small businessman to make it is if we have a planned program using the help we can get from [City Hall] and the Redevelopment Agency," noted hardware store owner Carlos Vela. He and some of his contemporaries clearly saw the SFRA's plan as a blueprint for progress. Still others sided with MCOR's agenda because they believed that the council would protect tenants as well as local businesses.[33] Notably, whether or not Latino property owners aligned with MCOR, one thing was clear: more among them supported state action in contrast to white counterparts in middle-class-identified organizations.

Responsible Merchants, Property Owners and Tenants (RMPT) functioned as the leading middle-class group in the Mission. Led by Jack Bartalini, an electrical contractor and Republican Party member, the RMPT maintained that redevelopment embodied an injurious form of government power—which would harm hard-working, middle-class citizens. "The tax-supported Redevelopment Agency is waging war," asserted Bartalini. The renewal process as war served as an apt allegory for a venture that his organization equated to the destruction of property and the middle class. Convinced that redevelopment would result in a loss of assets and economic security, Bartalini and his associates positioned the defense of property at the core of their political work. They coupled economic interests with citizenship, casting the potential outcomes of renewal (i.e., clearance and demolition) as infringements on their rights as Americans. The RMPT sought to preserve liberty and democracy, Bartalini expounded, including the "freedom of renting or owning a home or a store free from unnecessary governmental regimentation, free from the confiscatory and dictatorial power of the Redevelopment Agency."[34] This fervor encapsulated a sense of besiegement by a public agency that was considered tyrannical. Adding to their distress, RMPT members bemoaned how local legislators backing urban renewal undermined democratic rights by ignoring citizens' wishes and public disdain for the SFRA.

Two other organizations joined the RMPT in mounting a middle-class challenge to redevelopment. Parents and Taxpayers (PAT) and the SFCSRA likewise pulled homeowners and small business proprietors into their fold. Renetta Southcott and a cohort of homemakers founded PAT at mid-decade.[35] Though not based in the Mission, its keen attention to the proposal highlighted the plan's implications beyond the district. Southcott and her colleagues viewed the Mission as a stable community with a strong middle class.

They worried that if redevelopment touched the Mission, it would then spread into other communities like it. The SFCSRA concurred. Originally a Mission-based organization, it soon became a citywide coalition of middle-class groups. Its members resolved to defeat the Mission proposal and save the city's middle class from deceitful practices and abuse of power attributed to the SFRA.

Conservatives' condemnation and distrust of the SFRA exhibited some parallels with the critiques levied by MCOR. Like Missionites in the liberal coalition, conservatives cast the SFRA as an agent of downtown interests set on altering San Francisco's landscape. They rendered the SFRA as threatening to the public interest and devious in its operations. Southcott and others in PAT branded all renewal projects as profitable enterprises for real estate speculators and developers—"greedy and ruthless men" according to the SFCSRA—but disastrous for small businesspeople and ordinary homeowners. Furthermore, a "record of irregularities, half truths . . . and other evils," noted Becky Schettler, the RMPT's secretary, made her organization "unalterably opposed" to the agency's work."[36] Many in MCOR likewise determined that the SFRA's past efforts had involved chicanery and produced much hardship; they nevertheless imagined a different future if the renewal process came under communal control. Southcott, Schettler, and their allies could not entertain that possibility. They found no merit in redevelopment and deemed it dangerous to the property and livelihood of the middle class, irrespective of who controlled the initiative.

Activists in conservative organizations actually viewed MCOR as the impoverished counterpart of monied interests, which jointly jeopardized their well-being. Describing themselves as "true middle-class people" who could "provide for all their own needs," they assumed that the poor had much to gain from redevelopment. The program formed another component of the War on Poverty, deduced conservatives, as they warned against MCOR's agenda. Bartalini and his cohort believed MCOR's vision grew out of political opportunism and a desire to further welfare dependency through housing assistance. "Opportunists seek [a] government subsidy on the one hand, while some interests lobby for extreme land-usage controls on the other," professed Bartalini.[37] From this angle, redevelopment stood to boost opportunities for the wealthy and the poor—at the expense of middle-class residents' property and taxes.

Dissatisfaction over taxation offered more ideological sustenance to conservatives' challenge. San Franciscans in the RMPT, PAT, and the SFCSRA contended that middle-class residents found themselves beleaguered by an expansion and misuse of taxes. Their organizations challenged the fiscal soundness of spending tax dollars on "unwanted, unneeded" projects. Mary Hall, SFCSRA coordinator, admonished the use of public monies for renewal efforts viewed as expensive, wasteful, inefficient, and "morally wrong." Coupling charges of financial recklessness with a lack of civic integrity, Hall and her colleagues avowed it was unscrupulous for the state to rely on—and raise—taxes for projects that took years to complete and that the citizenry did not support.[38] Conservatives found it particularly perverse that they had to finance, involuntarily, renewal efforts that would result in the loss of homes and their decline as a class. Paralleling other taxpayer campaigns in 1960s California, they condemned public financing of initiatives deemed exclusively beneficial for the rich and the poor. "Federal Urban Renewal is weakening the middle class," affirmed PAT, "by forcing it to pay, through taxation, much of the cost of subsidized housing projects for the poor and the cost of the land being transferred to the big interests." The perspective solidly situated redevelopment within a liberal agenda rewarding "the favored ones" (i.e., downtown interests and impoverished minority communities) but disregarding the interests of the white middle class.[39]

The Supervisors Weigh In

Throughout the summer and fall of 1966, city supervisors held public hearings before deciding if they would forward the redevelopment application to Washington. While MCOR, the RMPT, and the SFCSRA offered community perspectives, elected officials also weighed opinions from scholars, church and labor leaders, and other citizen groups. They presented a host of viewpoints, placed the proposal in a citywide context, and impelled supervisors to consider whether the Mission might "become a repeat" of neighboring districts.[40]

Scholars and policy experts typically fell into two camps as they addressed two central questions: the SFRA's past practices and the fate of residents in other renewal areas. Social scientists often relayed the SFRA's tendency to sidestep its "stated intentions" and alter its plans after official approval of redevelopment proposals. Sociologist Harry Brill detailed how the SFRA undertook a demolition project in South of Market after originally announcing that clearance would not be required. In the Western Addition, displaced families found themselves without replacement housing, according to Edward Eichler, an urban affairs specialist. MCOR's insistence on community control and veto power thus represented logical protective measures given the SFRA's dubious record in other neighborhoods.[41] Policy analysts from the San Francisco Planning and Urban Renewal Association (SPUR)—a key proponent of redevelopment—downplayed these scholars' positions and insisted that citizens' desires had shaped past projects. Their assessment proved lopsided as the citizens who lobbied for "glamorous" and "high tax producing projects" were professional planners and downtown business leaders, not residents of renewal areas. SPUR nevertheless attempted to assuage Missionites' fears by claiming that the SFRA had historically operated with fairness and would now "formulate [its] plan in a glass house and . . . locate that house in the Mission."[42] A pledge of transparency rendered MCOR's demand for veto power unwarranted. But SPUR presented a myopic version of local history. MCOR sought community control precisely because the transparency touted for previous projects had not materialized.

In an unprecedented move, the supervisors' finance committee responded favorably to some of MCOR's demands. City leaders' openness, in effect, recognized MCOR as the Mission's representative body. The council's provisional support for the plan, in contrast to conservative groups who stood entirely against it, informed this receptivity. Legislators' accommodation irked Missionites who viewed MCOR in a different light. "The letterhead organizations claiming to represent the 'Greater Mission' (some kind of coalition of churches and social service groups)," relayed one activist from the SFCSRA, "hardly speak for the people and property owners of the Mission."[43] The comments encapsulated a popular perspective among conservatives: MCOR members were not true Missionites. Multiple factors shaped their opinion, including length of residence, class status, and racial identity; above all, their property investments made conservatives believe they had more at stake in the district. Supervisors on the finance committee thought otherwise. They legitimized MCOR for two reasons: compromise would move the proposal forward, and MCOR had greater grassroots support than conservative organizations.

The quest for community control took center stage as deliberations proceeded, even as all parties gradually learned that the law placed limits on the process MCOR envisioned. In summer 1966, Supervisor Jack Morrison consulted with the city attorney and the U.S. Department of Housing and Urban Development (HUD) to weigh "the legality of the various conditions" put

forth by the community, including the prospect of allotting a portion of planning funds to the council. MCOR had requested public monies for an independent technical assistance team, which would analyze all renewal plans
and make recommendations on whether to back or halt the SFRA's activities.
Local and federal administrators' responses were the same: neither California
nor federal law allowed for the disbursement of renewal funds to an entity
other than the city or the local public agency charged with redevelopment.
An alternate arrangement would signify an illegal extension of public powers
to a private body, explained the functionaries, and could "lead to confusion"
and misadministration of funds.[44] Morrison and his colleagues then considered another strategy in their attempt to establish a middle ground between
the SFRA's proposal and MCOR's demands. They attached a resolution to the
application, a measure with safeguards, such as relocation housing in the
Mission and a matching supply of new housing units at prices within reach
for existing residents.[45] MCOR welcomed these protections but reiterated
that it would not categorically endorse the application without full community control. Gridlocked and with the absence of veto power, the council
withdrew its conditional support on 26 September 1966. Since the law
blocked their vision of community control, MCOR reaffirmed its commitment to block urban renewal imposed from the outside.

Three months later—after more hearings, deliberations, and grassroots
mobilization—the full Board of Supervisors considered the plan and "killed"
it—an outcome shaped by legislators' stances on redevelopment, concerns
over political fallout, and their views on growth liberalism.[46] Some leaders
voting against the proposal validated community groups' anxieties about
clearance, relocation, and citizen participation. They agreed that urban renewal projects could not move forward as before. Referencing the "misera-
ble" experiences of Western Addition residents, Roger Boas warned against
supporting a project that might prove just as disastrous. John Ertola sided
with him and stressed that citizens had to "become involved in the planning
process."[47] For others, a negative vote grew out of political expediency and a
desire to remain in office. Joseph Casey and Kevin O'Shea originally suggested they might approve the application. But these men faced reelection
the following year, and citizen groups underscored that backing the Mission
proposal would have consequences at the polls.[48] San Franciscans elected
supervisors on an at-large basis during these years. Given the issue's potency
across the city, support for redevelopment could well mold a politician's
future.

In the minority, five supervisors voted "yes" and aligned themselves with the city's growth regime. These leaders continued to approach urban renewal vis-à-vis the traditional lenses of large-scale growth and top-down planning. They generally affirmed the SFRA's logic propelling the redevelopment agenda. Terry Francois emphasized the importance of surveying and planning to ensure that Missionites reaped the benefits of economic progress generated by BART. "A no-action program," he stated, would "represent a tragic failure to make use of the coming rapid transit." Francois and Jack Morrison also inverted concerns about displacement by arguing that existing residents would actually face greater obstacles without redevelopment. The private market alone would "force the present population out of the neighborhood," the men claimed, as housing prices were bound to rise.[49] As they saw it, district residents had to embrace the reality of inevitable change.

The six supervisors who voted down the proposal accepted that times had indeed changed. They understood a key development at mid-decade: the progrowth urban regime long dominant in the city now faced formidable resistance—from the left and the right. Through their visions, admonitions, and organizing efforts, citizens in MCOR, the RMPT, and the SFCSRA convinced a majority of legislators that urban renewal could no longer unfold in its traditional manner. Opponents of redevelopment could temporarily set their political differences aside and celebrate a joint victory for the Mission. "Redevelopment foes of all political casts," declared the *San Francisco Progress*, "from arch-conservatives to ultra-liberals—patted one another on the back for turning aside the Redevelopment Agency sponsored application."[50]

The triumph did not abate communal angst about redevelopment or the conflict over liberalism. Fears of displacement and the loss of community retained both emotional and political currency for decades to come. The discord concerning the weight and configuration of government aid likewise remained at the center of Mission political life. The struggle against redevelopment had exposed a diverse and deeply divided community, particularly along the axes of class, race, and ideological investments in liberalism. Debates about the district's relationship to the state, government assistance, citizen participation, and community control would only escalate during the Model Cities era.

Model Cities and the Mission Coalition Organization

Fourteen months after halting the redevelopment plan, Elba Montes, Mary Hall, and their activist networks resumed their organizing activities on learning about Mayor Joseph L. Alioto's aspiration to bring Model Cities to the Mission. Elected in November 1967, Alioto disclosed his intentions at a Spanish Speaking Issues Forum in February 1968. MAPA, LULAC, and other Latino organizations that backed Alioto's mayoral campaign coordinated the event. Alioto came to the conference to express his gratitude and affirm his promise to augment Latinos' well-being. His interest in turning the district into a Model Cities community formed part of that political commitment. Some Missionites welcomed the mayor's news; others responded with skepticism and bewilderment. The announcement sent shock waves throughout the neighborhood, and the mayor quickly found himself "under fire": community members demanded specific details, and many wondered whether Model Cities was a pretense for redevelopment. Montes, Hall, and most parties that had participated in the renewal fight soon began "to line up either to destroy the Model Cities proposal or to modify its basic structure."[51]

The civic feuds sparked by Model Cities drew on the institutional and philosophical legacies established during the renewal maelstrom. Many individuals and organizations that built MCOR reunited and assembled a comparable confederation of residents and community groups, soon known as the Mission Coalition Organization. The new alliance's ideological posture vis-à-vis Model Cities seemed strikingly familiar: the MCO sanctioned the program if it obtained community control and veto power over mayoral designs. Conservative groups, too, reanimated their base and undertook another challenge to state action. The RMPT, the San Francisco Committee (formerly the San Francisco Committee to Stop the Redevelopment Agency), and their partners enlarged their denunciations of government instrumentality and public welfare. Their censure of Model Cities incorporated pronounced racial hostilities and backlash against state aid to nonwhite residents. Neither white conservatives nor Latinos and their allies left any doubt that the Mission faced yet another round of controversy involving Great Society liberalism.

The Model Cities experiment eventually spawned a more tumultuous chapter of communal strife. Unlike the redevelopment proposal, Model Cities went from potentiality in 1968 to reality by 1970. Its auspicious beginning under the MCO's direction, however, proved fleeting: its implementation laid bare intense divisions within the coalition itself. Community activists and leaders who formed a united front before government authorities began to fight each other soon after Model Cities monies poured into the district. They clashed over the workings of community control, allocation of government funds, and prioritization of Latino cultural needs. Tensions and confrontation between the MCO's factions eventually transformed allies into adversaries. The acerbic state of affairs, escalating year after year, foreclosed the possibility of strengthening the alliance created to represent and mobilize the district's myriad interests and constituencies.

The MCO never spoke for all Missionites, even if City Hall anointed it as the envoy of communal will. White conservatives consistently spurned the coalition and so did Latino radicals. As public authorities legitimized the MCO, a new generation of Latinos denounced government assistance and impugned the coalition for its rapport with the liberal state. Politicized by the antiwar and student movements, young people in Los Siete Defense Committee (LSDC) and La Raza En Acción Local (LaREAL) deemed it essential to create programs and services for Latinos—ones driven by ethnoracial pride and the concept of self-determination. They nevertheless challenged the motives behind the Great Society and cast governmental aid as an impediment to Latinos' progress. Latino radicals fortified their positions as they witnessed the internal trials that engulfed the MCO. Standing on the far left, they added a new hue to a spectrum of political thought colored by competing investments in liberalism and latinidad.

The Model Cities Program

Created under the Demonstration Cities and Metropolitan Act of 1966, the Model Cities program promoted comprehensive and neighborhood-based approaches for community development. It encouraged cities to couple the physical revitalization of urban neighborhoods with the "human rejuvenation" of its residents. In other words, Model Cities amplified the framework guiding urban renewal—one that prioritized housing and land use—by advancing a paradigm that simultaneously stressed educational programming, health care, and other social services. This multipronged approach embodied "one of the major policy departures," according to political scientist Sidney Milkis, "that formed the heart of the Great Society."[52]

San Francisco's mayor and some city supervisors greeted the Model Cities concept with optimism. They saw the federal program as one that could bridge physical planning objectives with residents' social needs. Mayor Alioto's policy team noted, "City officials and agencies have long recognized the need for a comprehensive planning effort in the Mission area but previous efforts have been too limited or have failed for lack of support." Referencing the unsuccessful redevelopment proposal—endorsed by Alioto's predecessor—the new administration anticipated that the Model Cities format would garner greater public approval. Other elected officials shared the mayor's aspiration and applauded its breadth. Supervisor Ronald Pelosi, chairman of the Planning and Development Committee, stressed, "Model Cities is not confined to housing, or education, or job-training, or health facilities. [It] is a comprehensive attack for ALL of these problems."[53] Pelosi and redevelopment enthusiasts Jack Morrison and Terry Francois hoped that this programmatic fullness would convince other supervisors—and the citizenry at large—to side with the mayor's course of action.

In mid-April 1968, the mayor's office filed a grant application with HUD, citing broad community support for Model Cities. Alioto explained that meetings with Missionites in "a coalition of interests [and] organizations" revealed receptiveness to the program, which the application referenced.[54] The politically astute leader surely knew about varied communal desires and that a shared geography did not translate into ideological unity; after all, he had chaired the SFRA before taking office. What the community wanted remained anything but uniform. City supervisors had to underwrite the grant proposal before it could be evaluated by HUD; they learned that the new coalition's approval was conditional and that conservative groups repudiated the application altogether.

Missionites' reactions to mayoral gumption triggered a reenactment of the redevelopment showdown. The MCO, the San Francisco Committee, and their associates rallied their grassroots bases; citizens inundated their elected officials with letters and telephone calls, and they flocked to City Hall hearings. In written correspondence, press interviews, and testimonies before elected officials, activists and residents recast what had become the district's liberal and conservative stances on Great Society programs. The MCO conveyed its willingness to favor Model Cities if it obtained policy-making power over the effort. Two of its lead organizers, Elba Montes and Joan Boardman—both veterans of MACAP and MCOR—presented the coalition's position in early May 1968. They offered preliminary support for the application but underscored that their alliance wanted "guaranteed control over the proj-

ect."[55] City council members had heard this message before: liberal Missionites stood ready to embrace the government initiative if allowed to claim
ownership of it. Their conservative neighbors once again objected vociferously. Insisting that Model Cities would result in redevelopment on "a gigan-
tic scale," leaders from the San Francisco Committee and the RMPT
excoriated the mayor's proposal on procedural and fiscal grounds. Mary Hall
and Jack Bartalini characterized Alioto's action as "extreme INSOLENCE,"
alleging that the mayor proceeded without consent from taxpayers and the
citizenry. Government authorities had to honor residents' input and desires,
conservatives asserted. They made this point while discrediting the MCO's
equation of citizen participation via community control. Instead, Hall and
her allies now initiated calls for a district referendum, which would permit
Missionites to vote directly on the matter.[56]

The individuals voting that spring were their elected representatives. In
late May 1968, the supervisors approved the Model Cities application. It was
a tepid authorization. Five board members had strong reservations about the
proposal and opted to block it. Supervisors James Mailliard and Peter Tama-
ras pointed to a lack of a community "mandate" and questioned the fiscal
ramifications given "news from Washington about cutbacks in Federal
spending." William Blake sided with them and bluntly denounced Model
Cities as urban renewal in disguise. "It is not very new," he exhorted, "it's the
same old thing in new words."[57] Yet six supervisors assigned enough merit,
and possibly novelty, to move the request forward. Supervisor Pelosi's focus
on the program's comprehensive format and insistence that Model Cities was
not synonymous with redevelopment convinced some of his colleagues to
align with him, including Leo McCarthy and Roger Boas, who had opposed
urban renewal. While McCarthy found it reassuring to learn that the power
of eminent domain was not sewn into the application, Boas's disposition to
use public funds for social welfare led him to vote for it.[58]

Though they validated the mayor's basic blueprint, city legislators admitted that citizens' concerns called for assurances. An accompanying resolution
specified that grant funds, if offered by HUD, would not be accepted until the
city devised bylaws delineating the process of maximum feasible participation.[59] A viable arrangement for community involvement, elected officials
stressed, would have to be sanctioned by district residents and the supervisors as well. This provision left room for the MCO to intensify its campaign
for community control. That is exactly what the coalition did over the next
two years.

The Rise of the Mission Coalition Organization

"The potential opportunities in the [Model Cities] program combined with the fear that it could lead to uncontrolled bulldozing of homes," read an institutional chronicle from 1970, "led community leaders to get together and organize the MCO."[60] Here, the coalition relayed two key reasons behind its formation. Some leaders and institutions—especially those that had received War on Poverty funds—found the Model Cities concept appealing because it could infuse more federal funds into the district. Service agencies had great interest in the program "in terms of the money," recounted Ben Martinez— one of the MCO's principal organizers. Yet the specter of redevelopment remained palpable. Activists and groups previously involved in MCOR shared their conservative neighbors' consternation that Model Cities could spell urban renewal in its traditional form. This admixture of hope and panic brought together an amalgamation of thirty-five Mission community groups soon after the mayor's announcement in February 1968.[61]

The grassroots architects who assembled the MCO included seasoned MCOR activists (e.g., Elba Montes) and emergent organizers such as Martinez. Martinez had worked as a community liaison with the Organization for Business, Education and Community Advancement (OBECA) since 1965. Through that position, he developed relationships with community advocates, including Montes and David Knotts. A Presbyterian pastor, Knotts introduced Martinez to community organizing as championed by the Industrial Areas Foundation. This Chicago-based organization had been founded by Saul Alinsky in the 1940s and backed grassroots efforts promoting mass action and mobilization. Protestant leaders and congregations drawn to the Alinsky tradition had played crucial roles in building MCOR and did so again with the MCO.[62]

Embracing the tenets of mass organization and coalition politics did not mean all leaders and members identified themselves as Alinsky disciples. The MCO's builders definitely aspired to establish a mass action organization. Most coalition members wanted to ensure that Model Cities remained in the community's hands.[63] "[We were] running [along] two parallel tracks," recalled Martinez, in pursuit of "control [over] Model Cities" and aiming "to organize the community." Montes described a related impulse. Her time with MACAP and MCOR convinced her that small groups had to connect with unions, churches, and other collectives in order to effect long-lasting, structural progress. "We [therefore] organized the Mission Coalition," she explained.[64]

Seven hundred delegates from sixty-six organizations—including tenant groups, religious congregations, labor unions, social service agencies, and ethnic associations—attended the coalition's first annual convention on 04 October 1968. Gathered at Centro Social Obrero Hall, they formalized their relationship with the MCO, elected officers, and set up policies to govern the organization's work. Much of the preconvention groundwork had been carried out by Mike Miller, a white, Alinsky-trained organizer who began serving as staff director a few months before the event. Miller worked closely with Knotts, Martinez, Montes, and a few others who composed the MCO's organizing nucleus. These individuals collaborated with well-known community leaders, including Herman Gallegos, Lee Soto, and Abel Gonzales. Gallegos remained active in social service agencies like OBECA (headed by Soto) as he immersed himself in building the Southwest Council of La Raza, a regional body promoting the civic and political advancement of Mexican Americans. Gonzales still presided over the Latino branch of the Construction and General Laborers Union Local 261 (commonly known as Los Obreros). In concert, these organizers and leaders convinced their allies and constituencies that a people's organization would enable Missionites to design their future together.[65]

"Our Convention is the first step toward building a new Mission," averred Martinez days before the assembly.[66] Elected as the MCO's first president, Martinez's conviction relied on the distinctiveness of the alliance: it was multi-issue, multiracial, cross-class, dependent on representative democracy, and intent on fighting for all Missionites. These characteristics would fuel myriad grassroots campaigns and accomplishments. Over the next five years, the MCO engaged more than ten thousand residents—through its member organizations and its various committees—and orchestrated what one scholar described as "the largest urban popular mobilization in San Francisco's" late postwar period. To be sure, the coalition's multiracial composition did not translate into an absence of racial friction. And its entanglement with Model Cities often diverted its multi-issue orientation. As Miller later put it, "No single interest more defined the character of the MCO than Model Cities."[67]

The MCO crafted a Model Cities strategy marked by openness and contingency, ambivalence and firmness. Its members proceeded from a place of uncertainty as they weighed the initiative's value. "The Model Cities program can be either an asset or a liability for the Mission District," stated a resolution drafted at the first convention.[68] Many Missionites at that gathering agreed that the plan's impact ultimately depended on who managed it. They remained convinced that Model Cities could well result in redevelopment if implemented from outside the district. "We are determined to keep the bulldozers from coming into our community," read a position statement disseminated in 1969. "That is why we have demanded strong controls over the Model Cities Program."[69] The hard-line stance against a top-down approach did not foreclose other arrangements. With insight from the recent past, the MCO conditionally sanctioned Model Cities if it acquired official power over program planning and administration.

Coalition leaders and activists adopted a course of action transposed from MCOR's ideological playbook: they pressed for community control and veto power. HUD accepted the planning application in November 1968 and expressed readiness to allocate funds once San Francisco had both its city demonstration agency (CDA) and procedures for citizen participation in place. The Model Cities guidelines called for the creation of a CDA—a public body charged with program planning and distribution of funds—and underscored the indispensability of citizen participation. Like MCOR, the MCO equated citizen participation with comprehensive control at the community level. The coalition reasoned that as the "voice" of the Mission it should be allowed to directly appoint two-thirds of the CDA's members and be granted "the right to approve or veto" all plans.[70] Mayor Alioto and his policy team responded coolly. They recognized the MCO as the vehicle of broad community participation but were not keen on endowing it with wide-ranging authority. Coalition leaders insisted their organization would not budge. "If the people of the community cannot control programs that are supposed to be for their benefit," Martinez emphasized, "then we would rather not have these programs."[71]

The MCO relied on town hall meetings, press conferences, and demonstrations to broadcast its position and display its range of popular support. Its march and rally of May 1969 transpired during the culmination of a heated, six-month process of mobilization and negotiation. It took place days after coalition leaders carved out an agreement with the mayor's office and in preparation for its review by city supervisors. The compromise acknowledged mayoral prerogative over all appointments to the CDA, but two-thirds of its members would be selected from an MCO-approved roster. Of utmost significance, the coalition obtained full review of and veto power over all programmatic plans. This accord evidenced a mutual investment in Model Cities

Figure 8. Flor de Maria Crane (front left) and members of the Mission Coalition
Organization (MCO) speaking with elected officials, late 1960s. Spence
Limbocker MCO Photograph Collection. Courtesy of Spence Limbocker.

and the mayor's acceptance that Missionites should participate "as equals."[72]
Mayor Alioto surely wanted to proceed with the effort and forestall an escalation of tensions. His accommodation in fact corresponded with developments in other cities, where mayors also bargained with forceful grassroots
organizations such as the MCO.[73]

Persuading the city's Board of Supervisors to endorse the Alioto-MCO
arrangement would consume the coalition for another six months. Many

supervisors remained receptive to Model Cities; others questioned the official role bestowed on the coalition. MCO leaders now had to convince these elected officials and corroborate they had a grassroots base behind them. Hundreds of residents regularly "traveled in busloads to be at City Hall" whenever coalition leaders testified at public hearings.[74] The most dramatic civic performance before the full board took place on 01 December 1969. Joined by over seven hundred residents, spokespersons from all seventy-eight organizations in the coalition offered short statements endorsing the Alioto-MCO agreement and confirmed a staggering aspiration to take charge of Model Cities.[75] Seven supervisors interpreted the bundle of testimony as a communal decree; they voted to move ahead with the plan and approved the CDA's bylaws. A majority of legislators also seconded the mayor's recognition of the MCO as the Mission's representative body, and acceded to the coalition's credo of citizen participation via community control.

Federal administrators did not prove amenable to this approach. In March 1970, HUD officials rejected the city's Model Cities plan, objecting to the CDA's structure, its level of autonomy, and the veto power extended to the MCO. The decision affirmed Washington's view that citizen participation could not be equated with categorical neighborhood control. "People in minority ghettos are going to continue to talk about control," relayed one HUD bureaucrat back in 1968. "But beneath the rhetoric, there can be no exclusive control by citizens, or by any single citizen group."[76] San Francisco's elected officials had exhibited more flexibility because they had to balance the city's interest in federal aid with the clamor and resistance mounted by the MCO. They now returned to the negotiating table because, as one mayoral deputy put it, the city "[was] not for losing Model Cities in the Mission after all this time."[77]

It turned out the MCO did not wish to lose Model Cities either. Coalition members expressed a willingness to cooperate with the mayor's team and work out the "bureaucratic hitch." In an uncharacteristic move, the MCO retreated from its previously unyielding stance and chose not to insist on across-the-board veto power. This concession stemmed from material considerations as well as adjustments to the workings of community control. On one hand, "the social agencies and the majority of the membership" urged the organization to compromise because they clung to the potential benefits presented by Model Cities. They did not want the Mission to forfeit its "access to the desperately needed public resources."[78] On the other hand, coalition leaders realized that the MCO could still exert significant control and exercise an indirect form of veto power through its appointments to the CDA.

The revised plan preserved the MCO's ability to mold the CDA's board composition; final authority over program development and administration rested with the mayor's office. Montes discussed the coalition's altered perspective in April 1970. "This is a workable compromise," she told supervisors. "It gives the city the authority and responsibility that [HUD] thinks it should have and we retain the right to nominate a majority of the directors and to recall our delegates if we wish."[79]

After another round of review, the supervisors accepted the amended arrangement in summer 1970. Federal authorities followed suit in the fall and authorized $150,000 in initial study funds during fiscal year 1970 to 1971. These monies covered planning and staffing costs to conduct a needs assessment in the district. During the first Model Cities action year (1971–1972), the Mission Model Neighborhood Corporation (MMNC)—the name given to the CDA—received $2.8 million to run twelve childcare programs, a language center, two job training projects, a housing development corporation, a community hiring hall, and various educational programs.[80] The programmatic successes notwithstanding, the life of Model Cities remained muddled in controversy. Political divisions within the MCO itself, in fact, became pronounced once negotiations with both local and federal governments subsided.

Ethnic Liberals and Populist Radicals in the MCO

In June 1972, the *San Francisco Examiner* lauded the MCO for mobilizing a heterogeneous community, where Latinos were in the majority, and teaching its members that "power comes from coming together." Features writers commended the coalition for practicing "true democracy at the grass-roots level" and for its Model Cities win. Praise aside, journalists acknowledged the existence of competing approaches for acquiring power, factional rifts within Latino organizations, and generational differences among district leaders. They treated these factors as descriptive layers of the MCO, not as elements that bred serious disharmony and trouble. Their interpretation conformed to what community advocates themselves reported. Whereas some downplayed "the clashes" as insignificant, others pointed out that disagreement was a "healthy sign" of a vigorous organization.[81] Leaders and activists either wanted to preserve the MCO's image and integrity or held onto optimism that they could weather organizational challenges. Political discord within the MCO, however, proved to be quite meaningful and corrosive.

The impressive grassroots experiment begun in 1968 had become "an organizational battleground" by 1972.[82] MCO members simply did not share a uniform political philosophy; this reality created space for thoughtful deliberation but also left the federation vulnerable to rupture. Individuals and organizations entered the coalition with varied allegiances, ideas about the purpose of grassroots mobilization, perspectives on state action, and attachments to latinidad. Prolonged negotiations with the state—and an emphasis on maintaining a communal, united front—restrained members' distinct views for a few years. Once Model Cities became a reality, the organization had to contend with its ideological diversity and gradually met dissension. Disputes over leadership, appointments to the MMNC, employment opportunities within Model Cities projects, the programmatic focus of those projects, and eventually the coalition's identity as the community's representative all consumed the MCO as the years wore on. Ironically, organizations that opposed Model Cities had regularly questioned the MCO's representativeness. These unaffiliated groups situated their criticism within larger political visions about government instrumentality and racial dynamics, issues that the coalition had to grapple with as well.

Differences over the community's relationship to the state and the centrality of latinidad defined much of the MCO's internal strife. Coalition members shared a conviction that the government had an obligation to ameliorate Missionites' socioeconomic challenges. Assigning an instrumental role to the state in effect positioned the MCO as a champion of Great Society liberalism. Yet leaders and activists disagreed about the deeper, politicized implications of Model Cities—ramifications that went beyond an enhancement of residents' well-being. They tussled over the MCO's connection with government authorities and its entanglement with Democratic machine politics. This concern intersected with dissonance over designing Model Cities as a people's program or a Latino program. Coalition founders did not set out to be an exclusively Latino body; some of its members nevertheless expected that Model Cities would be structured foremost as a program for Latinos. To be sure, there were other sources of division (e.g., personality clashes, allocation of funds). Rifts over "serving Spanish [i.e., Latino] interests" and "differences concerning social action" vis-à-vis state power, however, most deeply strained the MCO's existence.[83]

Prominent member organizations, such as LULAC, OBECA, and some institutions created during the War on Poverty, treated the MCO as an engine to secure public funds for Latinos' social welfare. The influence of groups adhering to "an ethnic style of organization" had grown during the early to mid-1960s; these networks advocated for greater governmental attention to Latinos as they fastened their ties to the Democratic Party. Ethnic mobilization and the consolidation of an ethnic bloc became mechanisms to obtain public resources in exchange for political allegiance.[84] Latinos were not alone in doing so. African Americans likewise engaged in political patronage to make demands on the liberal state.[85] Their embrace of this model of political work marked many Latinos in the MCO as ethnic liberals.

Leading ethnic liberals actually engineered a Model Cities action plan many months before the MCO's emergence. In 1967, Soto, Gallegos, and other leaders from OBECA sent Martinez to Washington to learn more about Model Cities. Martinez recalled how this decision arose from leaders' investment in "bringing [more] money to the Mission" to sustain the social service infrastructure created during the War on Poverty. MACAP director Alex Zermeño concurred. That same year, Zermeño, Bob Gonzales (MAPA), and Abel Gonzales (Los Obreros) sat down with then-candidate Joseph Alioto to discuss the mayoral campaign. Alioto purportedly asked, "Okay, guys, what do you guys want in exchange for your support?" Their wish list included Model Cities and Latino appointments to the San Francisco Board of Education and Board of Supervisors. Bob Gonzales confirmed having participated in the meeting and remarked, "There was essentially an agreement that the Mission would be the designated area for Model Cities." Their recollections revealed that Model Cities did not arrive in the Mission by chance. Instead, the plan originated from political maneuvering and patronage. As the election season progressed, these ethnic liberals and their allies mobilized and swayed Latinos to support Alioto. The new mayor made his Model Cities announcement during his second month in office and then labored tenaciously to make his promise a reality. "That's the kind of politics I like," stressed Zermeño. "[Alioto] paid up and we worked our ass off for it."[86]

Bringing Model Cities to the Mission was only the beginning. Ethnic liberals expected to take charge of the program and ensure it remained within their sphere of influence. They believed neighborhood institutions— supported by the state but managed by community representatives—would best serve Latinos' needs. Part of this outlook stemmed from a distrust of public agencies' ability to extend culturally appropriate services. They also knew that some Latinos had reservations about turning to city-run departments for assistance because of linguistic barriers, immigration concerns, or bureaucratic bewilderment. Controlling the stream of government money presented another advantage: it made it possible for ethnic liberal leaders to sustain a network of client-patrons through the provision of services. These "political power brokers," as Miller identified them, sought "to gain control over the distribution of services as a means by which they could develop a base."[87] This venture had roots in the War on Poverty. Ethnic liberals now aspired to enhance and widen that base by controlling Model Cities. They joined the MCO because a neighborhood alliance signaled broad support for the government program and a large organization could more forcefully clamor for community control.

If ethnic liberals saw the MCO as the conduit to Model Cities, the MCO's pioneer organizers saw Model Cities as the catalyst to build a grassroots movement. The coalition's founders, too, set out to establish a base: one that would operate independently from social service agencies and ethnic-centered political groups. Montes, Martinez, Miller, and others drawn to Alinsky's teachings sought to mobilize residents and collectively press public and private authorities to address their plight. Montes detailed how she and like-minded activists wanted to "form a power base that would bring about changes to the Mission by putting pressure on the city" and its institutions.[88] The emphasis on pressure, confrontation, and grassroots power encapsulated the approach guiding Alinsky-inspired radicals. Their language and tactics instilled "a mass psychology of urban populism," to build on historian Michael Kazin's insight, which energized residents to challenge inequality and exploitation. After all, "the purpose of the mass organization," as Miller explained it, was "to confront unresponsive power."[89]

As populist radicals, Montes and her counterparts exalted direct action as the premier method to acquire power and effect change, while insisting on grassroots organizing beyond ethnicity. They were populists because they committed themselves to building a people's movement that incorporated residents from all backgrounds. "We were an Alinsky organization," stressed Luisa Ezquerro, and that "mold" encouraged the merger of diverse constituencies in pursuit of common interests. Active in the teachers' union, Ezquerro—and others involved in the labor movement—found the MCO's emphasis on organizing around economic issues particularly appealing. Focusing on the economic well-being of all Missionites offered an avenue to glue residents together across a myriad of social differences. This did not mean racial disparities were of secondary concern. But populist radicals did not want their efforts to prioritize or be driven by an exclusive focus on one ethnoracial group. "We [were] not only representing Latinos in the Mission District," Montes remarked. "We [were] representing the Mission, period."[90]

The radicalism of Montes, Ezquerro, and others drawn to Alinsky-style organizing hinged on their prescriptions of mass protest, defiance, and aggressive engagement with government authorities and the private sector. They strove to reform the workings of government, democracy, and capitalism, but did set out to overturn the existing political and economic systems. Unlike ethnic liberals, Montes and her counterparts did not intend to wed themselves to the Democratic Party machine. Populist radicals aspired to maintain an independent and sometimes adversarial relationship to the state; they turned to direct action to amass political muscle and push for governmental reform. Political scientist Frederick Wirt referenced the divergence between populist radicals and ethnic liberals in 1974. Activists following Alinsky's model, Wirt suggested, "wished to work outside the traditional structures in the city and to substitute alternative structures to solve old problems."[91]

One additional element distinguished some populist radicals from their ethnic liberal allies: they had reservations about the doctrine of community control. Championing the notion of "institutional change," such individuals as Martinez, Miller, and Ezquerro thought the MCO should focus its energies on "forcing the public institutions to modify their policies under pressure from the grassroots, but without actually involving the community organization in the daily management" of Model Cities. This perspective aligned with their inclination to prioritize mass organizing and ensure that the MCO did not itself become a social service agency. Under their ideal arrangement, the MCO would use Model Cities funds as leverage for improved public services and programs. "We should be just a conduit for the funds and let the city run the programs," elucidated Larry Del Carlo." Twenty-one years old at the time of the MCO's founding, Del Carlo had worked for a youth program established by MACAP and went on to lead the MCO's employment committee. He acknowledged "institutional change people" like him were in the minority; their outlook departed from the vision supported by ethnic liberals and publicly avowed by the MCO.[92] They deferred to the philosophy of community control given its currency among most MCO members and the communal distrust of governmental bureaucracies. The MMNC's final structure created a middle ground between the advocates of institutional change and community control. "[The] MCO would not itself administer programs," observed Miller, "but through the MMNC it would monitor and evaluate programs and withhold funds when necessary." This compromise minimized the factional schism in the short term; the ideological disjuncture later fed into the competition over who controlled the MCO and, by extension, Model Cities.[93]

Left and Right of the MCO

Distinctions between ethnic liberals and populist radicals mattered little to activists unaffiliated with the MCO. Latinos in the LSDC and LaREAL instead zeroed in on MCO members' common stake in Model Cities. These organizations generally bucked the coalition's agenda and questioned its engagement and negotiation with the state. Their members did so because they did not accept the governmental rationale for Great Society programs and doubted the motivations propelling the MCO's interest in Model Cities.

The LSDC and LaREAL emerged as the MCO's prominence crystallized. In mid-1969, student activists organized the LSDC as an advocacy group for seven young Latinos (*los siete*) charged with murdering a police officer. A number of those accused had participated in recent campus strikes demanding "relevant education" and had been "actively working for the unity and advancement of the community."[94] Students at Mission High School, Balboa High School, San Francisco State College, City College, and the College of San Mateo began mobilizing for curricular and personnel changes as early as fall 1968. They used the slogan of "relevant education" to press for La Raza studies (present-day Latino/a studies) and more Latino teachers. Associating themselves with the LSDC became a logical segue for many of these young organizers, especially since the men on trial had supported their campus cause.

Activists soon combined their campaign to exonerate *los siete* with efforts to address "the needs of the people." Francisco Flores and Donna Amador agreed that their organization very quickly decided "to be a defense group of the community."[95] They set out to rally and protect Latinos against structural inequities while enhancing their community's everyday conditions. Inspired and supported by the Black Panthers, the LSDC blended grassroots activism—focused on such issues as police brutality and inadequate education—with projects such as free breakfast programs, a mobile clinic, and after-school tutoring. This mixture of action and service aimed to fortify "brown people" on a political and material level. "We saw ourselves as the true saviors," recalled Amador, "the true avengers of the community."[96]

Contemporaneously, activists whose political work occurred outside campus movements formed LaREAL in 1970. Founders Al and Gary Borvice saw their organization as a vehicle to serve Latinos and "to mobilize the people" toward social change.[97] The Borvice brothers had ties to the Peace and Freedom Party and La Raza Unida Party, independent political bodies that developed as alternatives to the Democratic Party. The Peace and Freedom Party opposed the Vietnam War and energetically promoted civil rights; La Raza Unida turned to Chicano nationalism as the basis to organize and empower Mexican Americans. The latter party's appeal in San Francisco did not match its force across Southern California or in Texas localities, but a comparable emphasis on ethnicity undergirded outfits such as LaREAL. "Unity within the Spanish-speaking community (ethnic solidarity)," professed LaREAL's leaders, represented "the basic building block, the power base, for community development."[98] With this precept, they launched a leadership development program, a silk-screening center, and projects that mirrored the LSDC's tutoring and legal assistance efforts.

The parallels between LaREAL and the LSDC were not just practical but ideological. Latinos in these collectives shared critiques of or ambivalence about liberalism, an embrace of or openness to socialism, and a Latino nationalist zeal that positioned them as ethnic radicals. Their political sensibilities had been nurtured through campus activism, involvement in the antiwar movement, and by witnessing the mobilization of other Bay Area youth. Many of their outlooks and activities aligned with ones of like-minded youth organizations elsewhere, especially the Young Lords and the Brown Berets.[99] Carmen Carrillo joined the LSDC while working on a master's degree at San Francisco State, and Pete Gallegos gravitated toward LaREAL while studying at City College. Gallegos's political formation actually began in high school, when he "questioned why [he] hadn't been taught anything" about his cultural heritage or offered a more balanced view on the Cold War. Many young Latinos like him grew to oppose the Vietnam War and became supportive of the Cuban Revolution. While they assailed the armed conflict in Asia as immoral, undemocratic, and driven by American imperial ambitions, they hailed the experiment in Cuba for its defeat of capitalism and U.S. imperialism. Disapproval of U.S. intervention in Latin America and a "very active [engagement] in antiwar activities" likewise molded Carrillo's activist path. She belonged to two Latino groups at San Francisco State and served as treasurer of the Third World Liberation Front.[100] A collective of students of color, the Liberation Front co-led a successful campus strike (November 1968 to

March 1969) demanding an ethnic studies curriculum. The liberation of nonwhite peoples functioned as a call to resist and end all forms of racist oppression and aggression, whether in the city's classrooms and streets or in the fields in Vietnam.

Ethnic radicals regularly distinguished themselves from ethnic liberals, whom the LSDC and LaREAL identified as the community's "old guard." Differences over state authority, the Vietnam War, and the Democratic Party—as well as variations in organizing style and tone—fueled much of the divergence. At a deeper level, while ethnic liberals put faith in liberal reform and in the workings of American democracy, ethnic radicals called that conviction into question. Gallegos expanded on this philosophical disjuncture. He noted, "The 'old guard' believed that you could make change by working with the system and the 'radicals' were convinced that in order to make change you needed to change the system." Carrillo echoed Gallegos's perspective. "Our generation was more militant," she said. "We [didn't] want to buy into the same old oppressive politics and the same old class structure."[101] To be sure, agendas for societal transformation varied and encompassed a broad set of goals. These included an overhaul of educational curricula, the creation of workers' cooperatives, engagement in third-party politics, and, for some, the advocacy of a socialist revolution.

Revamping "the system" generally involved a challenge to liberalism and a repudiation of public benevolence as manifested at the time. Activists in the LSDC and LaREAL had reservations about the Great Society on the grounds that governmental initiatives deepened their community's dependency on the state. They surmised that enhancing Latinos' well-being would best occur without government interference. Ethnic radicals typically opted to fund their projects through foundation grants, fundraising activities, and pro bono services. Full control of community institutions and programs, they argued, could not be realized with oversight and prerequisites from the state. "We saw ourselves as more progressive than [the backers of] Model Cities," explained Al Borvice. "We saw them as part of the city. . . . We wanted alternatives to that."[102] Such opinions implicitly cast the MCO as part and parcel of the political establishment and the Democratic Party, attachments that ethnic radicals did not aspire to cultivate.

Some ethnic radicals went further, arguing that cooperation with the government would do little to alter structural inequities. Part of their position stemmed from an assumption that state assistance to inner-city neighborhoods did not result from an altruistic concern for people's welfare. Government authorities had an investment in controlling and manipulating poor and minority peoples, according to many of these radical activists. "Many believed the money was a way for the federal government to quell urban unrest," observed Pete Gallegos. "Federal aid was a way for the federal government to buy off community leaders and turn them into docile, dependent, poverty pimps." The "poverty pimp" label became a popular moniker for the personnel at community agencies reliant on government money. It specifically served to cast ethnic liberal leaders as a self-interested cohort—individuals who capitalized on the poor's plight in exchange for political influence and their own professional standing. Ethnic radicals came to view the social service corps at government-funded organizations as the ultimate beneficiaries of state aid—who purposely failed to address the root causes of socioeconomic marginalization. The real objective of Model Cities, Flores concluded, involved the solidification of "a Latino middle class who would serve . . . the interest of *the system* in the community" and "create that link between the Mission and the powers downtown."[103] This perspective coincided with the misgivings about patronage disseminated by populist radicals. Yet ethnic radicals generally saw anyone interested in Model Cities as part of the old guard and backers of the existing political order.

If ethnic radicals positioned themselves at the vanguard of change, white conservatives viewed organizations such as the LSDC as emblematic of the "subversive" and "militant groups threatening" public safety and communal life. Calls for law and order and disdain for social movements challenging the status quo became more prevalent features of conservatives' agenda at the turn of the decade. The antiwar movement's amplification, an escalation of tensions on college campuses, and urban riots near and far all contributed to this development. At the same time, residents drawn to the RMPT and the San Francisco Committee remained vehemently opposed to the Great Society. Initiatives such as Model Cities reignited their passions against government intervention and social welfare. "The promotors [sic], the speculators, the chislers [sic] and unscrupulous politicians," related the RMPT, had lined up anew to exploit and profit from the middle class. In its members' estimation, law-abiding, tax-paying Missionites now found themselves threatened by radical leftists as well as liberals.[104]

Conservatives singled out the MCO as the district's leading chiseler. The San Francisco Fairness League (SFFL)—which succeeded the San Francisco Committee in 1969 and remained under Mary Hall's leadership—and its allies consistently accused the coalition of falsely professing to represent all

Missionites. Still predominantly white, SFFL and RMPT members insisted that the MCO did not speak for the entire community.[105] Conservatives concurrently charged the coalition with creating fraudulent organizations to bolster membership claims and garner support from city leaders. Hall apprised the mayor of this perspective during early deliberations over the Model Cities application. "Self-serving people, who neither work (in), live (in), nor understand the Mission District ar [sic] trying to convince you of community-wide acceptance," Hall wrote in May 1968. The "so-called coalition," she continued, actually "consists of many 'paper groups' which appear to have suddenly materialized out of thin air."[106] Her missive had two aims. Hall sought to discredit the MCO by classifying it as a body of outsiders and charlatans. And she called into question the coalitional process itself: many conservatives simply did not regard it as the most appropriate channel for citizen participation and expression of communal will.

The MCO's representativeness and motivations met challenge from ethnic radicals too. A number of key positions disseminated by the LSDC mirrored ones circulated by their conservative adversaries. In 1970, the LSDC-run ¡Basta Ya! suggested "big politics" sustained the MCO and underscored that the coalition "hardly represents the Mission at all." Its reporters concurrently deduced that Model Cities would result in the district's destruction. Echoing the SFFL and the RMPT, LSDC members equated Model Cities with urban renewal. "We were very suspicious of groups like the Mission Coalition," detailed Amador, "because we were worried that they were inviting" BART and redevelopment.[107] She and her colleagues arrived at this conclusion by connecting Alioto's past work with the SFRA and the MCO's willingness to compromise with the mayor. All the maneuvering taking place "behind the scenes" and the MCO's 1970 decision to give "the veto power away completely" led the LSDC to assume that the coalition would cave in to the mayor's prodevelopment vision.[108]

Ethnic radicals married their resistance to Model Cities to their contempt for the Alioto machine and patronage politics—a linkage made by white conservatives as well. Jack Bartalini and his associates indicted Model Cities for "carry[ing] the stench of graft, corruption and political patronage" as early as 1968. Two years later, Hall added that the coalition "knowingly or unknowingly, was being used all along to help the Mayor show community support where none existed." Her young radical foes held a comparable impression. "They were set up to get Model Cities money into the Mission," stressed Flores.[109] These allegations synchronously branded the program as a mayoral scheme and the MCO as Alioto's community-based pawn. Ethnic radicals and white conservatives essentially believed that the MCO had not developed organically and that the mayor himself determined the contours of community representation.

A wholesale negation of the MCO's agency, vision, and work seemed misguided. Critics' assumptions nevertheless contained some kernels of accuracy. Patronage politics certainly contributed to the MCO's standing and its interest in Model Cities. The coalition functioned as the Mission's representative body precisely because it collaborated with the mayor and sanctioned the designs of local and federal authorities, even if not always harmoniously. Ethnic liberals and radical populists, after all, embraced the tenets of Great Society liberalism—a position ethnic radicals and white conservatives refused to assimilate.

The growth of the welfare state continued to aggravate conservatives, who remained convinced that liberal government abused and ignored the white middle class. Members of the RMPT and the SFFL censured Model Cities as the latest liberal venture that compromised their economic assets and bypassed their wishes. Conservatives reproduced the perspectives promulgated during the redevelopment fight; Model Cities, they insisted, brushed aside their citizenship and property rights. Outrage over a program they viewed as redevelopment in disguise reignited their ire about taxation. "The taxpayers [are] tired of being bilked and bamboozled," clamored Bartalini. His comrade Marilla Parratt emphatically concurred. The tax burden faced by property owners, she decried, made them feel "handcuffed and literally destroyed by the octopus of gov't programs."[110] Embittering them further, Bartalini, Parratt, and their counterparts saw Model Cities as failing to advance the prosperity of the "native" and "real residents" of the Mission.[111] These racially coded outlooks were not new: they had surfaced during the urban renewal fight. White conservatives now intensified such views, postulating that the liberal state prioritized the interests and desires of nonwhites and foreigners at their expense.

Latinidad, Self-Determination, and Citizenship

Racial politics and the force of latinidad permeated community politics. Mission leaders and activists constructed a variety of "racial projects" to grapple with race, socioeconomic inequality, state indifference, and political power.

Social scientists Michael Omi and Howard Winant hold that "a racial project is simultaneously an interpretation, representation, or explanation of racial dynamics, and an effort to reorganize resources along particular racial lines."[112] The Model Cities program functioned as a state-sponsored racial project: it aimed to improve life opportunities for racial minorities, and it operated as a governmental pipeline to cultivate nonwhites' political loyalties by sponsoring community-based social welfare. Mayor Alioto used Model Cities as "the channel," as sociologist Manuel Castells put in 1980, "through which funds and jobs could be distributed to the blacks and Latinos in exchange for their political allegiancy."[113] Ethnic liberals understood and accepted this compact. Their racial project therefore wove latinidad into Model Cities: they expected to direct the program and tailor their efforts to enhance life conditions for *la raza*.

Exalting and prioritizing *la raza* bridged the generational and political divide between ethnic liberals and ethnic radicals. Though immersed in separate organizations and holding incongruent ideas about state action, Latinos in LULAC and the LSDC, for example, converged on their emphasis of cultural affirmation, identity, and Latino pride. They "stood side by side" in promoting *la raza*'s cultural heritage and historical resilience, while stressing the contemporary needs of and challenges faced by Latinos. *La raza* typically conveyed a sense of peoplehood and community; for some Latinos, it also referred to a racialized location that exceeded the standard system of U.S. racial categorization. Community institutions had sometimes employed the term in decades past; it now regained popularity as racial identity took on greater political valence. "La Raza is the most widespread term in usage among Spanish-speaking/Spanish-surname people in the United States," announced LaREAL's leaders. "[We] are the children born from the union of the indigenous cultures and the African and European cultures."[114] Acknowledging a legacy of *mestizaje* proved particularly important for ethnic radicals who regarded racial mixture—and especially brownness—as a source of pride and a defiant departure from rigid understandings of race.

Invocations of *la raza* reinforced the imperatives of latinidad. "The liberation of *la raza*," some Latinos insisted, "depended on their unity to realize a prosperous "common destiny." Ethnic radicals and ethnic liberals alike committed themselves to the Latino collective and incorporated latinidad into their work. "Fused together by common language, history and cultural values," delineated activists in LaREAL, "we are more able to relate to Raza people and to mediate between our people and the major socio-political and economic institutions that affect us."[115] Comparable perspectives emanated from such bodies as OBECA and LULAC: their leaders assumed "Latin-oriented organizations" would proffer optimal "services and other assistance needed to improve the lives of Latin ethnics." This very sentiment guided their resolve to control Model Cities. Ethnic liberals reckoned that programs run by Latinos would "be more sensitive"—offering an antidote to the indifference and marginalization Latinos experienced in the city at large.[116] They arrived at this formulation by looking backward and forward: to a past record of public neglect and a future of communal autonomy. If unified, the argument ran, Latinos could confront the inaction and authority of white America by responding to their present and molding their future.

Latinidad bolstered claims to self-determination, another prevailing current within ethnic liberal and ethnic radical circles. Generally denoting communal sovereignty and empowerment, the philosophy of self-determination acquired formidable acceptance in minority communities across the country. Latinos who took up this banner believed they should "have full control over [their] lives and the decisions that affected [their] position in society."[117] For ethnic liberals, managing Model Cities represented the zenith of self-determination. Many in the MCO, in fact, construed community control as the means for Missionites to "determine their own destinies." The maxim that Latinos should forge their own communal fate flourished in ethnic radical circles too. LaREAL's and the LSDC's prescription for self-determination, of course, did not rest on accessing public monies and controlling government programs. Independent organizing and autonomous community institutions, these groups argued, would permit Latinos to "take our future into our own hands" and "determine [our] own destiny."[118] The LSDC's establishment of a community-run clinic during the 1970 strike at San Francisco General Hospital, for example, substantiated its members' pledge to serve the poor and to inspire Latinos to attend to their own health needs. Two years into its operation, the clinic stood as a testament of "very hard work and struggle and a desire to have self-determination."[119]

Latino activists adhering to Alinsky's principles understood the ambitions nourished by latinidad but found ethnic liberals' enterprise limiting. They valued residents' affirmation of ethnoracial pride and supported the creation of culturally appropriate programs. Some actually identified an emotive appeal in latinidad yet cautioned against emphasizing Latinos' predicament or prioritizing their needs over those of other Missionites. As Montes told a news reporter in 1970, "My first feeling is for the Spanish-speaking people, La Raza.

But I look at the economic problem rather than the race. I look at the Mission District rather than [only at] the Spanish-speaking community." Luisa Ezquerro and Ben Martinez held similar perspectives. Alongside non-Latino populist radicals, they preferred to underscore those challenges shared by all district residents. An effective grassroots movement and solid agenda for change, they reasoned, depended on solidarity built on mutual interests rather than ethnic ties.[120]

Populist radicals did not presume ethnicity was irrelevant. They recognized the potency of ethnic identities and knew about concerns involving Mexican American hegemony and clout in the district's public sphere. At the time, most Latino leaders and directors of service agencies were ethnic Mexicans. The MCO's founders attempted to balance this situation by incorporating a string of ethnicity-based vice presidencies into the coalition's governing structure. Ethnic vice presidencies applied to Latino subgroups as well as Italian Americans, African Americans, Filipinos, and other ethnoracial groups. "We had a lot of Central Americans, some people from South America and [we] really needed to have some kind of representation from all these different groups," specified Martinez. Populist radicals essentially aspired to deflect unease over the preponderance of Mexican American leadership and to cement the MCO's identity as a people's organization, not a Latino body. Their arrangement aimed to make all residents feel included and formally represented. By accounting for ethnicity from the outset, Alinsky's enthusiasts hoped the MCO could pursue a populist program—driven by a class strategy instead of an ethnic one.[121]

Middle-class white conservatives found neither the MCO's populist orientation nor its claims of representation convincing. While some working- and middle-class whites participated in the MCO, their conservative peers chose to disseminate racially charged judgments about the popular alliance. Activists in the RMPT and the SFFL impugned the MCO by casting doubt on its members' integrity and citizenship. Identified as the district's "honest, decent citizens," white conservatives implied that MCO members were deceitful—in their intentions and claims of belonging. Conservative activists simultaneously framed Model Cities as a program for nonwhites who contributed little to society yet depended on public assistance. Parratt from the RMPT reproached the government's readiness "to allow hordes of immigrants, minority groups, etc. already swelling our Welfare Rolls, to displace those who pioneered and built this city."[122] Alluding to political supplantation by nonwhites, Parratt and like-minded folks indicted the welfare state for aiding racial minorities they considered shiftless and undeserving. Casting themselves as pioneers further substantiated their identity. Their history, rootedness, and citizenship, white conservatives alleged, distinguished them from the interlopers and foreigners in the MCO.

Intent on putting their citizenship into action, white conservatives mounted a "Right to Vote" drive from 1968 to 1969. Hall, Bartalini, and their allies insisted that citizens' wishes should be gauged through a plebiscite, which would grant "bona fide" Missionites a direct say on Model Cities. By equating citizen participation with voting, Hall and her associates set out to supersede the MCO's process, rooted in grassroots mobilization and community control. "Giving residents of the area a vote is the American Way," conservatives underscored.[123] They assumed that the will of the majority (i.e., white Missionites eligible to vote) would reveal that Model Cities had no community support—at once unveiling the MCO's chicanery and invalidating the mayor's proposal. Pursuing direct democracy became conservatives' recourse to capsize the MCO's authority and dissolve "the COLOR of citizen participation." Consciously or not, the stress on color betrayed white conservatives' conviction that the MCO represented nonwhites and "outsiders" with questionable citizenship.[124]

White conservatives' strategy failed. Their franchise campaign garnered little attention from public officials. The governmental rebuff was a product of national policy and local circumstances. Federal guidelines did not include neighborhood referenda as a means to assess citizen support. And white conservative organizations had neither a grassroots base comparable to the MCO's nor the ear of the Democratic mayor. In 1969, Mayor Alioto referred to the "homeowners groups led by Mrs. Hall and Mr. Bartalini as little more than a radical fringe group." The defeat did not silence them: conservatives continued to insist that the MCO did not speak for them. In May 1970, Hall challenged the MCO's identity as a field of inclusion, cooperation, and selflessness. "Many 'sour lemons' and 'thorns' will appear in this 'garden,'" she augured.[125] She was not wrong. In a twist of historical irony, some of the same conservative charges levied against the MCO soon emerged within the coalition itself.

Alinskyites, Agency People, and the
Elusiveness of Community Unity

Five months after Hall's prophesy, in October 1970, the MCO held its third annual convention—the first public event laying bare the existence of organizational strife. Many members expected the gathering would be a celebratory one: coalition leaders had completed negotiations with government authorities months earlier, and the Model Cities planning phase would begin that very fall. Instead, the assembly came to be eclipsed by frustration and dissension. The annual presidential election and Ben Martinez's decision to run for a third term, which required an amendment to coalition bylaws, presented the discernible sources of contention.[126] Martinez faced opposition from Elba Montes, serving as executive vice president at the time, and from Manuel Larez, LULAC's local director. While Martinez had the backing of most populist radical delegates, Montes garnered support from some delegates representing block clubs, tenant groups, and other clusters engaged in grassroots organizing. Their ethnic liberal rival, Larez, rallied delegates from "a handful of established, Latino-oriented, community agencies" and other Latino-focused associations. Those who stood with Martinez believed his leadership and know-how were vital to the MCO's stability and continued success. Montes's and Larez's followers thought otherwise: they likened the founding president to a Latin American dictator and charged the bylaws committee, chaired by Martinez, with procedural foul play and irregularities in the vote count. Some one hundred delegates from a dozen member organizations actually left the convention before voting began; others walked out in protest after Martinez's reelection had been confirmed.[127] The victor and his base insisted all proceedings had transpired fairly and democratically. Neither questions nor ill feelings would dissipate. Though the day's events may have preserved institutional continuity, they cemented the "split [of] the organization into a lot of pieces."[128]

Ethnic liberal dissidents aligned with Larez promulgated other critiques and concerns. For several months before the election, rumors had circulated "that many of the 72 organizations that made up the MCO were only *on paper.*"[129] Insinuations of duplicity had typically originated from outside the MCO; they now began to surface internally. Some ethnic liberals espoused this view in an attempt to dismantle populist radicals' clout and leadership. The charge escalated in the wake of what many disgruntled MCO members viewed as an illegitimate and rigged election. Delegates from LULAC, the Mission Neighborhood Health Center, and the Latino Local Development Corporation, among others who sided with Larez, especially fretted over the "Alinskyite cadre's anti-agency, centralizing strategy." These ethnic liberals worried that populist radicals led by Martinez aspired to aggrandize the MCO at their expense. More specifically, Larez and his supporters feared that "the Alinskyites would take exclusive control of the MMNC and use that control to exclude LULAC and others not only from Model Cities money, but also perhaps from other federal program money." Their apprehension merged with allegations of cultural indifference and appropriation. Ethnic liberals claimed that the MCO's leaders were "insensitive to the Latino culture" and accused them of "using a Latino image . . . to win power in city hall for a non-Latino organization."[130] Rhetorically potent yet factually imprecise, these views inspired a vociferous camp to challenge populist radicals' power. Though they lost in 1970, they set a precedent for future internecine confrontations over authority, legitimacy, money, and latinidad.

Populist radicals' deprecation and marginalization of "agency people"—a label used to disparage the directors and staff of social service agencies—fed many ethnic liberals' anxieties. Some MCO leaders who embraced Alinsky's principles regarded service agencies' personnel as incompetent, opportunistic, and predisposed to "enhancing their [individual] organizations." Their assessments guided the preparations for Model Cities in late 1970 and early 1971. Pointing to the challenges and friction experienced during the War on Poverty, populist radicals opted to exclude many ethnic liberals from programmatic planning and development.[131] The initial framework for Model Cities thus prioritized: 1) new community-based agencies (e.g., the Mission Housing Development Corporation) under direct oversight by the MMNC; 2) service projects run by public bodies (e.g., the San Francisco Unified School District) out of deference to institutional change; and 3) funds for already existing neighborhood agencies that supported Martinez's third-term presidency (e.g., OBECA). Notably, despite their reproach of ethnic liberals' reliance on political patronage, populist radicals began to engage in a similar process by rewarding their allies. Loyalty to those in power now translated into appointments to the MMNC, access to funds, and positions in the funded agencies. MCO leaders systemically set out "to make sure that loyal people were placed in positions of authority in the Model Cities program."[132] Populist radicals' efforts to maintain their influence antagonized ethnic liberals, whose fears of exclusion shifted from speculation to reality.

Rivalries and bitterness typically escalated and proved most pronounced during the annual convention seasons. At the fifth convention in November 1972, ethnic liberals managed to gain control of the MCO by mobilizing a bloc called the Alianza caucus. They raised the banner of latinidad and brought together many Latino-centered agencies and associations. But Alinskyites still ran the MMNC, which resulted in ongoing quarrels and polarization. Populist radicals consistently chastised the new MCO leaders for failing to honor the distinct roles assigned to the coalition and the MMNC. Ethnic liberals apparently sought "greater involvement in the day-to-day administration of Model Cities" and jockeyed to place their people in Model Cities–funded projects and agencies.[133] Critics of the new regime elided a key fact: past MCO administrations had engaged in parallel machinations, thereby stoking tensions between factions.

The once mighty MCO imploded by fall 1973. That November, many populist radicals boycotted the annual convention and organized an ad hoc committee of concerned members—challenging what they identified as unethical practices by a bloc set on retaining its power. Ezquerro and other populist radicals claimed that the Alianza caucus sidestepped parliamentary procedures and relied on "phony delegations" to build up its electoral strength. "Paper organizations" with voting power, delineated Ezquerro and her allies, raised questions about whether "the current membership of the MCO represent[ed] the Mission Community."[134] The charge of fraudulence and misrepresentation had come full circle. White conservatives and ethnic radicals had offered comparable perspectives when the MCO first emerged. Some ethnic liberals levied similar accusations in 1970 as conflicts with populist radicals mounted. The tables had turned: populist radicals doubted the honesty and legitimacy of ethnic liberals now leading the coalition.

Coalitional rupture seemed irreparable. Presiding over the MCO, Carlos Carrillo assailed populist radicals' critiques as "destructive rumors," which tarnished the MCO's image. He and other ethnic liberals stressed that their foes' accusations could result in the loss of Model Cities funding.[135] Model Cities had actually been subjected to budgetary cutbacks and greater mayoral oversight since early 1973. These developments formed part of an ongoing overhaul of Great Society programs by the Nixon administration. The MCO's downfall, then, did not stem from shrinking Model Cities funds. Whether members accepted it or not, the coalition's demise resulted from the political infighting between ethnic liberals and populist radicals.

Contemporary observers sometimes found it easiest to explain the communal troubles and disunity through the lenses of personality and self-interest instead of ideology. Writing for *El Mundo* in January 1974, Raúl Moreno interpreted the coalition's "decadence" as a product of "envy, favoritism, and selfishness."[136] Personal motivations and clashes over temperament certainly caused friction, but individual ambitions were often fueled or justified by one's political visions. The strength and unity once exhibited by the MCO proved challenging and fleeting because populist radicals and ethnic liberals attached divergent values to governmental assistance and latinidad. To complicate matters further, the benefits of community control and the potential for institutional change came to be clouded by activist factions' ongoing struggle for influence. White conservatives and ethnic radicals, watching from the sidelines, found some ideological comfort in the MCO's fate. They had, after all, consistently challenged the coalition's prominence, its engagement with the liberal state, and its claims of unity and representation.

Now bracing themselves for a post-MCO future, Missionites could agree on one thing: their model neighborhood stood bruised and deeply divided. The Model Cities era had exposed and heightened fissures over community control, representation, liberalism, and latinidad.

CHAPTER 6

"Oppressed by Our Latino Culture"

Tradition and Liberation
During the Sexual Revolution

Elba Montes's decision to leave the MCO in 1970 involved more than critique of organizational procedure: it also represented a challenge to male authority. Having proven her organizing talent, gumption, and political commitment since her days in MACAP, she found that some "men that were in power" resisted the possibility of a woman presiding over the MCO.[1] Hers was not a singular experience. Other Latina activists met parallel circumstances—inside and outside the coalition. Circumscribed leadership and decision-making roles fit within a gamut of gendered opportunities available to women and girls at this time. Long-standing cultural prescriptions and expectations regarding women's place at home and in public life circulated alongside entrenched assumptions about sexual identity, choices, and practices. But established customs involving gender, sex, and family did not go unquestioned or unshaken, especially in a city where the sexual revolution unfolded with much force. Montes's defiance of male power offered but one manifestation of a juncture reached by Latinas and Latino men in the late 1960s and 1970s. Her ethnic kin now stood at the crossroads between tradition and liberation, between cultural conservatism and cultural liberalism.

On the eve of Montes's protest, Latinas and Latino men found themselves weighing and grappling with worldviews on gender, sexuality, and family with greater regularity and intensity. Cultural politics and "intimate matters" intersected with and influenced broader deliberations of power, communal welfare, and liberalism.[2] Whether Latinos publicly admitted it or not, gendered and sexual conventions shaped their lives, opportunities, and political identities. As the sexual revolution unraveled around them, some activists and residents upheld the cultural status quo while others set out to alter it. Their views on gender, family, and sexual life informed understandings of and prescriptions for well-being and advancement.

Through an ideological tug-of-war pitting cultural tradition against sexual liberation—one that was sometimes tacit and rarely face-to-face—Latinos calibrated their alignment with an evolving liberal project. They generally accepted that the dominant strand of 1960s liberalism encompassed support for racial equality and economic melioration—even as some radical activists criticized the motives and limitations of that political endeavor. Incorporating sexual equality and freedom into a progressive agenda, in contrast, took on disparate significance and urgency. The contest between tradition and liberation now impelled Latinos to qualify—often implicitly—their connection to American liberalism vis-à-vis sexual politics.

Deliberations and conflict involving gender relations, family life, and the sexual realm had previously occurred in private, individually, and intermittently; they acquired more public, communal, and forceful attention as the sexual revolution intensified. Latinos typically learned and reproduced scripts about sex, desire, the body, and morality in their families, recreational venues, and religious settings. Numerous community-based initiatives—including ones funded by public monies—likewise promoted gender conventions, a limited range of sexual autonomy, and heterosexuality as the acceptable form of sexual expression. Synchronously, though not necessarily in tandem, policymakers, social workers, poverty warriors, and people of faith affirmed and reproduced a set of traditional values about sex and family. They generally treated their approaches as apolitical matters. By the early 1970s, Latinas with a feminist orientation began to critique this cultural matrix. Latino/as who identified as gay or lesbian followed suit by mid-decade. Fusing sexual politics into community politics, these activists advanced a culturally liberal agenda stressing equality between women and men, sexual expression and freedom, open discussions about sex, and a moral code built on honesty and dignity. Their visions ran counter to the culturally conservative outlooks and assumptions pervasive in Latino life. Feminists, gay men, and lesbians thus politicized topics related to gender and sexuality, and labored to revise and expand various cultural layers of latinidad.

Tradition and authority became increasingly debatable in the late postwar era. At mid-century, ecclesiastical mandates and expert knowledge on gender and sexuality flowed from religious authorities and social welfare professionals. Few Latinos, if any, took part in crafting authoritative frameworks, which colored and reinforced traditional understandings of gender, household dynamics, and sexual life. Community advocates often relied on such perspectives when designing programs for youth development, familial stability, and overall community advancement. Latina feminists and gay- and lesbian-identified Latino/as mounted a public challenge to this state of affairs in the 1970s. Offering alternative and liberal outlooks, they widened the scope of Latino politics—and recast sociopolitical analyses of individual, familial, and communal welfare.

Human Renewal, Family Rehabilitation, and Catholic Orthodoxy

In an age when urban renewal elicited much anxiety, policymakers and social workers focused on another arena some observers identified as a site of deterioration: family life. Increased public attention to female-headed households and out-of-wedlock pregnancy led welfare professionals to recommend a strengthening of poor (and often minority) families through "human renewal." Proponents of this approach relied on counseling and other social services to promote traditional domestic arrangements and gender relations and to counter "inadequate family composition," "sexual maladjustment," and dependency.[3] They simultaneously called for a modification of cultural values and sexual practices considered detrimental for individual and familial improvement. Social workers maintained that the psychological and economic well-being of poor, minority families depended on establishing two-parent, nuclear households fostering economic productivity, Americanization, and heterosexuality. If urban planners saw redevelopment as the solution to physical decay, social welfare experts favored human renewal as the appropriate course to treat what they regarded as familial, interpersonal, and sexual manifestations of blight.

Human renewal acquired ideological fuel from two postwar frameworks linking race, poverty, and family structure. The problem of dependency and the culture of poverty—often seen as mutually reinforcing—functioned as potent explanations for the life challenges faced by some minority families. Ongoing reliance on public welfare, according to personnel at municipal and state agencies, stemmed from familial problems, such as separation, divorce, "illegitimate parenthood," and desertion. Though they did not discount the role of lagging economic growth and unemployment in producing poverty, the existence of generational poverty dismayed them. Building a causal link between family structure and dependency, social welfare experts determined that growing up in "broken homes" and environments with a "distorted family life" predisposed children to emulate those familial dynamics and replicate the cycle of dependency as adults.[4] Social workers who assisted Spanish-speaking families at the MNC reached similar conclusions. Among them, Arletta Dawdy and Irving Kriegsfeld made a neat correlation between female-headed households, dependency, and teenage pregnancy. "Reliance on public welfare has characterized some families, especially where the mother is the only parent at home," they noted. "For the pregnant teenager in an AFDC [Aid to Families with Dependent Children, a federal assistance program] family, her inclusion in the mother's budget assures financial assistance for her unborn child, but also continues the generational pattern of use of public welfare." These patterns of "social dysfunction" worried MNC staffers, who joined public authorities in their quest to reform family life.[5]

Concerns over generational poverty and the cycle of dependency fit within broader deliberations about the culture of poverty. This paradigm offered academics and policymakers a rubric for linking cultural values, family dynamics, and economic misfortune. Departing from structuralist perspectives, which emphasized labor market conditions and racial discrimination as the bases for economic hardship, the culture of poverty thesis cast economic burdens as ones principally shaped by cultural life and family structure. It posited that cultural attributes and dispositions (e.g., present-time orientation, fatalism, and irrational thinking)—transmitted from generation to generation—resulted in low aspirations and a lack of economic success. Proponents also impugned female-headed households and other non-nuclear-family arrangements for supposedly failing to foster self-sufficiency, male responsibility, and a socially acceptable work ethic. Their mutually constitutive judgments reinforced and advanced the framework: the culture of poverty fed the cycle of dependency, and dependent families made it possible for that cultural system to thrive.[6]

These intellectual currents did not circulate exclusively within academic circles. They informed various programs carried out by bodies offering social services to poor and minority families. In the early 1960s, the city's Public Welfare Department initiated its Family Rehabilitation Program (FRP), which revamped existing public assistance efforts and amplified strategies to offset "the breakdown of healthy family life." Programs such as these flourished during the postwar decades, and according to historian Jennifer Mittelstadt, "Tapping into broader social debates about the importance of families in American society and the role of parents and children within families, welfare reformers attempted to 'rehabilitate' welfare clients whose family patterns deviated from white, middle-class norms."[7] Latinos came under the FRP's purview in relatively small numbers. In 1962, less than 10 percent of all 5,500 families in the program were identified as Mexican or "other"; the majority of families who received public assistance were either African American (56 percent) or white (35 percent). Latinos seldom accessed public aid for multiple reasons, including their lack of familiarity with these services and welfare personnel's inability to meet their linguistic needs. Those who did it—typically women—received vital relief. In doing so, they subjected themselves to varying levels of counseling, instruction on homemaking skills, lectures on "acceptable child-rearing practices," and a multitude of judgments about their families.[8]

Champions of the rehabilitation agenda lauded traditional gender roles and heterosexual marriage as the optimal pathways to create "healthy, happy, useful, and independent" families. Guided by the normative expectations of white, middle-class America, they marked female-headed households as deficient because these familial arrangements lacked a male breadwinner and father figure. Cognizant of present realities, engineers of the therapeutic project focused much attention on curbing women's sexual behavior. Social workers used economic and cultural arguments to counsel against future out-of-wedlock pregnancies. Fewer children would supposedly make it more feasible for an unmarried woman to procure employment. Altering reproductive practices, welfare authorities insisted, was integral for the reconditioning process—one set on countering cultural sanctions of "illegitimate parenthood." Furthermore, welfare custodians assumed that children raised by a single parent grew up with less love and emotional support. These youngsters, "bereft of the family care, affection, and understanding guidance," would supposedly encounter difficulties in becoming productive, self-sufficient members of society.[9] Such assessments encapsulated the anxieties and resolve guiding the rehabilitation effort. Dependent, deficient households stood to reproduce themselves by passing on their characteristics and problems to successive generations. Social welfare professionals therefore deemed it imperative to intervene and repair these families.

A rehabilitative ethos guided the architects of the War on Poverty as well. Though the federal initiative offered opportunities for programmatic experimentation, numerous projects deferred to conventional wisdom on gender relations and sexuality as promoted by public welfare and religious bodies. Recent scholarship by Eileen Boris reveals that the builders of the Great Society believed "economic opportunity was never dependent on workplace alone" and hoped "the War on Poverty would rehabilitate families and rebuild communities in the process of providing education, training, and jobs."[10] San Franciscans who sat on the city's Economic Opportunity Council expected that the anti-poverty crusade would strengthen family life and "motivate dependent families to become more self-sufficient." Some among them placed great faith on the rehabilitative ethos: "broken" and ailing families needed counseling, coaching, and behavior modification to successfully break the cycle of poverty. In the process, anti-poverty planners envisioned that women would become dependent on men rather than the state; men and women would adhere to traditional gender roles; and they would establish two-parent, heterosexual households.[11]

Religious authorities likewise worried about "family disintegration." Though domestic fissures presented themselves in various ways, unmarried parenthood regularly received the most attention. "We are alarmed at the increase in the number of young unwed mothers coming to our Catholic Charities agencies for help," noted Father James Flynn in 1964.[12] Flynn directed Catholic Social Service (CSS), a private welfare agency offering services to Catholic families, individuals, and children throughout the city. Its contact with Latinos proved extensive given its Mission location and the presence of three Spanish-speaking caseworkers by the mid-1960s. Throughout that decade, approximately one-fourth of its clientele was of Latin American heritage. Priests often referred their parishioners there, and the agency nurtured ties with such organizations as the CCSS. All these factors made the CSS a more accessible place for Latinos confronting life challenges, including marital problems and unwed motherhood, emotional and spiritual troubles, and a host of economic worries.[13]

Public and faith-based blueprints for enhancing family life overlapped and diverged. Like the administrators and coordinators of the FRP, Catholic officials, priests, and caseworkers sought to prevent and counseled against "family breakdowns." They concurred on the significance of marriage: they regarded it as the foundation for familial stability and propitious child development. San Francisco's archbishop, Joseph T. McGucken, identified it as part of God's law and joined other Catholic bishops in casting heterosexual matrimony as an "inalienable right."[14]

Catholic orthodoxy nevertheless stood at odds with governmental openness to and, in some instances, advocacy of family planning and contraception. State administrators typically correlated family size with economic independence; counseling sessions at welfare offices and county hospitals sometimes integrated information and provision of birth control. Some members of the local EOC, too, placed family planning and discussions about "unregulated family expansion" within a comprehensive anti-poverty agenda.[15] The Catholic establishment resoundingly opposed this orientation and practice. In 1964, McGucken reminded all in his archdiocese that "artificial birth control" defied church doctrine and was "always immoral and . . . not justifiable under any circumstances." Viewing it as a violation of natural and divine law, Catholic authorities decried "Government's stepped-up intervention in family planning." The state's promotion of birth control, clergymen claimed, infringed on citizens' freedom and "the right of human privacy" by interfering with and attempting to regulate intimate decisions, "new life," and God's plan for an individual family. Sidestepping its own role in limiting personal autonomy and regulating sexual behavior, the Church's hierarchy urged all Catholics to resist the efforts of state agencies endorsing "birth prevention as a public policy."[16]

Latinos and other San Franciscans who identified as Catholic confronted and maneuvered religious doctrine in varied ways. Faith-centered mandates guided the services offered by such agencies as the CSS and likely influenced the personal decisions made by some individuals and families. Moral considerations likewise seeped into the anti-poverty projects carried out under the auspices of MACAP. In this way, Catholic teachings came to influence public yet community-driven plans to assist poor families. Private, secular efforts at the MNC, in contrast, tended to correspond closely with the impulses guiding public welfare authorities. Notably, the MNC's staff discovered that their clients did not entirely embrace either therapeutic or religious views on family and sexuality. Social workers' observations, in fact, acknowledged the workings of individual and quiet resistance to expert opinion and Catholic orthodoxy.

Americanization, Gendered Opportunities, and Immorality in the Mission

Aligned with a twentieth-century tradition of settlement-house work, the MNC extended an array of social services to aid residents in bettering their urban lives. The agency offered educational programming, psychosocial counseling, and varied leisure activities. Latinos accessed these neighborhood-based services with some regularity. By the mid-1960s, immigrants from Latin America and their second-generation offspring—adolescents and children alike—formed the largest client base at the agency's divisions for children, youth, and families.[17]

A professional and civic impulse to Americanize and acculturate newcomers guided much of the neighborly assistance. As like-minded institutions had done decades before, the MNC stressed English-language acquisition, coordinated citizenship classes, and encouraged communal cohesion and national belonging. Americanization entailed more than just English proficiency, civic lessons, and patriotism. Its proponents also sought alterations in nutrition, recreation, family life, and sexuality. Conversant with culture-of-poverty perspectives, social workers identified their services as interventions to offset the "cultural disadvantages" of residents whose lives deviated "from [their] American middle-class contemporaries."[18]

Comprehensive Americanization rested on familial and sexual rehabilitation. Paralleling the inclinations of public authorities, MNC caseworkers labored to reverse "family dysfunction" and sexual behavior considered aberrant. Their drive to impede the reproduction of values and practices viewed as problematic prompted them to launch various projects targeting adolescents. In clubs for young mothers and fathers, teenage parents received guidance on child-rearing, health education, and birth control, and lectures on the presumed advantages of two-parent households and sex within the confines of marriage. These sessions imparted some beneficial information. But the MNC's team sought to manage and control adolescents' sexuality, not promote sexual discovery and autonomy. At the same time, caseworkers consistently prescribed traditional gender relations as the building blocks for familial stability, urging the cultivation of homemaking skills among women and emphasizing men's roles as breadwinners and providers.[19]

The promotion of traditional gender roles and valorization of marital sex went hand in hand with an assumption that heterosexuality represented the only problem-free expression of erotic desire and intimacy. Social workers at the MNC typically handled homosexuality through crisis management and referrals to public authorities for medical intervention. The city's health department took a more stringent approach for remedying what they identified as "sexual maladjustment." Its personnel relied on psychiatric counseling and various forms of behavior modification to treat homosexuality, promiscuity, and other "sexual problems."[20] The classification of homosexuality as a disease retained its potency in the 1960s, even as queer San Franciscans experienced budding social freedoms. There were some strides in tolerance for homosexuality during this period, including the repeal of California's vagrancy law and a de-escalation of police harassment.[21] Yet in diagnosing "inadequate sex orientation" and unwed parenthood as behaviors in need of overhaul, social workers and public health experts circumscribed the identities, decisions, and outlooks of individuals whose lives they sought to enhance.[22]

Missionites who passed through the MNC's doors did not necessarily concur with professionals' worldviews or attach the same meaning to the services they received. Though client accounts and recollections have proved difficult to locate, staff reports incorporated fragments of clients' counterpoints.[23] Social workers in the Mission fleetingly, yet tellingly, acknowledged their clients' contrasting views on family and sexuality. "Spanish-speaking and Negro families," noted Dawdy and Kriegsfeld in 1966, shared "a strong sub-cultural tradition . . . to suggest nothing unusual or problematic in a single-parent (mother) head of household." And while social welfare professionals equated a complete family unit with a nuclear family, their clients often identified grandparents, aunts, uncles, and even friends as part of their "total family."[24] Such observations belied expert assessments and recommendations. Latinos and African Americans did not appear to stigmatize female-headed households, nor did they regard nuclear families as superior to extended households or fictive kin arrangements. Grassroots warriors such as Elba Montes did not view households consisting of a mother, her children, and a grandmother as single-parent families. As she remembered, "I [saw] two people that definitely [were] committed to raising the children."[25] Her comments homed in on how professionals' frameworks could well contradict poor people's understandings of themselves.

Another disjuncture between authoritative dispositions and residents' everyday orientations exhibited itself in considerations of family planning. In counseling sessions with young Latinas, MNC caseworkers learned that many clients found birth control to be desirable and necessary. The women disclosed how pragmatic needs sometimes led them to "choose to disobey the religious ban against contraceptive pills or devices."[26] The revelations made clear that religious mandates were not accepted blindly or without some negotiation. Of course, the MNC's clientele represented just one subset of district residents, but they were not the only ones interested in more family-planning education and access to birth control. In late 1966, as anti-poverty programming unfolded, Missionites in Bernal Heights Action for Progress, a grassroots collective sponsored by MACAP, proposed setting up a birth control clinic and information center. MACAP's governing board neither prioritized nor allocated funds for such services, in marked to contrast to all other poverty target areas.[27] This decision stemmed from district leaders' religious identities and acquiescence to church mandates. Members of the CCSS sat on the board, and MACAP staffers cultivated strong ties with the CSS. Deference to Catholic doctrine meant that most "health professionals in the Latino community at that time were fairly conventional and conservative in their approach," explained Joanna Uribe, a childcare specialist who arrived in the Mission around 1970. Still, some residents and activists engaged in anti-poverty work consistently urged program board members to weigh "the need for a family planning center."[28] These Missionites obviously believed sex education and birth control fit within an anti-poverty agenda, even though most community leaders continued to resist or evade that proposition.

MACAP leaders' reluctance to grapple with the tensions between religiosity and sexuality proceeded alongside their promotion of traditional gender roles. Paradoxically, the district's anti-poverty program facilitated women's participation in policymaking and grassroots organizing even as some of its projects affirmed gendered assumptions about women's spheres, talents, and futures. In 1995 sociologists Jill Quadagno and Catherine Fobes analyzed the Job Corps—another initiative created under the 1964 Economic Opportunity Act—and demonstrated how the War on Poverty reproduced "a gendered division of labor by channeling women into low-paying jobs and training them to become family caregivers."[29] Some undertakings in the Mission and across the city paralleled that endeavor. Among these, the Bernal Heights Neighborhood Leaders Training Project offered educational and recreational opportunities while replicating a matrix of gendered expectations. The initiative targeted young girls and adult women and proposed to encourage new skills, interest in civic affairs, and teamwork across ethnoracial backgrounds. In actuality, most activities focused on generating and expanding interest in homemaking. Participants learned to sew, cook, and "acquire skills important to them as future wives and mothers." Project directors' ties to the local Young Women's Christian Association informed much of their vision. Guided by a maternalist orientation stressing domesticity and child-rearing, they presented young women with a wholesome set of after-school alternatives.[30] Their curriculum approached women's leadership potential and future employment in narrow ways. The project prepared young girls for domestic labor—which would further women's economic inequity and dependence on men—instead of introducing a breadth of options to foster female independence and occupational diversity. And by equating women's leadership with home management and rearing upstanding children, coordinators continued to assume that marriage and motherhood formed part of women's destiny and self-development.

Faith-based civic associations, too, stressed the importance of strengthening marriage. In the late 1960s, the CCSS began sponsoring "marriage encounters" encouraging heterosexual Latinos to evaluate their marital relationships and commit themselves to "the renewal of their family life." The effort signaled laypersons' response to communal concerns about divorce, as well as their inclination to lean on spirituality to fortify family ties and obligations. It dovetailed with the emergence of the Movimiento Familiar Cristiano (MFC), a religious initiative begun in Houston in 1969 that soon spawned regional groups in localities with sizable Latino communities.[31] With backing from the CCSS, San Francisco's MFC organized weekend retreats, couples' groups, lectures, and events for families. These forums encouraged partners' dialogue and reflection on their marriage, offered peer modeling and support, promoted increased involvement in children's lives, and provided ongoing instruction on Christian values as the foundation for family life. By participating, husbands and wives stood to become catalysts for socioreligious rejuvenation. Sister Maria Mercedes Reygadas, who coordinated modules and activities into the mid-1970s, emphasized that the MFC was "helping the Spanish speaking couples to form Christian families who [would] be a leaven to the Church and to Society." Program strategies and aims were straightforward: by amplifying conjugal communication, practicing perseverance, and clinging to faith, couples would fend off infidelity, separation, disconnection from children, and any consideration of birth control. Honoring marriage promises and "progressing along the ways of God," MFC participants heard, depended on valuing chastity, celebrating fecundity, adhering to Catholic teachings, and instilling moral values in children.[32]

If some Latinos relied on their sacred arsenal to bolster marital and parental relationships, others rallied against social forces viewed as profane and harmful to family life. A boom in commercialized sexuality, public assertions and consummation of erotic desires, and a celebration of homosexuality, among other manifestations of sexual transformation, troubled and exasperated many culturally conservative San Franciscans. Individuals, parents, and small business owners who naturalized and revered privatized, marital, procreation-centered heterosexuality therefore pledged to stamp out sexual openness, nonconformity, and rebellion in their midst. As the sexual revolution intensified, Latinos and other city residents took part in what historian Josh Sides has identified as a "bitter contest about sexual expressions in public spaces." Many neighborhood battles over sexuality hinged on the expansion of a public sex culture beyond the Barbary Coast and the Tenderloin—areas long identified with commercialized sex—and into districts such as the Mission.[33]

The sprouting of pornographic venues in the Mission, beginning in the late 1960s, alarmed some district residents and prompted an early wave of anti-porn organizing. In 1968, a contingent of Latinos and other Missionites mobilized within the MCO to curb the trend. The coalition's community maintenance committee, chaired by Ophelia Balderrama, functioned as a communal watchdog; it set out to regulate businesses engaged in sex-related enterprises and monitor their compliance. The committee drafted numerous resolutions calling for "quality, clean" businesses. One of these demanded that district theaters cease the screening of adult movies during weekend matinees, school holidays, and summer vacation. Another one urged stores displaying "lewd type magazines" to halt the practice and remove these materials from public view. Establishments that disregarded the committee's designs became targets of picketing and mass protest, as experienced by the Crown Theater, near 21st and Mission, in 1969. Balderrama and her colleagues justified their tactics as indispensable for "the defense of the people of the neighborhood." The promotion and consumption of sex, they determined, threatened Mission residents, morally, culturally, and economically.[34]

Communal denunciations of sex in the public sphere remained prominent as the new decade began. In April 1971, representatives from various media outlets, social clubs, and social service organizations came together under the Clean Up the Mission Committee, pledging to purge immorality from the district. Shielding families from subject matter and entertainment marked as disgraceful, offensive to cultural sensibilities, and inappropriate for children functioned as the front-line rationales propelling the anti-porn drive. "Let's raise the flags of decency," proclaimed Francisco Marín in *El*

Mundo, a prominent newspaper backing the "laudable" campaign against pornography. The committee impugned all forms of erotica, including live sex shows, and called on residents to protest and expunge this "trash" from their community. "The morality and urbanity of our women and children is headed down a path of corruption," added Willy Alfredo Lopez, a local radio host and committee member. He warned his Spanish-speaking audience that the "cancer" of pornography would only grow if Missionites "remained quiet" and indifferent to the detriments purportedly spawned by commercialized sexuality.[35]

The clean-up committee's consternation did not end there. Its members identified pornography as just one facet of a subterranean marketplace run by criminal organizations simultaneously engaged in the sale of drugs and in human trafficking. They assumed all these activities converged to destabilize socioeconomic life, by fostering delinquency on one hand and prompting disinvestment of "clean" businesses on the other. Marketing sexuality raised alarm for yet another reason: it cast the sexual realm as a site of pleasure while exposing a diversity of sexual desires and practices. The material Marín and associates found particularly troubling included that which "no longer depict[ed] normal relations between persons of different sexes, but rather aberrations . . . found in Sodom and Gomorrah."[36] Some producers and consumers of porn surely disagreed with this assessment; they did not regard pornography as immoral or homosexuality as abnormal. Here lay a central yet implicit anxiety generated by a sexualized public sphere: it served to advertise and validate alternative views on sexuality and desire. And the proliferation of eroticism in public life countered, and could potentially decenter, a conservative and traditional impulse to keep sex hidden—beholden to the mandates of church and family.

Everyday Lessons on Gender and Sexuality

Conservative directives and cultural codes governing family life, gender relations, and sexuality did not emanate exclusively from community defense groups, social service agencies, religious bodies, and the media. Institutional agendas and messages entered the public record more frequently, making these easier to access by historians. But Latinas and Latino men received everyday instruction about gender roles, sexual autonomy, and heterosexuality at home, in the streets, and in other places of daily social interaction. The transfer and reproduction of gendered expectations and sexual scripts thus occurred symbiotically and across multiple fronts, in institutional settings and from the bottom up.

In the 1970s, Latinas augmented public discussions about the workings of traditional gender roles and sexual conservatism, and the limitations these practices presented in their lives. Typically in their twenties or early thirties, some women had been involved in community activism since the mid- to late 1960s; others' political engagement commenced in the new decade. Their analyses of gender conventions and inequity often began by identifying the family as a site in which women received ongoing, quotidian lessons on gender and sexuality. Maria Del Drago explained that many Latinas witnessed the sanctioning and reproduction of male privilege during childhood. "Our position within the family circle is learned early," Del Drago noted. "At the table, the men and boys are served first, the best cuts of meat (or the only meat), the freshest fruits, the strongest coffee."[37] Such mundane circumstances were not inconsequential. They impressed on young girls that men's and boys' wants and needs came before theirs, and conveyed greater valorization of men's health, nutrition, and, in effect, male well-being. At the same time, girls and women regularly performed a host of household chores, whereas boys and men had greater leeway to play and engage in pursuits outside the familial milieu.

Gendered tasks and opportunities within Latino families intersected with instruction and ideas about women's bodily and interpersonal comportment. "If we are women, we are taught to be gentle, quiet, [and] shy," bemoaned Del Drago. Other Latinas concurred and joined her in challenging these teachings, which they viewed as reproducing female dependence and curtailing personal initiative. "We were not created to be docile, or submissive," stressed Rebecca Carrillo. Rather, as Ana Montes put it, Latinas were "brave, with ambition and hope" and should "no longer [be] the silent one[s]." Discrediting notions of women's essence or natural temperament, these individuals gestured toward a social construction of personality and behavior. They believed women's abilities were inexhaustible—not predestined—and insisted that realizing their "full potential [as] creative human beings" demanded a new consciousness and political action.[38]

Latinos and Latinas who identified as gay or lesbian also found their lives circumscribed by rigid gender roles and compounded by commonplace perceptions of homosexuality as aberrant and foreign. Rodrigo Reyes, Diana Felix, Eddi Baca, and others who discussed their gayness in public often commented on the ignorance, aversion, "ugliness and fear our *gente* [people] have towards homosexuality." Same-sex desire and intimacy, they recounted, was typically viewed as incompatible with, and external to, Latino cultures.[39] These individuals drew particular attention to the practice of "heterosexual chauvinism," which they first encountered in their families and at an early age. "As young children we are channeled into heterosexual molds by parents, peers and society at large," detailed the Gay Latino Alliance (GALA), a collective founded by Reyes, Felix, and their counterparts in 1975. "By the age of two we have already been conditioned into believing that it is wrong for people of the same sex to love each other."[40]

Placing emphasis on the processes of molding and conditioning, gay-identified Latinos laid bare and critiqued the cultural power and construction of heteronormativity and traditional gender roles. Assumptions of heterosexuality as the standard and healthy form of sexual desire and expression permeated Latino life and mainstream America in the early to mid-1970s. The circulation of such attitudes, their legitimization by multiple institutions, and their transmission across generations, GALA members determined, worked in tandem to equate heterosexuality with "natural instincts." Prescriptive heterosexuality concurrently hinged on and reinforced gendered scripts. Homosexual Latinos, observed Baca, did not subscribe to "strict roles for men and women."[41] This was certainly the case in terms of sexual object choice as most heterosexual Latinos held onto a notion that biology and anatomy dictated desire for the opposite sex. At the same time, some gay men and lesbians refrained from traditional expressions and performances of gender, including ones pertaining to bodily comportment, affect, and dress.

Gay people's divergence from gendered expectations and their involvement in intimate, same-sex relations incurred, more often than not, opprobrium. Baca discussed this reality by stressing that many heterosexual Latinos found homosexuality to be in conflict with "the concepts of honor, dignity and machismo of Latino culture."[42] The reproach called into question gay-identified individuals' personhood, psychosocial disposition, and reputation. Assessments of gay men as weak and docile and lesbians as independent and intractable cast doubt on their manhood or womanhood, as well as on their allegiance to kin. These impressions fit within a cultural worldview emphasizing duty and gendered obligations (e.g., men should protect, women should obey), loyalty to family, deference to tradition and accretion of respect, and the importance of progeny.[43] Revelations or rumors of same-sex attraction resulted in ostracism and shame from family members, neighbors, and others who regarded gay people as living outside—and betraying—this value system. One of GALA's key tasks would entail formulating an alternative worldview and linking its political vision to all Latinos' ongoing quest for advancement.

Communal blueprints for empowerment and progress designed by prominent Latino organizations rarely incorporated questions of gender and sexuality. An array of rationales informed this situation. The logic of latinidad emphasized unity and solidarity vis-à-vis ethnicity. And a significant faction of Latinos contemporaneously gravitated toward a class-centered program for change. Most Latino activists and leaders, then, approached or understood inequality, disadvantage, and exclusion primarily through the lenses of race, ethnicity, and class. A self-identified feminist and participant in the LSDC, Carmen Carrillo discussed how concerns involving gender relations and sexual life did not receive "high priority" in her collective and others like it. Those spheres of social existence, she explained, were not viewed as generating "the worst problem[s] in the community . . . or the worst form[s] of discrimination."[44] Others did not find it necessary to prioritize because they regarded sexual politics as inconsequential to or disconnected from their lives.

These various impulses fit within national currents of Latino political action at a time of impressive grassroots ferment. In his classic analysis of the Chicano movement, Ramón Gutiérrez demonstrated how Mexican Americans constructed a political and moral community by emphasizing an ethos of collectivism, cultural bonds, and common predicaments begot by white racism. Yet the movement relied heavily on sexism and homophobia, making the pursuit of equality and self-actualization applicable first and foremost to heterosexual men.[45] Feminists, gay men, and lesbians in San Francisco's Latino community met a comparable set of circumstances. Their lived experiences impelled them to propose a more ample—and more liberal—outlook on equality and human potential. In so doing, they would advance a framework that neither denied nor ranked sexual inequities but instead considered the intersectional workings of oppression.

Though marginalized, gender and sexuality matters were not absent from community politics. Male privilege, a gendered division of labor, gay men's and lesbians' involvement in community organizations, and sex-related programming all received public consideration, even though most discussions went unrecorded in written sources. The deliberations often took place informally, fleetingly, or in the interstices of broader reflections on power, representation, and well-being. Scattered and ephemeral attention to gender and sexuality should not be interpreted as irrelevant. Historian and theorist Emma Pérez urges us to attend to fragments, silences, and gaps in the historical record in order to "decolonize our history and our historical imaginations." By uncovering what has not been "written in history," she posits, scholars "honor multiple experiences" and acknowledge the agency of historical actors whose labors and visions may have been discounted by their contemporaries.[46] Her framework proves instructive even for a mid- to late twentieth-century context. In 1970s San Francisco, well-known entities such as the MCO refrained from addressing sexual politics in official proceedings and records. Yet activists' personal recollections made clear that gender and sexuality factored into community politics in myriad ways and occasions.

At the forefront of the city's Latino movement, the MCO became a pivotal site in which Latinas initiated a public challenge to male authority and traditional gender roles. In mid-1970, Elba Montes announced her aspiration to become the coalition's next president. Montes formed part of the MCO's founding team and had become a prominent community figure by this time. Her experience notwithstanding, some leaders, officers, and delegates proved resistant to the idea that a woman could be president on a permanent basis. Gender appeared to have outweighed her know-how and dedication to the organization. Montes recounted how "the males, not all of them, but a big percentage of them" saw her as "very useful to them as long as [she] didn't try to outdo them." Her opinionated and "feisty" style, she suggested, may also have been off-putting to some colleagues in the MCO. Notably, weeks before the election, the *San Francisco Examiner* ran a five-part story on women of *la raza,* with a focus on Latinas' participation in political life. "Latino men recognize women have the ability to lead, as they accept the involvement of women," Linda Marquez, another veteran of MACAP, told reporters. She then added, "But not the overbearing types."[47] Montes and Marquez basically pointed to gendered expectations about women's personality and behavior, their amiability, and deference to men. In Montes's case, her disposition may have been viewed as unwomanly, unmannerly, and potentially detrimental for engaging in negotiations with government officials. Her charge of male chauvinism and men's usurpation of power fell on deaf ears: she lost the election and then opted to leave the MCO. The gendered critique went unaddressed and did not receive any coverage in the press.

Two years later, a related scenario surfaced when Flor de Maria Crane made a bid for the presidency. Luisa Ezquerro described Crane as a "very in-dependent" woman and contrasted her style with the deference exhibited by some women whose political work depended on whether or not their hus-bands' approved. The caucus backing Crane's candidacy implicitly supported feminism. Ezquerro relayed, "We thought we were introducing that [femi-nism] with the activism of Flor and trying to move [women] into high lead-ership inside the MCO but it didn't take off."[48] The challenge met by Crane involved more than gender politics; her campaign occurred at the height of tensions between activists who differed over whether to structure the Model Cities program along ethnoracial or class lines. Ezquerro's comments never-theless revealed the currency of gender ideologies in circumscribing women's roles within the MCO. While some women chaired committees and directed Model Cities agencies, the MCO never elected a woman as its president.[49]

The perspectives offered by Montes and Ezquerro were neither isolated cases nor particular to the MCO. Women in the LSDC and LaREAL con-fronted rigidly defined gender roles and men's resistance to female leadership as well. Judy Zalazar Drummond participated in the LSDC and described the group as a "very traditional" space, one where "the women did all the work and the men did all the talking." Here, she echoed the experiences and frus-tration of Latinas engaged in community activism in Los Angeles, Chicago, and other localities. Zalazar Drummond detailed the operation of a gendered and unequal division of labor between men and women. "Women did all the typing, they took all the phone calls, and did all the shit work," but "there [were] no women in leadership." Donna Amador, also active in the LSDC, shared parallel memories. "Our group," explained Amador, "was incredibly macho and male-dominated."[50] Both women recalled men's dismissals and ridicule whenever they attempted to discuss gender inequality and to intro-duce a more equitable set of arrangements. Many male activists refused to consider and accept that some of their attitudes and behaviors proved detri-mental to women and the community as a whole. The situation led some fe-male activists to create a women's caucus within the LSDC; others simply decided to leave the collective.

Latinas' challenge to gendered dynamics within community organizations raised important questions about the range of community control and self-determination. As discussed in Chapter 5, these philosophies fueled grass-roots campaigns and community-based programs from the mid-1960s to the mid-1970s. Women's experiences and critiques, however, demonstrated that some Latino men understood community control only in relationship to government power. These male activists evidently believed community control could proceed without revamping the workings of male authority. In a related fashion, standard invocations of self-determination focused attention on the external, dominant agents of oppression (e.g., the state, white American culture, the capitalist economy). Yet male advocates of self-determination frequently overlooked or dismissed the communal and cultural practices circumscribing women's participation, agency, and freedom.

A pervasiveness of male authority and rigid gender roles overlapped with a hesitancy, if not outright resistance, to situate sexuality matters within an agenda for community development. Activists and observers generally agreed that cultural prohibitions and religious values hindered the creation of projects addressing sexual health and sexual autonomy. Religious instruction at home and at church emphasized the sanctity of reproduction, sex as a sacred activity, the innateness of heterosexuality, and overall privacy surrounding sexual life. Catholic teachings about sexuality made it almost impossible to engage in public and frank discussions about sexual practices, choices, and decision-making. Religion exerted great influence over people's lives, explained Carmen Carrillo, and it impeded attempts to address "sexuality [and] being open about or dealing with it." A young researcher at the University of California, Berkeley, offered a related assessment in the early 1980s. "Conservative Catholic doctrine," detailed Fernando Tafoya, "continues to be the dominant force in determining Raza's moral convictions and in socializing attitudes toward sexual issues."[51]

Well aware of the delicate issues before them, some community advocates recognized the need to incorporate material about sexuality into their service projects. "We want to set up a Planned Parenthood type program with sex education," Esperanza Echavarri told a news reporter in 1970. At the time, she worked with the Real Alternatives Program, which offered a variety of educational and recreational services to at-risk youth. Echavarri continued, "It will be hard to do it but it has to be done." The setbacks she referenced did not necessarily involve resources; rather, they hinged on her community's guardedness and discomfort with public discussions of sex. Gladys Sandlin, a health educator, likewise understood the cultural and religious taboos surrounding sex education and family planning services. She relied on alternative strategies to circumvent the situation. In 1971, while collaborating with the Mission Neighborhood Health Center, Sandlin coordinated a smoking prevention project for teenagers. Promoting her endeavor as basic health education, some workshops included information on anatomy, reproduction, and contraception. "That was a way to enter into the family [and] the home but not call it sex education," Sandlin explained.[52] Her efforts evinced a resourcefulness among community workers who wove sexual topics into broader initiatives for community health. By doing so, they avoided scrutiny for upending cultural sanctions against discussions of sex in the public sphere.

Misgivings and tiptoeing around sex education materialized as denunciations of homosexuality expanded. At a time when the city's gay and lesbian movement flourished, Latinos received, and many of them reproduced, a set of unfavorable appraisals about same-sex desire. Judgments from religious authorities, journalists, and health professionals converged in marking gay people as sinful, abnormal, and ill. The negative opinions were not necessarily new; they simply circulated with more regularity as the visibility of gay people—though not necessarily gay-identified Latinos—grew in the early 1970s. In communications with clergymen and laypeople, Archbishop McGucken cast homosexuality as an "evil," one sustained by "deviant habits and attitudes." Their church and faith "neither approves nor condones" the practice, expounded the *Catholic Monitor*'s editor, who worked closely with McGucken, because "it is in direct contradiction to [God's] moral law."[53] Such sentiments trickled down to Latinos in their parishes and at home. Youth activist Pete Gallegos identified Catholic teachings as foundational for his and his peers' understanding of same-sex relations as "unnatural" and a negative behavior. The messages permeated community life, Gallegos noted, and went overwhelmingly unquestioned; even radical organizations like his (La-REAL) did not "consider [homosexuality] a thing that was debatable."[54]

Catholic authorities sometimes reinforced their doctrine with prescriptions for medical intervention. They believed gay people's "deviation" could be cured through spiritual advice and prayer as well as psychiatric treatment if needed. While religion functioned as the key cultural apparatus furthering stringent and conservative views on homosexuality, many health professionals continued to rely on a medical outlook characterizing gay people as clinically ill. Two years before the American Psychiatric Association's 1973 declassification of homosexuality as a mental disease, staff at the Mission Neighborhood Health Center apprised residents of services available for persons who exhibited "sexual problems" and "perversions," such as homosexuality, promiscuity, and transsexuality. Like individuals engaged in criminal conduct and drug abuse, explained Luis Echegoyen, the health center's spokesman, gay men and lesbians needed medical evaluation and psychological treatment.[55] The assessments at once pathologized all sexual behavior occurring outside heterosexual marriage and bolstered the linkage between queer sexualities and crime. Popular commentators seized on religious and clinical perspectives, condensing and disseminating them in newspapers like *El Mundo* and *Tiempo Latino*. Though the Spanish-language press only took up homosexuality sporadically, columnists usually cast it as indicative of depravity and illness, or simply as a sexual transgression. The convergence of popular and authoritative messages meant most Latinos continued to assume there was "something wrong or deficient" about gay men and lesbians.[56]

For all the negative connotations attached to homosexuality in Latino life, gay people took part in grassroots organizing and community development efforts. Doing so typically demanded that their sexual identities remain undisclosed or undiscussed. A number of heterosexual activists from the MCO, LaREAL, and the LSDC referenced this reality and acknowledged it would have been challenging to be openly gay in their organizations. "There were a number of women in our group who may have been lesbian," remarked Amador. "But I don't think they would ever have felt comfortable saying anything."[57] Indeed, activists and community workers who were gay-identified, or involved in same-sex relations, had to make strategic decisions. Favorable and unquestioned engagement in public life hinged on keeping their personal affairs private. Homosexuality, after all, generated concerns about one's trustworthiness, judgment, and integrity. A cohort of Puerto Rican lesbians in 1970s New York City analogously conveyed how maneuvering homophobia required a set of personal concessions. Committed to public service, they "all expressed great fear that their leadership position vis-à-vis the Puerto Rican community would be jeopardized if their sexual orientation and preference were discovered." The women underscored how they could lose respect and leadership if their romantic and sexual lives became known.[58] Their counterparts in San Francisco confronted comparable pressures and likely made similar compromises.

Some community workers' sexual identities acquired political significance, even if they themselves did not intend to politicize their personal lives. Organizational accounts generally left concerns over homosexuality unaddressed, but such individuals as Ramón Barbieri and Joanna Uribe witnessed the scrutiny and apprehension involving gay people. Hired by the Model Cities program, Barbieri and Uribe observed how objections to homosexuality fed into deliberations involving authority, culture, and well-being. Barbieri worked as an accountant for the MMNC and detected unease over the selection of Juan Pifarre as that agency's executive director in 1971. "Juan Jorge

Pifarre was a gay guy," recounted Barbieri. "A gay guy as a leader [was] un-heard of," he continued; some in the Mission simply "could not understand this give—this tolerant view."[59] His comments referenced a potent, if implicit, assumption that the community's assets and enterprises should be under het-erosexual stewardship. Yet he also confirmed that Latinos' attitudes toward homosexuality were not homogenous or invariable. Though many Latinos did not situate tolerance for gay people within their liberal vision, others had started to do so. Pifarre's appointment, after all, owed much to the backing from Luisa Ezquerro and others who did not think gayness should automati-cally disqualify a person from employment or leadership.

Pifarre's case did not signal a progressive course, especially when com-pared with Susan Castro's experience. In 1972, Castro became director of the Mission Childcare Consortium, a cluster of childcare centers funded with Model Cities monies but with oversight from the mayor's office. Uribe served as a teacher and remembered the intense opposition to Castro's leadership and presence in the agency. The logic of community control and cultural anxieties over homosexuality fueled the antipathy. Some Mission leaders purportedly argued that Castro was not "community-grown," viewing her appointment as mayoral repudiation of Missionites' control and a reaffirmation of white power dynamics. Furthermore, some Latinos regarded her as an outsider be-cause she was white (her Spanish surname notwithstanding), supposedly held Communist views, and was rumored to be a lesbian.[60] Allegations of homosexuality raised particular alarm given the aversion to placing gay peo-ple in social service positions, especially ones involving contact with chil-dren. Objections to employing gay men and lesbians as teachers fit within a national, non-Latino-specific worldview. Research findings from a 1970 study funded by the National Institute of Mental Health revealed that nearly three-quarters of adults nationwide believed gay people sought children for sexual purposes or other illicit aims.[61] Some Missionites shared such senti-ments and thought Castro "[was] gonna lead our children astray." The "ho-mophobic stuff" together with other charges marginalized Castro, making her work in the consortium thorny and short-lived.[62] Her experience con-veyed unmistakable messages about the weight of cultural nationalism and defensive heterosexuality, offering a public reminder about the professional stakes confronting individuals perceived or identified as gay. A few more years would pass before gay and lesbian Latinos began to confront hetero-sexual privilege and homophobia head on.

Latina Feminists in the 1970s

Castro's exit from the Mission coincided with a flourishing of Latina feminist visions, which offered new formulations on gender, sexuality, and liberation. Latinas established at least four collectives—Concilio Mujeres, the Puerto Rican Women's Organization (PRWO), the Women's Caucus of the LSDC, and El Comité de Mujeres Latinas—aimed at countering conservative perspectives on gender relations, family life, and sexuality. The founders and co-ordinators of some groups had amassed work experience within Great Society experiments; others' activism originated on college campuses or in organizations wary of government authority. Some Latinas participated in a broader, second-wave feminist movement in varying ways and degrees; others found the mainstream feminist organizations ill-suited or unresponsive spaces for their work. "None of the predominantly white, middle-class, professional women's groups have come to grips with racism in American society," expounded Velia García Hancock in 1971.[63] Trained as a social worker at San Francisco State University, she voiced a common critique levied against white feminist activists. Latinas and other women of color often found white women to be oblivious or indifferent to issues involving race and class. In her analysis of 1970s Chicana feminism, sociologist Alma Garcia discerned that many Chicana activists regarded white women's singular "emphasis on gender oppression" as limiting because it "overlooked the effects of racial oppression experienced" by women of color.[64] A similar political mind-set led some Latinas in San Francisco to view white women's agendas as irrelevant or limited in scope. As Carmen Carrillo put it, "It was almost impossible to relate to the topics that white women wanted us to talk about." Such perspectives prompted Latinas to form their own organizations, collaborate with other women of color, and seek to apply feminist principles within progressive milieus.[65]

Identifying herself as "a feminist all the way," Carrillo admitted she regularly "raise[d] the Latino banner" over the feminist one.[66] Many of her contemporaries appear to have held similar sentiments. By and large, Latina feminists did not treat their work as separate from a Latino political project. They saw their efforts as an expansion of a shared quest for progress. Still, many understood that feminism—as ideology and political praxis—posed challenges for many Latino men and some Latinas as well. Dorinda Moreno, founder of Concilio Mujeres, related, "We knew we were feminist but we never used the word because it seemed to cause a lot of controversy." The strife she referenced exhibited itself in dismissals of feminist aims, mockery, and charges that feminism ran counter to Latinos' cultural heritage. Moreno and like-minded activists hoped to capsize these reactions and ideas. Doing so sometimes required casting the feminist label aside. "I was not into defending the word," explained Moreno, "as much as I was into causing change."[67]

Whether or not publicly identified as feminist institutions, Latina organizations tackled inequities at home, in the community, and in society at large. Some groups went further and upended silences and conservatism surrounding female sexual autonomy, sex education, and other topics considered private or culturally taboo. Among them, Concilio Mujeres generated the most comprehensive body of Latina feminist thought. Students at San Francisco State University founded the "self-organization" in 1970; their educational status may have afforded more time and space to reflect on their political philosophy. Led by Chicanas but open to all Latinas, it "committed [itself] to the development of the individual and the community." Concilio soon affiliated with La Comisión Femenil Mexicana, a national network of Chicana feminist groups created in 1971 and based in Los Angeles. Its mission aligned closely with La Comisión's, which sought "to provide a platform for women to use for thinking out their problems, to deal with issues not customarily taken up in regular organizations, and to develop programs around home and family needs."[68]

Concilio crafted a political program guided by the tenets of equality, mutuality, and a coeval struggle against racial and gender discrimination. Its members regularly discussed their aims and visions in nonfiction articles, poetry, and other forms of literary production published in *La Razón Mestiza*. Like other Chicana-focused outlets of this era, this journal allowed women to analyze the manifestations, effects, and interplay of sexism, racism, and economic marginalization in daily life.[69] Its editors at once identified the intersectional workings of women's oppression and argued against gradations of freedom and equity. "Sexual equality is inherent in racial equality," they declared in 1975. Acknowledging an inseparability between gender and racial parity, Concilio's members underscored the imperative of tackling both forms of prejudice and exclusion. Furthermore, they insisted that this endeavor demanded collaboration among women and men. "Our mutual culture has been our survival mechanism," they asserted. "Priorities and direction can only be established through our mutual quest towards overcoming the inequities in the total society."[70]

Calls for unity and collaboration positioned Concilio's vision within a broader agenda for Latino advancement. Its members nevertheless faced criticism for drawing attention to gender inequity, family dynamics, and sexual politics. Allegations that feminist goals diluted cultural traditions and splintered mobilizations for social change proved common in Latino communities at this time. In Chicago, as Lilia Fernández has documented, critics of Latina feminism cast it "as a threat to the family and cultural norms" and a program that "drained resources and energy from larger community struggles."[71] Women in San Francisco contended with a comparable set of charges. Some "traditionalists," recounted Moreno, had problems with "[our] ideology because they thought that we were separating the movement." The accusation was both dismissive and simplistic; after all, the city's Latino movement was heterogeneous and already divided along ideological and generational lines. Latina feminists consistently responded by affirming their desire to solidify, not divide, the communal pursuit of progress. "The New Woman," proclaimed Ana Montes, committed herself to "fighting for equality" and "working for a better world." This endeavor could not be realized separately from men. "Let's do it together," Montes insisted. "Together we will prevail."[72]

The two hundred women gathered at a conference in August 1974 heard a similar message. Sponsored by the PRWO, the event offered a large, public demonstration of "a movement for rights" led by Latinas. The PRWO had formed at least a year earlier, following discussions between Elba Montes, Norma Ortega, and other female activists. Montes and her allies had ties to a broader women's movement but found "there were hardly no Hispanics involved" in those feminist networks. They therefore decided to build an organization for Puerto Rican and other "Latino women."[73] Ethnic bonds, they deduced, could be used to introduce more Latinas to feminist aims and to ground goals in their everyday lives. The initial response, as reflected by attendance at the conference, confirmed the merit of their strategy.

At the gathering, organization leaders stressed that Latinas could not "afford to lag behind in the Women's Movement." Improving the status and lives of all women and Latinas in particular simply could not be left up to others. "We cannot be neutral," asserted Montes. She and her comrades coupled their incitation to take feminism seriously with proposals for a political partnership with Latino men. "We must have the help and understanding of our man leaders," Carmen Maymi, a federal government official, told the audience while delivering the keynote address. "We must all work together in combined brotherhood and sisterhood, to achieve the highest level of human dignity for all."[74] Her message of solidarity conveyed two key points undergirding the PRWO's feminist vision: it neither excluded men nor could it succeed without men's support. The organization certainly did not set out to disengage from or to discontinue collaborations with men. Instead, its members sought to remove barriers impeding women's development as individuals, workers, and leaders. And they hoped men would stand behind them in this effort.

The PRWO espoused what some scholars have termed "liberal feminism" given that the organization principally attended to gender inequities in public life.[75] Much of its agenda centered on questions of access and opportunity: members aspired to boost women's prospects in employment, education, and other public realms. In turning to government agencies for assistance, they professed faith and expectation that the state would aid them in carrying out their work. One early project offered Latinas employment counseling and job referrals; its funding came from the Women's Bureau of the U.S. Department of Labor, a division headed by Maymi.[76] Alongside efforts to augment job opportunities, the PRWO pressed for women's promotion to decision-making ranks—at work, in their neighborhoods, and in the city. "One of the things that we were looking at was how to be in leadership being a woman, a Latino woman," recalled Montes. Given the challenges Latinas had encountered in bodies such as the MCO, the group deemed it important to organize discussions on the obstacles, including gendered assumptions, women faced in positions of authority; such forums became invaluable spaces for mentorship and peer support. The focus on Puerto Rican and other Latina women did not preclude building relationships with non-Latinas. In fact, some of the PRWO's educational workshops specifically targeted white women. Montes and her colleagues coordinated sessions on cultural outreach and sensitivity "so that they would understand the Latino."[77]

As they cultivated alliances, the PRWO heralded what many Latinas and other nonwhite women knew: gender was just one determinant of opportunity and their overall existence. One marker of social difference (e.g., gender, race, class) alone could not explain Latinas' lived experiences; instead, these factors overlapped, shaping their identities and the inequities they confronted. Women-of-color feminists across the country posited as much in the 1970s. Black feminists in Boston's Combahee River Collective, for example, underscored it was "difficult to separate race from class from sex oppression."[78] The women in the PRWO likewise understood that gender inequity could not be disentangled from constraints posed by poverty and racial discrimination. Montes colloquially contrasted poor and working-class Latinas' struggles with those faced by middle-class white women. She recalled, "We were fighting to get in the door, they were fighting for management jobs; we were just trying to clean the floors." Research data corroborated some of Montes's anecdotal evidence. In 1975, coordinators of the Chicana Rights Project, based in the city and sponsored by the Mexican American Legal Defense Fund, found that Chicanas and other Latinas met consistent hurdles in hiring and promotion to higher-paying positions. Employment and language-training programs for Latinas, researchers concluded, were not "equal in quality and number to the men's programs."[79] The study quantified what the PRWO and other Latina organizations conveyed in qualitative terms: Latinas trailed both Latino men and white women in terms of job opportunities and prospects for economic self-sufficiency.

Concilio Mujeres, too, sought greater access to education, jobs, and other arenas that would grant Latinas "full participation in society." Its members kept themselves abreast of the PRWO and the Chicana Rights Project and championed their work. Generally speaking, Concilio's base was younger, college educated, and drawn to cultural production. Its performing arts troupe, Cucarachas en Acción, used dance, poetry, and music to showcase women's talents, highlight their activism, and popularize their feminist vision. The troupe strove "to preserve, promote and enrich the cultural heritage of La Raza people."[80] Cultural production only became a central component of Concilio's work after 1973; it had not served as the impetus for creating the organization. The group's agenda in 1970 underscored the indispensability of offering academic and social support to college-bound Latinas. Concilio encouraged young women to enroll in college, complete their degrees, and enter nontraditional professional careers.[81] At the same time, its members urged Latino parents to reframe the cultural messages transmitted to young women—attending less to marriage prescriptions and instead motivating them to pursue higher education and other interests outside the domestic sphere.

A confluence of structural and cultural factors continued to narrow life opportunities for women and girls. Most Latinos accepted that racism and poverty spawned manifold barriers for advancement. Feminist activists now impelled Latino parents and the community at large to recognize how certain cultural practices hindered women's potential and well-being. In a piece for *La Razón Mestiza*, Maria Del Drago identified the gender biases commonly experienced by young girls in traditional Latino households. "Sacrifices are made for a boy's education, but rarely for a girl's," she wrote.[82] A valorization of boys' education reproduced gendered outlooks about women's capacities, contributions, and adult futures circumscribed by marriage, child-rearing, and domesticity. This cultural trend at once reified assumptions about female dependence on men and curbed women's potential to study, consider nontraditional pursuits, and be fully independent.

More and more Latinas questioned "old attitude[s]" in the 1970s—within organized settings or through individual assessments and courage. Community advocate Linda Marquez quietly rebelled against traditional views "that the man is educated and the woman gets married and has a family."[83] Breaking away from tradition and embarking on a different life course than her sister, Marquez conveyed to her family and neighbors that women could be successful and fulfilled without marriage and children. Defying parental expectations could be emotionally and financially difficult. Given challenges such as conflict with parents, the peer support, help with procuring financial assistance, and other services offered by Concilio and like-minded collectives proved particularly vital.

Activists in Concilio wanted Latinas to consider new ways of living and being. They promoted women's autonomy, dispelled stereotypes about women's abilities, and worked against traditional gender roles. A focus on women's independence and agency did not necessarily correlate with advocacy of an individualist ethos. Most Latina feminists did not aspire to forsake ties and commitments to their ethnoracial community. They sought an equal place in Latino life, as well as the unbounded ability to advance personally and communally. "We have so much to say, us, women of the movement," affirmed Concilio's members. Nourishing and tapping into Latinas' limitless ideas, capacities, and resourcefulness depended on moving away from traditional gender roles and expectations. "Sex-role stereotyping" limited women and girls, Concilio consistently affirmed, while stressing that strict gender roles stifled boys and men as well. Some of its youth workshops addressed these topics directly; the collective concurrently partnered with other groups promoting alternatives to the cultural reproduction of gender. Change for Children, for example, "encourage[d] children to develop a sense of identity and purpose according to their own talents and interest[s] rather than their sex."[84] Concilio's collaboration with this collective further confirmed its members' dedication to challenge conventional cultural paradigms by promoting more open and expansive views on gender, selfhood, and self-actualization.

Laboring to broaden conceptions of gender and identity, some feminists also set out to liberalize cultural mores built on religious doctrine, silence, and sexual repression. Standing up to tradition was inherently a political act: it meant challenging Catholic orthodoxy and deep-seated worldviews concerning sex, the body, and free will. Noticeably, not all women drawn to feminism took up this call. "There were issues that you could never touch," observed Montes. Latinos' religious values would make it difficult to organize around birth control and abortion, she noted, and one "needed to be careful" with these matters. Moreno and her colleagues in Concilio thought differently and placed themselves on a "very militant, radical side of [those] issue[s]."[85] Donna Amador and others in the women's caucus of the LSDC likewise tackled some culturally sensitive topics. The LSDC's socialist leanings and critique of religious authority surely influenced these activists' decisions. Concilio's members, for their part, found inspiration in analyses offered by Chicana feminists at conferences and in published materials. Attendees at a Chicana Regional Conference in 1971, for example, levied charges against religious authorities for "defining and limiting" women's lives. They asserted, "The Church has supported the necessity to keep the woman ignorant, barefoot and pregnant by condemning legal abortions and birth control."[86] Conference participants and their allies in Concilio cast this state of affairs as an impediment to women's autonomy and self-determination, pertaining to their bodies specifically and life conditions more broadly.

Many Latina feminists found the convergence of conservative cultural values, gender role socialization, and constraints on female sexual autonomy troubling. The interplay of these social forces, explained Del Drago, Anna Lange, and other contributors to *La Razón Mestiza*, stymied women's identities, choices, and experiences. Gendered scripts about comportment and corporeality, they noted, produced a marked divergence in men's and women's sexual subjectivities. Del Drago specifically criticized the workings of a traditional matrix dependent on disparate codes and messages concerning sex, body, and desire. The framework encouraged sexual experimentation, knowledge, competency, and control among men, yet emphasized virginity, innocence, submission, and silence for women. "We Latinas are not encouraged to be articulate about any part of our experience," Del Drago lamented. "We are painfully shy about our bodies and about sex." Others concurred. Anna Lange deplored how "knowledge about our bodies has been denied to us." She continued, "It is particularly galling that knowledge peculiar to ourselves, i.e., about our reproductive system, should be withheld."[87] Lange and her allies challenged this status quo by questioning religious teachings and culturally constructed practices viewed as natural and accepted for time immemorial. In countering conservative principles pertaining to female sexuality, Latina feminists hoped to turn silences into communication, deference into autonomy, and notions of fixed traditions into considerations about well-being and cultural regeneration.

Guided by a culturally liberal ethos, Latina feminists created spaces and projects offering information, peer support, and services addressing questions of self-image, the body, and sexual life. Well-established community institutions continued to defer to cultural conservatism; their staffs generally avoided discussions about reproductive rights, mounted limited sex education programming, and replicated sexual silences. Feminists in Concilio and the LSDC departed from these conventions; they believed women's health, autonomy, and overall sense of self depended on open dialogue and knowledge about the sexual realm. Concilio offered counseling and workshops on human sexuality, parenting, and sex roles. The sessions led by Moreno and her counterparts included "talking about abortion, family [life], preventive pregnancies, the whole thing." Female health educators at the LSDC's free clinic offered related advice and pointed women to Planned Parenthood. Among them, Amador counseled Latinas on "how to take care of themselves personally so that they didn't have to have fifteen kids or how to help their husbands also understand [their] role."[88] As these activists saw it, discussion and information about reproductive rights, family size, and sexual decision-making would prove healthier for women and their loved ones—emotionally, psychologically, and economically. Their labors became the manifestation of their feminist vision—bucking cultural conservatism in the name of self-determination, well-being, and social change.

The Birth of the Gay Latino Alliance

Latina feminists in Concilio and the LSDC typically approached questions of gender and sexuality through a heterosexual lens. Assumptions about opposite-sex relationships and households often colored their deliberations on family dynamics and gender roles. Though feminist activists critiqued male power and privilege, challenging the workings of heterosexual privilege and the silences surrounding sexual identity proved more limited. Latina feminists' diverse stances on homosexuality influenced, at least in part, this situation. Some activists approached the issue neutrally while others viewed homosexuality as incompatible with Latino cultures. In February 1975, *La Razón Mestiza* announced the publication of a poetry collection by a gay Chicana. The only commentary accompanying the notice read, "Whether Chicana gay is here to stay or not is hardly the question."[89] Acknowledging the diversity of Latinas' sexual lives on one hand, editors intimated the existence of conflicting perspectives on gayness on the other.

Indeed, some feminists raised concerns about the compatibility between homosexuality and their cultural heritage. Patricia San Miguel Gonzalez, writing in 1975, derided increased attention to lesbianism and sexual pleasure. "I do not believe we need the experience of self diversion of sexual energies or with others of the same sex," she expounded. "We have our own culture and we should be respected for our beliefs." She may have been responding to growing considerations of sex as a leisure activity or the radical proposition that women's full equality depended on complete extrication from men—one made by lesbian separatists.[90] By suggesting that lesbianism was incongruent with her culture, she conveyed a commonplace perspective held by many heterosexual Latinos. They branded homosexuality as a foreign practice and incompatible with Latino cultural life. Under this traditional perspective, Latinos could not be gay or lesbian, or, put differently, homosexuality existed outside the cultural matrix of latinidad.

Men and women involved in the Gay Latino Alliance testified otherwise and set out to shatter that worldview. Created in 1975, GALA became the city's first organization of gay Latino men and lesbian Latinas—and one of the earliest outfits of its kind in the nation. Some fifty individuals attended planning meetings to establish a group to challenge Latino cultural conservatism and dedicate itself "to the struggles of our rights as Gay Latinos."[91] Strongly attached to their cultural heritage and proud of their gayness, activists pledged to fight racism, homophobia inside and outside Latino settings, and other injustices faced by other oppressed peoples—locally, nationally, and abroad. Their initial locus of activity became their ethnoracial community. After all, as Eddi Baca put it, "We are oppressed within our own Latino culture. [There is] the denial that we exist."[92] Baca and his comrades in GALA made clear that they did.

GALA emerged as Latinos expanded their quest for political empowerment and the city's gay liberation movement flourished. Its founders proclaimed, "Gay Latinos, inspired by the struggles and victories of oppressed people throughout the world have said '*BASTA YA*' and have joined the liberation struggles." The pursuit of emancipation demanded that their sociopo-

Figure 9. Gay Latino Alliance marching in the 1979 Gay Freedom
March and Rally. Courtesy of Archivo Rodrigo Reyes, under the
stewardship and courtesy of L. A. Campos de la Garza.

litical collective address the personal, cultural, and structural obstacles
confronted by its members and others not yet ready to join the group. Attending to multiple layers of social existence, activists consistently affirmed
the "humanity of gay people" and worked to dismantle damaging attitudes
and practices, which often resulted in fear, rejection, and violence.[93] GALA
coordinated social functions, offered peer support to individuals as they
came to terms with their sexual identities, referred gay Latinos to places
where they could access social services, participated in gay pride events, and
built alliances with other local gay organizations. Its members also engaged
in community education, advocacy, and electoral politics. They undertook
all these activities while claiming "their right to a place" in Latinos' social
world. "Early on we decided that we were to be an organization that was part
of the Latino community," detailed Rodrigo Reyes, one of the collective's
founders. "We did not want to become another sub-group of the white gay
community."[94]

GALA's engagement with its ethnoracial community proceeded at an ideological level and through everyday interactions. Its members first sought to

fracture culturally conservative views about homosexuality and then link gay oppression to other forms of inequality. The collective identified and denounced cultural conventions that silenced, devalued, and harmed gay men, lesbians, and other queer people. It specified, "Throughout our growing up experience we are taught that men do not cry . . . that they cannot have gentle feelings towards other men. As women we are taught not to be aggressive . . . or independent. Non-conformists are pressured into place through ridicule, physical and mental assaults and even murder."[95]

Gay Latinos endeavored to curb harmful attitudes, expectations, and practices by upending traditional understandings of culture, history, and fate. Cultural codes and customs involving gender and sexuality, they told their straight counterparts, were not "natural instincts." Instead, institutions invested in maintaining their stronghold over familial and sexual life, including the Church and the state, constructed and reproduced value systems sanctioning some sexual practices and proscribing others. GALA members went further and argued against the assumption that "heterosexuality is manifest destiny."[96] Pointing to the existence of homosexuality in other historical and cultural contexts—as well as their own lived experience—they disputed two common notions held by heterosexual Latinos. Sexual identity was not predetermined by God, gay activists insisted, and heterosexuality did not represent the only normal, stable course of human development.

These perspectives formed part of GALA's ideological armor, which activists used to mount their appeal for justice, equity, and freedom. Pressing for an inclusive and diverse recognition of sexual desires and identities, the organization raised the banner of self-determination to advocate for lives devoid of prejudice and repression. Adopting this potent philosophy aligned gay Latinos' pursuit of freedom and autonomy with the aspirations of their heterosexual counterparts and other marginalized populations. "We claim the right to shape our own destinies," read GALA's constitution. In making this assertion, the collective conveyed that a quest for self-determination should not be bounded by sexual identity or dependent on heterosexuality. It concurrently linked the eradication of all forms of injustice with a full realization of freedom. Urging solidarity among all marginalized peoples, gay Latinos underscored how a truly open, fair, and equitable world hinged on acknowledging everyone's humanity, supporting others' programs for liberation, and engaging in coalitional work. "If we are to succeed in the struggle for a society free of exploitation and oppression by one people over another," GALA noted in 1976, "we must all, gay and straight, young and old, join hands."[97]

Dispelling culturally conservative views about homosexuality and finding common cause with other Latinos could not occur through philosophical discussions alone. GALA members understood so and therefore immersed themselves in community politics as openly gay people; this decision became their grounded strategy to foster greater interaction and garner support from straight Latinos. From the mid-1970s into the early 1980s, they participated in organizing drives that did not center exclusively on questions of homosexuality. Gay Latinos collaborated with Latina feminists to halt violence against women; worked to elect a heterosexual Latino to the San Francisco Board of Supervisors when the city transitioned to district elections in 1977; and supported Central Americans' opposition to authoritarian regimes in the isthmus.[98] The organization also moderated heightened frictions between Latinos and a growing gay population settling in the Mission District. In the process, GALA reminded the public of two indisputable facts: not all Latinos were straight, and not all gay people were white.

Through their public presence, personal reflection, and political work, GALA members pushed heterosexual Latinos to reconsider their views on homosexuality and gay people in Latino life. Paralleling Latina feminists' agenda, these activists challenged conservative perspectives concerning gender roles and sexual subjectivity. Traditional censures of same-sex relations, they argued, harmed members of their own ethnoracial community, compromised a commitment to civil rights, and impeded Latinos' overall quest for progress. Cultural conservatism and repression, gay Latinos felt, had to be replaced with a valorization of everyone's humanity and all peoples' quest for autonomy and freedom. In the early 1980s, reflecting on the significance of the Fourth of July, Reyes made a powerful correlation between racial and sexual injustice. Racism and homophobia "reduce us to less than human beings," he declared. "They both stem from feelings of superiority."[99] As he and others in GALA had done since the mid-1970s, his comments urged heterosexual Latinos, white gays and lesbians, and other marginalized communities to acknowledge the relational workings of oppression and commit themselves to a comprehensive vision for liberation.

The terms of engagement between culturally conservative Latinos and their culturally liberal counterparts generally proved tepid. Though passionate about their positions, individuals and groups from both camps regularly spoke over each other. They occasionally listened to opposing views yet frequently dismissed clashing perspectives. Still, their ideological tug-of-war exposed crucial reflections and divisions over tradition and liberation in

Latino life. Attention to gender and sexuality matters politicized dominant cultural outlooks and assumptions regarding male authority, female autonomy, family life, and heterosexuality. Culturally conservative Latinos stressed that communal well-being and advancement depended on the promotion of conventional family arrangements, adherence to long-standing cultural traditions, and an affirmation of religious morality. Feminists, gay men and lesbians, and their allies disagreed. Progress and liberation, they argued, lay in the erosion of gender inequity, female dependence on men, heterosexual bias, and repression of sexual life. These divergent perspectives held important consequences for the course of community politics. Cultural values and sexuality would soon figure prominently—and more heatedly—in struggles over housing, education, and civil rights.

CHAPTER 7

"We Must Unite with All Struggling People"

Gentrification, Gay Rights, and Neighborhood Politics

Eddi Baca and other GALA members positioned themselves at the center of a confrontation involving public accommodations, homosexuality, and Latino cultural sensibilities in fall 1976. Controversy ensued as Mrs. V. Bourgeault and Meg Goldfeather attempted to open a new bar and eatery in the Inner Mission. The entrepreneurs hoped the venue at 24th Street and South Van Ness Avenue would cater to women and primarily attract a female clientele. Upon learning of this plan, LaREAL initiated a "campaign to prevent SISTER'S SPEAKEASY from becoming a lesbian restaurant." The radical, nationalist organization led by brothers Al and Gary Borvice summoned concerned residents, merchants, and community organizations to a forum in mid-September, where they discussed the "adverse effects" the restaurant would supposedly generate. A gay business located within a hub of Latino commercial and public life, attendees concluded, would "threaten the family and cultural character of this community." Branding gayness as antifamily and outside the sociocultural cartography of latinidad, they pledged to impede the opening of this establishment and others like it.[1] Mounting antagonism, negative publicity, and an alleged arson attempt quickly convinced the owners "to change the character of the new restaurant from 'gay' to 'family' style." LaREAL and its allies rejoiced over this decision, even as they found themselves on the defensive. A subsequent meeting in late September brought the "anti-gay" contingent face to face with well-known gay and lesbian leaders, Mission residents with more open perspectives, and, most important, given the issues at hand, gay Latinos. Emphatically claiming a place in the

Mission, culturally and geographically, Baca and his counterparts told the audience gay people belonged in the district. They pressed for recognition and the protection of all gay persons' rights. In so doing, gay Latinos asked their straight counterparts to think capaciously about inclusion, nondiscrimination, and civil rights. Some went further and identified a need and potential for coalitional work. Among them, Jack Trujillo "called for cooperation and understanding to solve the mutual problems of discrimination."[2]

The potential for solidarity was not yet discernible to forces opposed to Sister's Speakeasy. Their resistance actually hinged on much more than cultural politics. Activists and residents who viewed gayness as culturally foreign coupled those perspectives with economic anxieties largely grounded in housing predicaments. Construing homosexuality as an affront to Latinos' cultural and moral traditions, the bar's foes concomitantly posited that gay people posed a risk to communal cohesion and residential viability. "We do not want what happened in the Eureka Valley to happen in the Mission," heralded a flyer disseminated by LaREAL. Here, the organization referenced the changes unfolding in the Castro—a neighborhood rapidly transforming into an epicenter of gay male life—and portrayed gay migration and settlement as processes that resulted in the dislocation of families and an escalation of rental prices.[3]

Some gay Latinos refuted these views easily and unequivocally. Others held more nuanced positions and did not discount the possibility that white gay men and lesbians influenced—and perhaps constrained—the economic circumstances of all Latinos, irrespective of sexual identity. Baca himself acknowledged that the "touchy situation" ignited by the bar raised questions about how newcomers' opportunities and profits affected long-term residents.[4] The causal linkage between gay-identified people and housing troubles, then, seemed debatable and qualifiable. One thing was definitely clear: the contention over a social venue for lesbian women had little to do with leisure and merriment. Instead, it exposed how historical actors deployed their social identities to register a sense of place, to claim rights, and to safeguard resources amid a climate of economic vulnerability.

In the mid- to late 1970s, housing, political representation, and civil rights converged and swayed Latinos' political energies. Bleak housing prospects and rising rents generated ongoing communal concern during these years—a blanket preoccupation that fit within a long-standing fear of displacement. Outlooks on gay rights, on the other hand, proved more variable. Latinos simply did not adhere to a unified or unwavering position on homosexuality. Cultural conservatism remained potent, but it was not absolute; in fact, a deference to civil rights tempered and sometimes overrode it. The range of nondiscrimination and mounting housing anxieties took center stage—sometimes overlapping—in campaigns for neighborhood power, electoral reform, gay rights, and rent control. By participating in these drives, more and more Latinos, both gay and straight, collaborated with other San Franciscans drawn to a progressive, coalitional ethos. The editors of *El Teco-lote*, a leftist newspaper and media collective, underscored the imperative of building common cause among residents—irrespective of race, class, and sexual orientation—early on. "We must unite with all struggling people," they told their readers in 1976.[5] Other community organizations, activists, and residents soon followed suit. Together, they set out to capsize discrimination and exclusion based on multiple social differences, and challenged the manifestations of a political economy—including housing speculation and regressive taxation—that harmed working people and racial minorities. Reminiscent of progressive unionists of the 1930s and 1940s, Latinos and their allies in a 1970s' coalitional front sought economic stability and fairness, while pressing for an expanded commitment to civil rights.

Displacement, Planning, and Sexualized Spaces in the Early to Mid-1970s

Few issues spawned persistent disquiet and received continuous attention as much as those involving housing. Fears of displacement proved common and potent, even a decade after Missionites defeated the SFRA's urban renewal plan. Community activists and organizations remained vigilant about new proposals or ventures that could result in higher rents, evictions, and dislocation. *El Tecolote* consistently detailed Latinos' housing woes and preoccupations as the 1970s wore on. Its team also played a key role in sustaining the memory of the 1960s' urban renewal fight and linking that struggle to contemporary housing tribulations—in both written and visual forms. A July 1976 review of Latinos' living conditions included a photograph of a bilingual poster that read "*No Queremos Salir* (We Don't Want to Go)."[6] This could well have been a banner from 1960s campaigns or from recent demonstrations.

In November 1973, a group calling itself the Mission Defense Committee (MDC) disrupted the ceremonies to mark the opening of two BART stations. Local politicians and transit agency officials, including Mayor Alioto, praised the transportation system and reiterated their boilerplate messages. They emphasized that BART would serve as an engine of economic growth and "reconstruction" of the Mission. Residents in tenant groups, LaREAL, and others drawn to the MDC agreed that the transit system would propel change, but they did not believe the prosperity would benefit them. Municipal and metropolitan growth, they deduced, would occur at their expense. Their placards conveyed their views acutely; some of these read "BART Means People Removal" and "Housing for People, Not Profit for BART."[7] These sentiments were not new; BART's completion merely intensified citizens' furor and anxiety.

Though public officials and their supporters downplayed the critiques, communal restlessness persisted and invigorated calls for rent control. Some Missionites increasingly deduced that displacement could well occur without a formal urban renewal program. The forces of growth liberalism, it appeared, remained intent on fortifying a political economy built on market yields rather than public good. Rent control presented a key antidote to this profit-driven orientation. Prosperity depended on stability and community, the MDC, LaREAL, *El Tecolote*, and other like-minded institutions noted, not on vulnerability and potential uprootedness. In advocating rent control, community activists stressed a desire to protect and prioritize the housing needs of existing residents, who could well find themselves displaced by speculation and new construction stimulated by BART.

Tenants were not the only ones who feared displacement. Joseph Bonilla, James Ursino, and other small business owners harbored related apprehensions. Their premonitions found an anchor in plans to open a McDonald's at 24th and Mission Streets, directly across from a new BART station. Five months before the station opened, in June 1973, restaurant owners Bonilla and Ursino petitioned the city's Board of Permit Appeals to revoke the municipal permit for the fast-food restaurant. Their challenge was simple: they attacked McDonald's for its practice of undercutting competitors and for paving the way for other chain businesses to enter the neighborhood, which the men believed would spawn the closure of locally owned establishments. The MDC, the MCO, LaREAL, and other community organizations concurred. Bonilla and Ursino do not appear to have belonged to these groups; their action nevertheless garnered impressive grassroots support.

Halting McDonald's arrival turned into a communal campaign. Community groups bolstered the economic analysis with a cultural argument. The chain restaurant profited from selling homogenized, inferior food, critics asserted, that did not "cater to the ethnic tastes of our multi-ethnic community."[8] Missionites' opposition to the fast-food chain resonated across the city. Only two McDonald's stores operated in San Francisco in 1973; other communities, including Nob Hill, had managed to convince public servants to deny permits for the franchise's expansion. Bonilla, Ursino, and their supporters hoped to build on this precedent; they instead met bureaucratic delays and court hearings spanning one year. In June 1974, the permit appeals board finally heard the case—allotting time for public comment—and then voted to allow the McDonald's plan to proceed.[9]

The decision hinged on a number of factors, some concrete and others more conjectural. Some business owners, especially ones in the Mission Merchants Association (MMA), actually backed McDonald's. The MMA had long supported redevelopment and ventures viewed as a potential boost for the district's economic landscape. "I don't see why people want to obstruct progress," Frank Hunt told a reporter many months before the public hearing. Actively involved in the MMA and the proprietor of a doughnut shop, Hunt owned the land where McDonald's would sit. He and his allies likely exerted more influence with the permit board—made up of political appointees—because their association had a history of cultivating relationships with political and economic power brokers outside the Mission. Permit board members, of course, may have independently concluded that this district, unlike high-income Nob Hill, needed a big-profile and profit-yielding business to spur more outside investment. Such an assessment would have legitimized the vision of BART promoters, redevelopment proponents, and the MMA. The alignment of these interests seemed quite clear to many restaurant opponents. "McDonald's is just the beginning of the massive BART-related redevelopment scheme that the city planners have concocted for the Mission," noted an *El Tecolote* writer even before the appeals board issued its decision.[10]

McDonald's impending opening disillusioned many Missionites but did not cripple their resolve to influence local development initiatives—be they residential, commercial, or physical in nature. The MCO had nurtured much of this conviction, especially through its housing and planning committees. Activists in these circles led the way in mobilizing residents and crafting an agenda that prioritized the construction of affordable housing, encouraged homeownership, and promoted community-owned enterprises. The MCO as a whole supported these priorities and believed it critical to protect neighborhood businesses from corporate encroachment, which explained its disapproval of McDonald's. Many coalition members likewise worried that BART's presence would result in high rents and that its operation, combined with heavy automobile traffic on such streets as Bryant and Guerrero, would turn the Mission into "a highway for S.F. peninsula commuters."[11]

Proactively and on various fronts, the MCO's action committees and the Mission Housing Development Corporation—a community agency created with Model Cities monies—set out to direct local planning and zoning processes. Their proposals ran the gamut from big to small. In the early 1970s, the MCO, the development corporation, and their community partners sought public funds to build 130 units of subsidized, low- and moderate-income housing on a site where a brewery had once operated, at 20th and Harrison Streets. The coalition obtained support and buy-in from the city's planning department and the SFRA, an impressive sign of consensus given the history of tensions between official planning bodies and Mission organizations. To their frustration, federal officials at HUD rejected the request on grounds that the property was too costly and that its industrial location "would have a deteriorating effect on housing." Coalition members and their allies disagreed with this particular evaluation, even as they acknowledged the existence of other obstructions to Missionites' quality of life. Virginia Orozco and others working with the MCO's planning committee identified traffic conditions as one such obstacle. In November 1973, they persuaded the city's Public Works Department to adjust the flow and design of four blocks along Harrison and Bryant, near 24th Street. Changing the traffic lanes from four to two, adding diagonal parking, and widening the sidewalk, Orozco and her neighbors explained, "would promote safety" and "provide more open space and greenery."[12] Given the number of blocks covered, the project and public functionaries' assent presented a small but significant triumph. It surely inspired other residents to consider similar experiments. And it reminded all Missionites of their potential to shape what their district looked like and whose needs should be prioritized.

One of the most watched—and victorious—campaigns at mid-decade involved the land-use classification of twelve blocks abutting the 24th and Mission BART station. In late 1974, LaREAL and the Mission Planning Council (MPC) filed a joint application with the city's planning department, proposing to rezone Capp and Bartlett Streets directly east and west of Mission. The MPC emerged earlier that year and aimed to improve the built environment "for all people who now live or work in the district."[13] Its founders, Latinos and whites, had been active in the MCO's planning committee but became disillusioned with the coalition as ideological divisions made day-to-day organizing difficult. Luisa Ezquerro, Toby and Jerry Levine, Ramon Barbieri, Jack and Bonnie Bourne, and others gravitated to it because they felt the MCO had abandoned its original philosophy. The coalition "was too disrupted," recalled Toby Levine, "[and] we weren't able to do what we thought we needed to do."[14] In collaborating with LaREAL, MPC members found themselves collaborating with activists who had once criticized them. Their independence from the MCO and knowledge of planning matters must have been appealing for activists in the nationalist organization. LaREAL's maturation as a community institution likely encompassed an understanding that engagement with the state did not automatically equate with dependence on government money.

Finding common ground on Mission rezoning, the two groups rallied tenants and homeowners and set out the change the classification of a dozen blocks from commercial to residential. The initiative grew out of now-familiar, grassroots concerns: BART-driven development, land speculation, and displacement. Although the blocks in question primarily served a residential function at this time, the commercial designation left the area open for new business activities and speculative enterprises. Activists and residents worried that private developers would purchase this valuable land, evict tenants from existing housing, and raze old structures to make room for large department stores, office buildings, and parking lots.[15] Redevelopment and displacement could potentially proceed entirely under private hands—a possibility that unsettled the MPC-LaREAL alliance and propelled their response.

Community groups once again "lock[ed] horns" with Mission development boosters. The MMA and the Greater San Francisco Chamber of Commerce insisted that rezoning would "strangle the Mission shopping district" by not allowing the commercial sector to expand. Avoiding questions of speculation and displacement, merchants cast rezoning as a restraint on job creation and "the death knell of Mission Street as YOUR business community." Economic development, the merchants suggested, justified compromising on residential stability.[16] Planning authorities and most elected officials disagreed with business stakeholders on this occasion. In April 1975, the city's Planning Commission voted unanimously to rezone the area; an overwhelming majority of supervisors (ten out of eleven) followed suit eight weeks later. Municipal leaders' impressive decision boiled down to philosophical outlooks and pragmatic considerations. Some supervisors committed themselves to the preservation of family housing and possibly shared residents' presentiments about speculation and displacement. Others relied on extant evidence: 84 percent of the Capp and Bartlett area was already residential, and the rezoning plan did not affect main arteries, such as Mission, South Van Ness, or Valencia Streets. Elected officials' individual rationales ultimately appeared less newsworthy than their collective approval of the communal petition. In late May 1975, *El Tecolote* commended LaREAL, the MPC, and their allies for convincing the supervisors "not to sacrifice 700 low and moderate housing units ... to speculators seeking to increase land values because of BART."[17]

Divided over land use near the BART corridor, the MPC, LaREAL, and the MMA did identify a foe they all considered detrimental to residential and commercial life: pornography. Two months after the rezoning fight ended, these organizations joined forces with block clubs and religious congregations to halt the presence and "proliferation of pornographic book stores and movies" near the 16th and Mission Street area. Communal unease over pornography, as discussed in Chapter 6, was not new. The differences now lay in greater organizational coordination and the strategies used "to keep other smut businesses" from locating in the Mission. Branding itself Operation Upgrade, the alliance of civic, religious, and business groups identified a desire to "live in a healthy, safe, friendly and stimulating environment" as its "common denominator."[18] Reverend John Loya at El Buen Pastor, Toby Levine from the MPC, and their allies believed the "pornie parlors" jeopardized the community's well-being in myriad ways. Pornography, its critics charged, harmed children's development by exposing them to sexually explicit material, offended residents' moral sensibilities, deterred "clean businesses" from opening or remaining in the district, and attracted "elements"—city residents as well as suburbanites—who engaged in disorderliness, drug dealing, and other perilous activities.[19]

Others in the city and country shared some or all of these sentiments. Earlier in the decade, residents and merchants in North Beach asked the Board of Permit Appeals to revoke the permits of three adult movie houses in that district and met with success. A concentration of porn shops, they had argued, "hamper[ed] the [area's] beautification" and "disturbed residents and visitors alike."[20] Missionites in Operation Upgrade built on such precedents and organized to defeat a theater permit for the Mission News Adult Store in July 1975. For two summers, anti-porn activists also staged "'community pornographic tour[s]'" and "clean up" meetings. The events publicized organizational aims, sensationalized the situation, and conveyed communal determination to halt porn shops' operation and expansion.[21] By 1977, Operation Upgrade and its citywide counterparts bid welcome to Supervisor Dianne Feinstein's proposal to "prevent undue concentration of [porno-graphic] enterprises." The linchpin of the "Feinstein Porno Ordinance," as some observers labeled it, required all new porn businesses be located at least a thousand yards from one already in existence. Unanimous approval by the city's Board of Supervisors and Mayor George Moscone's signature in Octo-ber 1977 confirmed for many that San Francisco had gotten "tough with porn."[22] Loya, Levine, and other Missionites applauded the development.

Activists and community groups connected with Operation Upgrade, re-markably, did not focus their attention on commercial establishments and social spaces accessed by gay men and lesbians. This state of affairs proved striking given earlier linkages between pornography and homosexuality and objections to both. Overlooking leisure spaces frequented by gay people could have indicated a lack of concern, an evolving set of views on homo-sexuality, or perhaps a form of compromise since views on gayness were not as clear-cut as those involving porn.

Mission-based venues for gay sociality flourished at mid-decade. The Inner Mission housed five bars or restaurants frequented by gay people in 1974. Four of these leisure spots (Dogpatch Saloon, Kelly's Saloon, Connie's Why Not, and Fickle Fox) were located within a small quadrant bounded by Mission and Valencia Streets (east to west) and 18th and 20th Streets (north to south). Three of these establishments catered to lesbians; none appear to have operated or marketed themselves as gay Latino or lesbian Latina spaces.[23] In-dividuals seeking spiritual nourishment could turn to the local congregation of the Metropolitan Community Church—a gay-affirming ministry founded in Southern California in 1968. Services began taking place on Guerrero Street, between 22nd and 23rd Streets, in 1973 and the church remained there for years. Men whose interests lay in carnal pleasures could find fulfillment at the 21st Street Baths, near Bartlett Street and only three blocks away from the new 24th and Mission BART station. This bathhouse had been operating there since at least the early 1970s.[24] To be sure, the men and women who gathered in these places came from various neighborhoods and suburban areas. But some gay-identified San Franciscans, including Latinos, lived in the Mission. More sought to do so as the controversy over Sister's Speakeasy erupted in September 1976.

An "Influx of Gays," the "Speculation Cancer," and Gentrification

Sister's Speakeasy obviously did not signal the onset of gay-oriented leisure spaces in the Mission. On the contrary, the businesswomen attempted to expand an existing commercial landscape. The outcry from LaREAL activists, their allies, and the residents they mobilized, on the other hand, was indeed novel. Their hostility did not hinge exclusively or predominantly on homophobia and cultural conservatism. Many heterosexual Latinos may well have been unaware of gay venues already in operation. Yet it seems implausible that activists familiar with commercial life, including the arrival of Mc-Donald's and the Mission News Adult Store, did not know about any of the aforementioned spaces catering to gay people. Kelly's Saloon and its counterparts were located in the heart of the Mission, not in the district's periphery. The 24th Street strip arguably held more cultural and emotive significance because key institutions, including St. Peter's Church and the CCSS, sat in close proximity to where Sister's Speakeasy would have operated.

Controversy over gay people in St. Peter's parish had actually ensued years earlier. In 1973, heterosexual Catholics from near and far protested a decision to allow the city's Dignity chapter—an organization for gay Catholics—to use church space for its meetings. Notably, dissent did not come from Latinos, who represented the largest ethnoracial group in the parish. Latino Catholics failed to notice, chose to ignore, or tolerated the presence of Dignity at St. Peter's. Neither individual parishioners nor the CCSS raised complaints with the Catholic hierarchy or mounted any collective protest.[25] Turning a blind eye to Dignity or Kelly's Saloon, of course, signaled neither acceptance nor an embrace of homosexuality. But the practice suggested that cultural conservatism in itself was not enough to ignite the challenge to a new lesbian bar.

The roots of resistance to Sister's Speakeasy lay in a long-standing struggle against displacement, economic precariousness, and trepidation about the breakup of an ethnoracial enclave marked as Latino. A history of opposition to urban renewal, BART, McDonald's, and porn shops was not just contextual but central to this 1976 contest. "Our community has the right to self-determination," noted LaREAL and its followers. "We have struggled against: Redevelopment, Bart, Pornography, Pawn Shops, and Drug Addiction in the past and will continue to do so."[26] These Latinos viewed this bar's operation as the latest manifestation of an enduring scheme to deracinate them and their culture from the Mission. Timing proved essential here: activists learned about plans for this lesbian establishment as restlessness over housing speculation, displacement, and gay migration to the district intertwined and escalated. The *Bay Area Reporter*, a mainstream gay newspaper, later identified Latinos' commotion over Sister's Speakeasy as a turning point in citywide deliberations over "Gay impact on San Francisco's housing patterns."[27]

Latino homophobia was by no means inconsequential. LaREAL's activists relied on religious dogma to cast homosexuality as immoral, arouse residents, and bring them into their campaign.[28] In this way, cultural conservatism functioned as a catalyst for action. It was neither the core nor the underlying cause for resentment and opposition to Sister's Speakeasy. High rents generated by real estate speculation "have been at the root of the hostility of ethnic minorities against gay people," concluded Manuel Castells in his scholarly investigation of tensions between Latinos and white gay men migrating from the Castro into the Mission. The sociologist did not discount the significance of Latino cultural conservatism, but he did not classify it as the principal determinant of troubles either. "Class hate, ethnic rage, and fear of displacement by the invaders," Castells concluded, "have clearly held greater sway than prejudices from family traditions or machismo ideology."[29]

The Castro as a gay—and predominantly white and male—enclave took shape in the 1970s. Long known as Eureka Valley, the area west of Dolores Park and south of upper Market Street experienced a large-scale migration and residential concentration of gay men during this decade.[30] Gay bars, restaurants, a variety of specialty shops, and community institutions clustered on and near Castro Street. This development first led to a territorial designation of Castro Village, and eventually just the Castro. The success of the "gay mecca" and "gay ghetto," as some observers and scholars dubbed it, could be seen in its popularity, vibrant commercial life, renovated Victorian buildings, increased property values, and a rental market steadily on the rise. Soaring rents, speculators' and realtors' business acumen, and gay residents' desire to live in close proximity to the Castro merged and produced a "spill-over effect" by the mid- to late 1970s.[31] Missionites and African Americans in the lower Western Addition (often called the Fillmore and later the Lower Haight) increasingly witnessed the arrival of new people, which a television reporter described as "affluent . . . white . . . male . . . and gay."[32]

White gay people certainly formed a significant and noticeable share of new residents in the Mission, but the newcomers were not all wealthy or male. Some had never lived in the Castro and had settled in the neighboring district earlier in the decade. "Since the early seventies the Mission District has seen a steady influx of gays," detailed a collective known as Lesbians Against Police Violence (LAPV). Organized in the late 1970s, its members clarified that white lesbians found it difficult to afford rents elsewhere and turned to "Latino neighborhoods, because that is the only place they can live as well."[33] Lower earnings sustained by a gender pay gap typically impelled lesbians, single mothers, and other women who lived apart from men to procure cheaper housing. Some lesbians concurrently found gay men's social world uninteresting or unwelcoming and desired to create lesbian spaces. According to historian Anne Enke, lesbians and feminists of the 1970s sought "social space in which to assemble independently of men" and create "meeting grounds to encourage lesbian, feminist lesbian, and/or feminist activism and self-determination."[34] Feminist lesbian Ruth Mahaney arrived in San Francisco in 1971 and quickly discovered that "more of the women's stuff" existed in the Mission. She recounted, "In the early 70s that's where most of the lesbians were sort of moving or had apartments."[35]

Lesbian bars, women-owned bookstores, and feminist institutions had sprouted in the district—especially on or just off Valencia Street—by mid-decade.[36] Notably, the women who created and supported these venues did not necessarily expect to replicate the Castro's trajectory. They did not envision changing the Mission's name; establishing a neighborhood economy built around consumption, sexual excess, and profit; or elevating property values and rental prices. LAPV activists actually contrasted white lesbians' settlement from that of "white male homosexual professionals." Most Latinos did not tease out these class distinctions or consider the implications of gender in gay and lesbian life. LAPV assumed as much and acknowledged, "These two separate migrations are as seen as one by the Latinos being displaced and pinched economically, and hostility is directed against 'white queers' indiscriminately."[37]

Blocking Sister's Speakeasy exemplified one manifestation of Latino animus. Yet it did not deter white gays' settlement in the district or the establishment of new venues for sexual minorities. One of the most well-known feminist lesbian institutions—Old Wives' Tales Bookstore—opened its doors on Valencia Street in October 1976, a month after frictions over Sister's Speakeasy abated. By 1978, almost a dozen restaurants and bars catering to gay men and lesbians dotted the Inner Mission. One of these stood at 25th and South Van Ness, one block south from where the lesbian bar attempted to operate two years earlier.[38]

A painful episode, the Sister's Speakeasy fracas prompted some proactive responses and relationships in the long run. As 1976 came to a close, Operation Upgrade members affirmed a commitment "to decrease the hazards of our neighborhood life" and invited everyone who called the Mission home to join them. "We are not exclusionists," they stressed, vowing to respect residents' diversity—be it of "background, experience, ethnic identity [or] lifestyle." The lifestyle rubric implicitly included gays and possibly hippies and other nonconformist individuals. Missionites in Operation Upgrade essentially conveyed an acceptance of difference while denouncing "abuse of people in any form, personal or institutional."[39]

Activists in LaREAL, for their part, started to reassess their cultural intolerance and assumptions about homosexuality. They slowly came to understand that plans for "saving Latino culture and the Latino community" could proceed without reverting to homophobia. Face-to-face engagement with gay Latinos—first in tension and later in collaboration—proved critical here. "GALA really made its presence felt," remarked Reyes; its leaders pushed heterosexual Latinos to reconsider and expand notions of self-determination, equality, and community. Discussions with LaREAL were not easy, stress free, or immediately transformative. Yet GALA managed to garner "some hesitant respect" and kept lines of communication open.[40] Nurturing a relationship with LaREAL and other Latino groups may have been more imperative for GALA—at least at first—because gay Latinos also regarded the Mission as their cultural and political base. "GALA was rooted in the Mission, where many of its members lived and socialized," explained scholar-activist Horacio N. Roque Ramírez many years later.[41] Though sexual identities separated them, a strong identification as Latinos and concordant attention to their precarity soon served to foster alliances.

Community activists, residents, and chroniclers of everyday life—gay and straight alike—shared deep concerns about the vexing housing situation Latinos found themselves in. Holding onto and finding affordable housing proved increasingly challenging. Journalists offered extensive coverage of dire housing prospects and linked their observations to a budding demographic current. "Housing Problems Overwhelm San Francisco's Latino Community" and "Latinos Pushed Out" read two of countless news headlines from the late 1970s. In a reversal of trends from the early postwar period, residents of the Mission and the Western Addition—central-city areas once considered obsolete, unsafe, and unappealing by many whites—witnessed how parts of their districts became increasingly desirable and expensive. High demand and short supply yielded speculation, spiraling rents, and evictions. "While this problem has affected all city neighborhoods," wrote Margarita Sandoval in *El Mundo*, "it is the minority areas and the elderly on fixed incomes who have suffered the most painful and saddest consequences."[42]

Feeding off each other, the triumvirate of speculation, higher rents, and evictions spelled gentrification. Urban sociologists took up the term *gentrification* in the late 1970s to highlight the increase of white-collar professionals in low-income neighborhoods in the central city. The course of events in the Mission, Brooklyn's brownstone neighborhoods, and Chicago's Lincoln Park presented local variations of an emergent nationwide phenomenon.[43] Politically savvy writers for *El Tecolote* made sure to apprise Latinos of the racial and economic stakes. In 1978, they told readers that Latino families were "being forced out in order to make room for gentrification, or the rediscovery of inner city neighborhoods by young, white, affluent professionals." Some activists and journalists wondered, astutely, if the process amounted to redevelopment in new clothes or "urban renewal made simple." Residents themselves offered less bookish but still powerful analyses. The "final goal" of individuals profiting from the real estate bonanza, deduced Alfredo Vega, "is to drive us out of the neighborhood."[44]

Displacement and gentrification functioned as two sides of the same coin—one minted and manipulated by speculators, developers, and realtors. As the decade wore on, poor and working-class Latinos and other Missionites with limited means found themselves burdened by sharp and unexpected hikes in rents and property tax assessments. The choices before them proved limited and costly, materially and emotionally. They could opt to pay more for housing but compromise other life necessities (e.g., food, health care); vacate voluntarily or by force (i.e., evictions) if they rented; or sell quickly—and cheaply—if they had managed to become homeowners, which few of them had. Their former residences then underwent quick facelifts and mild improvements before new residents with higher incomes and more financial resources moved in. A 1978 political cartoon concisely depicted and impugned the process at work: the structures that once housed "the former element" (i.e., Latinos) only needed new paint to get them ready for the "young hip set [who] really go for these old Victorians."[45]

The movement of people by private, profit-driven hands presented significant gains for those who excelled at maneuvering the housing market: speculators and developers. Business-driven perspectives cast speculation as a financial gamble for private investors, one that could potentially spur economic improvement. Activists and advocacy journalists brushed aside this view. They instead branded the practice as degenerative, dangerous, and corrosive to the social fabric of working-class, ethnic communities. "Speculation is like a malignant cancer," admonished *El Tecolote*. "It starts quietly, low-keyed; but then moves quickly, spreading out, growing more and more vicious until finally destroying the body it's in."[46] The body in question was the Mission; its cancerous cells included high and rising rents and the frequent turnover of property. Ongoing metastasis, the media collective predicted, would result in wholesale displacement, the death of the Mission as they knew it, and its metamorphosis into a gentrified district.

Witnessing the transformation around them, some Latinos made a simple deduction and pegged gay people as the underlying source of higher rents and dislodgement. "The housing condition is terrible," a Latino tenant told a documentarian. "The gays have moved into this neighborhood . . . and consequently . . . the rents have gone up." Implicitly and explicitly, many Latinos also understood gentrification as a racial phenomenon. They knew so by witnessing the demographic shifts, talking to their neighbors, reading press coverage, and reviewing cartoons like the one discussed earlier. In what may have been the most potent statement on gentrification, race, and sexuality, one or more Missionites spray-painted the following phrases on a Liberty Street wall: *Es Mi Barrio. Stop White Gay Racism.*[47] These seven words conveyed critical messages that likely resonated with many Missionites. Latinos laid claim to the district and continued to regard it as their home. They felt beleaguered by the ongoing migration of white gay people who displaced them and gentrified the Mission. The gentrification transpiring before their eyes offered yet another example of racism at work because it hinged largely on the expulsion and exclusion of people of color.

White gay men and lesbians who identified themselves as antiracist, anti-imperialist, or socialist empathized with racial minorities' plight, and some of their political formulations overlapped with ones offered by Latinos. San Franciscans affiliated with Bay Area Gay Liberation (BAGL), Lesbian and Gay Action (LGA), and LAPV generally sought to connect gay liberation with "the liberation of Third World people and the working class as a whole."[48] How to best link multiple struggles against oppression and build solidarity sparked much reflection and generated philosophical and strategic variation among these groups. Their members did find common ground on some issues, including housing matters. Real estate speculation, gentrification, and the tensions arising between gay people and communities of color, they agreed, demanded keen attention. "We need to involve ourselves in the issue[s]," remarked Mark Freeman of the Housing Rights Study Group (HRSG), "because Gay people are intimately affected by changes in the neighborhoods." Activists from BAGL and LGA formed the HRSG in early 1977 to examine the "housing dilemma," as Gayle Rodgers noted. Through inquiry and activism, the HRSG and its partners aspired to claim a central place in deliberations about displacement and gentrification. They likewise hoped to foment collaborations between people of color—irrespective of sexual orientation—and white, working-class gay residents.[49]

A progressive vision guided left-leaning gay men's and women's analysis of the housing crisis. Their work proceeded from a commitment to recognize and value San Franciscans' diversity. Ethnic neighborhoods "make our city strong," asserted BAGL and LGA members in a joint statement. Yet skyrocketing rents, evictions, and "people removal" threatened local cultural richness and the preservation of a heterogeneous population, which they regarded as positive components of twentieth-century urban life. Activists in these circles concurrently underscored the heterogeneity of gay people, most of whom simultaneously lived as women, nonwhite persons, and working-class residents.[50] This acknowledgment proved imperative for countering misrepresentations of a homogenous gay subject (i.e., wealthy white male) encroaching on minority neighborhoods only populated by heterosexual residents. Simplistic assessments about gay people, in fact, deflected focus from the root of housing problems: speculation.

"Real estate speculators are playing monopoly with our homes—buying and selling overnight for huge profits," warned members of BAGL, LGA, and the HRSG. Women in LAPV soon issued an even more scathing indictment. "Speculators, often gay, have bought the old multi-family flats," detailed the lesbian collective, "[and] done superficial renovation while doubling or tripling the rents, thus forcing the Latinos out." Their observations affirmed what Latino activists suspected: the improvement efforts under way exemplified private redevelopment free of state oversight. And it amounted to ethnoracial cleansing. Speculators' and landlords' "game is racist," decried BAGL and LGA, "and anti-gay."[51]

Offering an insightful perspective on the housing quagmire, San Franciscans in these networks posited that speculation and gentrification harmed gay people as well. A housing shortage, varied income levels, and discrimination based on sexual orientation all limited the residential options for gay men and women. Speculators took advantage of these factors, activists in BAGL and LGA postulated, and used gay people "to 'bust' neighborhoods, pitting them against their neighbors." These schemes sustained a lush cycle of profits and a succession of displacement. "Gays themselves are [eventually] moved," HRSG members detailed, "unless they are the professional types preferred by real estate agencies" and had incomes that withstood unrestricted rental increases. Exploited by speculators and landlords, poor and working-class gay people concomitantly bore the brunt of rancor from long-standing residents in districts undergoing neighborhood change. Leftist activists' antidote for this state of affairs was multipronged: public education, community organizing, and cooperation among working people across racial and sexual identities. The housing crisis "provide[s] an urgent opportunity for united action," delineated the HRSG, "against the speculators, be they gay or straight, who are trying to ruin our neighborhoods in the name of Progress."[52]

The Promise and Disillusionment of District Elections

Mission activists had correlated housing predicaments, redevelopment, and electoral representation for years. In 1973, amid the McDonald's melee, a community reporter reproached an open-ended redevelopment agenda designed by banks and land developers and rubber-stamped by supervisors "'elected' by us, who do not live in or care about our community." Interrogating the extent to which current city leaders actually represented the citizenry, the commentator inferred that supervisors might behave differently if elected and held accountable at the community level.[53] The nearly one hundred activists gathered at Centro Latino—a community center offering basic social services (e.g., meals, recreational activities) to Latinos of all ages—in early January 1976 shared a similar instinct. Eight months before it derailed Sister's Speakeasy, LaREAL embarked on a more momentous and sustained campaign to elect supervisors by districts and replace the existing at-large process. Its partners included the host agency, the MPC, youth-serving organizations like Real Alternatives Program and Mission Youth Project, and Centro de Cambio—which offered supportive services to persons confronting drug addiction—among other groups backing the plan. Activists from Concilio Mujeres and GALA likely attended this event as well, even if sexuality, homophobia, and Latino cultural life were not issues under consideration. The same could not be said about race, class, housing, and redevelopment.

"Third World neighborhoods like the Mission," critics of the at-large system insisted, needed direct and robust representation in City Hall. Many Missionites remained convinced that working people's concerns took less precedence than, or came to be eclipsed by, the ambitions of corporate folks, wealthy residents, and suburbanites. They backed up these assertions by pointing to downtown development projects, the construction of BART, and supervisors' reluctance to advance "pro-working class reforms as rent control."[54] Leaders and members of the Mission's most prominent organizations therefore pledged to join an emergent citywide movement to place the district elections proposal on the November ballot. In so doing, they set out to wrestle formal political power from downtown interests and distribute it across city neighborhoods.

For twenty months, between January 1976 and August 1977, Latinos active in the aforementioned groups, connected with other circles, or as individuals participated in a citywide alliance known as San Franciscans for District Elections (SFDE). This citizens' federation included minority organizations, political clubs, labor unions, civic associations, gay groups, and other collectives from virtually every neighborhood. Its origins lay in earlier efforts, back in 1972 and 1973, to institute district elections, which fell short of popular support.[55] This time, the drive's leaders augmented grassroots outreach and brought many more community groups into its fold. The aim was straightforward: first, divide the city into eleven electoral districts; then, elect one supervisor from each district—individuals who lived in the area they sought to represent. Al Borvice, president of LaREAL, served on SFDE's steering committee, and his organization played a leading role in incorporating Latinos into the campaign. "At the very heart of district elections," he explained, "rests the firm belief that the people of San Francisco know better how to manage their affairs than the present aloof and special interest dominated majority on the Board today."[56]

Borvice's remarks acquired ideological sustenance from two crucial points disseminated by all in SFDE. First, the existing, at-large arrangement spawned a city council that was out of touch with most constituents. Second, district elections would rectify this situation by allowing voters to select "supervisors who must know about and respond to neighborhood problems to stay in office."[57] LaREAL, the MPC, and the Greater Mission Democratic Club were but a handful of Mission organizations promulgating these messages. Some district activists also joined other SFDE allies in gathering more than thirty-five thousand signatures to place the proposal—soon known as

Proposition T—on the fall ballot. The opposition, including conservative politicians, downtown business interests, and citizens content with the status quo, attacked Proposition T from multiple angles, often contending that the established method worked well and ensured "every voter has eleven supervisors who care about his or her views." Citizens' leverage in City Hall, they claimed, would diminish by only having one supervisor answerable to them. And they believed district elections would introduce "corrupt ward politics," which would supposedly result in supervisors and district political bosses fighting over services and resources.[58] Their arguments failed to convince a simple majority. Fifty-two percent of San Franciscans voting in November 1976 backed Proposition T. They reaffirmed this position the following summer when faced with an aggressive repeal initiative mounted by downtown forces. In August 1977, 58 percent of the city's electorate staved off a plan to invalidate Proposition T. More impressively, 75 percent of voters in the new District 6—which included the Mission and parts of South of Market—did so, "upholding district elections [by] 3 to 1."[59]

Aspirations for greater citizen representation and a diversified City Hall energized many Missionites and impelled them to favor—and stick with— Proposition T. SFDE leaders had regularly pointed out that district elections would "ensure a Board of Supervisors more representative of the city's diverse communities." Most Latino activists clung to this outlook and took it further. Editors at *El Tecolote* actually viewed the lack of minority representation on the legislative body as evidence of "racism [being] part and parcel of the at-large system." A city with a total nonwhite population hovering around 43 percent, according to some community advocates, needed more supervisors of color or representatives who took "minority viewpoints" seriously.[60] In 1976, two nonwhite supervisors (Terry Francois and Bob Gonzales) sat on the board; both men had been 1960s mayoral appointees and then elected through at-large voting. Gonzales's original appointment owed much to the maneuvering of Latino power brokers; he now allegedly "admit[ted] that he was not elected to articulate the interests" of Latinos or the Mission. Gonzales and Francois opposed district elections and aligned with forces seeking to repeal Proposition T—a position that stood at odds with most Latinos and African Americans at the grassroots.[61] In blocking the repeal effort in summer 1977, proponents of district elections could now focus on the upcoming fall campaign to choose their new supervisors.

Latinos inside and outside the Mission found the prospect of electing one of their ethnic kin to "defend our interests at City Hall" exhilarating. Raúl Moreno, former president of the CCSS and a regular columnist for *El Mundo*, acknowledged an intense communal "desire for one of our own to win and to represent us at the municipal palace." The fervor inspired six Latinos to seek the District 6 seat; seven others likewise expressed interest in serving as the area's next supervisor.[62] Latinos formed the largest ethnoracial group in the Mission—and the new electoral district—but they did not represent an absolute majority. Official figures placed them under 50 percent on both counts.[63] Yet "throughout the city, the Mission was seen as a Latino community," observed Al Borvice. "Therefore it should've had a Latino representative." Moreno agreed. "Propelling a Latino to victory," explained the news columnist, "is of vital importance for the city's most Spanish-speaking district."[64] These men traveled in different circles and had divergent political trajectories. Unlike Moreno, Borvice had never participated in the MCO or the CCSS. Still, they both believed that a Latino supervisor would be most responsive to Latinos' concerns. Sending a Latino from the Mission to City Hall held symbolic and emotive power. Latinos had long been excluded from the upper echelons of political office and now confronted the reality of displacement. A supervisor with cultural roots in the Mission, some Latinos thought, would work to protect them against further expulsion while signaling greater inclusion in San Francisco's civic life.

Latinos' ethnoracial allegiances continued to intersect with ideological differences and organizational histories. The four best-known Latino candidates each relied on a base with distinct generational and ideological characteristics. A former editor of *America* newspaper, George Medina had been a political operative in the Spanish Speaking Citizens Foundation and member of MAPA. He represented an older and more deferential constituency, including some small business owners and persons wary of confrontational politics. Ray Rivera stood on the opposite end of the political spectrum: he appealed to activists who had participated in Los Siete Defense Committee, young Latinos involved in revolutionary circles, and artists immersed in a rich cultural movement flourishing at the time. "Rivera had support [from] . . . the college students' base, the more sort of left political base, [and] he had the arts people," recalled Larry Del Carlo. Once active in War on Poverty efforts and a key player in the MCO, Del Carlo's candidacy offered a middle ground between Medina's traditionalism and Rivera's radicalism. "I was probably the most moderate," Del Carlo noted. He received backing from labor unions, some churches, and others in what he called his "natural base."

That natural base, as Al Borvice understood it, included "the traditional, Model Cities leadership" and activists from the MCO, which had disintegrated by this time.[65] Yet some former MCO activists, including Luisa Ezquerro and David Sánchez Jr., actually backed Gary Borvice, who had cofounded LaREAL with his brother, Al. This slate of candidates and the blocs they mobilized exposed the ongoing significance and reproduction of political visions—and tensions—circulating in Latino life since the 1960s. To be sure, not everyone looked to the past when deciding whom to endorse. Some residents took a more pragmatic approach by considering who had the best chance of winning. In so doing, they aligned with the candidate with the most presence in Latino civic life in 1977: Gary Borvice.

The Borvice brothers and the collective they founded in 1970 had become principal actors in community affairs and grassroots action by middecade. LaREAL co-led a rezoning initiative in 1974 and 1975, joined a communal front to keep McDonald's and porn shops out of the district, and devoted great energy to the Proposition T campaign. Along with El Tecolote, LaREAL played an instrumental role in explaining, promoting, and defending district elections.[66] These efforts unfolded as the organization continued to coordinate an array of programs, including legal assistance, a graphic arts workshop, and citizenship classes. For Gary Borvice, the supervisorial bid represented a logical extension of community service and an attempt to fuse the ideology of self-determination—which guided much of his work—with electoral politics. The logic undergirding district elections, in fact, melded quite well with a philosophy emphasizing communal autonomy and control over socioeconomic affairs. Ideology aside, economic vulnerability marked the lived reality of many Latinos, especially amid growing inflation and fears of displacement. Borvice knew so and "[saw] housing and jobs as the biggest problems in the Mission." He pledged to tackle this situation head-on if elected to the board. "Speculation is driving rents up," he said. "[And] there is no equal advance in terms of wages."[67]

Borvice also took a strong and expansive stand on civil rights, a remarkable development for someone who led the offensive against Sister's Speakeasy. The candidate made his position known in El Mundo, a mainstream publication with a wider circulation than El Tecolote. "We need a tough affirmative action policy in terms of human rights, for gays and women as well as minorities," Borvice told a news reporter. His brother, Al, likewise stressed that "Gary's agenda included gay rights." The broad-mindedness may have been a simple political calculation. But Borvice could have also chosen to remain hostile to or noncommittal on gay issues. In fact, not all candidates in District 6 or other districts incorporated gay rights into their platforms.[68]

Significantly, no other candidate had a working relationship with GALA. Rodrigo Reyes and others in GALA viewed Borvice's personal evolution and public position on gay rights as a progressive development in Latino civic life. The advances evinced the fruits of gay Latinos' political labors. Now, with their eyes set on sending a Latino to City Hall, GALA members threw their support "solidly behind Gary Borvice" and labored to help elect him. The collective found great appeal in Borvice's messages about cultural pride, higher wages, protection against speculation, and civil rights. Gay Latinos, once at odds with Borvice, now regarded him as the best candidate for all Latinos and for the Mission. Not everyone in District 6 shared this view or proved willing to move beyond Borvice's antigay past.[69]

The most formidable challenge to Borvice came from Carol Ruth Silver, a Jewish attorney with a staunch commitment to civil rights and "a long-time supporter of liberal causes," including gay rights. Silver's professional and political trajectory included participating in African Americans' freedom struggle in Mississippi, offering legal assistance and representing farmworkers in rural California, and working to repeal laws criminalizing homosexual behavior. She had supported the Proposition T campaign and knew that the Mission "had been carved out as a Hispanic district"—by many Latino organizations and some in the Democratic Party machine. The district's heterogeneity, she explained, called for a supervisor who "would represent the needs of Hispanics, the Germans, the Italians, the blacks, the gays, every group that [was] here."[70] Pursuing a big-tent strategy, Silver challenged some Latinos' exclusionary sentiments and questioned the usefulness of fusing Latino affinity and cultural pride into this political race. But not all white residents found Borvice's or other candidates' reliance on latinidad problematic. Toby Levine from the MPC actually "work[ed] for Gary to get him elected." Other prominent Mission activists, including Luisa Ezquerro, downplayed Silver's message of inclusion and instead saw her as an "opportunist" and clever candidate. She "saw an opportunity," noted Al Borvice, to "pick up white votes, including from those that had moved in from the Castro, white seniors," and others.[71]

Leaving gay Latinos out of her equation, Silver acknowledged that the residents "who voted for [her] were significantly more gays and lesbians than Hispanic." Her campaign workers conducted outreach throughout the electoral district, devoting particular attention to areas ignored by some Latino contenders (e.g., the southern end of South of Market, the western Mission) and targeting those pockets where they could find more registered voters. Campaign ads targeting gay people underscored that Silver was "a friend when we needed friends," and reminded gay voters that "now we need her more than ever."[72] The candidate herself did not raise questions about Borvice's political past and the brawl over Sister's Speakeasy. Silver did not have to; the gay press did it for her. "The large Gay population living in the western section of the District," the *Bay Area Reporter* underscored, would prove critical in deciding whether District 6 was represented "by an anti-Gay, Gary Borvice, or a long-time friend of Gay rights, Carol Ruth Silver."[73]

Other gay newspapers joined the *Reporter* in endorsing Silver, while leaving GALA's endorsement and canvassing on behalf of Borvice unaddressed. Reporters either cared little about gay Latinos' views or chose the path of journalistic expediency. Revisiting Borvice's past actions and questioning his capacity to reform proved relatively simple. Explaining why many gay Latinos supported the straight Latino candidate demanded more nuance, as well as a recognition that the election was not merely about gay rights. GALA activists themselves consistently identified race, cultural pride, and displacement as central issues in the contest.[74]

In an ironic display of political dislocation, the population that LaREAL had once sought to keep out of the Mission now blocked Borvice's supervisorial aspirations. Overwhelming support from white gay residents and a crowded field of Latino candidates propelled Silver to victory in November 1977. She garnered 35 percent of votes cast; Borvice and Del Carlo trailed her with 23 percent and 17 percent, respectively.[75] Irrespective of sexual identity, many Latinos interpreted the outcome as another indicator of their deracination from the district. Most *Bay Area Reporter* readers turned their attention elsewhere: they treated Silver's win as a triumph for gay people.

Gay Rights as Human Rights

The following year, all Californians had to consider gay people's standing in their state while reflecting on the scope of civil and human rights. Amid a mounting nationwide backlash to rescind rights and liberties that gay men and lesbians had fought for, state senator John Briggs led a statewide drive to codify discrimination and exclusion in the name of morality and the protection of children. Briggs represented parts of Orange County and chaired

California Save Our Children, the organization leading the drive paralleling Anita Bryant's crusade in Florida. Also known as the Briggs Initiative, the proposition's intent was clear-cut: any person who engaged in "public homosexual activity or conduct" would be dismissed from or refused employment in the state's public schools.[76] Gay people and their allies began organizing against the proposed measure long before its backers gathered enough signatures to place it on the November 1978 ballot. In mid-March, hundreds of gay and straight San Franciscans assembled at a church in the Western Addition and pledged to defeat the proposition. Froben Lozada, a Chicano studies professor and member of the Socialist Workers Party, joined Harvey Milk and other community leaders in speaking out against it. Pointing out that Briggs's plan threatened gay Californians, they underscored how its passage could well "embolden other Right Wing [forces] to increase their attacks on civil liberties and all oppressed groups."[77]

Californians drawn to Save Our Children refuted charges that their effort amounted to persecution and instead identified homosexual teachers and their allies as a societal threat. They presented themselves as guardians of public welfare, arbiters of morality, and warriors against social death. Relying on fundamentalist Christianity and psychological theories already abandoned by the scientific establishment, Briggs and his supporters equated homosexuality with evil, disease, and ruin. They believed gay teachers would cripple and corrode children's moral and psychosocial development and should therefore be removed from public service. In addition, they consistently accused gay people of seeking to recruit young persons and to normalize a sinister existence that would result in destruction. "When children are constantly exposed to [these] homosexual role models," opined Briggs, "they may well be inclined to experiment with a life-style that could lead to disaster for themselves and, ultimately, for society a whole." He branded gay persons as "anti-life" because they had turned away from divine, heterosexual mandates and did not procreate.[78] Based on this logic, gay people's determination to live freely and openly represented a scheme to corrupt and destroy humanity that had to be halted.

Gay and straight San Franciscans rebuked Briggs's design and resolved resoundingly to thwart it. The senator regularly chastised their city for its liberality and the visibility and political clout of its gay and lesbian population. Many local residents reciprocated the antipathy, charging Briggs and his supporters with intolerance and the promotion of state-sanctioned bigotry. They mobilized their opposition within existing political collectives and new alliances that pulled diverse constituencies into the fight. One well-known coalition, the Bay Area Committee Against the Briggs Initiative (BACABI), counted civil rights groups, labor unions, and religious bodies among its members and endorsers. Staging community meetings, press conferences, and rallies throughout 1978, BACABI coordinators consistently underscored the imperative of assembling a united front to defeat Briggs's forces. "Women, minorities and organized labor especially must unite with the gay movement," they proclaimed in May 1978.[79] After all, Proposition 6 raised paramount questions involving equity, prejudice, worker rights, and constitutional protections.

Gay Latinos understood the initiative's multiple ramifications and joined the "No on 6" campaign in various ways. They spoke emphatically against it, beseeched Latinos to remember their experiences—past and present—of being devalued and hated, and labored to dispel the myth of gay people as sexual predators. In a press interview, Eddi Baca emphasized: "The greatest danger for the Latino child is the educational system, crime, violence and drugs, not homosexuals." Challenging Briggs's position head-on, he simultaneously stressed that the senator's allies also opposed the advancement and civil rights of racial minorities. "The followers of Anita Bryant and Senator Briggs supported Nixon, are ultra-right-wing conservatives," Baca relayed, and were "the true enemies of all oppressed people."[80] His comrades in GALA shared his sentiments. The three-year-old alliance urged heterosexual Latinos to stand up for gay rights and in all likelihood sponsored forums—akin to ones concerning district elections and antigay violence—to educate Latinos about Proposition 6.

In late June 1978, the Gay Freedom Day March and Rally offered the opportunity to affirm everyone's humanity, participate in a "massive and visible" demonstration against Proposition 6, and make clear that the quest for gay liberation was not over. Weeks before the event, Diana Felix invited "non-gay Latinos as well as our gay sisters and brothers" to join the GALA contingent there.[81] BACABI acknowledged "the day's political content and significance" and encouraged its allies to march as well. The coalition drew members from across the Bay Area and of varying sexual identities; most individuals involved in its day-to-day activities, however, lived in San Francisco and were gay or lesbian. Some of them were Latinos, including residents involved in the media and precinct work committees. By devising media strategies, canvassing voters, and rallying at public events, such activists as Lorraine Ramirez and Pablo Ruiz did their part to stop "this highly dangerous proposition."[82]

Another contingent of Latinos assumed a leading role in the campaign against Proposition 6: education professionals. The initiative's spotlight on teachers, teachers' aides, counselors, and administrators generated intense opposition from those laboring in the educational sector. While gay rights advocates deduced that the proposal imperiled gay people of all occupational backgrounds, educators concluded that it would harm everyone in their ranks irrespective of sexual identity. "Briggs Hurts Us All," declared the *San Francisco Teacher*, the voice of the American Federation of Teachers Local 61. The labor union branded Proposition 6 as an "anti-teacher, anti-gay, anti-individual rights measure." Its statewide partner, the California Federation of Teachers, concurred; so did the city's Latin American Teachers Association (LATA).[83] Likely an outgrowth of a Latino caucus within Local 61, its members expressed solidarity with gay coworkers early on, attended rallies, and conveyed their viewpoints to friends and family. In one-on-one conversations and before large crowds, Roberto Lemus, one of LATA's representatives, explained why his colleagues spurned the initiative. It authorized discrimination against a minority population, threatened job security irrespective of work performance, embodied an invasion of personal privacy, and violated First Amendment rights. Lemus and many teachers found the language of "homosexual conduct" as grounds for dismissal particularly loathsome: anyone who expressed favorable views about gay people, discussed homosexuality as a normal expression of human sexuality, or challenged discrimination based on sexual orientation stood to lose their job.[84]

An impressive roster of Latino educators—including Rosario Anaya, Luisa Ezquerro, Rosa Perez, and David Sánchez Jr.—echoed LATA's perspective. "Proposition 6 is a serious threat to the civil rights for which we have fought for in this country," relayed Perez, an assistant dean of students at San Francisco City College. "Anyone who has felt the pain of discrimination must understand the importance of voting NO."[85] Her appeal shared much in common with Eddi Baca's from GALA. But the respect afforded to teachers in Latino life and the prominence of such community leaders as Ezquerro and Anaya, who sat on the city's school board, meant their perspectives carried greater weight. If some heterosexual Latinos, especially ones with children, discounted Baca's position without much thought, Latino educators' opposition pushed them to reflect more deeply about the stakes before them.

Other labor groups, civil rights organizations, and Catholic leaders, too, voiced opposition to Proposition 6. BACABI actually established a labor committee to educate all union members and ensure they understood how the measure "would pave the way for the firing of workers by other employ-ers based on any differences in life styles or political views." Jose Gonzalez participated in it; he represented Northern California's chapter of the Labor Council for Latin American Advancement. Founded in 1972 and tied to the AFL-CIO, the council aimed to pull more Latinos into the labor movement and coordinate interunion campaigns; its first president, Ray Mendoza, was a hod carrier from Orange County. Mendoza's counterparts in San Francisco belonged to the Construction and General Laborers Union Local 261, and backed BACABI's efforts. Their stand against the proposition demonstrated that even Latino laborers in a hypermasculine industry found it dangerous and prejudicial.[86] The Puerto Rican Women's Organization and MAPA surely applauded construction workers for siding with them; these were two addi-tional organizations condemning the initiative for its infringement on civil and human rights. Pointing out that it was discriminatory at a juridical level and an affront to a minority group's welfare, they reminded Latinos about their own quest—past and ongoing—for equal protection of the law and human dignity. Monsignor James Flynn and other prominent Catholic fig-ures held related perspectives. Well respected among Latinos since the 1960s, Flynn now directed the archdiocese's commission on social justice. He joined religious leaders of varying faiths in toppling Briggs's supporters' moral claims. Attacks on gay people's personhood, disregard for their well-being, and limitations on employment, they explained, all added up to violations of human rights. "A vote for Proposition 6 is not a vote for morality," Flynn stressed, "but an act of discrimination."[87]

For non-faith-based, secular views on Briggs's measure, Latinos could turn to at least four Spanish-language or bilingual newspapers. None of the dominant publications endorsed the proposition, though some chose not to address it. *El Mundo* and *El Bohemio* had a record of covering electoral poli-tics and statewide initiatives; they remained silent on this matter. By doing so, editors conveyed that Proposition 6 was not of concern to Latinos, too contentious for consideration, or both. Their counterparts at *Tiempo Latino* acknowledged the controversy while opting for neutrality. Reminding the public of the "many things at play," including children's education and "the human factor of homosexuals themselves," editors encouraged readers to consider their conscience and use "common sense" when making their deci-sions. A commentator known as Don Kuka, writing for this same newspaper, struck a different tone and circuitously recommended voting against it. Kuka used parody, innuendo, and homophobia (mocking gay people and branding

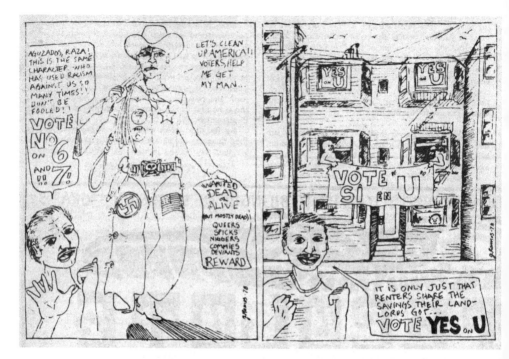

Figure 10. "NO en 6, SI en U," cartoon by Gerardo Ramos, *El Tecolote*,
November 1978. Courtesy of Acción Latina and Nettie Lee Benson
Latin American Collection, University of Texas at Austin.

homosexuality as a sexual deviation) to make his case. He told his audience
"fairies had a right to work"; if passed, the proposition could be "easily borrowed to make a 'bed' for anyone" accused of philandering or being sexually
adventurous.[88] Gerardo Ramos, a cartoonist for *El Tecolote*, likewise relied on
humor to convey his message. Politically sharp and coalitional in orientation,
his cartoon cast all oppressed peoples as Briggs's targets. "Attention, Raza!"
read a speech balloon, "This guy is the same one who has persecuted us!!! Vote
NO on 6." Ramos's recommendation fell fully in line with *El Tecolote*'s position. Its team did not mince words: Proposition 6 was antigay, anti-labor, dangerous for all teachers, and backed by "conservative elements in our state."
They wanted Latinos to recognize the proposition's importance, understand
how it "would directly affect our lives," and vote it down.[89]

The range of outlooks appearing in the press mirrored Latinos' varied positions and assessments. Some Latinos likely supported the proposition or

abstained from voting on it. More among them turned to the recommendations of teachers, labor unions, and religious leaders and opposed it. Part of the reflection recommended by *Tiempo Latino*, after all, involved weighing what educators and moral teachers had to say. Residents who wavered or found themselves in the middle simply could not ignore the perspectives disseminated by community groups, neighbors, friends, and relatives who stood adamantly against Proposition 6. In the end, three-quarters of San Francisco voters rejected it; almost 60 percent of California's electorate did so. The outcome in districts with a high concentration of Latinos paralleled the citywide margin.[90] Non-Latinos of course lived in the Mission, Bernal Heights, and adjacent neighborhoods. Still, electoral results alongside the responses from individuals and institutions connected with Latinos suggested that more of them opted to acknowledge gay people's humanity, protect labor rights, and stand on the side of equality and justice.

Rent Control and the 1970s Popular Front

El Tecolote's political education primer of fall 1978 encompassed much more than the antigay Proposition 6. Apprising Latinos about the discriminatory nature of that statewide initiative, the media collective concurrently advised readers to stand behind Proposition U, a local proposal known as the rent rebate ordinance. Proposition U originated in direct response to Proposition 13—a property tax limitation measure passed in June that year. Weeks after a majority of California voters approved it, San Franciscans for Renters Property Tax Relief drafted a municipal measure requiring landlords to extend rental rebates based on "the savings attributable to Proposition 13." The alliance of tenants and housing advocates viewed their plan as an equitable and appropriate way to assist renters, especially since landlords regularly rationalized rent hikes by citing increased property taxes. Now that property owners would benefit from a tax reduction, the group argued, there should be some compensation "to the tenants who really pay these taxes."[91] Their position reframed recent deliberations on civic responsibility, fairness, and state power. Supporters of Proposition 13 had abridged governmental authority to tax property, even if doing so compromised the public good. In turn, San Franciscans backing Proposition U amplified the terms of landlords' obligations to tenants and sought state action to mandate those duties. Some homeowners, too, viewed the initiative as a matter of "tax justice."

Charlene Martinez from Bernal Heights belonged to an ad hoc group of homeowners who believed "renters ought to get the same property tax benefits owners have just gotten under Prop. 13." *El Tecolote*'s team could not agree more. "One must vote YES on U," the newspaper told its audience. "It is fair that we the lessees also reap benefits with reductions in rent."[92]

Latinos' involvement in a citywide housing movement had fully blossomed by 1978. Composed of an interlocking network of organizations—some with a citywide reach and others targeting specific neighborhoods—housing activists, tenants, and some allied homeowners focused their energies on three principal goals: safeguards against evictions, antispeculation legislation, and rent control.[93] Advocates' and residents' interest in establishing a mechanism to regulate rental prices, backed by state power, had been around for at least a decade. In the late 1960s, the MCO's Housing Committee acknowledged the need for low-rent housing and urged the coalitional body to conduct research on how to reduce housing expenses across the city. District activists and social service providers offered a host of concrete recommendations in the ensuing years: these included rent stabilization and low-cost homeownership programs, an expansion of public housing, and "safeguards against arbitrary rent hikes."[94] The elements of a rent control plan, in effect, had currency even before that term had solidified. By late 1973, residents and activists refusing to celebrate BART's opening instead offered celebrants the following dictum: "Rent Control Not Redevelopment." Some of these Missionites soon connected with the San Francisco Rent Control Committee, which emerged in spring 1975. This committee drafted an early full-fledged rent control proposal, but it failed to collect enough signatures to place the measure on the ballot.[95] Though public oversight of the private rental market garnered little interest outside tenant and housing circles in 1975, more and more San Franciscans took up the issue by the decade's end. This shift owed much to the escalation of rents, consternation over speculation, and the rising tide of gentrification. The housing crisis "has become a major social problem," opined Harvey Milk, the iconic gay supervisor, in March 1978. "Everyone knows that the price of San Francisco housing, and thus renting, has risen to a point where even the major media are talking about rent control."[96]

In 1978, housing advocates pursued two avenues to alleviate the housing crisis: an antispeculation ordinance and rental rebates vis-à-vis Proposition U. Early that year, the San Francisco Housing Coalition (SFHC)—an umbrella group of tenant unions, block clubs, and community organizations concerned about the diminution of affordable housing—formulated a policy proposal to levy hefty municipal taxes on real estate speculators. Its signature provision called for the imposition of an 80 percent tax on the profits of all property bought and sold within one year; this duty formed part of graduated tax rate "bottoming at 15%, if [landholdings] sold within five years."[97] Activists and organizations alarmed by the speculation craze viewed the SFHC's plan as one panacea to housing troubles. In late March 1978, city residents and activists of all backgrounds—including Latinos, African Americans, seniors, and gay people—descended on City Hall, took turns in discussing "the disastrous effects of speculation," and beseeched supervisors to pass an antispeculation ordinance. Harvey Milk, Carol Ruth Silver, and a few other supervisors stood with these constituencies; they found themselves in the minority.

Even with district-based elections in place, the real estate industry and other profit-centered bodies held sway over many legislators—and the electorate. Opponents of the antispeculation initiative rejoiced when the proposal failed to become law owing to limited support from the sitting supervisors. Realtors, developers, and their allies celebrated again later that year when voters rejected Proposition U. The rent rebate initiative, its opponents had argued, was really a circuitous and "disastrous" path to rent control. The proposed measure included a provision capping rents at June 1978 levels to ensure that rental prices did not rise and counterbalance the rebates. Critics rebuked the plan and claimed that Proposition U would actually harm renters, by either spurring landlords into condominium conversion or deterring them from making property improvements. Those scenarios would diminish either the quantity or the quality of rental housing. Some detractors went further and shrewdly placed Proposition U on par with Proposition 6. They cast the initiatives as comparable "means [of] more governmental interference in people's personal and private lives."[98] Regulating the rental market and attempts to curtail gay people's civil rights, the opposition contended, both exemplified violations of freedom. This constellation of arguments worked. Fifty-three percent of voters in November 1978 turned down Proposition U, dealing yet another setback to the housing movement.[99]

San Franciscans who sought to ameliorate the housing crisis felt disillusioned but not vanquished. Proposition U lost by a small margin, indicating that a different outcome might be possible if housing advocates devoted more time to political education and community organizing. Part of the educational work included ongoing dialogue about the frictions between white gay people and minority communities. In March 1979, Al Borvice from LaREAL,

Gwen Craig from the Harvey Milk Democratic Club, Randy Stallings from the SFHC, and other activists came together at a forum on housing issues. Panelists acknowledged the reality of intergroup tensions while underscoring the need for greater collaboration to confront skyrocketing rents, evictions, and other unfair housing practices. Keeping a lesbian bar from opening, as LaREAL had learned, bred discord but ultimately did not curb rising rents and displacement. Minority residents and gay people had to "join together and quit attacking each other," Randy Stallings implored in a news column later that spring; otherwise "we will continue to play right into the hands of those who grow rich off of our common misery."[100] A coalitional impulse was not new. But activists still had much work to do. Simplistic, ill-informed binaries—Latinos versus gays, blacks versus gays—retained much currency at this time, making it easy for opponents of housing reform to stoke and profit from those sentiments.

Raising the coalitional banner in 1979, San Franciscans for Affordable Housing (SFAH) embarked on a crusade to push local government "to control runaway housing costs that are squeezing everyone, renter and owner." Some fifty community organizations formed part of this new citizens' alliance, a spin-off of similar bodies leading the antispeculation and rent rebate efforts in 1978. SFAH described itself as "the most broadly-based grouping in the City's history to come together to deal with the housing crisis." The MPC, MAPA, the Mission Deanery for Community Concern, San Francisco Gay Liberation (formerly BAGL), and the Third World Gay Caucus were but a handful of organizations on its steering committee. For many months in 1979, SFAH organized community forums in each supervisorial district, consulted with residents and obtained input on its comprehensive housing reform plan.[101] The end product became a blueprint for a housing ordinance, which SFAH managed to place on the November ballot.

A multipart initiative, the best-known piece of Proposition R involved rent control. The proposition placed a cap on yearly rent adjustments by tying these to local inflation rates based on "the percentage increase in the Rental Component of the Consumer Price Index."[102] In 1980, when SFAH expected the ordinance to take effect, landlords would not be allowed to raise rents above 5 percent of the existing base rent. Proprietors could still turn to a Rental Housing Board—elected by local residents—and make a case for why their rents had to be higher. The proposal also delineated just causes for eviction (e.g., failure to pay rent, damage to property) and fined those landlords who violated this provision. Furthermore, Proposition R set limitations on the conversion of apartments into condominiums, stipulating that the process could not occur unless 80 percent of existing tenants opted to purchase their apartments. Such robust measures, housing advocates explained, would truly signal an investment in affordable housing and offer much relief to San Franciscans "caught in the housing squeeze."[103]

Latinos from various walks of life found inspiration in Proposition R and backed it with gusto. Community leaders, activists, and residents connected with organizations long favoring rent control immediately threw their support behind it. Whether linked to SFAH, involved in other groups, or as individuals, most Latinos regarded the proposed ordinance as beneficial to them. "Proposition R is a people's program," asserted Rene Ramos, a Mission resident. "It was written by tenants, homeowners, unions, church people, seniors, minority, disabled, and other grassroots groups." Referencing the process leading up to the initiative, Ramos underscored that the plan prioritized the needs of average people and vulnerable populations. Older Latinos, including those in the Latin American National Senior Citizens Association, appeared to have been particularly receptive to Proposition R. Many of them and other senior citizens lived on limited and fixed incomes. Graciela Cashion, president of the association, together with leaders of other elderly organizations urged the public to "help us stay" in the city. "We've lived here a long time," they said. "We deserve some protection."[104] Shielding residents against displacement, of course, had been one of Latinos' political priorities since the mid-1960s.

Proposition R introduced an apparatus for socioeconomic stability and augmented everyday San Franciscans' repository of rights. "A tenant traditionally is in a powerless position with respect to his/her landlord," SFAH representatives explained. The housing reform plan therefore offered tenants a bill of rights, including safeguards against landlord intimidation, control over condominium conversion, and a democratically elected Rental Housing Board. Community advocate Eulalio Frausto, an attorney who regularly represented working-class and minority residents, welcomed this resolve. In a joint statement, Frausto, Monsignor James Flynn, and a dozen other community-based workers applauded Proposition R for giving "tenants the rights they need." The rights in question, as these individuals indicated, had to be considered with an eye on humanity and survival, not economic privilege and profit. As they urged voters to back the initiative, Frausto and his colleagues reminded the public that "housing is more than a commodity or service . . . it is a necessity."[105]

Professing to comprehend existing housing ills, the anti–Proposition R forces mounted an artful critique centered on questions of opportunity, well-being, freedom, and bureaucracy. Groups such as San Franciscans for Sensible Housing Policy (SFSHP)—backed by real estate and other commercial interests—generally bypassed discussions of profit, speculation, and inequity. Instead, they painted rent control as threatening to the public—materially and socially—and dangerous in terms of governance. Rent control would exacerbate the housing crisis by crippling the rental market, stressed SFSHP and its partners. Here, the opposition refined the arguments made against Proposition U a year earlier. Proposition R's passage would allegedly forestall new construction and its restrictions on landlords' revenue would hinder owners' capacity to maintain their units, thereby spawning "housing decays."[106]

Rent control as a harbinger of slums unsettled many residents and became a powerful weapon in the opposition's ideological arsenal—one legitimized by such expert politicians as Mayor Dianne Feinstein. Fusing public distaste for blighted neighborhoods and long-standing fears about the Manhattanization of their city, Feinstein told the citizenry, "Rent control in New York meant 300,000 units of abandoned housing and new slums." The new mayor concurrently lent credence to a perception that the proposed ordinance would result in "more bureaucracies, more government cost, [and] more government interference with your life." Connecting these charges with ones leveled against Proposition U, critics excoriated what they viewed as excessive governmental regulation, an infringement on property rights, and a curtailment of citizens' freedom "to choose where and how we live."[107]

Some opponents also branded Proposition R's directives as unnecessary because a rent stabilization ordinance already existed. Indeed, in June 1979, as momentum for Proposition R built up, the supervisors passed a law with rental increase guidelines, a recognition of landlords' prerogative to "raise rents as much as they wish," and a rent arbitration board appointed by the mayor. Supervisors Carol Ruth Silver and Harry Britt regarded that statute as "a feeble, short-term stopgap measure" and believed Proposition R presented a better and stronger alternative.[108] Many of their constituents in the Mission, South of Market, the Castro, Noe Valley, and the Haight concurred. A majority of voters from these districts backed rent control as prescribed by Proposition R. They found themselves in the minority once again. The sentiments and hypotheses circulated by SFSHP, Feinstein, and their friends persuaded 60 percent of voters citywide to repudiate the measure in November 1979.[109]

The outcome stunned San Franciscans who expected that Proposition R's

passage would affirm the strength and unity of working people and intro-
duce a new era of progressivism. Activists, residents, and politicians linked
with the citywide housing movement had had good reasons to believe they
would be victorious. Support for rent control had grown since 1975; the
housing crisis occupied the minds of nearly all residents; and almost two-
thirds of San Franciscans were renters. Polls conducted just weeks before the
election had suggested that the measure might "well pass." In their search
for explanations, SFAH and their allies identified "comparative low registration and low voter turnout in lower-income, minority, and renter precincts"
as the critical determinants behind the loss.[110] The aggressive, savvy, and
well-funded appeals disseminated by SFSHP and its allies surely influenced
some voters as well. Some renters may also have chosen to stay away from
the polls owing to landlord harassment and fear of retaliation. A year earlier,
weeks after the vote on rental rebates, *El Tecolote* reported that some "tenants [had] been threatened with rent increases if people were to vote YES on
Proposition U." This compendium of factors and the opposition's determination resulted in the rejection of a robust rent control ordinance, which proponents had cast as imperative for the preservation of "our working class,
multi-racial City."[111]

At a deeper level, the defeat of Proposition R offered some clues about the
state of grassroots organizing, political identities, and liberalism as the postwar era came to end. Liberal and progressive San Franciscans coalesced into
overlapping coalitions at this time—ones promoting district elections, defending gay rights, and pushing for rent control. These alliances and their
member organizations undertook vigorous political education and advocacy
work. Their direct-action components, however, proved more limited. For
decades, Latinos and other San Franciscans had relied on a network of labor
unions and outfits such as the MCO to educate, defend, incite, and rally
them. A wider array of political strategies in the mid- to late 1970s may have
prompted more residents to register and vote for initiatives beneficial to working people. Still, neither "working-class" nor "tenant" functioned as primary
or meaningful identities for the city's renter majority. *El Tecolote* and other
left-leaning collectives had often identified district elections and rent control
as products of "working-class power."[112] Yet some backers of district elections
did not support rent control. And while some middle-class San Franciscans
voted for Proposition R, some working-class residents turned against it.
These decisions resulted, at least in part, from the varying levels of importance that diverse constituencies placed on class-based and "noneconomic

political objectives." Above all, the electorate's decision not to enact a strong, citizen-created rent control ordinance exposed both evolving and divided attachments to liberalism. The city's rejection of "propositions to set up rent control . . . to tax business more heavily, and to provide binding arbitration of wage and working-conditions disputes with the police and fire unions," concluded a *New York Times* writer, meant San Francisco now said " 'NO' to the old liberalism."[113]

Most Latinos chose to stick with the "old" liberalism while affirming—and expanding—a commitment to the new one. Their support for rent control fit within a long trajectory of championing state regulation of the economy and backing public initiatives to augment the citizenry's socioeconomic well-being. By upholding the old liberalism, Latinos revealed a continued embrace of the tenets and promise of New Deal and Great Society liberalism. Residents such as Betty Anello insisted that government had to do more to meet "people's basic needs" and to ensure their welfare. Deeply concerned about the housing crisis, she stated, "I have to question the values of our economic system where property rights and real estate rights are the most protected and most sacred, while the most basic rights like the right to decent housing are the least protected and most disregarded."[114] The pursuit of civil rights, which the East Coast reporter presumably placed in the new liberalism column, had likewise consumed Latinos' political energies for decades. In the 1970s, many Latino San Franciscans found themselves having to reconcile their cultural conservatism with their long-standing promotion of civil rights liberalism. The process was neither automatic nor easy. Yet LaREAL's collaborations with GALA, communal disapproval of Proposition 6, and the growth of a lesbian community along Valencia Street offered indications that many heterosexual Latinos would make some room for gay people—even if grudgingly—and yield to gay rights. In December 1978, weeks after Mayor Moscone's and Supervisor Milk's assassinations, Juan Gonzales of *El Tecolote* asked Latinos to side with nonviolence, oppose exploitation, and focus on "promoting the well-being of many rather than the comfort of a few."[115] That is precisely what residents involved in the Proposition R campaign set out to do. Raising the banner of the old liberalism and aligned with the new one, Latinos took their place, once again, alongside the progressive forces of "this most liberal of California cities."[116]

EPILOGUE

Fifteen years after the defeat of Proposition R, in June 1994, I traveled to San Francisco for the first time. My knowledge of its place in late twentieth-century America was paltry, my sense of its history rudimentary. As a teenager in the late 1980s, I had delighted in sanitized, buoyant images of the city propagated by the television sitcom *Full House*. I had also heard gay people lived there; I do not recall what or who transmitted that information to me. Once in college, a dear friend told me Central Americans had been living in this metropolis for generations and encouraged me to conduct research on the subject. Her revelation piqued my interest, though scholarly investigations were not on my agenda in 1994. The trip would not be a tourist adventure either. I came to San Francisco to be an activist. That summer, as Californians clashed over the motives and dangers of Proposition 187—a statewide initiative that sought to deny public benefits, education, and health services to undocumented immigrants—and as San Francisco's LGBT community commemorated the twenty-fifth anniversary of the Stonewall Uprising, I immersed myself in homeless advocacy work. The organization sponsoring my internship placed me at a Latino homeless project in the Mission, one block east of the 16th and Mission BART station. I could not have imagined that this intersection, the transit system, housing matters, or the city's Latino population would one day consume much of my professional life.

The Latino community I encountered in the mid-1990s had experienced remarkable developments and continuities since the late 1970s. One phenomenon proved palpable as the 1980s began. In 1981, the *San Francisco Examiner* reported on what many Latinos were witnessing firsthand: a "new wave of Salvadoran immigrants" had reached the city.[1] What became a twelve-year civil war in El Salvador (1980–1992) spurred a large-scale exodus from that country in the twentieth century's closing decades. Concurrent armed conflict and economic distress prompted Nicaraguans and Guatemalans to migrate as well. San Francisco became a logical destination for those seeking safety and stability given the long-standing presence of Central

Americans there. One early study found that approximately 15,000 Central American immigrants entered the city between 1980 and 1985 alone; activists and social service providers often questioned such figures owing to the high rates of unauthorized migration and public authorities' traditional undercounting of immigrant populations. Newcomers settled in the Mission and adjacent neighborhoods as their predecessors had done in decades past. They relied on existing social and institutional networks for support and interacted in varying degrees with established Latino residents and more recent Mexican immigrants.[2] The latter continued to arrive steadily throughout the 1980s and 1990s, though their migration to the metropolis was not marked by the acceleration presented by the Central American case. Mexicans sought to escape economic instability, to obtain better employment than found in California agriculture, or to reconnect with kin. Seen from one perspective, these population flows merely reproduced Latinos' heterogeneity along lines of national origin. But they diversified the local Latino population as well. The latest migrants represented a distinct generation, included a larger pool of undocumented immigrants, and found themselves having to compete for social services in a context of shrinking governmental commitment to the public welfare.

Latino San Franciscans' quotidian existence in the 1980s and 1990s presented a study in contrasts. In 1990, approximately one-third of them lived in the Mission; the district remained "the heart," as historian Cary Cordova has put it, of the community.[3] Cultural life during these decades exhibited great effervescence and multilayeredness. Three Kings Day celebrations in January, street fairs, a Mardi Gras–style Carnaval every May since 1979, and an array of cultural productions at the Mission Cultural Center (founded in 1977) offered examples of festive and creative abundance. Leisure and nightlife for queer Latinos flourished as well. By the late 1980s, there were three venues near 16th and Mission, including Esta Noche and La India Bonita, catering to gay Latino men and sometimes frequented by lesbian and transgender Latinas.[4] Most Latinos and other San Franciscans knew about this Mission zone for other reasons: drug dealing, crime, and homelessness. These societal ills were not specific to Latinos or the Mission, but they marked the district as unsavory and dangerous. So did the spike in gang activity; at least seven gangs with hundreds of young Latinos as members existed by 1995. Neighborhood service providers offered numerous explanations for this development, including peer pressure, a lack of social connectedness, poverty, and a desire "to defend [their] territorial autonomy" from outsiders.[5]

Economic disparities beset Latinos across the city, and the specter of displacement continued to bedevil those living in the Mission. While Latino rates of labor force participation matched those of white residents, annual per capita incomes did not. Latinos earned roughly half of what whites made in 1980; the figure was decidedly less than half ten years later.[6] The most economically vulnerable among them (e.g., residents with lower levels of education, recent immigrants) typically resided in the Mission. Notably, rising rents and real estate speculation persisted even as many San Franciscans cast the Mission as economically depressed and undesirable. "Gentrification is definitely here," one nonprofit worker told *El Tecolote* in late 1986. Four years later, the *San Francisco Chronicle* noted how "Hong Kong investors, Asian grocers and bohemian artists" increasingly found the Mission attractive because of its "sunny weather, relatively affordable housing and busy shopping districts."[7] Many Latinos did not regard their housing options, in the Mission or elsewhere, as inexpensive. One-half of all Latino households citywide paid "unaffordable rent" by 1990: they used more than 30 percent of their earnings to cover lodging. Low incomes, occupational segregation in service and clerical sectors, and high housing expenses placed many in an ongoing state of economic precarity.[8]

Activism in response to employment and housing realities appears to have been subdued in the 1980s, though other issues consumed Latinos' political energies. Commenting on housing pressures in the mid-1980s, one observer noted, "People are not organized to fight back."[9] Others stressed how American foreign policy, immigration, AIDS, and education pulled Latinos in multiple directions. A considerable number of them, including recent immigrants, mobilized against U.S. intervention in Central America and in support of the thousands fleeing war. Some participated in the Bay Area's Sanctuary Movement, an organized effort of churches and community groups offering social services to Central American refugees, sheltering them from deportation, and advocating for fair and humane immigration policies. Humanity and death took on political urgency amid the AIDS crisis. Former members of GALA—which disbanded in 1983—joined other gay Latinos in organizations such as Comunidad Respondiendo a AIDS/SIDA, founded in 1987, to devise communal responses to the epidemic, push local agencies to offer treatment and prevention services, and educate all Latinos about the disease.[10] Educational reform and Latino representation on municipal bodies responsible for public education became the priorities for others. Political scientist Richard DeLeon, writing in 1992, concluded that Latinos had recently "made their greatest political inroads in that field." Some activists advancing the long-standing ambition to solidify their community's clout citywide belonged to the Latino Democratic Club. Luisa Ezquerro, Al Borvice, and other seasoned leaders created the club in the early 1980s, which had a life span of about a decade. Its members registered voters, endorsed candidates, and pressed politicians to seriously tackle issues affecting Latinos.[11]

Immigrant rights, AIDS, and educational improvement remained critical concerns in the 1990s, while youth violence, work life, and gentrification garnered mounting attention. Throughout this decade, the Mission witnessed the unfolding of the Community Peace Initiative, a violence prevention effort funded by a private foundation. Missionites from all walks of life, including former gang members, took part in it. The initiative's team coordinated community forums and peace rallies, conducted street outreach and mobilized young people around a host of interrelated issues (e.g., educational inequities, mass incarceration), and advocated for policies to treat violence as a public health issue. As a new generation of youth became politically engaged, Latino workers did as well, especially those in service-sector jobs. Growing numbers of housekeepers, food service workers, dishwashers, and janitors responded positively to the unionization drives carried out by the locals of the Hotel Employees and Restaurant Employees Union and the Service Employees International Union. The development confirmed the potential of organizing a new generation of unskilled, immigrant workers and reviving the tradition of class-based solidarity.[12] Mobilizing Missionites against displacement regained prominence as gentrification escalated in the late 1990s. By summer 2000, residents, artists, community groups, and neighborhood business owners came together under the Mission Anti-Displacement Coalition. MAC protested the housing crisis spawned by the dot-com boom and demanded a moratorium on the construction of new market-rate housing, live-work lofts, and digital office space.[13] It proved clear that direct action and policy advocacy could be channeled yet again to propose human-centered alternatives to the inequities bred by capitalism as the twenty-first century began.

Months after MAC's emergence, San Franciscans once again elected their supervisors at the district level. The original experiment with district elections (1977–1980) had been short-lived; the city reverted to at-large elections for twenty years. Electoral results in December 2000, following many run-off contests, shifted the city's "political power base decisively to the left." Voters in

the seven districts that sent left-leaning representatives to City Hall—
including the new District 9 encompassing the Mission and Bernal Heights—
celebrated the prospect of a new progressive agenda, one with initiatives
"ranging from clamping down on dot-com development to easing up on
homeless scofflaws."[14] It was an exhilarating period to be in the city—as a
resident, an activist, or a scholar.

The early research phases for what would form part of this book began
around that time. It was tempting to become absorbed in the activism of the
early 2000s, but scholarly priorities directed me to the archives. I had returned
to the city to understand what had transpired at least two generations earlier.
San Francisco as research site originally drew me because of its motley Latino
population. Historical scholarship on the alliances and tensions between Latino subgroups did not exist fifteen years ago, and it still remains rather slim. I
also wanted to approach political action from multiple angles. The work on
1930s labor organizing and 1960s social movements fascinated me; yet most
historians treating unionization rarely took their analyses beyond the early
1950s, and studies of social movements typically proceeded from the mid-
1960s forward. At the same time, examinations of communal deliberations
over gender and sexuality tended to emanate from literary and cultural studies
fields. I set out to integrate these layers of political life and to historicize their
connections and imbrication. Many years into the project, I realized that liberalism and latinidad were the threads holding my analysis together. Liberalism and latinidad, as I have argued, consistently framed and influenced
Latinos' aspirations and the trajectory of their political engagement.

Latinos and the Liberal City joins the flourishing fields of U.S. Latino/a
history and American political history. It offers an interpretation based on
my scholarly preoccupations, the archival material I accessed, and the historical actors who shared their memories with me. There remains material to
be found and sifted. In retrospect, there are numerous topics I wish had expanded on, questions I had asked, and places I had turned to for additional
evidence.

Two areas stand out for brief reflection here. First, given the prominence
of labor organizing from the 1930s to the 1950s, it would have been advantageous to tease out labor unions' modified place in Latino life in the 1960s and
1970s. Latinos remained involved in ILWU and ILGWU locals during the
mid- to late postwar era; others belonged to organizations representing construction workers, hotel employees, and teachers. This reality demanded
more probing into how union members approached and made sense of the

War on Poverty, urban renewal, and campaigns for district elections and rent control. Correspondingly, some attention to sexual politics before the 1960s would have added interpretive texture. Concerns over pay equity and sexual harassment on the job, as briefly noted in Chapter 3, were not absent from workers' consciousness and day-to-day existence. And Latinos may have labored alongside gay unionists of the MCS, presenting one site from which to potentially examine how they grappled with sexual identity and difference at mid-century.[15] These fragments point to the possibility of widening the account of Latino perspectives on gender and sexuality.

I now understand that my initial trips to San Francisco took place as its residents confronted the transition and adjustments to a neoliberal order. Gentrification, homelessness, and decreased opportunities for social mobility, as many social scientists have shown, are largely products of neoliberalism.[16] Historians explain that this "new" political ethos is rooted in classical liberalism; it promotes economic deregulation, a retreat from social welfare spending, rollbacks in state protection for workers, and a reverence for the free market.[17] Many San Franciscans living at the turn of the twenty-first century sought to buck this current, and hoped the left-leaning supervisors who took office in 2001 would steer the city back on a progressive course.

Impressive changes certainly occurred in the new century, often in response to the demands and mobilizations of such groups as MAC and the San Francisco Living Wage Coalition. Between 2001 and 2008, the city initiated a program to offer health care to all uninsured residents, passed laws prohibiting the use of Styrofoam containers and plastic bags at grocery stores, mandated restaurants to display nutritional information on their menus, initiated an instant-runoff voting system, and widened supervisors' authority over appointments and confirmations to city commissions.[18] These developments reaffirmed a municipal commitment to social welfare, environmental regulation, and democratic reform. Wages and housing, of course, remained utmost priorities. In 2003, voters approved a citywide minimum wage ($8.50 an hour in 2004, $10.74 an hour by 2014) applicable to all employers, tied to inflation, and higher than state and federal levels. The policy came on the heels of an "inclusionary housing ordinance," enacted in 2002, requiring private developers to offer 15 to 20 percent of new units at below market-rate prices. Residents in the Mission, Potrero Hill, and South of Market concurrently welcomed land use controls, temporary moratoriums on large office developments and live-work lofts, and public bodies' increased efforts to engage them in community planning. Notably, as late as 2008, planning officials continued to express confidence in the city's ability "to house diverse groups of people and address the citywide need for more affordable housing."[19]

Neither the housing crisis nor income inequality abated. By the mid-2010s, San Francisco could boast about its advantage in the digital economy, a boom in construction, its exceptionally low unemployment rate, and plans to increase the local minimum wage to $15 an hour effective July 2018. It had also become the nation's costliest city for renters and one of the most economically unequal places in the country.[20] Politicians, policy experts, and activists have proposed myriad solutions to navigate this reality. Some of these include building higher and relaxing land-use restrictions, halting condominium construction in the Mission and other in-demand neighborhoods, expanding rent control protections, and investing in a future middle class by turning low-wage service jobs into higher-paying jobs. Scholars and commentators, for their part, have pondered one question time and time again: "What's the matter with San Francisco?" A popular account in an online magazine offered the simplest yet most telling response. "We've come so far on social issues, but gone backwards on the financial problems," noted a *Paste* writer. Pointing out that much of San Francisco's early twenty-first-century progressivism is actually neoliberalism, he underscored this observation: "We have progressive cultural values but conservative economic ones."[21]

Latinos experience the contemporary conundrum of liberalism on a daily basis. While the economic crisis is felt most acutely by those in low-wage service industries, Latinos and other San Franciscans who are administrative assistants, teachers, nonprofit workers, artists, and small business owners increasingly find the city unlivable. The long-standing, twin-headed "monster" of gentrification and displacement continues to cause turmoil and garner national attention. "Gentrification Spreads an Upheaval in San Francisco's Mission District" read the headline of a *New York Times* article in May 2015, noting that the chronic issue "now seems to be accelerating in its pace and scope."[22]

Latinos and their allies have engaged in vigorous community mobilization to confront the present situation—as done in the past—and have met backlash against their efforts. Still, they have acquired a fair amount of political clout at the municipal level. In recent history, many Latinos backed and had the ear of socially and economically progressive legislators, including John Avalos and David Campos. Avalos represented the Excelsior and other southern neighborhoods; he ran a promising but unsuccessful mayoral campaign in 2011 and served as supervisor until 2016. Campos became the first gay Latino supervisor elected in the Mission; he served from 2008 to 2016. But political influence has not translated into economic security or guaranteed a future in San Francisco. Popular and scholarly projections point to a diminishing Latino population in the coming decades—a product of economic inequity and housing unaffordability.[23] This book stands as a reminder of past prospects, ambitions, and possibilities—when Latinos and other ordinary residents believed equality, opportunity, and social mobility were within their reach.

NOTES

Introduction

1. Ship Scalers Union (SSU), International Longshoremen's and Warehousemen's Union (ILWU) Local 2, untitled statement, ca. October 1940, Maritime Federation of the Pacific (MFP), box 31, folder 23, Labor Archives and Research Center (LARC), San Francisco State University.

2. Bay Area Committee Against the Briggs Initiative (BACABI), "No on 6"; Gay Student Community et al., "Rally Against Prop. 6," both flyers, November 1978, ephemera collection, Briggs file, BACABI and Prop. 6 folders, Gay, Lesbian, Bisexual, and Transgender Historical Society of Northern California (GLBTHS), San Francisco; "Rosario Anaya for School Board," pamphlet, 1978, San Francisco Ephemera Collection, November 1978 elections file, candidates folder, San Francisco History Center, San Francisco Public Library (SFPL).

3. Steve Fraser and Gary Gerstle, eds., *The Rise and Fall of the New Deal Order, 1930–1980* (Princeton, NJ: Princeton University Press, 1989); Alan Brinkley, *Liberalism and Its Discontents* (Cambridge, MA: Harvard University Press, 1998), x.

4. An important sample includes Stephen J. Pitti, *The Devil in Silicon Valley: Northern California, Race, and Mexican Americans* (Princeton, NJ: Princeton University Press, 2004); Camille Guerin-Gonzales, *Mexican Workers and American Dreams: Immigration, Repatriation, and California Farm Labor, 1900–1939* (New Brunswick, NJ: Rutgers University Press, 1994); and Mae M. Ngai, *Impossible Subjects: Illegal Aliens and the Making of Modern America* (Princeton, NJ: Princeton University Press, 2004), especially chapter 4.

5. Guadalupe San Miguel Jr., *Chicana/o Struggles for Education: Activism in the Community* (Houston: University of Houston Center for Mexican American Studies, 2013); Sonia Song-Ha Lee, *Building a Latino Civil Rights Movement: Puerto Ricans, African Americans, and the Pursuit of Racial Justice in New York City* (Chapel Hill: University of North Carolina Press, 2014), chapter 5.

6. Mackenzie Weinger, "Poll: Latinos Say They're More Liberal," *Politico*, 04 April 2012, https://www.politico.com/story/2012/04/poll-latinos-say-theyre-more-liberal-074835, accessed 16 December 2017; Pew Research Center, "Democrats Maintain Edge as Party 'More Concerned' for Latinos, but Views Similar to 2012," October 2016, http://www.pewhispanic.org/2016/10/11/democrats-maintain-edge-as-party-more-concerned-for-latinos-but-views-similar-to-2012/, accessed 16 December 2017; Roberto Suro, "Whatever Happened to Latino Political Power?" *New York Times (NYT)*, 02 January 2016, SR1.

7. Tomás F. Summers Sandoval Jr.'s *Latinos at the Golden Gate: Creating Community and Identity in San Francisco* (Chapel Hill: University of North Carolina Press, 2013) and Cary Cordova's *The Heart of the Mission: Latino Art and Politics in San Francisco* (Philadelphia: University of Pennsylvania Press, 2017) offer key social and cultural histories.

8. William Issel, *Church and State in the City: Catholics and Politics in Twentieth-Century San Francisco* (Philadelphia: Temple University Press, 2013); Richard Edward DeLeon, *Left Coast City: Progressive Politics in San Francisco, 1975–1991* (Lawrence: University of Kansas Press, 1992). On the 1934 strikes, see Bruce Nelson, *Workers on the Waterfront: Seamen, Longshoremen, and Unionism in the 1930s* (Urbana: University of Illinois Press, 1988), chapter 5.

9. Alice Echols, "Hope and Hype in Sixties Haight-Ashbury," in *Shaky Ground: The Sixties and Its Aftershocks* (New York: Columbia University Press, 2002), 17–50; W. J. Rorabaugh, *American Hippies* (New York: Cambridge University Press, 2015), especially chapters 4–5; Josh Sides, *Erotic City: Sexual Revolutions and the Making of Modern San Francisco* (New York: Oxford University Press, 2009).

10. Reuel Schiller, *Forging Rivals: Race, Class, Law, and the Collapse of Postwar Liberalism* (New York: Cambridge University Press, 2015), 4.

11. Lorrin Thomas, *Puerto Rican Citizen: History and Political Identity in Twentieth-Century New York City* (Chicago: University of Chicago Press, 2010); Steven Gregory, *Black Corona: Race and the Politics of Place in an Urban Community* (Princeton, NJ: Princeton University Press, 1998), 11.

12. Meg Jacobs and Julian E. Zelizer, "The Democratic Experiment: New Directions in American Political History," in *The Democratic Experiment: New Directions in American Political History*, ed. Meg Jacobs, William J. Novak, and Julian E. Zelizer (Princeton, NJ: Princeton University Press, 2003), 6–8; Issel, *Church and State in the City*, 1.

13. Robert W. Cherny, "Patterns of Toleration and Discrimination in San Francisco: The Civil War to World War I," *California History* 73 (Summer 1994): 130–41; Issel, *Church and State in the City*, 1–3.

14. Gary Gerstle, "The Protean Character of American Liberalism," *American Historical Review* 99 (October 1994): 1043–73; William H. Chafe, ed., "Introduction," in *The Achievement of American Liberalism: The New Deal and Its Legacies* (New York: Columbia University Press, 2003), xi–xviii; Doug Rossinow, "Partners for Progress? Liberals and Radicals in the Long Twentieth Century," in *Making Sense of American Liberalism*, ed. Jonathan Bell and Timothy Stanley (Urbana: University of Illinois Press, 2012), 17–37.

15. Agustín Laó-Montes, "Niuyol: Urban Regime, Latino Social Movements, Ideologies of Latinidad," in *Mambo Montage: The Latinization of New York City*, ed. Agustín Laó-Montes and Arlene Dávila (New York: Columbia University Press, 2001), 119–45; Nicholas De Genova and Ana Y. Ramos-Zayas, *Latino Crossings: Mexicans, Puerto Ricans, and the Politics of Race and Citizenship* (New York: Routledge, 2003), chapter 7.

16. Gerstle, "Protean Character of American Liberalism," 1045; Chafe, "Introduction," xii; Robert O. Self, *American Babylon: Race and the Struggle for Postwar Oakland* (Princeton, NJ: Princeton University Press, 2003), 13–14.

17. The great exception here is Thomas's *Puerto Rican Citizen*.

18. Gary Gerstle and Steve Fraser, "Introduction," and Maurice Isserman and Michael Kazin, "The Failure and Success of the New Radicalism," both in *Rise and Fall of the New Deal Order*, ed. Fraser and Gerstle, xx–xxi and 228–37.

19. Alan Brinkley, *The End of Reform: New Deal Liberalism in Recession and War* (New York: Alfred A. Knopf, 1995), 3–14; Gerstle, "Protean Character of American Liberalism," 1044–45, 1068–69.

20. Matthew J. Countryman, *Up South: Civil Rights and Black Power in Philadelphia* (Philadelphia: University of Pennsylvania Press, 2006), 21–35; Mark Brilliant, *The Color of America*

Has Changed: How Racial Diversity Shaped Civil Rights Reform in California, 1945–1978 (New York: Oxford University Press, 2010), 7–8, 158–59.

21. Sidney M. Milkis, "Lyndon Johnson, the Great Society, and the 'Twilight' of the Modern Presidency," in *The Great Society and the High Tide of Liberalism*, ed. Sidney M. Milkis and Jerome Mileur (Amherst: University of Massachusetts Press, 2005), 1–37; Self, *American Babylon*, 198–210.

22. Countryman, *Up South*, 4.

23. Robert O. Self, *All in the Family: The Realignment of American Democracy Since the 1960s* (New York: Hill and Wang, 2012), 219–47; Susan M. Hartmann, "Liberal Feminism and the Reshaping of the New Deal Order," in *Making Sense of American Liberalism*, ed. Bell and Stanley, 202–28.

24. John D'Emilio and Estelle B. Freedman, *Intimate Matters: A History of Sexuality in America* (Chicago: University of Chicago Press, 1988).

25. De Genova and Ramos-Zayas, *Latino Crossings*, 1, 175; Laó-Montes, "Niuyol," 120–21; Deborah Paredez, *Selenidad: Selena, Latinos, and the Performance of Memory* (Durham, NC: Duke University Press, 2009), xiii; Juana María Rodríguez, *Queer Latinidad: Identity Practices, Discursive Spaces* (New York: New York University Press, 2003), 9–10.

26. Cristina Beltrán, *The Trouble with Unity: Latino Politics and the Creation of Identity* (New York: Oxford University Press, 2010), 6.

27. Pitti, *Devil in Silicon Valley*; George Sánchez, *Becoming Mexican American: Ethnicity, Culture and Identity in Chicano Los Angeles, 1900–1945* (New York: Oxford University Press, 1993); Gabriela Arredondo, *Mexican Chicago: Race, Identity, and Nation, 1916–39* (Urbana: University of Illinois Press, 2008); Thomas, *Puerto Rican Citizen*; Carmen Teresa Whalen, *From Puerto Rico to Philadelphia: Puerto Rican Workers and Postwar Economies* (Philadelphia: Temple University Press, 2001). The key exception to date is Lilia Fernández, *Brown in the Windy City: Mexicans and Puerto Ricans in Postwar Chicago* (Chicago: University of Chicago Press, 2012).

28. Ngai, *Impossible Subjects*, 7–8.

29. Raúl Coronado, *A World Not to Come: A History of Latino Writing and Print Culture* (Cambridge, MA: Harvard University Press, 2013), 29–30.

Chapter 1

1. The account is reconstructed from information provided by the Valle siblings to immigration authorities on arrival in San Francisco. S.S. *Venezuela* Passenger Manifest, 08 April 1924, list 3, "Passenger Lists of Vessels Arriving at San Francisco, CA, 1893–1953," Records of the Immigration and Naturalization Service, 1891–1957, RG 85, microfilm 1410, roll 182, National Archives and Records Administration, Washington, DC (hereafter NARA).

2. "El Sr. Gobernador Johnson," *La Crónica (LaC)*, 24 October 1914, 2. Titles of Spanish-language or bilingual news articles and essays will be cited as they appeared in the original source.

3. On the Panama Canal's construction, see Julie Greene, *The Canal Builders: Making America's Empire at the Panama Canal* (New York: Penguin, 2009).

4. U.S. Department of Commerce, Bureau of the Census, *Thirteenth Census of the United States Taken in the Year 1910, Statistics for California* (Washington, DC: Government Printing Office, 1914), 592; Bureau of Census, *Fourteenth Census of the United States, State Compendium: California* (Washington, DC: GPO, 1924), 25; State of California, Departments of Industrial Relations, Agriculture, and Social Welfare, *Mexicans in California: Report of Governor C. C. Young's Mexican Fact-Finding Committee* (San Francisco: State Printing Office, 1930), 46; Paul

Radin, *The Italians of San Francisco: Their Adjustment and Acculturation* (Sacramento: State Employment Relief Administration, 1935), 36.

5. San Francisco's economic preeminence at this time is discussed in William Issel and Robert Cherny, *San Francisco, 1865–1932: Politics, Power, and Urban Development* (Berkeley: University of California Press, 1986), chapter 2.

6. See Sánchez, *Becoming Mexican American*, chapters 1–3; Arredondo, *Mexican Chicago*, chapter 1; and Thomas, *Puerto Rican Citizen*, chapter 1.

7. International Institute of San Francisco (IISF), Annual Report to the National Board of the Young Women's Christian Associations, 1922, H–3, Records of IISF, collection 1066, box 1, Immigration History Research Center, University of Minnesota, Minneapolis (hereafter IHRC); "Repatriación de obreros mexicanos," *LaC*, 18 December 1915, 2. On immigration restriction debates, see Ngai, *Impossible Subjects*, chapter 1.

8. On Italians, see Dino Cinel, *From Italy to San Francisco: The Immigrant Experience* (Stanford, CA: Stanford University Press, 1982).

9. On San Francisco during these years, see Michael Kazin, *Barons of Labor: The San Francisco Building Trades and Union Power in the Progressive Era* (Urbana: University of Illinois Press, 1987), 234–45. For a critical comparison, see Lizabeth Cohen, *Making a New Deal: Industrial Workers in Chicago, 1919–1939* (New York: Cambridge University Press, 1990), chapter 1.

10. Julio G. Arce, "Entrando a la nueva decada," *Hispano América (HA)*, 19 April 1924, 1.

11. For a general introduction to the Native peoples residing in and brought to San Francisco during the late eighteenth and early nineteenth centuries, see Richard Levy, "Costanoan," in *Handbook of North American Indians*, vol. 8: *California*, ed. Robert Heizer (Washington, DC: Smithsonian Institution, 1978), 485–95.

12. Discussions of the founding of the mission and presidio can be found in Frank Soulé, John H. Gihon, and James Nisbet, *The Annals of San Francisco* (New York: D. Appleton, 1855), 46–48; John S. Hittell, *A History of the City of San Francisco* (San Francisco: A. L. Bancroft, 1878), 47–49; Hubert Howe Bancroft, *History of California, Volume 1: 1542–1800* (San Francisco: A. L. Bancroft, 1884), 279–92.

13. Soulé et al., *Annals of San Francisco*, 60–61; Hittell, *History of the City*, 72–78, 83–84. On mission secularization, see Steven Hackel, *Children of Coyote, Missionaries of St. Francis: Indian-Spanish Relations in Colonial California, 1769–1850* (Chapel Hill: University of North Carolina Press, 2005), chapter 9. Important scholarly accounts about the Californios include Leonard Pitt, *The Decline of the Californios: A Social History of the Spanish-Speaking Californians, 1846–1890* (Berkeley: University of California Press, 1966); and Douglas Monroy, "The Creation and Re-creation of Californio Society," in *Contested Eden: California Before the Gold Rush*, ed. Ramón Gutiérrez and Richard Orsi (Berkeley: University of California Press, 1998), 173–95.

14. Hittell, *History of the City*, 106; Soulé et al., *Annals of San Francisco*, 162–63, 167–71.

15. On the U.S.-Mexico War, see Thomas Hietala, *Manifest Design: American Exceptionalism and Empire* (Ithaca, NY: Cornell University Press, 1985); and Amy Greenberg, *A Wicked War: Polk, Clay, Lincoln, and the 1846 U.S. Invasion of Mexico* (New York: Vintage, 2012).

16. Soulé et al., *Annals of San Francisco*, 176–77; Hittell, *History of the City*, 117.

17. Soulé et al., *Annals of San Francisco*, 243; Radin, *Italians of San Francisco*, 29.

18. Roger Lotchin, *San Francisco, 1846–1856: From Hamlet to City* (New York: Oxford University Press, 1974), xix. On violence in gold country, see Pitt, *Decline of the Californios*, 56–58; and Susan Lee Johnson, *Roaring Camp: The Social World of the California Gold Rush* (New York: W. W. Norton, 2000), 196–208.

19. Soulé et al., *Annals of San Francisco*, 471.

20. Hubert Howe Bancroft, *History of California, Volume VII: 1860–1890* (San Francisco: History Co., 1890), 700; David Weber and Arnoldo de León, eds., *Foreigners in Their Native Land: Historical Roots of the Mexican Americans*, rev. ed. (Albuquerque: University of New Mexico Press, 2004).

21. Lotchin, *San Francisco*, 114; *El Eco del Pacífico*, ca. 1856–59, cited in Pitt, *Decline of the Californios*, 200; and Roberto Trevino, "Becoming Mexican American: The Spanish-Language Press and the Biculturation of Californio Elites, 1852–1870," Working Paper Series No. 27, Stanford Center for Chicano Research, 1989, 9.

22. IISF, Annual Report of the International Institute Branch of the Young Women's Christian Association, 1925, collection 1066, box 1, IHRC; Radin, *Italians of San Francisco*, 36; Henrietta Horak, "S.F. Spanish Colony Sorrows over War," *San Francisco Chronicle (SFC)*, 06 September 1936, 10.

23. J. Piña, "La fuerza de estas tierras," *LaC*, 31 December 1916, 5.

24. The literature on Mexican immigration during these decades is extensive. A sample of important works includes Sánchez, *Becoming Mexican American*; Zaragosa Vargas, *Proletarians of the North: A History of Mexican American Industrial Workers in Detroit and the Midwest, 1917–1933* (Berkeley: University of California Press, 1993); Pitti, *Devil in Silicon Valley*; and Arredondo, *Mexican Chicago*.

25. "Repatriación de obreros."

26. For an introduction to the Mexican Revolution, see John Mason Hart, *Revolutionary Mexico: The Coming and Process of the Mexican Revolution* (Berkeley: University of California Press, 1987).

27. "Los mismos . . . los mismos . . . y los mismos," *HA*, 7 January 1919, 1; Leonard Austin, *Around the World in San Francisco* (Palo Alto, CA: James Ladd Delkin, 1940), 105.

28. Laura Hoffman Zarrugh, "*Gente de Mi Tierra*: Mexican Village Migrants in a California Community," PhD dissertation, University of California, Berkeley, 1974, 11–14.

29. On the significance of the railroads, see Sánchez, *Becoming Mexican American*, 20–22.

30. Robert Willson, "San Francisco's Foreign Colonies–No. 3–Spanish-Mexican," *San Francisco Examiner (SFE)*, 02 December 1923, K3.

31. See Lillian Guerra, "The Promise and Disillusion of Americanization: Surveying the Socioeconomic Terrain of Early-Twentieth-Century Puerto Rico," *Journal of the Center for Puerto Rican Studies* 11, no. 1 (Fall 1999): 9–31; and Cesar Ayala, *American Sugar Kingdom: The Plantation Economy of the Spanish Caribbean, 1898–1934* (Chapel Hill: University of North Carolina Press, 1999).

32. "The Porto Rican Exodus," *NYT*, 04 April 1901, 5.

33. "Porto Ricans Go to Hawaii," *NYT*, 07 December 1900, 1; "Puertorriqueños que van a Hawaii," *La Correspondencia*, 17 December 1900, and "Report of the Commissioner of Labor on Hawaii," July 1903, both in History Task Force, *Sources for the Study of the Puerto Rican Migration, 1879–1930* (New York: Centro de Estudios Puertorriqueños, 1982), 20, 57. On the migration to Hawaii, see Carmen Teresa Whalen, "Colonialism, Citizenship, and the Making of the Puerto Rican Diaspora: An Introduction," in *The Puerto Rican Diaspora: Historical Perspectives*, ed. C. T. Whalen and Victor Vásquez-Hernández (Philadelphia: Temple University Press, 2005), 3–12.

34. "La colonia portorriqueña de California cuenta con dos grades sociedades," *La Correspondencia*, 12 October 1925, in *Sources for the Study of the Puerto Rican Migration*, 183.

35. "Porto Rican Colony of This City," *San Francisco Call*, 28 May 1905, 5; "La colonia puertorriqueña en California," *La Correspondencia*, 03 November 1923, in *Sources for the Study of the Puerto Rican Migration*, 176.

36. On Puerto Rican migration during the World War I era and the 1920s, see Whalen, "Colonialism, Citizenship," 13–20; Virginia Sánchez Korrol, *From Colonia to Community: The History of Puerto Ricans in New York City* (Berkeley: University of California Press, 1994), chapters 1–2; Thomas, *Puerto Rican Citizen*, chapter 1.

37. "Trabajadores de Puerto Rico vendran a los Estados Unidos," *HA*, 10 February 1918, 12; IISF, Annual Report of I.I. for 1930, 28, collection 1066, box 1, IHRC. On Puerto Ricans in Arizona, see Whalen, "Colonialism, Citizenship," 21–22.

38. To date, historians have devoted little attention to Central Americans. Most scholarship has emanated from sociologists, anthropologists, and cultural studies scholars, and has been situated in the late twentieth and early twenty-first centuries. See, for example, Cecilia Menjívar, *Fragmented Ties: Salvadoran Immigrant Networks in America* (Berkeley: University of California Press, 2000); and Nora Hamilton and Norma Stoltz Chinchilla, *Seeking Community in a Global City: Guatemalans and Salvadorans in Los Angeles* (Philadelphia: Temple University Press, 2001).

39. IISF, Annual Reports of I.I. for 1925 and 1926, collection 1066, box 1, IHRC.

40. For a general introduction to early twentieth-century Central America, see Héctor Pérez Brignoli, *Breve historia de Centroamérica*, 3rd ed. (Madrid: Alianza Editorial, 1988), chapter 4. On Nicaragua and El Salvador, see Jeffrey Gould and Aldo Lauria-Santiago, *To Rise in Darkness: Revolution, Repression, and Memory in El Salvador, 1920–1932* (Durham, NC: Duke University Press, 2008); and Jeffrey Gould, *To Lead as Equals: Rural Protest and Political Consciousness in Chinandega, Nicaragua, 1912–1979* (Chapel Hill: University of North Carolina Press, 1990), chapters 1 and 3.

41. Brian Godfrey, *Neighborhoods in Transition: The Making of San Francisco's Ethnic and Nonconformist Communities* (Berkeley: University of California Press, 1988), 139; Center for Education and Lifelong Learning, *Resource Guide of the Hidden Neighborhoods of San Francisco: The Mission* (San Francisco: KQED, 1994), 1.

42. Enid Valentine, "The Possibility of a Club for the Latin Americans of San Francisco," *Centro América*, 20 February 1921, 8.

43. "Bars Let Down for Refugees," *SFC*, 11 November 1929, 7; "Murder Plot Charged by Nicaraguans," *SFC*, 18 October 1929, 7; "El caso de El Salvador," *HA*, 04 April 1932, 3.

44. Bancroft, *History of California, Volume VII*, 700.

45. Ian Haney López, *White by Law: The Legal Construction of Race* (New York: New York University Press, 1997); Laura Gómez, *Manifest Destinies: The Making of the Mexican American Race* (New York: New York University Press, 2007), 4–5, 83–87.

46. Soulé et al., *Annals of San Francisco*, 506; Bancroft, *History of California, Volume VII*, 700; Radin, *Italians of San Francisco*, 28.

47. Soulé et al., *Annals of San Francisco*, 258, 472; Bancroft, *History of California, Volume VII*, 700; Vicente Pérez Rosales, *Recuerdos del Pasado* [ca. 1880s], translated and published by Edwin Morby and Arturo Torres-Rioseco as *California Adventure* (San Francisco: Book Club of California, 1947), 68.

48. Soulé et al., *Annals of San Francisco*, 53–54, 472; Herbert Asbury, *The Barbary Coast: An Informal History of the San Francisco Underworld* (Garden City: Garden City Publishing, 1933), 33.

49. Elizabeth Haight Strong, "Little Mexico in the Ruins of a Church," *San Francisco Call*, 13 January 1907, 9; "Porto Rican Colony of This City."

50. Strong, "Little Mexico"; Enos Brown, "Under Our Flag: Uncle Sam's White, Brown and Black Children Throughout the World," *San Francisco Call*, 30 June 1907, 4–5. On the ideology of civilization, see Gail Bederman, *Manliness and Civilization: A Cultural History of Gender and Race in the United States, 1880–1917* (Chicago: University of Chicago Press, 1995), chapters 1–2.

51. Information is drawn from extensive review of passenger lists. Some examples include the S.S. *Peru* Passenger Manifest, 30 July 1916, list 5; S.S. *Sachem* Passenger Manifest, 04 May 1920, list 7; and S.S. *Venezuela* Passenger Manifest, 08 April 1924, list 3, all found in "Passenger Lists," RG 85, microfilm 1410, rolls 90, 134, and 182, respectively, NARA.

52. Thomas Guglielmo, *White on Arrival: Italians, Race, Color, and Power in Chicago, 1890–1945* (New York: Oxford University Press, 2003).

53. Genevieve Green, "Around the Exposition," *San Francisco Call*, 17 June 1900, 8; Green, "Pan–Latinism," *San Francisco Call*, 27 April 1903, 4; Adriana Spadoni, "The Sunday Night Baile in San Francisco's Spanish Colony," *San Francisco Call*, 20 October 1907, 8.

54. Issel and Cherny, San *Francisco*, 55–56. On Asian Americans, see Judy Yung, *Unbound Feet: A Social History of Chinese Women in San Francisco* (Berkeley: University of California Press, 1995); and Yong Chen, *Chinese San Francisco, 1850–1943: A Trans-Pacific Community* (Stanford, CA: Stanford University Press, 2000). On African Americans, see Douglas Henry Daniels, *Pioneer Urbanites: A Social and Cultural History of Black San Francisco* (Berkeley: University of California Press, 1991); and Albert Broussard, *Black San Francisco: The Struggle for Racial Equality in the West, 1900–1954* (Lawrence: University Press of Kansas, 1993).

55. Ads in *El Nuevo Mundo*, 16 September 1864, 4; 18 December 1864, 4.

56. Clementina Garcia Landgrave, "A Temple with Much History: Church of Our Lady of Guadalupe," *El Latino*, December 1999, 5–11; Strong, "Little Mexico"; Amelia Ransome Neville, *The Fantastic City: Memoirs of the Social and Romantic Life of Old San Francisco* (Boston: Houghton Mifflin, 1932), 34, 43; Asbury, *Barbary Coast*, 33; Robert O'Brien, *This Is San Francisco* (New York: Whittlesey House, 1948), 118.

57. "Census Spanish Church," January 1917, Our Lady of Guadalupe general file, Archives of the Archdiocese of San Francisco, Menlo Park, CA (hereafter AASF).

58. Ads in *LaC*, 31 October 1914, 4; 05 December 1914, 5; 01 October 1916, 13–14; and 05 November 1916, 13–15; "El banco de los españoles y latino americanos," Bank of America ad, *HA*, 18 April 1931, 2.

59. Shone Martinez, "History of San Francisco's Spanish Speaking People," 1972, 2, unpublished paper, Mission History Vertical Files Collection, Mission Branch, SFPL.

60. Issel and Cherny, *San Francisco*, 65.

61. S.S. *San Jose* Passenger Manifest, 11 July 1916, list 9; S.S. *Sachem* Passenger Manifest, 04 May 1920, list 8, both in "Passenger Lists," RG 85, microfilm 1410, rolls 90 and 134, NARA.

62. Ads in *LaC*, 17 October 1914, 4; 31 October 1914, 4.

63. "De viaje," *HA*, 10 January 1920, 4; S.S. *Sachem* Passenger Manifest, 04 May 1920, list 7, "Passenger Lists," RG 85, microfilm 1410, roll 134, NARA; Austin, *Around the World* (1940), 102.

64. Issel and Cherny, *San Francisco*, 58, 66.

65. Ad in *HA*, 28 August 1920, 4.

66. S.S. *Corinto* Passenger Manifest, 19 April 1927, lists 2 and 5; and S.S. *Sachem* Passenger Manifest, 04 May 1920, list 9, all in "Passenger Lists," RG 85, microfilm 1410, rolls 220 and 134,

respectively, NARA. Butter was born in El Salvador, racially classified as Spanish American, and described as having a dark complexion. His non-Hispanicized surname may have been a product of familial intermarriage or a spelling error on the part of immigration authorities.

67. Issel and Cherny, *San Francisco*, 58–60.

68. S.S. *Venezuela* Passenger Manifest, 08 April 1924, list 5; and S.S. *Newport* Passenger Manifest, 30 April 1922, list 7, both in "Passenger Lists," RG 85, microfilm 1410, rolls 182 and 159, respectively, NARA.

69. On commercialized leisure, see Jessica Sewell, *Women and the Everyday City: Public Space in San Francisco, 1890–1915* (Minneapolis: University of Minnesota Press, 2011). Beyond San Francisco, see Kathy Peiss, *Cheap Amusements: Working Women and Leisure in Turn-of-the-Century New York* (Philadelphia: Temple University Press, 1986); and George Chauncey, *Gay New York: Gender, Urban Culture, and the Making of the Gay Male World, 1890–1940* (New York: Basic, 1994).

70. Judy Yung has noted that "almost all" of Chinese Americans' social activities "occurred in a segregated setting." See *Unbound Feet*, 146–48.

71. Feliciano Hernández, "Consultas," *HA*, 10 May 1919, 2. On African Americans, see Broussard, *Black San Francisco*, 19–20, 71–73

72. "Gran baile popular y fiesta de carnaval," *LaC*, 13 November 1915, 1; "La fiesta del Club Alegría," *HA*, 08 October 1921, 4; "El baile del Club Primavera, *HA*, 19 August 1922, 4; and "El Club Ideal," *HA*, 01 October 1927, 8.

73. "Gran baile de inauguración del Club Juventud y Reforma," *LaC*, 15 October 1916, 4. On Progressive reform work targeting young people, see Peiss, *Cheap Amusements*, chapter 7.

74. "Club Social Centro-Americano," *Centro América*, 20 February 1921, 5.

75. C. A. García, Ramón Corvera, et al. to Archbishop of San Francisco, 15 August 1909, Guadalupe general file, AASF.

76. Henry Langley, *The San Francisco Directory* (San Francisco: Commercial Steam Presses, Valentine & Co., 1863), 509; Langley, *The San Francisco Directory* (1875), 979; Directory Publishing Company, *Langley's San Francisco Directory* (San Francisco: Francis, Valentine, 1880), 1120; H. S. Crocker Company, *Crocker-Langley San Francisco Directory* (San Francisco: H. S. Crocker, 1905), 41.

77. "Celebración de aniversario," *HA*, 23 June 1918, 4; "La colonia portorriqueña de California," 184; "La Sociedad Española de Beneficencia Mutua en San Francisco," *LaC*, 08 August 1914, 2; "Baile de la Sociedad 'La Alianza,' " *HA*, 27 May 1922, 4.

78. "Invitación a la colonia hispano-americana," *LaC*, 17 July 1915, 4; Austin, *Around the World* (1940), 99.

79. "La colonia portorriqueña de California," 185; "Notas de la colonia portorriqueña," *HA*, 23 August 1924, 4.

80. Fernando García, "Qué papel desempeña el Centro Benéfico, que no practica la caridad?" *LaC*, 05 December 1914, 1.

81. Ibid., 4; "Pabellón de la unión ibero americana y monumento de Isabel la Católica," *LaC*, 28 November 1914, 2.

82. "El Club Azteca de Sras dará un gran baile de caridad," *HA*, 12 October 1918, 4; "Trabajos del Club Azteca de Señoras por la caridad," *HA*, 09 October 1920, 4; and "Una hermosa fiesta de caridad," *HA*, 05 January 1924, 1.

83. Austin, *Around the World* (1940), 105–6.

84. Ads in *HA*, 25 November 1922, 2, 4; 24 February 1923, 2; 16 August 1924, 2, 4.

85. Martinez, "History of San Francisco's Spanish Speaking People," 1; employment ads in *HA*, 27 January 1918, 14; 02 February 1924, 2; 23 January 1926, 3.

86. "Vida social," *HA*, 14 September 1918, 2.

87. Michael Kazin, *Barons of Labor: The San Francisco Building Trades and Union Power in the Progressive Era* (Urbana: University of Illinois Press, 1987), 162–71; Broussard, *Black San Francisco*, 13, 48.

88. "Repatriación de obreros."

89. Kazin, *Barons of Labor*, 24, and fn. 38, 34.

90. On unionization in the early 1900s, see Issel and Cherny, *San Francisco*, 88–92.

91. Arthur Puga and Jose Martinez to San Francisco Labor Council (SFLC) secretary, 16 December 1909; and Frank Morrison, AFL secretary, to Andrew Gallagher, SFLC secretary, 29 December 1909, both in SFLC Records, carton 17, Ship Scalers Union (SSU) folder, Bancroft Library, University of California, Berkeley (hereafter BANC).

92. Humberto Costa and J. Calvo to Andrew Gallagher, 21 April 1910; and Jose Castillo to John Nolan, SFLC secretary, 19 June 1912, both SFLC, carton 17, SSU folder, BANC. On the origins of the eight-hour workday campaign, see Leon Fink, *Workingmen's Democracy: The Knights of Labor and American Politics* (Urbana: University of Illinois Press, 1983), chapters 1–2.

93. Shelton Stromquist, *Re-inventing "The People": The Progressive Movement, the Class Problem, and the Origins of Modern Liberalism* (Urbana: University of Illinois Press, 2006), 168.

94. Costa and Calvo to Gallagher; and J. Calvo to Andrew Gallagher, 13 December 1910, SFLC, carton 17, SSU folder, BANC.

95. Frank Morrison to Andrew Gallagher, 02 February 1911; and Costa and Calvo to Gallagher, 13 December 1910, both SFLC, carton 17, SSU folder, BANC.

96. J. Piña, "Del estado de oro," *LaC*, 08 October 1916, 4; Mario T. García, *Memories of Chicano History: The Life and Narrative of Bert Corona* (Berkeley: University of California Press, 1994), 95.

97. "Huelgas al por mayor," *HA*, 04 October 1919, 1; "Se abriran pronto 'los Shipyards,'" *HA*, 08 November 1919, 1. On the shipyard workers' strike, see Kazin, *Barons of Labor*, 246–47.

98. "La proyectada unión de trabajadores de la raza," *HA*, 15 February 1919, 1. On postwar labor unrest and repression, see David Montgomery, *The Fall of the House of Labor: The Workplace, the State, and American Labor Activism, 1865–1925* (Cambridge: Cambridge University Press, 1987), chapter 8.

99. "Baile de la Sociedad 'La Alianza,'" *HA*, 27 May 1922, 4; "Baile de la Alianza de Auxilios Mutuos," *HA*, 16 June 1923, 4; "El baile de 'La Alianza,'" *HA*, 28 April 1928, 8. To date, I have not located any additional materials on La Confederación.

100. Fernando García Muñoz, "Pro raza," *LaC*, 25 April 1914, 1–2; "'Hispano-América' y 'Mefistofeles' se han unido," *HA*, 27 July 1918, 1.

101. "Los abusos de los negreros con los trabajadores de Alaska," *HA*, 24 September 1918, 1; "Como fueron explotados los trabajadores que marcharon a Alaska," *HA*, 28 September 1918, 1.

102. Julio G. Arce, "Se hará justicia a los trabajadores?" *HA*, 18 January 1919, 1.

103. "Alaska y los trabajadores," *HA*, 05 January 1924, 1, 3.

104. "El Sr. Gobernador Johnson"; "¡Importante á los ciudadanos!" *LaC*, 17 October 1914, 4.

105. "Rolph candidato para Mayor," *HA*, 20 September 1919, 1; "Rolph debe ser reelecto," *HA*, 27 October 1923, 1; "La lucha electoral en S.F.," *HA*, 29 October 1927, 1. On Rolph's administration, see Issel and Cherny, *San Francisco*, 166.

106. "Como debe votarse en las elecciones próximas," *HA*, 30 October 1920, 1. On Asian immigrants' ineligibility for citizenship, see Ngai, *Impossible Subjects*, 37–50.

107. See Benedict Anderson, *Imagined Communities: Reflections on the Origin and Spread of Nationalism* (New York: Verso, 1991); Eric Hobsbawn, "Inventing Traditions," in *The Invention of Tradition*, ed. Eric Hobsbawn and Terence Ranger (Cambridge: Cambridge University Press, 1983, 2003), 1–14.

108. García Muñoz, "Pro raza," 1–2.

109. Julio Arce, "La unión de los pueblos hispanos del continente," *HA*, 27 July 1918, 1. An overview of U.S. intervention in Latin America during these years can be found in John Charles Chasteen, *Born in Blood and Fire: A Concise History of Latin America*, 2nd ed. (New York: W. W. Norton, 2006), 200–9.

110. Miguel Ruelas, "Abierta y cordial contestación de 'Hispano América' a 'El Imparcial,'" *HA*, 4 June 1927, 1; "Nuestro saludo a los pueblos centroamericanos," *HA*, September 1927, special ed., 4.

111. "La Sociedad Española de Beneficencia Mutua en San Francisco"; "La fiesta del Club Social América," *HA*, 23 September 1922, 1.

112. "Club Político Hispano-Americano," *HA*, 03 November 1923, 4.

Chapter 2

1. "Alaska Cannery Workers Battle Cops at the Docks," *Western Worker (WW)*, 14 May 1934, 1, 5; "Los Obreros de Alaska Baten A la Policía En los Muelles," *Lucha Obrera (LO)*, May 1934, 1.

2. Nelson Lichtenstein, *State of the Union: A Century of American Labor* (Princeton, NJ: Princeton University Press, 2002), 32–33. On the New Deal, see William Leuchtenburg, *Franklin D. Roosevelt and the New Deal, 1932–1940* (New York: Harper & Row, 1963); Brinkley, *End of Reform*; and Cohen, *Making a New Deal*.

3. Issel and Cherny, *San Francisco*, 214.

4. Nelson, *Workers on the Waterfront*, especially chapter 5.

5. Arrendondo, *Mexican Chicago*, 59–61, 159–60; Thomas, *Puerto Rican Citizen*, 93, 128. The literature on agricultural workers during the 1930s is much more extensive. A sample includes Guerin-Gonzales, *Mexican Workers and American Dreams*; Neil Foley, *The White Scourge: Mexicans, Blacks, and Poor Whites in Texas Cotton Culture* (Berkeley: University of California Press, 1999); and Pitti, *Devil in Silicon Valley*.

6. Robert Korstad, *Civil Rights Unionism: Tobacco Workers and the Struggle for Democracy in the Mid-Twentieth-Century South* (Chapel Hill: University of North Carolina Press, 2003); Zaragosa Vargas, *Labor Rights Are Civil Rights: Mexican American Workers in Twentieth-Century America* (Princeton, NJ: Princeton University Press, 2007), especially chapter 4.

7. "Celebración de la independencia del Peru," *HA*, 23 July 1932, 8; "Las fiestas patrias en el California Hall," *HA*, 10 September 1932, 8; "Obsequio a la colonia latinoamericana" and "Baile de Halloween," both *HA*, 15 October 1932, 8.

8. Pitti, *Devil in Silicon Valley*, 105–6.

9. "La falta de trabajo y la inmigración," *HA*, 28 February 1931, 1; Antonio Escobar, "La depresión económica," *HA*, 28 February 1931, 3; IISF, Annual Report for 1930, 28, and Service to Individuals: Case Work, ca. 1934, 4, collection 1066, boxes 1 and 15, IHRC.

10. "La ciudad da empleo a cientos de hombres para ayudarles," *HA*, 14 February 1931, 1; "El éxodo de extranjeros," *HA*, 28 February 1931, 1; Austin, *Around the World* (1940), 104. On public relief efforts, see Issel, *Church and State in the City*, 27.

11. For an overview of the repatriation movement, see Francisco E. Balderrama and Raymond Rodríguez, *Decade of Betrayal: Mexican Repatriation in the 1930s* (Albuquerque: University of New Mexico Press, 1995). On efforts in Los Angeles, see Sánchez, *Becoming Mexican American*, 214–15.

12. Austin, *Around the World* (1940), 104. According to William Issel, San Francisco's response to rising unemployment proved more effective than in Los Angeles, Seattle, and Portland. See Issel, *Church and State in the City*, 27.

13. Annie Clo Watson, "Special Nationality Problems of the Pacific Coast," 22 May 1934, Annie Clo Watson Papers, IHRC; "El número de deportados en EE.UU. va en aumento," *HA*, 11 July 1931, 1. Ventura is a fictional surname; social workers identified them as the Ventanas (translation, "windows"), a decision driven by staff's desire to maintain anonymity.

14. "Las fiestas patrias en el California Hall Auditorium," *HA*, 13 September 1930, 8; "Salud California! Happy Days Governor Rolph!" *HA*, 08 November 1930, 1.

15. "El President Hoover," *HA*, 29 October 1932, 1; "El presidente electo de los E.U.," *HA*, 12 November 1932, 1. On the 1932 election, see Leuchtenburg, *Franklin D. Roosevelt and the New Deal*, chapters 1–2.

16. F.L.I.S., "La ley de recuperación industrial," *HA*, 08 July 1933, 8. On the NIRA, see Lichtenstein, *State of the Union*, 25, 36; Brinkley, *Liberalism and Its Discontents*, 27–29.

17. "Organizing the 'Front': The Next Steps," *The Waterfront Worker* (*TWW*), February 1933, 1; "Our Policy," *TWW*, June 1933, 5. On the MWIU, see Nelson, *Workers on the Waterfront*, 79–80, 107–8.

18. Alaska Packers Association, "¡Hombres sin trabajo! Id a Alaska!" *HA*, 29 April 1933, 4.

19. Cannery Workers Union (CWU), "To Whom It May Concern," ca. 1934, SFLC, carton 6, CWU folder, BANC; "Packed Court Sees Sentencing of Alaska Packers Job Sharks," *WW*, 26 March 1934, 4; "Se Organizan Los Obreros De Alaska Para Mejor Lucha Por Sus Intereses," *LO*, April 1934, 1.

20. On agricultural unions and Communists' support, see Cletus E. Daniel, *Bitter Harvest: A History of California Farmworkers, 1870–1941* (Berkeley: University of California Press, 1981), chapter 4; Pitti, *Devil in Silicon Valley*, 111–15; Vargas, *Labor Rights Are Civil Rights*, 64–65, 71–72. For an introduction to the TUUL, see Edward Johanningsmeier, "The Trade Union Unity League: American Communists and the Transition to Industrial Communism," *Labor History* 42, no. 2 (2001): 159–77.

21. "Se Organizan Los Obreros De Alaska."

22. "Packed Court Sees Sentencing of Alaska Packers"; SFLC, *Resolution on Alaska Cannery Workers*, 02 February 1934, printed in *Labor Clarion* (*LC*), 09 February 1934, 10; "Alaska Peonage Case Ends in Convictions," *LC*, 16 March 1934, 6.

23. "Packed Court Sees Sentencing of Alaska Packers."

24. "Unense Los Scalers En Militante Unión," *LO*, June 1934, 1.

25. "Coast Longshoremen on Strike!" *WW*, 14 May 1934, 1; "Longshoremen Strike After Futile Efforts to Secure Agreement," *LC*, 11 May 1934, 1–2; "Longshoremen's Strike Ties Up Pacific Coast Shipping," *LC*, 18 May 1934, 3.

26. "After Mediation What?" *TWW*, 07 May 1934, 1–2; "Arbitration? No. No!" *TWW*, 21 May 1934, 1–2; "14,000 Estibadores En Huelga En La Costa del Pacífico," *LO*, May 1934, 1; "Longshoremen Strike After Futile Efforts."

27. "Unense Los Scalers"; "Nathan Attempt to Stop Cannery Union Backing Stevedores," *WW*, 21 May 1934, 4.

28. "'The Strike Is out of Hand,' Says Chamber of Commerce," *WW*, 28 May 1934, 1; "5,000 Stevedores, Families, Sympathizers in S.F. Parade," *WW*, 21 May 1934, 2.

29. "Longshoremen! Seamen! Don't Be Tricked!" *WW*, 21 May 1934, 1.

30. "Attempted 'Opening' of Port of San Francisco Meets Resistance of Strikers and Sympathizers," *LC*, 06 July 1934, 1; "State Militia Occupies San Francisco Waterfront," *LC*, 13 July 1934, 1; Ira B. Cross, *A History of the Labor Movement in California* (Berkeley: University of California Press, 1935), 257.

31. "I.L.A. Pide Se Vote La Huelga General" and "No Debe Romperse El Frente Dicen Los Estibadores de S.F.," *LO*, June 1934, 1.

32. Cross, *History of the Labor Movement*, 259–61.

33. Issel, *Church and State in the City*, 54; Nelson, *Workers on the Waterfront*, 138.

34. R. L. Polk & Co., *Polk's Crocker-Langley San Francisco City Directory* (San Francisco, 1935), 1025; "Leaders," *Dispatcher*, 04 January 1944, 4.

35. Glenna Matthews, "The Fruit Workers of the Santa Clara Valley: Alternative Paths to Union Organization During the 1930s," *Pacific Historical Review* 54, no. 1 (February 1985): 53.

36. CWU, memorandum, 04 May 1934, SFLC, carton 6, CWU folder, BANC.

37. "Las Canerias Y Alaska Centros de Explotacion" *LO*, September 1934, 2; "Los Obreros De Alaska Deben Y Pueden Edificar Una Union," *LO*, February 1935, 2.

38. Jacinto Penalver and Mary Saldoval to John O'Connell, 11 September 1934; O'Connell to Frank Morrison, 23 October 1934; Morrison to O'Connell, 10 December 1934; O'Connell to Sandoval, 10 December 1934, all SFLC, carton 17, SSU folder, BANC.

39. CWU, "To Whom It May Concern" and memorandum, BANC.

40. "Ship Scalers' Locked Out!" *TWW*, 19 August 1935, 4; "Employers Back of Disruption at Scaler Meet," *TWW*, 30 September 1935, 4.

41. "Scalers Framed on Murder Charge," *TWW*, 21 October 1935, 3; Ship Scalers Defense Committee (SSDC), "To All Affiliated Bodies of the Maritime Federation Bay Area District Council #2," 18 December 1935; SSU, "Stop Work to Protest the Frame-Up of the Four Scalers," 19 December 1935; SSU, "Stop These and Future Frame Up-s," 20 December 1935, all MFP, box 31, folder 23, LARC.

42. "Fight Against Vigilante Terrorism," *TWW*, 16 September 1935, 5; "Four Victims of Scaler Frame-Up to Be Tried Wednesday," *TWW*, 09 December 1935, 2.

43. SSU, "Stop These and Future Frame Up-s" and "Stop Work to Protest," LARC.

44. "Four Union Men on Trial—for Life!" *TWW*, 16 December 1935, 1; "Strike Protesting Brings Release Near for Scaler Four," *TWW*, 23 December 1935, 2; SSDC, "To All Affiliated Bodies," MFP, box 31, folder 23, LARC.

45. "The Freedom of the Four Scalers Points the Way to Victory in the Modesto Case," *TWW*, 30 December 1935, 8.

46. John O'Connell to Alaska Cannery Workers and Fish Reduction Workers, 02 December 1936; Theodore Johnson to Mary Sandoval, 05 December 1936; O'Connell to Frank Morrison, 14 December 1936, all SFLC, carton 6, CPWU folder, BANC; "Del Rey Cannery Workers Sign into Union," *WW*, 27 April 1937, 7.

47. "S.F. Local Wins First Cannery Closed Shop," *WW*, 03 June 1937, 1.

48. On the 1937 cannery struggles, see Daniel, *Bitter Harvest*, 275–80; Glenna Matthews, *Silicon Valley, Women, and the California Dream: Gender, Class, and Opportunity in the Twentieth Century* (Stanford, CA: Stanford University Press, 2002), 71–73. On the Cal San contest, see Vicki Ruiz, *Cannery Women, Cannery Lives: Mexican Women, Unionization, and the California*

Food Processing Industry, 1930–1950 (Albuquerque: University of New Mexico Press, 1987), 75–77; Sánchez, *Becoming Mexican American*, 242–43.

49. "How Could LABOR Do This to Labor?" *Labor Herald* (*LH*), 15 June 1937, 1; "Shelley Raps Tactics Used by Vandeleur," *LH*, 22 July 1937, 1.

50. "A.F. of L. Tries to Break Tea Garden Strike," *Agricultural and Cannery Union News* (supplement in *LH*), 20 July 1937, A-1; Processing Workers Conference minutes, UCAPAWA District 2 Convention, 11 May 1940, 2, MFP, box 65, folder 6, LARC.

51. "Alaska Union Reports Unity," *WW*, 25 January 1937, 6; "Alaska Canner Union Sets Up Union Fund," *WW*, 29 April 1937, 7; "Union Ended Dope Racket in Canneries," *WW*, 02 September 1937, 7.

52. "Alaska Cannery Union Shows Great Gains in 18 Months," "Union Put in Regulations of Sanitation," "Profiteering Was Killed by Union," and "Alaska Union Provided Medical Aid to Members," all *WW*, 02 September 1937, 7.

53. "Alaska Cannery Workers Vote CIO 40 to 1," *LH*, 20 October 1937, 1; Jack Berolla to MFP, 20 November 1937, MFP, box 27, folder 15; Pete Garcia and Mary Sandoval to MFP, 11 October 1937, MFP, box 31, folder 23, LARC.

54. "CIO Authorizes Holding of National Convention" and "A Few Top AFL Men Against ALL Labor," both *LH*, 20 October 1937, 1.

55. On progressivism in 1930s San Francisco, see Issel, *Church and State in the City*, 40–60. For discussions of the Popular Front, see Michael Denning, *The Cultural Front: The Laboring of American Culture in the Twentieth Century* (New York: Verso, 1997), chapter 1; and Robin D. G. Kelley, *Hammer and Hoe: Alabama Communists During the Great Depression* (Chapel Hill: University of North Carolina Press, 1990), chapter 6. On the AFL and the New Deal, see Lichtenstein, *State of the Union*, 63–66.

56. Harry Bridges quoted in "S.F. Members of C.I.O. Form Organization," *SFC*, 02 August 1937, 2.

57. "700 Hundred S.F. Furniture Workers Join CIO," *LH*, 10 November 1937, 1; "Shelley Flays CIO Drive on Can Workers," *SFC*, 08 May 1937, 3.

58. Daniel Katz, *All Together Different: Yiddish Socialists, Garment Workers, and the Labor Roots of Multiculturalism* (New York: New York University Press, 2011).

59. "International Representative Honor Guest of Cloakmakers," *LC*, 09 February 1934.

60. "Jennie Matyas and the ILGWU," oral history conducted by Corinne Gibb, 1955, 126, 132, Regional Oral History Office, BANC.

61. International Ladies' Garment Workers Union (ILGWU) Local 101, ledgers of incoming members, 1933–1936, in Records of the San Francisco Joint ILGWU Board (hereafter SFILGWU), 2001/037, box 1, LARC.

62. "Jennie Matyas and the ILGWU," 141–47; ILGWU Local 101, ledger no. 829, 1936, SFILGWU, box 1, LARC. Matyas discussed a historical actor named Ada but did not identify her surname. The union's ledger lists an incoming member named Aida Hogan, whose linguistic preference and nationality were "Spanish." I have deferred to the union's record, though it is possible that these were two different individuals.

63. "Jennie Matyas and the ILGWU," 144, 148–50, 153.

64. "Broaden Out Anti-Picket Law Drive," *WW*, 18 January 1937, 1.

65. SSU, Resolution on Anti-Picketing Ordinance, 13 September 1936, in Mary Sandoval to John O'Connell, 14 September 1936, SFLC, carton 17, SSU folder, BANC.

66. SSU, Resolution, April 1937, SFLC, carton 17, SSU folder, BANC.

67. Ibid.

68. Committee "FOR" Anti-Picketing Ordinance, "Vote YES on Proposition 8," 1–2, San Francisco Registrar of Voters, *Propositions to Be Voted on at General Municipal Election to Be Held November 2, 1937*, San Francisco Ballot Propositions Database (hereafter SFBPD), SFPL.

69. "Proposition No. 8 Clashes with Constitutional Rights," "Hundreds of Clubs Join Battle Against Anti-Picket Measure," and "Citizens of Foreign Birth Fight Anti-Picketing Law," all *LH*, 27 October 1937, 1, 4.

70. "Unity Is the Only Solution," *WW*, October 1933, 1, 5.

71. ILWU, *The ILWU Story: Three Decades of Militant Unionism* (San Francisco: ILWU, 1963), 9; Nelson, *Workers on the Waterfront*, 259–60; Second National Convention of the UCA-PAWA, Constitution and By-Laws, amended 17 December 1938, cited in Ruiz, *Cannery Women*, 44–45.

72. "Real Unity: Alaska Cannery Workers Show It in Election," *LH*, 02 November 1937.

73. "Leaders of Alaska Cannery Workers Union," *WW*, 02 September 1937, 1; "Alaska Union Set for Real Negotiations," *WW*, 25 March 1937, 5.

74. "Leaders of Alaska Cannery Workers Union."

75. "Union Sends Two to Spanish Speaking People's Congress," *LH*, 03 December 1939.

76. El Congreso de los Pueblos de Habla Española de California, Preparation for the Second Congress of the Spanish Speaking People in California, 09–10 December 1939, Ernesto Galarza Papers, box 13, folder 9, Special Collections, Stanford University (SCSU). On El Congreso's origins, see Sánchez, *Becoming Mexican American*, 244–45.

77. El Congreso, Draft Program of the National Congress of Spanish Speaking Peoples and Resolutions on Discrimination and Civil Rights; Relief; Wagner Act; Congressional Investigations; and Labor Unity, 1939, Galarza Papers, all box 13, folder 9, SCSU.

Chapter 3

1. Bureau of the Census, *Sixteenth Census of the United States: 1940*, Population Schedule, California, San Francisco County, enumeration district 104-B, sheet 1A, family 7, http://1940census.archives.gov, accessed 18 October 2014.

2. "Simmons Bed Pact Stalled on Basic Pay," *LH*, 09 October 1942, 5.

3. List of UFW delegates to San Francisco CIO Council, 1946; Ralph Nuckols to SFCIO Council, 01 May 1946, both in San Francisco CIO Council Records (hereafter SFCIO), carton 6, UFW 262 folder, BANC.

4. Paul Schnur to Mayor Roger Lapham and Charles Dullea, 29 July 1946, SFCIO, carton 5, minorities folder, BANC.

5. Ibid.

6. On *pachucos* and youth culture, see Luis Alvarez, *The Power of the Zoot: Youth Culture and Resistance During World War II* (Berkeley: University of California Press, 2008).

7. Schnur to Lapham and Dullea, SFCIO, BANC.

8. Whalen, *From Puerto Rico to Philadelphia*, 185–88; Fernández, *Brown in the Windy City*, 79–82, 152–58.

9. "Tortilla Triumph," *LH*, 06 February 1942, 1; "Tamale Firms Sign, Strike Won by UCA-PAWA," *LH*, 20 March 1942, 5.

10. Countryman, *Up South*, 16–17.

11. Membership clearance cards for Anna and Bertha Castro, 1942–43, Automotive Machinist Union, Lodge 1305 Records, box 1, folder 7, LARC.

12. San Francisco Bay Area Council, *San Francisco Bay Area: Its Peoples, Prospects, and Problems* (San Francisco: Industrial Survey Associates, 1948), 11–14; Charles Wollenberg, *Golden Gate Metropolis: Perspectives on Bay Area History* (Berkeley: Institute of Governmental Studies, 1985), 251; Roger W. Lotchin, *The Bad City in the Good War: San Francisco, Los Angeles, Oakland, and San Diego* (Bloomington: Indiana University Press, 2003), 145–46; Self, *American Babylon*, 43.

13. San Francisco Department of City Planning, *The Population of San Francisco: A Half Century of Change* (San Francisco: City Printing Office, 1954), 11–12, table 2; Bureau of the Census, *Sixteenth Census of the United States: 1940, Population, Nativity and Parentage of the White Population, Country of Origin of the Foreign Stock, by Nativity, Citizenship, Age, and Value or Rent of Home, for States and Large Cities* (Washington, DC: GPO, 1943), 75; Bureau of the Census, *United States Census of Population: 1950*, vol. 2, *Characteristics of the Population*, Part 5, *California* (Washington, DC: GPO, 1952), 107.

14. Bureau of the Census, *Population, Nativity and Parentage of the White Population*, 75.

15. Austin, *Around the World* (1940), 104.

16. Wayne Cornelius et al., *Mexican Immigrants in the San Francisco Bay Area: A Summary of Current Knowledge* (San Diego: Center for U.S.-Mexican Studies, 1982), 2; Wollenberg, *Golden Gate Metropolis*, 251. On the Bracero program, see David Gutiérrez, *Walls and Mirrors: Mexican Americans, Mexican Immigrants, and the Politics of Ethnicity* (Berkeley: University of California Press, 1995), 133–38, 153–55; Ngai, *Impossible Subjects*, 138–47; and Deborah Cohen, *Braceros: Migrant Citizens and Transnational Subjects in the Postwar United States and Mexico* (Chapel Hill: University of North Carolina Press, 2011).

17. San Francisco Department of City Planning, *Population of San Francisco*, table 2.

18. Wollenberg, *Golden Gate Metropolis*, 251; Carlos Cordova, "Migration and Acculturation Processes of Undocumented El Salvadoreans in the San Francisco Bay Area," EdD dissertation, University of San Francisco, 1986, 129.

19. Andrade is a fictional surname created for narrative flow. Julio A. interview cited in Cecilia Menjívar, *Fragmented Ties: Salvadoran Immigrant Networks in America* (Berkeley: University of California Press, 2000), 11; "Union Strengthened by Enlarging Executive Board," *Dispatcher*, 22 September 1944, 6.

20. Austin, *Around the World* (1955), 94; John Dumitru and Richard Salisbury, *Adjustment of Immigrant Spanish-Americans in San Francisco: A Pilot Study* (Berkeley: Survey Research Center, University of California, Berkeley, 1960), 29.

21. Alberto Sandoval-Sánchez, personal communication with the author, 01 November 2014; Elba Montes, interview by the author, 07 February 2003, Orinda, CA. In the 1960s and 1970s, this historical actor was known as Elba Montes and Elba Tuttle; she later became Elba Montes Donnelly. Per her request, Montes will be used in this study. For an introduction to the postwar great migration, see Whalen, "Colonialism, Citizenship," 25–35.

22. ILGWU Local 101, ledgers of incoming members, 1940–1944, SFILGWU, LARC; Austin, *Around the World* (1940), 103.

23. U.S. Commission on Civil Rights, "Staff Report on Spanish-American Community of the San Francisco Bay Area," 28 April 1967, in *Hearings Before the United States Commission on Civil Rights, San Francisco, CA, May 1–3, 1967* (Washington, DC: GPO, 1967), 824.

24. San Francisco Department of City Planning, *Population of San Francisco*, table 2.

25. See commercial ads in *El Democrata (ED)*, 1949–1951.

26. Josie Sigala, "Canon Kip Community Center," and John Marshall, "Southside Youth Council," *Youth Council News*, July 1947, 2, in IISF Records, box 39, IHRC; Austin, *Around the*

World (1955), 61; St. Joseph's Parish Historical Report for 1953 and St. Peter's Parish Historical Report for 1958, parish historical files, AASF.

27. "Behren's Political Gossip," *SFC*, 03 March 1938, 14.

28. "S.F. Cops in Mass Attack, Club Pickets," "Boycott Urged on Products," and "Canceling of Alaska Salmon Fishing Hit," all *LH*, 10 May 1940, 1; "No Union Pact, Ships Won't Sail," *SFC*, 13 April 1940, 1, 6; "Fish Packers Abandon the 1940 Cruise," *SFC*, 05 May 1940, 1, 7.

29. Rose Pesotta, "Gantner-Mattern May Have a 'Buenos Dias' for the Employer but They're out to Win the Strike," *Justice*, 15 April 1940; Matyas interview, 226–27; Jennye Matyas, "The Gantner and Mattern Labor Trouble," *SFC*, 04 May 1940, 12.

30. "NLRB Will Cite Gantner and Mattern," *SFC*, 14 June 1940, 9; "Trial Examiner Vindicates Gantner, Mattern on Unfair Labor Complaint," *San Francisco Recorder*, 20 January 1941, 1.

31. Gantner and Mattern Strike Committee, "Gantner Workers Are Still on Strike," 10 April 1941; and John O. Gantner Jr. to Members of the California State Assembly, 22 April 1941, both in Leonard Collection, box 341, Gantner Case folder, LARC; Matyas interview, 246–50.

32. "CIO Ship Scalers Bare AFL Move to Slash Wages," *LH*, 15 March 1940, 1.

33. Pete Garcia to Maritime Commission, 15 October 1940; W. J. Bush to Pete Garcia, 17 October 1940; Harry Bridges to F. P. Foisie, 15 October 1940, all MFP, box 31, folder 23, LARC.

34. "It Didn't Pay; CIO Ship Scalers Expect Contract," *LH*, 25 October 1940, 1.

35. "Peace Moves Pushed on Two Fronts," *SFC*, 26 April 1940, 14.

36. "Seek Cash to Put Teeth in 'Unity for Victory,'" *LH*, 06 February 1942, 1; "Victory Rally to Be Held Tuesday," *LH*, 20 March 1942, 1.

37. "Victory Rally" and "Bridges Calls for Union Speed-Up," both *LH*, 20 March 1942, 1; report of Balloting Committee, 17 January 1941, and list of CIO officials, San Francisco, Calif., 28 May 1941, both MFP, box 50, folder 8, LARC.

38. Furniture Men Adopt Win-the-War Program," *LH*, 19 June 1942, 3.

39. "Alaska Cannery Union Gets Raise of 25 Percent," *LH*, 05 June 1942, 6; "Textile Union Raises Pay at 3 Bag Plants," *LH*, 09 October 1942, 5.

40. "Auto, Can Shutdowns Sabotage War Output," *LH*, 06 February 1942, 3; "Union Gets Contract, Firm Won't Cooperate," *LH*, 02 July 1942, 1; "American Can WLB Decision Is Expected," *LH*, 02 October 1942, 1. For a roster of Local 1684 members at American Can, see list of appellants, *In the Matter of the Appeals of John S. Aguilera et al.*, Case 5749, California Department of Employment, 08 July 1941, Leonard Collection, box 341, SWOC folder, LARC.

41. "'Hot Cargo' Bill Passed by Assembly," *Los Angeles Times* (*LAT*), 14 May 1941, 4; "'Hot Cargo' in Olson's Lap!" *LAT*, 18 May 1941, A4; "The 'Hot Cargo' Ban," *LAT*, 07 June 1941, A4.

42. Thomas Maloney quoted in "'Hot Cargo' Bill Passed"; "Unions File Petition Blocking Enforcement of Hot-Cargo Act," *LAT*, 13 September 1941, 1.

43. C. J. Haggerty, Edward Vandeleur, et al., Argument Against Referendum Measure Prohibiting Hot Cargo, Secondary Boycott, in California Secretary of State, *Proposed Amendments to Constitution, Propositions and Proposed Laws*, 03 November 1942, 5, California Ballot Propositions Online Database (CBPOD), University of California Hastings Law Library; "Election Results," *LAT*, 05 November 1942, 1.

44. "Hot Cargo by Counties," *SFC*, 05 November 1942, 9.

45. SFCIO Political Action Committee (PAC), "What Is Precinct Work?" pamphlet, 1943; SFCIO PAC, meeting minutes, 12 November 1943; lists of precinct workers during Havenner primary, 1944; lists of participants/volunteers by area, ca. 1944, all SFCIO, carton 17, multiple precinct work folders, BANC. Emphasis in original.

46. "Scalers Have Two Big Jobs; Work and Ring Doorbells," *Dispatcher*, 03 November 1944, 6.

47. Thomas, *Puerto Rican Citizen*, 39–40, 99–103; Sánchez, *Becoming Mexican American*, 261–62.

48. "Organizing Drive Speeding; New Offices Nearly Ready," *Dispatcher*, 08 September 1944, 6.

49. List of union volunteers against Rolph, 1944; Havenner Campaign Workers, meeting minutes, 25 May 1944; Havenner for Congress Campaign Committee, "Let the Record Speak," pamphlet, 1944, all SFCIO, carton 17, precinct work and Havenner–general folders, BANC.

50. SFCIO PAC, report on the 1946 Election Campaign, 15 November 1946; Havenner Campaign Committee, "Look at the Havenner Record (*Mire la obra de Havenner*)," pamphlet, 1947, both SFCIO, carton 5, PAC communications folder and carton 19, CIO Council endorsement–Mayor folder, BANC.

51. Brilliant, *Color of America Has Changed*, 129–32, 137–40.

52. "Furniture Men Adopt Win-the-War Program"; George Robertson, "Desegregating a Maritime Union: The Marine Cooks and Stewards," Waterfront Workers History Project, http://depts.washington.edu/dock/mcs_desegregation.shtml, accessed 01 March 2015; "Steel Workers Condemn Racial Discrimination," *LH*, 20 March 1942.

53. California CIO Council, *Proceedings of the 6th Annual "Support the President" Convention*, Fresno, CA, 21–24 October 1943, 22, 146–47, SFCIO, carton 17, "Support the President" Convention 1943 folder, BANC.

54. Ibid., 23, 146; Minorities Committee of California CIO Council, "Northern California Conference on Racial and Unity in Wartime," San Francisco, 08 August 1943, SFCIO, carton 17, Minorities Committee folder, BANC.

55. Council for Civic Unity of San Francisco, *We Are Many People Living Together* (San Francisco, ca. 1944), 4.

56. Bay Area Council Against Discrimination, *"We Must Begin Now": San Francisco's Plan for Democratic Racial Relations* (San Francisco, 1943), 4–5; "Civic Unity Group Opens Headquarters," *SFC*, 13 December 1944, 11.

57. "For Unity Among Americans," event flyer, 04 March 1946, SFCIO, carton 16, SF PAC letters and bulletins folder, BANC.

58. "Community Meetings for AB3 Set in Bay Area, Los Angeles," *LH*, 23 February 1945, 6; Chester Hanson, "Assembly Kills Plea to Revive Racial Measures," *LAT*, 14 June 1945, 2; Hanson, "F.E.P.C. Measure Killed by Assembly Committee," *LAT*, 16 February 1946, 2.

59. Robert Kenny and Bartley Crum, Statewide Committee for a California Fair Employment Practices Commission, letter to friends, 01 October 1945, SFCIO, carton 5, minorities folder, BANC; "CIO Fair Play Policy Protects Minority Groups," *LH*, 11 October 1945, 1.

60. SFCIO PAC, lists of participants/volunteers at various PAC activities, 1945–46; SFCIO PAC, report on the 1946 Election Campaign, both SFCIO, carton 17, member lists from various locals folder and carton 5, PAC communications folder, BANC.

61. Arguments in Favor and Against Proposition No. 11, in California Secretary of State, *Proposed Amendments to Constitution, Propositions and Proposed Laws*, 05 November 1946, 11–12, CBPOD; "Fair Practices Act Assailed as Public Menace," *LAT*, 27 October 1946, A2; "Farm Bureaus in State Oppose Proposition 11," *LAT*, 29 October 1946, 5.

62. "FEPC Report," *SFC*, 06 October 1949, 13; Fitzgerald Ames Sr., Mayor's Committee on Human Relations, statement before the County, State and National Affairs Committee of the

Board of Supervisors, 18 October 1949, file 4636, folder 5, Archives of the San Francisco Board of Supervisors (hereafter ASFBS).

63. San Francisco Board of Supervisors, *Resolution No. 8006*, 18 October 1948; Samuel Valadez et al. to Don Fazackerley, 19 January 1950, both file 4636, folder 5, ASFBS.

64. E. M. to Don Fazackerley, 04 January 1950; petitions of proponents, 1951, all file 4636, folders 5 and 6, ASFBS. Emphasis in original.

65. Almon Roth, statement before the County, State and National Affairs Committee of the Board of Supervisors, 13 December 1949; Erwin Easton to Dan Fazackerly (*sic*), 20 January 1950; C. F. De Lano to Board of Supervisors, 25 May 1951; Earl Wilson to Dan Fazackerley, 20 January 1950, all file 4636, folder 4, ASFBS.

66. Antonio Montoya, "El deber es de nosotros," *MCS Voice*, 11 May 1951, 13, 16; Montoya, "ANMA Acts for Equality," *MCS Voice*, 29 June 1951, 10. For more on ANMA, see Juan Gómez Quiñones, *Chicano Politics: Reality and Promise, 1940–1990* (Albuquerque: University of New Mexico Press, 1990), 50–51.

67. On the CIO's purge of eleven radical unions, see Steve Rosswurm, ed., "Introduction: An Overview and Preliminary Assessment of the CIO's Expelled Unions," in *The CIO's Left-Led Unions* (New Brunswick, NJ: Rutgers University Press, 1992), 1–17.

68. Re File No. 4636, 28 May 1951, *Journal of Proceedings of the San Francisco Board of Supervisors* 46, no. 20: 562; R. L. Turner to Don Fazackerley, 25 May 1951, file 4636, folder 5, ASFBS.

69. Fillmore Communist Party, FEPC Now!! event flyer, ca. 1950, file 4636, folder 5, ASFBS; Re File No. 4636, 23 January 1950, *Journal of Proceedings of the San Francisco Board of Supervisors* 45, no. 4: 64. On fellow travelers, see Denning, *Cultural Front*, 5–6.

70. San Francisco Citizens Committee for Equal Opportunity, Organizations Supporting FEPC Ordinance for San Francisco, 20 December 1949; Irving Rosenblatt Jr. et al. to George Christopher, 16 April 1951, both file 4636, folder 5, ASFBS; Ralph Reynolds et al., "To the Editor," *San Francisco News*, 27 January 1950.

71. "Fair Employment," *SFC*, 30 April 1951, 3; "Supervisors Reject FEPC," *SFC*, 29 May 1951, 1–2; Rosenblatt Jr. et al. to Christopher, ASFBS.

72. United Latin Americans of America, Inc., to Don Fazackerley, 30 April 1951, file 4636, folder 5, ASFBS; Manuel Maldonado, selected testimony, in John Thomas Berry, "Fair Employment Practice in California: A Study of the Groups and Pressures Influencing Opinion on This Issue," master's thesis, Department of Political Science, University of California, Berkeley, 1952, 56. On ULAA's origins, see Chapter 4.

73. "Setback for Local FEPC," *SFC*, 06 January 1950, 1; "Job Discrimination," *SFC*, 06 January 1950, 2; Ray Leavitt, "Local FEPC: S.F. Supervisors Vote Against Proposal, 7 to 4," *SFC*, 24 January 1950, 1.

74. "Fair Employment"; "Supervisors Reject FEPC."

75. "Almon Roth Calls Tune in Defeat of San Francisco FEP Ordinance," *Dispatcher*, 08 June 1951, 9.

76. SFCIO Council, Resolution on Anti-Labor Legislation, 17 May 1947, and Resolution on the President's Executive Order No. 9835 on Loyalty Dismissals, 18 April 1947, both SFCIO, carton 9, resolutions folder, BANC.

77. Ruiz, *Cannery Women*, 111–18; Vargas, *Labor Rights Are Civil Rights*, 270–73.

78. Pablo Valdez to SF PAC, 20 November 1944, SFCIO, carton 18, CIO unions folder, BANC; Pablo Valdez to SFCIO Council, 17 November 1947, carton 10, cannery workers folder,

BANC; "Portland Branch Meets" and "Local 7 Prepares for All-Out Fight," *Local Seven News*, December 1947, 1.

79. ILGWU Local 101, record books of incoming members, nos. 3–9 (1948–1962); ILGWU Local 352, meeting minutes (1942–49); Employees of Lilli Ann: Hiring and Pay Information, 1948–1951, all SFILGWU, 1991/096, box 1, folders 9 and 6, respectively, LARC; Dick Hemp, "Non-Discrimination for S.F. Employers," *SFC*, 16 April 1951, 36.

80. Employees at Morris Goldman Manufacturing Co. Entitled to Wage Adjustments, December 1951; Sam Kagel to Henry Zacharin (ILGWU) and Alfred Cohen (San Francisco Coat and Suit Association), 19 March 1952; Rate of Pay and Working Conditions Information, September 1954, all SFILGWU, 1991/096, box 1, folder 13, LARC.

81. Henry Zacharin to SFLC, 18 January 1952; Zacharin, proposed resolution, 1952; SFLC Executive Committee, Action Reports, 21 January 1952 and 30 July 1956, all SFLC, cartons 66 and 80, ILGWU No. 101 folders, BANC.

82. ILGWU Local 101 Elections and Objections Committee, 1956; Local 101 Elections, 1959, both SFILGWU, 1991/096, box 2, folders 5 and 8, LARC.

83. Counterproposal and proposal, ca. 1952, SFLC, carton 66, ILGWU No. 101 folder, BANC.

84. Ben Liebman to Bertha Metro, Local 283, ca. 26 January 1954; Metro to George Johns, 22 January 1954, both HERE Collection, box 33, folder 8, LARC.

85. San Francisco Committee on Political Education (SFCOPE), Spanish Speaking Committee, 03 September 1958; SFCOPE, list of volunteers, 1958, both SFLC, carton 17, COPE volunteer lists folder and carton 143, volunteer workers folder, BANC; Ena Aguirre, Luisa Ezquerro, and David Sánchez Jr., interviews with author, San Francisco, CA, 19 March 2003, 18 March 2003, and 10 June 2003, respectively.

86. "Supervisors Given New Fair Employment Proposal," *LC*, 21 December 1956, 3; "Labor Group Again Backs Local FEPC," *SFC*, 02 March 1957, 16.

87. Louis Garcia, statement before Committee on County, State and National Affairs of the San Francisco Board of Supervisors, 30 January 1957, file 15143, statements folder, ASFBS.

88. Richard Reinhardt, "Supervisors Delay Action on FEP," *SFC*, 28 May 1957, 1–2.

89. "City FEP Passes First Board Vote," *SFC*, 21 May 1957, 1, 4; "FEP Faces Vital Test," *LC*, 31 May 1957, 2.

90. "FEPC Backers Assail Ballot Move," *SFC*, 26 May 1957, 5; "City FEP Compromise Is Approved," *SFC*, 29 June 1957, 1–2; "FEPC Okayed," *LC*, 12 July 1957, 3.

91. "Brown Urged to Resist Labor Bosses' Pressure," *LAT*, 31 January 1958, B3; proposed amendment to Article I, in California Secretary of State, *Proposed Amendments to Constitution, Propositions and Proposed Laws*, 04 November 1958, 20, CBPOD.

92. San Francisco Chamber of Commerce, press release, 04 September 1958; Northern California Committee for Right to Work, "To All Who May Be Interested," memorandum, both file 855–58, ASFBS.

93. Northern California Citizens Committee Against Proposition 18, Letter to the Editor, *LC*, 18 September 1958; SFLC, "The Unpleasant Facts," position paper, 1958; William Becker, Rough List of Arguments Aimed at Minority Group People on the Issue of Right to Work, 1958, both SFLC, carton 143, campaign materials folder, BANC.

94. SFCOPE, Spanish Speaking Committee, 03 September 1958; SFCOPE, Latin American Committee, n.d.; Comite Latino-Americano para la Defensa de Nuestros Trabajos, "Seguridad ó Depresión?" campaign flyer, 1958, all SFLC, carton 117, COPE volunteer lists folder, and carton 143, campaign materials folder, BANC.

95. SFLC, "The Unpleasant Facts"; lists of precinct workers submitted by individual unions to SFLC, fall 1958; untitled campaign card in Spanish, 1958; lists of volunteer registrars, January–August 1958, all SFLC, carton 143, multiple folders, BANC.

96. "Props 16, 17 and 18 All Lose Decisively" and "How SF Voted," *SFC*, 05 November 1958, 1, 1A.

97. "Props 16, 17 and 18."

Chapter 4

1. Ricardo Morada, "First Progress Report," memorandum to Irving Kriegsfeld and Walter Lipton, 22 April 1962; Morada, "Survey Report," memorandum to Kriegsfeld, 06 April 1962; and Esther Arenas et al., "Profile Study of the Spanish-Speaking Community in the Mission District of S.F.," field report, 07 April 1962, all Mission Neighborhood Centers, Inc., Records (hereafter MNC), carton 6, ethnic-Latin folder; carton 7, Spanish-speaking contacts and directories folder, BANC.

2. Herman Gallegos, introductory address, fourteenth annual Latin American Leadership Conference, University of San Francisco, 23 October 1966, Herman Gallegos Papers, box A-13, SCSU.

3. Ibid.

4. "L.A. First Councilman of Mexican Descent Arrives," *SFC*, 02 October 1949, 2; "California Spanish Organization," *SFC*, 31 July 1949, 14. On the origins of the Community Service Organization (CSO), see Pitti, *Devil in Silicon Valley*, 149–58.

5. "Club United Latin Americans," *ED*, 07 July 1949, 8; "No olvideis," *ED*, 14 July 1949, 6; "Untitled," *ED*, 12 April 1951, 2.

6. Alfred Espinor to Don Fazackerley, 26 November 1949, file 4636, folder 5, ASFBS. On LULAC, see Gutiérrez, *Walls and Mirrors*, 74–87, 162–68.

7. Espinor to Fazackerley, ASFBS; "Una reunión histórica," *ED*, 28 July 1949, 1.

8. "El Democrata," *ED*, 29 March 1951, 5; "The Americas Youth Fellowship," *ED*, 11 August 1949, 5; "Grandes festejos al Divino Salvador del Mundo," *ED*, 11 August 1949, 6; "Fiesta del Club Nicaragua," *ED*, 29 March 1951, 6.

9. "United Latin Americans," *ED*, 29 March 1951, 6; "Conferencian los latino americanos," *ED*, 04 August 1949, 1.

10. Maldonado, testimony in Berry, "Fair Employment Practice," 56. On youth gangs and juvenile delinquency, see Thomas, *Puerto Rican Citizen*, 194–95; and Eric Schneider, *Vampires, Dragons, and Egyptian Kings: Youth Gangs in Postwar New York* (Princeton, NJ: Princeton University Press, 1999).

11. "Conferencian los latino americanos"; "Notas editoriales," *ED*, 04 August 1949, 5.

12. "Democrat Roybal Here, Asks Action on Jobless and Schools," *SFC*, 28 March 1954, 11; Earl Behrens, "Powers and Roybal Campaign in Bay Area," *SFC*, 18 May 1954, 14.

13. Edward Roybal to Henry Zacharin, 27 October 1954, SFILGWU, 1991/096, box 1, folder 28, LARC.

14. Northern California Latin Americans for Eisenhower to Friends, October 1956, George Christopher Papers, folder 7, San Francisco History Center, SFPL; "California Vote for President," *SFC*, 08 November 1956, 12.

15. Mexican American Political Association (MAPA), pamphlet, 18 September 1964; Manuel Ruiz, untitled paper, ca. 1961; Louis Vásquez to Robert Gonzales, 18 April 1966, all Manuel Ruiz Papers, box 6, folders 1 and 6; and box 9, folder 11, SCSU.

16. MAPA, State Constitution and By-Laws, as amended at the Second Annual Convention, 1961, Ruiz Papers, box 6, folder 6, SCSU; "American, Mexican Political Group Formed," *SFC*, 27 April 1960, 6.

17. David Braaten, "Close-Up of The Mission," *SFC*, 30 April 1962, 1, 12; Braaten, "San Francisco's Mission: A Place of Many Voices," *SFC*, 01 May 1962, 1, 7.

18. Gregory Hurst and Juan Pifarre, *The Mission District of San Francisco* (San Francisco: City Printing Office, 1972), 13.

19. Braaten, "San Francisco's Mission," 7; MNC, "'A Self-Portrait' of the Greater Mission District in Southeastern San Francisco," 1960, 3–4, MNC, carton 23, BANC.

20. MNC, "'Self-Portrait,'" 2–5, 10, BANC; Economic Opportunity Council of San Francisco (EOC), "The Area Development Program," 1965, section 1. 2, file 454-64, ASFBS.

21. On suburbanization, see Kenneth T. Jackson, *Crabgrass Frontier: The Suburbanization of the United States* (New York: Oxford University Press, 1985); Self, *American Babylon*; and Lizabeth Cohen, *A Consumers' Republic: The Politics of Mass Consumption in Postwar America* (New York: Vintage, 2003).

22. MNC, "'Self-Portrait,'" 2–5, 10, BANC; Hurst and Pifarre, *Mission District*, 13; Raul Ortega "Community History Unfolds," *El Tecolote* (*ET*), 22 December 1972, 1.

23. IISF, Adult Immigrants to San Francisco from Six Central American Countries and Mexico (1958 to 1960), in James Stirling, *Nicaraguans in San Francisco: A Pilot Study* (San Francisco: San Francisco Human Rights Commission, 1964), 12; Roger Ortega interview, James Stirling's field notes, 09 April 1964, MNC, carton 7, Nicaraguans folder, BANC; Ortega, "Community History."

24. Ortega interview, Stirling's field notes, BANC; Mildred Schroeder, "The New Spanish Influence in S.F.," *SFE*, 27 June 1967, 19; Bill Moore, "The Hidden Problems of S.F.'s Largest Minority," *SFC*, 17 February 1969, 1.

25. Far West Surveys, *A Report of the Latin American Population Living in the San Francisco Bay Area and Brand Preference Survey* (San Francisco: Far West Surveys, 1962), 4, 19, 23.

26. Research Unit of the United Community Fund of San Francisco, "The Range of San Francisco Population Social Characteristics in 1960," 1964, MNC, carton 2, census folder, BANC; Bureau of the Census, *1970 Census of Population and Housing*, vol. 2, *Characteristics of the Population*, Part 6, *California* (Washington, DC: GPO, 1973), 1165.

27. San Francisco Department of City Planning, *San Francisco 1970: Population by Ethnic Groups* (San Francisco: City Printing Office, 1975), 3, 9; Schroeder, "New Spanish Influence."

28. Catholic Social Service of San Francisco (CSS) and Presbyterian Inner-City Council of San Francisco, "A Program of Neighborhood Organization Among the Spanish-Speaking of the Mission District," ca. 1964, MNC, carton 6, ethnic–Latin folder, BANC; MNC, "'Self-Portrait,'" 7, BANC.

29. Reverend William C. Hughes, "General Report on Spanish Speaking Work," March 1962, 7, Catholic Council for the Spanish Speaking (CCSS) file, AASF; Hector Reyes and Jose Raul Arias interviews, Stirling's field notes, 25 February 1964 and 12 March 1964, BANC; Moore, "Hidden Problems"; U.S. Commission on Civil Rights, "Staff Report on Spanish-American Community of the San Francisco Bay Area," 28 April 1967, in *Hearings Before the United States Commission on Civil Rights, San Francisco, CA, May 1–3, 1967* (Washington, DC: GPO, 1967), 818.

30. Ed Dutton, "Problems of Spanish-Speaking Residents in San Francisco," report to MNC, April 1963; Ricardo Morada, "CALA Meeting," memorandum to Irving Kriegsfeld, 16 July 1964, both MNC, carton 6, ethnic–Latin folder, BANC.

31. Reverend William C. Hughes to Monsignor Leo T. Maher, 05 August 1961; Hughes to Most Reverend Joseph T. McGucken, 06 April 1962, both CCSS file, AASF; CSO of San Francisco, event invitation, 26 November 1961, MNC, carton 2, CSO folder, BANC; CSO, Report to CSO on Membership Paid from December 1961 to December 1962, Fred Ross Papers, box 5, folder 14, SCSU.

32. CSO, fact sheet, n.d., Ross Papers, box 10, folder 12, SCSU; CSO, petition to Governor Edmund G. Brown and Members of the California Legislature, ca. 1962–63; Elmer Gallegos, minutes of general meeting, 09 January 1963, both MNC, carton 2, CSO folder, BANC.

33. Ezquerro, interview; Gallegos, minutes of general meeting; Ricardo Morada, "El Buen Vecino," memorandum to Irving Kriegsfeld, 21 July 1964, MNC, carton 6, ethnic–Latin folder, BANC.

34. Hughes, "General Report," 13, AASF; William C. Hughes, "Memoranda of Spanish Speaking Activities to Date," 05 July 1961, 1–2, CCSS file, AASF.

35. CCSS, untitled report, ca. 1964, 2–5, CCSS file, AASF; Ricardo Morada, "Centro Catolico Latino Americano," memorandum to Irving Kriegsfeld, 06 June 1963, MNC, carton 7, Spanish-American folder, BANC.

36. Roger Granados interview, Stirling's field notes, 05 March 1964, BANC; CSS and Presbyterian Inner-City Council, "Program of Neighborhood Organization," BANC.

37. Centro Activista Latino Americano (CALA), Acta de Fundación, 1964, MNC, carton 6, ethnic–Mexicans folder, BANC.

38. Ibid.

39. Will Stevens, "Return from Oblivion—SF's 'Los Olvidados,'" SFE, 23 March 1965, 4; Lawrence Palacios and Fitz-Gerald Ames to Conrad Rheiner, June 1965; Spanish Speaking Citizens Foundation (SSF), Preamble, ca. 1964, both MNC, carton 7, ethnic–SSCF folder, BANC.

40. SSCF, Preamble; SSCF, Articles of Incorporation and By-Laws, ca. 1964, both MNC, carton 7, ethnic–SSCF folder, BANC.

41. President Johnson's national declaration of a "war on poverty" occurred on 08 January 1964 during his annual State of the Union address. The Economic Opportunity Act was signed into law on 20 August 1964. Important scholarly treatments of the War on Poverty include Allen Matusow, The Unraveling of America: A History of Liberalism in the 1960s (New York: Harper & Row, 1984), chapters 4, 8–9; Michael B. Katz, In the Shadow of the Poorhouse: A Social History of Welfare in America (New York: Basic, 1986), 259–82; Thomas F. Jackson, "The State, the Movement, and the Urban Poor: The War on Poverty and Political Mobilizations in the 1960s," in The "Underclass" Debate: Views from History, ed. Michael B. Katz (Princeton, NJ: Princeton University Press, 1993), 403–39; and Annelise Orleck and Lisa Gayle Hazirjian, eds., The War on Poverty: A New Grassroots History, 1964–1980 (Athens: University of Georgia Press, 2011).

42. Gene Bernardi, "San Francisco: A Preliminary and Partial Socioeconomic Profile with Emphasis on Poverty Segments of the Community and Program for Alleviation," report to the California State Social Welfare Board (CSSWB), April 1964, 8; CSSWB Committee on Social and Economic Problems, Unedited Notes on Conversations with 'Poverty-Prone' Segment of San Francisco Community, 16 April 1964, 2–4, both MNC, carton 40, folder 4, BANC.

43. U.S. Office of Economic Opportunity, The First Step . . . on a Long Journey: Congressional Presentation (Washington, DC: GPO, 1965), 47.

44. Adam C. Powell, opening statement, U.S. House of Representatives, Committee on Education and Labor, Examination of the War on Poverty Program: Hearings Before the Subcommittee on the War on Poverty Program (Washington, DC: GPO, 1965), 2.

45. Annelise Orleck, "Introduction: The War on Poverty from the Grass Roots Up," in *War on Poverty*, ed. Orleck and Hazirjian, 2, 14–15. For a critical discussion of the War on Poverty in San Francisco, see Jackson, "The State, the Movement, and the Urban Poor."

46. EOC, "Area Development Program," introduction, ASFBS.

47. Willie Thompson, *Enemy of the Poor: A Report of the Struggle of the War on Poverty in San Francisco* (San Francisco: Citizens United Against Poverty, 1965), 7–9, 21–24.

48. William H. Bradley Jr., Citizens United Against Poverty (CUAP), to Adam Clayton Powell, 16 April 1965; CUAP, press release, ca. April 1965, both in Committee on Education and Labor, *Examination of the War on Poverty Program*, 807–8.

49. John F. Shelley quoted in "Mayor: 'A Power Play' on Poverty,'" *SFE*, 15 May 1965, 1.

50. Thompson, *Enemy of the Poor*, 4, 10–11.

51. Ibid., 35–36; John F. Shelley quoted in Harry Johanesen, "Shelley Yields in Poverty War," *SFE*, 02 September 1965, 1.

52. Ricardo Morada, "Spanish Speaking Citizens' Foundation Meeting in Judge Ames' Chambers," memorandum to I. Kriegsfeld, 12 August 1964, MNC, carton 7, SSCF folder, BANC.

53. Jess Hernandez, letter to the community, ca. 1964–65, MNC, carton 7, SSCF folder, BANC.

54. CSO, fact sheet, SCSU; CCSS, Report to Monsignor Bowe, 14 February 1964, CCSS file, AASF.

55. Herman Gallegos, address before MAPA's Executive Board, 06 December 1964, Galarza Papers, box 14, folder 11, SCSU.

56. Morada, "SSCF Meeting"; Lawrence Palacios and Fitz-Gerald Ames, "Representation of the Foundation on the Executive Committee of the EOC of SF," memorandum to EOC, ca. May 1965, both MNC, carton 7, SSCF folder, BANC; CSS and Presbyterian Inner-City Council, "Program of Neighborhood Organization," BANC.

57. Mission Area Community Action Board (MACAB), "Poverty Program Report," submitted to the Social Services Committee of the San Francisco Board of Supervisors, 18 August 1966, 1, file 454-64, ASFBS; Palacios and Ames, "Representation of the Foundation," BANC.

58. Ruth Krusa, "SSCF Meeting, July 21, 1965"; "CCSS Meeting, August 9, 1965"; "CSO Meeting, August 18, 1965," all memoranda to Irving Kriegsfeld, MNC, carton 7, Spanish speaking contacts folder, BANC; Palacios and Ames, "Representation of the Foundation," BANC.

59. Thomas, *Puerto Rican Citizen*, 218.

60. EOC, "A Preliminary Report on the Activities of the Economic Opportunity Council of San Francisco, Inc.," 1966, 51, file 454-64; MACAB, "Poverty Program Report," 1, both ASFBS.

61. Mission Area Structure Committee, "Proposed Structure for Permanent Area Organization," 30 October 1965, 2, MNC, carton 13, BANC; Ralph Kramer, "Community Case Study of the San Francisco Economic Opportunity Council," in Kramer, *Participation of the Poor: Comparative Case Studies in the War on Poverty* (Englewood Cliffs, NJ: Prentice-Hall, 1969), 42.

62. Herman Gallegos, remarks at Mission Dolores Hall, 17 January 1966, Gallegos Papers, carton 14.5, SCSU; Lawrence Palacios to SSCF Membership, November 1965, and SSCF, "Amigos Latinos," letter to the community, November 1965, both MNC, carton 7, SSCF folder, BANC.

63. Kramer, "Community Case Study," 43; Frances Fox Piven and Richard A. Cloward, "The Politics of the Great Society," in Milkis and Mileur, eds., *Great Society and the High Tide of Liberalism*, 256.

64. Alex Zermeño, interview by the author, 04 June 2003, Oakland, CA; Mike Miller, *An

Organizer's Tale: The Story of the Mission Coalition Organization (San Francisco: M. J. Miller, 1974), 5.

65. Kramer, "Community Case Study," 42; American Indian Council, "Community Action for the Urbanized American Indian," and Potrero Hill Neighborhood House, "Potrero Hill Manpower and Employment Research and Demonstration Project," MACAP project proposals, 1966, file 454-64, ASFBS; "Mission English Language Center," project description, 16 August 1966, in MACAB, "Poverty Program Report," 46, ASFBS.

66. MACAB, "Poverty Program Report," 6, 14, ASFBS.

67. Zermeño, interview; MACAB, "Poverty Program Report," 12, ASFBS.

68. Montes, interview.

69. "Organize to Help Yourself," *MACAP Newsletter,* December 1966, 4, MNC, carton 13, BANC.

70. MACAB, "Poverty Program Report," 21–24, ASFBS.

71. "Potrero Hill Movement Strike," *MACAP Newsletter*, December 1966, 5.

72. San Francisco Planning and Urban Renewal Association (SPUR), "The City's Anti-Poverty Program: A Report on the Economic Opportunity Council of San Francisco, Inc.," 1968, 10, file 194-68-3, ASFBS.

73. Kramer, "Community Case Study," 44; Brian Cahill, "Community Social Work," graduate student essay, 14 May 1968, 9, personal collection of B. Cahill.

74. For a comparison with experiences in Oakland and Philadelphia, see Self, *American Babylon*, 198–214; Countryman, *Up South*, 274–77, 295–300.

75. Katz, *In the Shadow of the Poorhouse*, 262–68; Piven and Cloward, "Politics of the Great Society," 259.

76. Lauren Horan, Office of Economic Opportunity, to San Francisco Board of Supervisors, 16 February 1968, file 194-68A, ASFBS.

77. Zermeño, interview.

78. "Conferencian los latino americanos"; SSCF, "Summary of Activities," report, ca. mid-1966, MNC, carton 7, SSCF folder, BANC.

79. Miller, *Organizer's Tale*, 5; Montes, interview; Zermeño, interview.

Chapter 5

1. "March Here for Model Cities," *San Francisco Sunday Examiner and Chronicle*, 18 May 1969, 10.

2. The Great Society refers to a series of federal initiatives focused on ending racial inequality, poverty, and related social inequities in housing, education, and health care. See essays in Milkis and Mileur, eds., *Great Society and the High Tide of Liberalism*.

3. Thomas J. Sugrue, *The Origins of the Urban Crisis: Race and Inequality in Postwar Detroit* (Princeton, NJ: Princeton University Press, 1996).

4. "March Here for Model Cities."

5. On the Chicano movement, see Ernesto Chávez, *"¡Mi Raza Primero!" (My People First!): Nationalism, Identity, and Insurgency in the Chicano Movement in Los Angeles, 1966–1978* (Berkeley: University of California Press, 2002); Lorena Oropeza, *¡Raza Sí! ¡Guerra No! Chicano Protest and Patriotism During the Viet Nam War Era* (Berkeley: University of California Press, 2005); and Pitti, *Devil in Silicon Valley*, chapter 8. On the Puerto Rican movement, see Whalen, *From Puerto Rico to Philadelphia*, chapter 7; Thomas, *Puerto Rican Citizen*, chapter 6; and Fernández, *Brown in the Windy City*, chapter 5.

6. Mission Coalition Organization (MCO) and Stanford University, *Summary of Trends in Housing and Population in the Mission Model Neighborhood, 1940–1970* (Stanford, CA: Stanford University Press, 1972), 7, 10.

7. Thomas J. Sugrue, "All Politics Is Local: The Persistence of Localism in Twentieth-Century America," in Jacobs et al., eds., *Democratic Experiment*, 302.

8. Donald Canter, "Near-Eruption at Hearing on Renewal Plans in the Mission," *SFE*, 28 June 1966, 10.

9. Sharon Gold, "The Story of a Fight Against Redevelopment in the Mission District of San Francisco," 1966, 1, Walter Goldwater Radical Pamphlet Collection, Special Collections, Peter J. Shields Library, University of California, Davis.

10. Orleck, "Introduction: War on Poverty," 2.

11. Lisa McGirr, *Suburban Warriors: The Origins of the New American Right* (Princeton, NJ: Princeton University Press, 2001), 147–216; Self, *American Babylon*, 256–90; and Sugrue, *Origins of the Urban Crisis*, 209–29.

12. Seminal works on urban renewal include Jon C. Teaford, *The Rough Road to Renaissance: Urban Revitalization in America, 1940–1985* (Baltimore: Johns Hopkins University Press, 1990); June Manning Thomas, *Redevelopment and Race: Planning a Finer City in Postwar Detroit* (Baltimore: Johns Hopkins University Press, 1997); and Alison Isenberg, *Downtown America: A History of the Place and the People Who Made It* (Chicago: University of Chicago Press, 2004), chapter 5.

13. On citizens' protests, see Thomas, *Redevelopment and Race*, 104–11; Self, *American Babylon*, 143–39; Eric Avila, *Popular Culture in the Age of White Flight: Fear and Fantasy in Suburban Los Angeles* (Berkeley: University of California Press, 2004), 161–70; and Fernández, *Brown in the Windy City*, 114–23.

14. DeLeon, *Left Coast City,* 40–46; Chester Hartman, *City for Sale: The Transformation of San Francisco* (Berkeley: University of California Press, 2002), 1–14, 25, 63–64; and John H. Mollenkopf, *The Contested City* (Princeton, NJ: Princeton University Press, 1983), 173.

15. San Francisco Department of City Planning (hereafter SF Planning), *Housing and Neighborhood Conditions in San Francisco: A Classification of Areas for Urban Renewal* (San Francisco, 1955), 6; San Francisco Board of Supervisors, *Resolution No. 707-63*, 31 December 1963, file 35-63, ASFBS.

16. Rai Okamoto and William H. Liskamm, *Mission District Urban Design Study* (San Francisco: City Planning Commission, 1966), 25, 31; San Francisco Redevelopment Agency (SFRA), *Resolution No. 67-66*, 17 May 1966, file 148-66-3-1, ASFBS.

17. SF Planning and SFRA, "A Survey and Planning Application for the Mission Street Survey Area," 1966, file 148-66-3, ASFBS.

18. Mission District Renewal Commission, "1966 Report of the Mission District Renewal Commission," February 1966, 1, file 148-66, ASFBS.

19. Greater Mission Citizens Council (GMCC), Resolutions, 28 April 1966 and 27 June 1966, file 148-66-3A, ASFBS.

20. Gold, "Story of a Fight," 1. On Alinsky's principles, see Saul D. Alinsky, *Reveille for Radicals* (Chicago: University of Chicago Press, 1946).

21. Jerry Pence and Herman Gallegos to Jack Morrison, appendix, 26 September 1966, 1, file 148-66-3, ASFBS.

22. MCOR, "Mission Council on Redevelopment Asks for Federal Investigation," ca. mid-1966, press release, file148-66-3A; Miller, *Organizer's Tale*, 7–8.

23. Gold, "Story of a Fight," 2. On the city's progrowth urban regime, see DeLeon, *Left Coast City*, 40–43.

24. Pence and Gallegos to Morrison, appendix, 1, ASFBS.

25. Manuel Cirilo, Antonio Morales, Maria Lucero, and Andres and Lucy Torres to San Francisco Board of Supervisors, 08 to 10 June 1966, file 148-66-3A, ASFBS.

26. MACAB, "Poverty Program Report," 25, ASFBS; Gold, "Story of a Fight," 3.

27. Eduardo López, testimony before San Francisco Board of Supervisors, 29 June 1966, 1, file 148-66-3, ASFBS.

28. Ibid., 1–2.

29. Gold, "Story of a Fight," 18.

30. López, testimony, appendix II, 29 June 1966, 2, file 148-66-3, ASFBS. On Great Society liberalism, see Self, *American Babylon*, 198–210; and Milkis, "Lyndon Johnson," 1–49.

31. Sugrue, *Origins of the Urban Crisis*, 218–29; McGirr, *Suburban Warriors*, 149–63.

32. San Francisco Committee to Stop the Redevelopment Agency (SFCSRA), Agenda for Third General Membership and Rally Meeting, 19 December 1966, file 148-66-3; Jack Bartalini to Planning and Development Committee, 19 September 1966, file 148-66-2, both ASFBS.

33. Carlos Vela, statement before Finance Committee, 30 November 1966, file 148-66-3A; López, testimony, 3, both ASFBS.

34. Jack Bartalini, "Enough Is Enough," broadside, August 1966, file 148-66, ASFBS.

35. "Confusion at Hearing on Renewal," *SFC*, 10 December 1965, 45.

36. Parents and Taxpayers (PAT), "Help Save the Mission from the Redevelopment Agency," broadside, 22 July 1966; SFCSRA, "A Bedtime Story," broadside, 24 December 1966; Becky Schettler to San Francisco Board of Supervisors, 04 October 1966, all file 148-66-3, ASFBS.

37. PAT, "Why the Inner Mission Needs a Federally Assisted Code Enforcement Program Rather Than a Redevelopment Project," broadside, November 1966, file 148-66-3; Bartalini, "Enough Is Enough," both ASFBS.

38. Jack Bartalini, "Regarding a Proposed Urban Renewal Project in San Francisco's Mission District," memorandum to Mayor John F. Shelley and the San Francisco Board of Supervisors, n.d., file 148-66; Mary Hall to Finance Committee, 30 November 1966, 1–2, file 148-66-3, both ASFBS.

39. PAT, "What Is a City Demonstration Program?" September 1966, broadside, file 148-66-3; PAT, "Help Save the Mission," both ASFBS. On middle-class taxpayer campaigns, see Becky M. Nicolaides, *My Blue Heaven: Life and Politics in the Working-Class Suburbs of Los Angeles, 1920–1965* (Chicago: University of Chicago Press, 2002), 302–3; McGirr, *Suburban Warriors*, 237–39; and Self, *American Babylon*, 316–26.

40. E. Cahill Maloney, "Mission Redevelopment," *San Francisco Progress* (*SFP*), 30 November–01 December 1966, 4.

41. Harry Brill, "Regarding Redevelopment Agency's Application for a Planning Grant in the Mission," memorandum to San Francisco Board of Supervisors, 15 June 1966, 1, file 148-66-1; Edward Eichler, "Urban Problems in the Mission," testimony before Finance Committee, 29 June 1966, 4–5, file 148-66-3A, both ASFBS. For contemporary scholarly treatments of these episodes, see DeLeon, *Left Coast City*, 46–7; Hartman, *City for Sale*, 41–55.

42. San Francisco Planning and Urban Renewal Association, "SPUR Report," December 1966, 1–2, file 148-66-3A, ASFBS.

43. Joe J. Heizer to Finance Committee, 08 August 1966, file 148-66-3A, ASFBS.

44. Jack Morrison to Thomas O'Connor, 08 July 1966; Morrison to Robert Weaver, 08 July 1966; Don Hummel to Morrison, 05 August 1966, all file 148-66-3, ASFBS.

45. Finance Committee, proposed resolution (sixth draft), 30 November 1966, 1, file 148-66-3.1, ASFBS.

46. Mel Wax, "Supervisors Kill Mission District Renewal Project," *SFC*, 20 December 1966, 1.

47. Roger Boas and John Ertola quoted in "Supervisors Split on Mission Plan," *SFC*, 06 October 1966, 1.

48. Wax, "Supervisors Kill Mission District Renewal Project."

49. Terry Francois, testimony before Finance Committee, 30 November 1966, 1, 3, file 148-66-3, ASFBS; Russ Cone, "Supervisors' Vote on Renewal Shocks Mayor," *SFE*, 20 December 1966, 8.

50. John Jordan, "Mission Renewal Vetoed," *SFP*, 21–22 December 1966.

51. "Mayor Is Under Fire in Mission," *San Francisco Argonaut*, 06 March 1968; "Renewal Foes Rally," *San Francisco Argonaut*, 08 May 1968.

52. John Evans, "Impact of the Model Cities Program on Construction Safety," remarks before National Safety Congress, Chicago, 29 October 1968, file 274-68A, ASFBS; Milkis, "Lyndon Johnson," 14.

53. Office of the Mayor, "Application to the Department of Housing and Urban Development for a Grant to Plan a Comprehensive Model Cities Program: Mission District" (hereafter Mission Model Cities Application), 15 April 1968, 5; Ronald Pelosi statement in San Francisco Committee, "Transcript of San Francisco Board of Supervisors Meeting on May 20 1968," 2, both file 274-68, ASFBS.

54. "Model Cities for Mission," *SFP*, 08–09 May 1968; "Renewal Foes Rally"; Mayor's Office, Mission Model Cities Application, 1, ASFBS; Joseph L. Alioto to Mary Hall, 02 May 1968, file 274-68, ASFBS.

55. "Renewal Foes Rally"; Jack Bartalini to San Francisco Board of Supervisors, 11 May 1968, file 274-68, ASFBS.

56. Responsible Merchants, Property Owners and Tenants (RMPT), "It's up to You!" informational pamphlet, May 1968; Mary Hall to San Francisco Board of Supervisors, 13 May 1968; Bartalini to San Francisco Board of Supervisors, 03 May 1968, all file 274-68, ASFBS.

57. Supervisors' statements in San Francisco Committee, "Transcript of San Francisco Board of Supervisors Meeting on May 20, 1968," 2–3, 6–7, ASFBS.

58. Ibid., 11; Roger Boas cited in Jerry Burns, "S.F. to Link Renewal, Aid to the Poor," *SFC*, 08 May 1968.

59. San Francisco Board of Supervisors, *Resolution No. 377-68*, 20 May 1968, file 274-68, ASFBS.

60. MCO, "Mission Coalition Organization: Three History–Making Years (Tres Años de Hacer Historia)," Third Annual Convention Program, 1970, n.p., personal files of Luisa Ezquerro.

61. Benino (Ben) Martinez, interview by the author, 17 July 2003, Oakland, CA; "Mayor Is Under Fire."

62. Miller, *Organizer's Tale*, 14; Martinez, interview.

63. Miller, *Organizer's Tale*, 14.

64. Martinez and Montes, interviews.

65. MCO, "The Mission Coalition Organization," ca. 1969, 2, MCO Vertical Files, Mission

Branch, SFPL; "Coalition—Convención," *New Nueva Mission* (*NNM*), November 1968, 1; Miller, *Organizer's Tale*, 16.

66. Ben Martinez quoted in "CESAR CHAVEZ Habla en la Mission (Cesar Chavez to Speak to Mission Residents)," *NNM*, November 1968, 1.

67. Manuel Castells, "Urban Poverty, Ethnic Minorities and Community Organization: The Experience of Neighbourhood Mobilization in San Francisco's Mission District," in Castells, *The City and the Grassroots: A Cross-Cultural Theory of Urban Social Movements* (Berkeley: University of California Press, 1984), 106; Miller, *Organizer's Tale*, 34.

68. MCO, "Policy and Resolutions Report," ca. 1968, 8, MCO Vertical Files, SFPL.

69. "Mission Coalition Organization," ca. 1969, 2, SFPL.

70. "Mission Group's Tough Demands," *SFC*, 04 November 1968; "Convention Blasts Alioto," *NNM*, December 1968, 1.

71. Martinez quoted in "Coalition," *NNM*, November 1968, 6.

72. Ben Martinez quoted in Scott Blakey, "Model Cities Plan Clears One Hurdle," *SFC*, 10 May 1969, 1; Miller, *Organizer's Tale*, 38–39.

73. A similar scenario unfolded in North Philadelphia. See Countryman, *Up South*, 300–302.

74. "Supervisores aprobaron el programa Ciudades Modelos," *La Prensa Libre*, 04 September 1969, 1; "Model Cities Soon!" *NNM*, September/October 1969, 1.

75. Miller, *Organizer's Tale*, 39; Castells, "Urban Poverty," 114.

76. Scott Blakey, "S.F. Model City Plan Rejected," *SFC*, 06 March 1970, 4; H. Ralph Taylor, remarks before the National Association of Housing and Redevelopment Officials, Minneapolis, 27 September 1968, file 274-68, ASFBS.

77. John Tolan quoted in "Setback for Model Cities in the Mission," *SFP*, 06 March 1970.

78. Ben Martinez quoted in Blakey, "S.F. Model City Plan Rejected"; Castells, "Urban Poverty," 115.

79. Elba Montes quoted in Jerry Burns, "Another Battle over Mission Planning Study," *SFC*, 29 April 1970, 4.

80. Joel Tlumak, "How the Coalition Turned It Around," *SFE*, 21 June 1972, 1; "Mission Model Cities Report," *Impacto*, 09 August 1972, 3.

81. Tlumak, "How the Coalition Turned It Around," 1, 7; Dexter Waugh, "Lesson: Muscle Equals Power," *SFE*, 20 June 1972, 1, 18.

82. Castells, "Urban Poverty," 116.

83. Frederick M. Wirt, *Power in the City: Decision Making in San Francisco* (Berkeley: University of California Press, 1974), 247–48.

84. Zermeño, interview; Gutiérrez, *Walls and Mirrors*, 181.

85. Countryman, *Up South*, 23–24, 213–14, 297–99.

86. Martinez and Zermeño, interviews; Bob Gonzales, interview by the author, 10 June 2003, San Francisco. Mayor Alioto appointed David Sánchez Jr. to the Board of Education in 1968 and Bob Gonzales to the Board of Supervisors in 1969.

87. Miller, *Organizer's Tale*, 66.

88. Montes, interview.

89. Michael Kazin, *The Populist Persuasion: An American History* (New York: Basic, 1995), 202; Miller, *Organizer's Tale*, 65.

90. Ezquerro and Montes, interviews.

91. Wirt, *Power in the City*, 248.

92. Castells, "Urban Poverty," 112; Larry Del Carlo, interview by the author, 09 July 2003, San Francisco.

93. Castells, "Urban Poverty," 114; Miller, *Organizer's Tale*, 75.

94. "Free Los Siete!" and "Our brothers . . . their cops," both *¡Basta Ya!* June 1969, 1.

95. Francisco Flores, interview by the author, 16 March 2003, San Francisco.

96. "Brown Power to Brown People!" *¡Basta Ya!* June 1969, 1; Donna Amador, interview by the author, 11 June 2003, San Francisco.

97. Al Borvice quoted in Djamilla Anne, "La Raza," 1985, 1, Community Organizations and Resources Vertical Files, Mission Branch, SFPL; La Raza En Acción Local (LaREAL), "La Raza Tutorial Program," ca. 1970, 1, La Raza Information Center (LRIC) files, San Francisco.

98. LaREAL, "Introduction to La Raza En Acción Local," ca. 1971, 1, LRIC files.

99. Amador, interview. On the Brown Berets and Young Lords, see Chávez, "*¡Mi Raza Primero!*" chapter 2; Fernández, *Brown in the Windy City*, chapter 5; Thomas, *Puerto Rican Citizen*, 231–40.

100. Pete Gallegos, interview by the author, 21 May 2003, San Francisco; Carmen Carrillo, interview by the author, 31 March 2003, Oakland, CA.

101. Pete Gallegos, "El Movimiento: 1960 to 1980 en la Mission," master's thesis draft, December 2002, 15, used with permission of the author; Carrillo, interview.

102. Al Borvice, interview by the author, 02 April 2003, San Francisco.

103. Gallegos, "El Movimiento," 23; Flores, interview. Emphasis is mine.

104. Marilla Parratt to Planning and Development Committee, 06 May 1968, file 274-68; RMPT, "It's up to You!", both ASFBS.

105. Blakey, "Model Cities Plan"; Mary Hall, " 'Which Citizens Participating?' " *SFP*, 13 May 1970.

106. Mary Hall quoted in "Model Cities for Mission."

107. "The Truth Behind MCO," *¡Basta Ya!* November 1970; Amador, interview.

108. "Truth Behind MCO."

109. Jack Bartalini to Harry R. Taylor, assistant HUD secretary, 12 July 1968, file 274-68, ASFBS; Hall, " 'Which Citizens Participating?' "; Flores, interview.

110. Bartalini to Taylor; Parratt to Planning and Development Committee, both ASFBS.

111. San Francisco Committee, memorandum to San Francisco Board of Supervisors regarding file 274-68, "Application for Federal Funds in sum of $400,000. to plan Model City programs for Mission District & Hunter's Point & Bayview Residential Dist," May 1968, file 274-68, ASFBS.

112. Michael Omi and Howard Winant, *Racial Formation in the United States: From the 1960s to the 1990s*, 2nd ed. (New York: Routledge, 1994), 56.

113. Castells, "Urban Poverty," 114.

114. Gallegos, "El Movimiento," 16; LaREAL, "La Raza Tutorial Program," LRIC files.

115. "Informational news organ for the liberation of LA RAZA," *¡Basta Ya!* June 1972, 1; LaREAL, "La Raza Tutorial Program," LRIC files.

116. Robert A. Rosenbloom, "Pressuring Policy Making from the Grassroots: The Evolution of an Alinsky-Style Community Organization," PhD dissertation, Stanford University, 1976, 225; Miller, *Organizer's Tale*, 62.

117. Gallegos, "El Movimiento," 19. On self-determination, see Self, *American Babylon*, 219–20; Thomas, *Puerto Rican Citizen*, 239–40.

118. "Mission Coalition Organization," Third Annual Convention Program, Ezquerro files; "Our brothers," 3; LaREAL, "Introduction to La Raza En Acción Local," 3, LRIC files.

119. "Centro de salud celebra segundo año," *¡Basta Ya!* May 1972, 2.

120. Elba Montes quoted in "The Women of La Raza: Part 1," *SFC*, 31 August 1970; Ezquerro and Martinez, interviews.

121. Martinez, interview; Rosenbloom, "Pressuring Policy Making," 309.

122. June York to San Francisco Board of Supervisors, 28 April 1970, file 210-70-2; Parratt to Planning and Development Committee, both ASFBS.

123. Hall, " 'Which Citizens Participating?' "; "Mission Model Cities," *Newsletter of Parents and Taxpayers,* April 1968, 3, file 274-68, ASFBS.

124. Bartalini to San Francisco Board of Supervisors, 03 May 1968; San Francisco Committee, memorandum to San Francisco Board of Supervisors, both ASFBS.

125. "Model Cities Fight Expected," *Argonaut,* 05 March 1969; Hall, " 'Which Citizens Participating?' "

126. Joel Tlumak, "Mission Coalition Splits over Third Term Bid by President," *San Francisco Sunday Examiner and Chronicle,* 18 October 1970; Anita Martinez, "MCO convention marred by walkout," *ET,* 19 October 1970, 1.

127. Rosenbloom, "Pressuring Policy Making," 216–17, 226–28; "MCO Walkout," *¡Basta Ya!* November 1970; Miller, *Organizer's Tale,* 139.

128. Montes, interview.

129. "MCO Walkout." Emphasis is mine.

130. Rosenbloom, "Pressuring Policy Making," 222; Castells, "Urban Poverty," 116.

131. Miller, *Organizer's Tale,* 127; Martinez, interview; Rosenbloom, "Pressuring Policy Making," 244–45.

132. Miller, *Organizer's Tale,* 142.

133. Ibid.

134. Luisa Ezquerro, memorandum to Executive Board of American Federation of Teachers Local 61, 28 November 1973, Ezquerro files.

135. Carlos Carrillo quoted in "MCO Split Develops: Legal Action Sought," *ET,* 21 November 1973, 12.

136. Raúl Moreno, "La M.C.O. en Decadencia," *El Mundo (EM),* 02 January 1974, 2.

Chapter 6

1. Montes, interview.

2. D'Emilio and Freedman, *Intimate Matters.*

3. Robert H. MacRae, "The Challenge of Change to Community Welfare Councils," lecture before National Social Welfare Assembly, 29 September 1962, Chicago, 3; MNC, "Prospectus for Pilot Project with Selected Multi-Problem Families," ca. 1959, 3; MNC, "A New Child Welfare Service Pilot Project for Pre-School Children Having Grossly Inadequate Parents," 1964, 2, all MNC, cartons 39 and 22, BANC.

4. San Francisco Public Welfare Department (SFPWD), "Rehabilitation for Independence: A Report of the Family Rehabilitation Program," 1962, 1–3; Earl Raab, "The 'X' Factor: One Key to a New Welfare Approach," 19 August 1964, 7, both MNC, carton 40, folder 4, BANC.

5. Arletta Dawdy and Irving Kriegsfeld, *Neighborhood Services for Teenage Parents and Their Babies* (San Francisco: Mission Neighborhood Centers, 1966), 10, 19.

6. For a classic discussion on this paradigm, see Oscar Lewis, *La Vida: A Puerto Rican Family in the Culture of Poverty—San Juan and New York* (New York: Random House, 1966). For recent scholarly treatments, see Alice O'Connor, *Poverty Knowledge: Social Science, Public*

Policy, and the Poor in Twentieth-Century U.S. History (Princeton, NJ: Princeton University Press, 2001), chapter 4; and Laura Briggs, *Reproducing Empire: Race, Sex, Science, and U.S. Imperialism in Puerto Rico* (Berkeley: University of California Press, 2002), chapter 6.

7. SFPWD, *Annual Report—Fiscal Year 1962–63* (San Francisco: City Printing Office, 1963), 14; Jennifer Mittelstadt, *From Welfare to Workfare: The Unintended Consequences of Liberal Reform, 1945–1965* (Chapel Hill: University of North Carolina Press, 2005), 12.

8. SFPWD, "Rehabilitation for Independence," 1–2, ; CSSWB Committee on Social and Economic Problems, Unedited Notes on Conversations with 'Poverty-Prone' Segment, 2, both BANC; Joyce Mallette, "Family Rehabilitation Services in an Intensive Casework Caseload," master's thesis, San Francisco State College, 1966, 3–6.

9. SFPWD, "Rehabilitation for Independence," 9, 18, BANC; Mallette, "Family Rehabilitation Services," 4.

10. Eileen Boris, "Contested Rights: The Great Society Between Home and Work," in Milkis and Mileur, eds., *Great Society*, 116.

11. Arthur Coleman, Statement of Basic Principles of the Economic Opportunity Council of San Francisco, 18 September 1964, 7, 11–12, MNC, carton 40, folder 6, BANC.

12. Joseph T. McGucken and James Flynn quoted in Catholic Charities, "News Release," 10 February 1964, Catholic Charities General Correspondence file, AASF.

13. CSS and Presbyterian Inner-City Council, "Program of Neighborhood Organization," BANC; CSS, 1966 Report, CSS file, AASF.

14. McGucken quoted in Catholic Charities, "News Release," AASF; Joseph T. McGucken, "Archbishop's Message," *Monitor* (San Francisco), 01 May 1964; National Conference of Catholic Bishops, "Statement on the Government and Birth Control," ca. 1966, 2, Birth Control file, AASF.

15. SFPWD, "Rehabilitation for Independence," 10; James Reston, "Washington: The Catholic Bishops on Birth Control," *NYT*, 20 November 1966, E12; Coleman, Statement of Basic Principles, 11.

16. McGucken, "Archbishop's Message"; National Conference of Catholic Bishops, "Statement on the Government and Birth Control," 3, 5–8, AASF.

17. MNC, " 'Self-Portrait,' " 4, 10, BANC; Dawdy and Kriegsfeld, *Neighborhood Services*, 4–6.

18. Irving Kriegsfeld and Lilian Katz, *Curriculum and Teaching Strategies for Non-English Speaking Nursery School Children in a Family School* (San Francisco: Mission Neighborhood Centers, Inc. and Telegraph Hill Neighborhood Association, 1965), 2–4.

19. Dawdy and Kriegsfeld, *Neighborhood Services*, 27–30; MNC, "Girls Club Project," multiple reports, 1963–1965; Arletta Dawdy, "Regarding the Status of Girls Club Project," memorandum to National Council of Jewish Women, November 1965, all MNC, carton 7, folder 15, BANC.

20. MNC, "Girls Club Project," reports, BANC; Marie Angell, City Clinic, San Francisco Health Department, "Self-Concept and Sexual Behavior," *ETC: A Review of General Semantics* 20, no. 3 (September 1963): 1–2, MNC, carton 39, BANC.

21. John D'Emilio, "Gay Politics and Community in San Francisco Since World War II," in *Hidden from History: Reclaiming the Gay and Lesbian Past*, ed. Martin Duberman et al. (New York: Penguin, 1990), 464–65; Nan Alamilla Boyd, *Wide Open Town: A Queer History of San Francisco to 1965* (Berkeley: University of California Press, 2003), 203, 216–18, 231–36.

22. Angell, "Self-Concept," 1.

23. In her now-classic study of unmarried mothers in early twentieth-century America, Regina Kunzel encouraged scholars to consider ordinary women's perspectives by recognizing the methodological limitations of impressions mediated by experts. See Kunzel, *Fallen Women, Problem Girls: Unmarried Mothers and the Professionalization of Social Work, 1890–1945* (New Haven, CT: Yale University Press, 1993), 6–8.

24. Dawdy and Kriegsfeld, *Neighborhood Services*, 9; Dawdy, "Regarding the Status of Girls Club Project," BANC.

25. Montes, interview.

26. Dawdy and Kriegsfeld, *Neighborhood Services*, 15.

27. "Bernal Heights Aims for Local Improvements," *San Francisco Progress*, 14 November 1966; MACAP, program pamphlet, ca. 1966; MACAB, meeting notes, 08 October 1966, 3–4, both MNC, carton 13, BANC; SPUR, "The City's Anti-Poverty Program," 6–8, ASFBS.

28. Joanna Uribe, interview by the author, 17 April 2003, Berkeley, CA; MACAB, meeting notes, 11 April 1968, MNC, carton 13, BANC.

29. Jill Quadagno and Catherine Fobes, "The Welfare State and the Cultural Reproduction of Gender: Making Good Girls and Boys in the Job Corps," *Social Problems* 42, no. 2 (May 1995): 175.

30. Bernal Action Against Poverty, "Neighborhood Group Leaders Training Project," project proposal, 1966, 1–3, 6, file 454-64, ASFBS.

31. Roger Hernandez to Archbishop Joseph T. McGucken, 04 October 1968, CCSS file, AASF; F. Arturo Rosales, "Movimiento Familiar Cristiano," in *Dictionary of Latino Civil Rights History* (Houston: Arte Público Press, 2006), 303.

32. Movimiento Familiar Cristiano (MFC), Report for 1971–1972; Maria Mercedes Reygadas to Archbishop McGucken, 02 October 1972; Reygadas to McGucken, 30 January 1975; Hernandez to McGucken, all CCSS file, AASF.

33. Sides, *Erotic City*, 5–6, 56–59.

34. MCO, "Policy and Resolutions Report," 1968, 10–11; Miller, *Organizer's Tale*, 62–63; MCO, "Mission Coalition Organization," Third Annual Convention program, 1970, n.p., Ezquerro files.

35. Francisco Marín, "Llamamiento A Campaña Contra la Inmoralidad En El Distrito Mission," and Willy Alfredo Lopez, "Comentario de la Semana," both *EM*, 08 April 1971, 1–2.

36. Marín, "Llamamiento A Campaña."

37. Maria Del Drago, "The Pride of Inés Garcia," *La Razón Mestiza (RM)*, special ed. (Summer 1975): 44.

38. Ibid.; Rebecca Carrillo, " 'I Had a Right to Defend Myself,' " *ET*, 14 October 1974, 3; Ana Montes, "La Nueva Chicana," *RM*, special ed. (Summer 1975): 54.

39. Gay Latino Alliance (GALA), "Understanding the Gay Latino Experience Part I," *ET*, June 1976, 3; GALA, "Understanding the Gay Latino Part II," *ET*, July 1976, 9–10; Eddi Baca, interview in "GALA Habla Acerca los Casos de los Homosexuales," *ET*, October 1977, 4.

40. GALA, "Gay Latino Experience Part I."

41. Ibid.; Baca, interview.

42. Baca, interview.

43. Historians and social scientists have approached these issues from various angles. A sample includes Ramón Gutiérrez, "Honor Ideology, Marriage Negotiation, and Class-Gender Domination in New Mexico, 1690–1846," *Latin American Perspectives* 12, no. 1 (1985): 81–104; Patricia Zavella, " 'Playing with Fire': The Gendered Construction of Chicana/Mexicana

Sexualities," in *The Gender/Sexuality Reader: Culture, History, Political Economy*, ed. Roger N. Lancaster and Micaela di Leonardo (New York: Routledge, 1997), 392–408; and Marysol Asencio, "'Locas,' Respect, and Masculinity: Gender Conformity in Migrant Puerto Rican Gay Masculinities," *Gender and Society* 25, no. 3 (June 2011): 335–54.

44. Carrillo, interview.

45. Ramón Gutiérrez, "Community, Patriarchy and Individualism: The Politics of Chicano History and the Dream of Equality," *American Quarterly* 45, no. 1 (March 1993): 46–50.

46. Emma Pérez, "Queering the Borderlands: The Challenges of Excavating the Invisible and Unheard," *Frontiers: A Journal of Women's Studies* 24, no. 2/3 (2003): 123–24.

47. Montes, interview; Linda Marquez quoted in Mildred Hamilton, "The Women of La Raza: Part 3," *SFE*, 02 September 1970, 32.

48. Ezquerro, interview.

49. Ezquerro herself eventually became the board chairperson for the MMNC.

50. Judy Zalazar Drummond, interview by the author, 24 March 2003, San Francisco; Amador, interview. On Los Angeles and Chicago, see Maylei Blackwell, *¡Chicana Power! Contested Histories of Feminism in the Chicano Movement* (Austin: University of Texas Press, 2011), 67–69; Fernández, *Brown in the Windy City*, 243–44.

51. Carrillo, interview; Fernando Tafoya, "Chicanos and the Function of Sexual Repression," 2, ca. 1980–1981, Gay Chicano Subject Files, Ethnic Studies Library, University of California, Berkeley.

52. Esperanza Echavarri quoted in Mildred Hamilton, "The Women of La Raza: Part 5," *SFE*, 04 September 1970; Gladys Sandlin, interview by the author, 21 July 2003, San Francisco.

53. McGucken to Mrs. Nicholas St. Amant, 29 January 1973; McGucken to Monsignor James Flynn, 23 January 1973; Gerard E. Sherry, draft editorial, late January 1973, all Dignity file, AASF.

54. Pete Gallegos, interview.

55. McGucken to Flynn, 30 January 1973, Dignity file, AASF; Luis Echegoyen, "Boletín de Servicio Comunitario," *EM*, 08 April 1971, 2.

56. Marín, "Llamamiento A Campaña"; Raúl Moreno, "Carnaval de brujas," *EM*, 10 November 1977, 4; Don Kuka, "Satélite," *Tiempo Latino*, October 1978, 9; Tafoya, "Chicanos and the Function of Sexual Repression," 5.

57. Amador, interview.

58. Hilda A. Hidalgo and Elia Hidalgo Christensen, "The Puerto Rican Lesbian and the Puerto Rican Community," *Journal of Homosexuality* 2, no. 2 (Winter 1976–77): 116.

59. Ramon Barbieri, "What is Model Cities for me?" unpublished manuscript, n.d., 14, courtesy of Ramon Barbieri.

60. Uribe, interview. Ramon Barbieri described Susan Castro as "a white middle class lady, having a Marxist view of the Social Agenda for the 60s and the 70s." He did not address concerns over her sexual orientation. Barbieri, "What is Model Cities for me?" 24.

61. Eugene E. Levitt and Albert D. Klassen, "Public Attitudes Toward Homosexuality: Part of the 1970 National Survey by the Institute for Sex Research," *Journal of Homosexuality* 1, no. 1 (1974): 32–33.

62. Uribe, interview.

63. Velia G. Hancock, "'La Chicana' Movement and Women's Liberation," *EM*, 15 July 1971.

64. Alma Garcia, "The Development of Chicana Feminist Discourse, 1970–1980," *Gender and Society* 3, no. 2 (June 1989): 229.

65. Hancock, "'La Chicana' Movement"; Carrillo, interview.

66. Carrillo, interview.

67. Dorinda Moreno, interview by the author, 04 June 2003, San Francisco.

68. "Concilio Mujeres, Dec. 1974," *RM* 1, no. 4 (December 1974): n.p; Shirlene Soto, "The Emerging Chicana: A Review of the Journals," *Southwest Economy and Society* 2, no. 1 (October/ November 1976): 41; Francisca Flores, "Comisión Femenil Mexicana," *Regeneración* 2, no. 1 (1971): 6–7.

69. Soto, "Emerging Chicana," 43.

70. "Editorial," *RM,* special ed. (Summer 1975): 2.

71. Fernández, *Brown in the Windy City*, 252.

72. Moreno, interview; Montes, "La Nueva Chicana."

73. "Primera Conferencia de Mujeres Puertorriqueñas (Puerto Rican Women Meet)," *ET*, 13 September 1974, 6; Montes, interview.

74. Montes and Carmen Maymi quoted in "Primera Conferencia de Mujeres."

75. See for example, Jane Sherron De Hart, "Second-Wave Feminists and the Dynamics of Social Change," in *Women's America: Refocusing the Past*, 6th ed., ed. Linda Kerber and Jane Sherron De Hart (New York: Oxford University Press, 2004), 598–623; Alice Echols, "Nothing Distant About It: Women's Liberation and Sixties Radicalism," in *Shaky Ground: The Sixties and Its Aftershocks* (New York: Columbia University Press, 2002), 75–94.

76. Montes, interview; "Carmen Maymi," *Notable Hispanic Women*, ed. Diane Telgen and Jim Kamp (Detroit: Gale Research, 1993), 265.

77. Montes, interview.

78. Combahee River Collective, "The Combahee River Collective Statement," in *Home Girls: A Black Feminist Anthology*, ed. Barbara Smith (New York: Kitchen Table—Women of Color Press, 1983), 264–65.

79. Montes, interview; "Law Project to Champion for Chicana/Latina Rights," *ET*, 22 August 1975, 3.

80. "Concilio Mujeres, Dec. 1974"; "Cucarachas en Acción," *RM* 1, no. 1 (March 1974): 2.

81. "Concilio Mujeres, Summer 1975," *RM*, special ed. (Summer 1975): back cover page.

82. Del Drago, "Pride of Inés Garcia."

83. Ibid.; Marquez quoted in, Hamilton, "Women of La Raza: Part 3."

84. "Concilio Mujeres, Feb. 1975," *RM* 2, no. 1 (February 1975): n.p; "Concilio Mujeres, Sept. 1974," *RM* 1, no. 3 (September 1974): n.p.; and "Change for Children," *RM* 1, no. 1 (March 1974): n.p.

85. Montes and Moreno, interviews.

86. "Chicana Regional Conference," *Hijas de Cuahtemoc* 2 no. 2 (May 1971): n.p.

87. Del Drago, "Pride of Inés Garcia"; Anna Beatrice Lange, "Chicana Self-Help Clinics," *RM*, special ed. (Summer 1975): 14.

88. "Counseling," *RM* 1, no. 4 (December 1974): n.p; Moreno and Amador, interviews.

89. Announcement, *RM* 2, no. 1 (February 1975): n.p.

90. Patricia San Miguel Gonzalez, "Soy Chicana y Ni Quien Melo Quite," *RM* special ed. (Summer 1975): 8. On lesbian separatism, see Anne Enke, *Finding the Movement: Sexuality, Contested Space, and Feminist Activism* (Durham, NC: Duke University Press, 2007), 81–82, 100–101, 260.

91. GALA, "GALA," ca. 1976, ephemera collection, GALA file, GLBTHS. On GALA's origins, see Horacio N. Roque Ramírez, "'That's My Place!' Negotiating Racial, Sexual, and Gender

Politics in San Francisco's Gay Latino Alliance, 1975–1983," *Journal of the History of Sexuality* 2, no. 2 (2003): 224–58.

92. Baca, interview.

93. GALA, "GALA," GLBTHS; Rodrigo Reyes, "Latino Gays: Coming Out and Coming Home," *Nuestro*, April 1981, 44.

94. GALA, "Gay Latino Experience Part I"; Reyes, "Latino Gays"; Rodrigo Reyes, videotaped interview by Richard Marquez, 14 June 1991, San Francisco, Archivo Rodrigo Reyes under the stewardship of Luis Alberto de la Garza, Berkeley, CA.

95. GALA, "Gay Latino Experience Part I."

96. Ibid.

97. GALA, "Gay Latino Experience Parts I and II."

98. Roque Ramírez, " 'That's My Place!' " 245–48.

99. Rodrigo Reyes, "On the Fourth of July: What America Means to Me," *Coming Up!* July 1982, 1–2.

Chapter 7

1. Paul Hardman, "Gay Restaurant Not Wanted in Mission," *Bay Area Reporter (BAR)*, 30 September 1976, 2 (capitalization appears in the original text); Concerned residents et al., untitled flyer, September 1976, Randy Alfred Papers, box 3, GALA file, GLBTHS.

2. Hardman, "Gay Restaurant Not Wanted."

3. Concerned citizens et al., untitled flyer, GLBTHS.

4. Baca quoted in Hardman, "Gay Restaurant Not Wanted;" Reyes, video interview.

5. "Open Letter to the Mission," *ET*, July 1976, 2.

6. "¿200 Años de 'Progreso' en la Mision?" *ET*, July 1976, 1.

7. "BART enriches the rich," *ET*, 21 November 1973, 2.

8. "McDonald's Invades the Mission," *ET*, 10 October 1973, 2; "Mission SI, McDonald's NO," *ET*, 24 February 1974, 2.

9. *Polk's San Francisco: City Directory 1973* (Monterey Park, CA: R. L. Polk, 1973), 657; Denise Holley, "Big Mac Goes to Court," *ET*, 21 November 1973, 6; Holley, "McDonald's appealed," *ET*, 10 June 1974, 4.

10. Frank Hunt quoted in "Mission SI, McDonald's NO"; Holley, "Big Mac Goes to Court."

11. Mission Housing Development Corporation (MHDC), *A Plan for the Inner Mission* (San Francisco, 1974), 15, 27, 38.

12. MHDC, *Plan for the Inner Mission*, 3; "Mission Protected Neighborhood Project," fact sheet, ca. 1973–1974, personal files of Toby Levine.

13. Toby Levine, Mission Planning Council (MPC) End of Year Report, 1974; MPC By-Laws, draft version, 19 February 1974, both Levine files.

14. Ezquerro, interview; Toby Levine, interview with the author, 04 April 2003, San Francisco.

15. "Redevelopment: BART and the Mission," *ET*, 28 March 1975, 2; "Moscone Supports Rezoning," *EM*, 21 May 1975, 2.

16. "Board of Supervisors to Hear Mission Rezoning," *EM*, 21 May 1975, 1; Mission Merchants Association, "Day of Mourning," ad, reprinted in *ET*, 28 May 1975, 1. Emphasis in original.

17. Cristina Valdes, "Latinos Win Rezoning Fight!!!" *ET*, 28 May 1975, 1.

18. "Porno fight in the Mission," *ET*, 22 August 1975, 4; Operation Upgrade, "A Position

Paper," December 1976, in MPC and Operation Upgrade, "Sixteenth Street: A Neighborhood Study," 1977, 89, Levine files.

19. Levine, interview; Miguel Torres, "Unsafe Buildings Target of Operation Upgrade," *ET*, March 1976, 8.

20. "Three Movie Spots Lose Permits," *SFE*, 26 May 1970, 8. For a contemporary examination of campaigns nationwide, see Louis A. Zurcher and R. George Kirkpatrick, *Citizens for Decency: Antipornography Crusades as Status Defense* (Austin: University of Texas Press, 1976).

21. "Porno fight"; MPC, calendar of events, June and July 1976, Levine files; Torres, "Unsafe Buildings."

22. Dianne Feinstein quoted in K. Connie Kang, "The Smut Dealers Will Have to Wait," *SFE*, 20 September 1977, 3; "Inside the Feinstein Porno Ordinance," *BAR*, 06 January 1977, 7; "S.F. Gets Tough with Porn," *SFC*, 06 October 1977, 3.

23. Bars and Restaurants Guide, *San Francisco Sentinel*, 01 February 1974.

24. "Metropolitan Community Church (MCC)" and "The Baths, multiple listings," *Polk's San Francisco* (1973), 675, 64; *1976 San Francisco City Directory* (R. L. Polk, 1976), 665, 62; "Guide to Restaurants and Bars," *San Francisco Crusader*, July 1976. For a basic history of the MCC, see http://mccchurch.org/overview/history-of-mcc, accessed 01 August 2016.

25. This assessment is based on a review of Dignity and CCSF files, AASF. See also Jeffrey M. Burns, "Qué es esto? The Transformation of St. Peter's Parish in the Mission, San Francisco, 1913–1990," in *American Congregations*, ed. James Wind and James Lewis (Chicago: University of Chicago Press, 1994), 434.

26. Concerned citizens et al., untitled flyer.

27. Bruce Petitt, "Does Improved Housing Displace Blacks?" *BAR*, 01 February 1979, 4.

28. Reyes, interview.

29. Manuel Castells, "Cultural Identity, Sexual Liberation and Urban Structure: The Gay Community in San Francisco," in *City and the Grassroots*, 167.

30. D'Emilio, "Gay Politics and Community," 468; Boyd, *Wide Open Town*, 238.

31. Martin P. Levine, "Gay Ghetto," *Journal of Homosexuality* 4, no. 4 (Summer 1979): 363–77; Randy Shilts, "Mecca or Ghetto? Castro Street," *Advocate*, February 1977, 20–23; Castells, "Cultural Identity, Sexual Liberation," 145–58; Godfrey, *Neighborhoods in Transition*, 171.

32. *I Left My Home in San Francisco*, documentary, produced by Tony Van Witsen, ca. 1980, GLBTHS.

33. Lesbians Against Police Violence (LAPV), untitled paper on the Mission District, n.d., 2; LAPV, untitled paper on police violence, n.d., 3, both LAPV files, GLBTHS.

34. Enke, *Finding the Movement*, 222.

35. Ruth Mahaney, interview by the author, 11 July 2003, San Francisco.

36. Ibid.; *The Mission*, video recording, written and produced by Pam Rorke Levy (San Francisco: KQED-San Francisco, 1994).

37. LAPV, untitled paper on the Mission District, GLBTHS.

38. Historical Note, "Guide to Old Wives' Tales Bookstore Records," GLBTHS; "Bars and Restaurants Guide," *San Francisco Crusader*, October 1977; "Bars and Restaurants Guide," *BAR*, 03 August 1978, 40.

39. Operation Upgrade, "Position Paper," 89, 92, Levine files; Godfrey, *Neighborhoods in Transition*, 168.

40. Al Borvice, interview; Reyes, interview.

41. Roque Ramírez, "'That's My Place!'" 243.

42. Margarita Sandoval, "Problemas de vivienda agobian a la comunidad latina en San Francisco," *EM*, 27 October 1977, 2; David Oberweiser, "Housing in the Mission District," *EM*, 27 April 1978, 1. See also "Mission Tenants Resist Eviction," *ET*, March 1977, 1; "Mudanza de Gente," *ET*, March 1978, 1; and "Latinos Pushed Out," *ET*, July 1978, 4.

43. On Brooklyn and Chicago, see Suleiman Osman, *The Invention of Brownstone Brooklyn: Gentrification and the Search for Authenticity in Postwar New York* (New York: Oxford University Press, 2011), 270-80; Fernández, *Brown in the Windy City*, 174-80.

44. "Anglo Professionals Move In," *ET*, July 1978, 4; Alfredo Vega quoted in Juan Cruz and G. Roginsky, "Mission Fires: Urban Renewal Made Simple?" *ET*, April 1977, 1, 10.

45. Untitled cartoon, *ET*, February 1978, 6.

46. "Housing Speculation—One More Neighborhood-Buster," *ET*, February 1978, 6.

47. Unnamed Latino informant #1 in *I Left My Home in San Francisco*; Randy Shilts, "A Confrontation of Cultures," *California Living Magazine*, 18, insert in *San Francisco Sunday Examiner & Chronicle*, 01 October 1978; *The Mission*, video recording.

48. Lesbian and Gay Action (LGA), Statement of Purpose, ca. 1976-1977, Paula Lichtenberg Papers, box 2, miscellaneous files, GLBTHS; Bay Area Gay Liberation (BAGL), "Progressive Gay Caucus—Principles of Unity," ca. 1976, ephemera collection, BAGL file, GLBTHS; LAPV, untitled paper on police violence, 2, GLBTHS.

49. Mark Freeman and Gayle Rodgers quoted in Housing Rights Study Group (HRSG), "Free Report on Housing Available," press release, 12 August 1977; HRSG, "Who's Moving? A Look at the Neighborhoods," report, 1977, 1, 9; "Housing and National Oppression Committee," *BAGL Newsletter*, Feb. 1978, 6, all Alfred Papers, boxes 4 and 1, GLBTHS.

50. BAGL and LGA, "Speculators Get Out of Our Neighborhood!" flyer, ca. 1978; "Come Out May Day Against Speculation in the Fillmore!!" *BAGL Newsletter*, May 1978, both Alfred Papers, boxes 4 and 1, GLBTHS; LGA, Statement of Purpose, Lichtenberg Papers, GLBTHS.

51. BAGL and LGA, "Speculators Get Out"; LAPV, untitled paper on Mission District, both GLBTHS.

52. BAGL and LGA, "Speculators Get Out"; "Come Out May Day;" HRSG, "Who's Moving?" 1, all GLBTHS.

53. Holley, "Big Mac Goes to Court."

54. Jim Shoch, "Campaign to Elect Supervisors by District Begins," *ET*, March 1976, 2; Centro Latino, press release, June 1970, Community Organizations and Resources Vertical Files, Mission Branch, SFPL.

55. Hartman, *City for Sale*, 228-29.

56. Al Borvice quoted in "Propositions T & 14—District Elections of Supervisors," *ET*, October 1976, 6.

57. San Franciscans for District Elections (SFDE), Argument for Proposition "T," in San Francisco Registrar of Voters (SFRV), *San Francisco Voters Information Pamphlet* (*SFVIP*), 02 November 1976, 18, SFBPD.

58. Citizens for a United San Francisco et al., Argument Against Proposition "T," in SFRV, *SFVIP*, 02 November 1976, SFBPD; "Propositions T & 14."

59. Hartman, *City for Sale*, 229-32; Mariam Morley, "Latino Activist runs for Mission Supervisor," *EM*, 29 September 1977, 1.

60. Nancy G. Walker, SFDE treasurer, Argument for Proposition "T," in SFRV, *SFVIP*, SFBPD; "Propositions T & 14." For a demographic snapshot based on the 1970 census, see SF Planning, *San Francisco 1970*, 2.

61. "Yes on T," *ET,* November 1976, 12; Dianne Feinstein et al., Argument for Proposition A, in SFRV, *SFVIP,* 02 August 1977, 12, SFBPD.

62. "Congreso de la Mision: Asuntos y Accion," *ET,* May 1977, 2; Raúl Moreno, "Intensifican campaña los candidatos del distrito 6," *EM,* 03 November 1977, 2.

63. SF Planning, *San Francisco 1970,* 9; Manuel Castells, "The Methodological Appendices," Table A.3., in *City and the Grassroots,* 352.

64. Al Borvice, interview; Moreno, "Intensifican campaña."

65. Del Carlo and Al Borvice, interviews.

66. Ibid.; "Congreso de la Mision: Asuntos y Accion."

67. Gary Borvice quoted in Morley, "Latino Activist runs."

68. Ibid.; Al Borvice, interview; George Mendenhall, "Milk Wins, 1st Gay Supervisor," *BAR,* 10 November 1977, 4.

69. Reyes, video interview; Wayne Friday, "District 6: Carol Ruth Silver in Tough Race," *BAR,* 29 September 1977, 10.

70. Carol Ruth Silver, interview by the author, 22 June 2003, San Francisco; Mendenhall, "Milk Wins"; "Carol Ruth Silver Statement on Gay Issues," *BAR,* 27 October 1977, 23.

71. Levine, Ezquerro, and Al Borvice, interviews.

72. Silver, interview; Carol Ruth Silver for Supervisor, campaign ad, *BAR,* 04 November 1977, 7.

73. Friday, "District 6."

74. Mendenhall, "Milk Wins;" "Sentinel Endorses," *San Francisco Sentinel,* 20 October 1977, 5; Roque Ramírez, "'That's My Place!'" 243.

75. Mendenhall, "Milk Wins"; Castells, "Methodological Appendices," Table A.10, in *City and the Grassroots,* 354.

76. "Initiative Aimed at Firing Homosexual Teachers Filed," *LAT,* 04 August 1977, D1; Text of proposed law and John Briggs et al., Argument in Favor of Proposition 6, both California Secretary of State, *California Voters Pamphlet, General Election November 7, 1978,* 29–30, CBPOD.

77. Bay Area Committee Against the Briggs Initiative (BACABI), "Speak Out Against the Briggs Initiative!" flyer, March 1978, ephemera collection, Briggs file, BACABI folder, GLBTHS.

78. John Briggs, "Deviants Threaten the American Family," *LAT,* 23 October 1977, Part VII, 5; statement of Senator John Briggs before Los Angeles Press Club, 07 September 1977, Lichtenberg Papers, box 1, folder 10, GLBTHS.

79. BACABI, "Unite to Defeat the Briggs Initiative," flyer, May 1978; BACABI and San Franciscans Against Proposition 6, "San Francisco Says NO to Proposition 6," pamphlet, 1978, Lichtenberg Papers, box 1, folder 12, both GLBTHS.

80. Baca, interview.

81. Paula Lichtenberg and Michael Mank to BACABI Members, ca. May–June 1978, Lichtenberg Papers, box 1, folder 12, GLBTHS; "Gay Latinos Call for Mission Support," *ET,* June 1978, 4.

82. Lichtenberg and Mank to BACABI members; BACABI, media committee roster, 1978, Lichtenberg Papers, box 1, folder 8; BACABI, "Unity Now," pamphlet, 1978, ephemera collection, Briggs file, BACABI folder, all GLBTHS.

83. "Briggs Hurts Us All—No on 6," *San Francisco Teacher,* October 1978, 2; BACABI, "Unite to Defeat the Briggs Initiative," GLBTHS; "Gay Rights," *California Teacher,* November 1977, 2.

84. Lesbian Schoolworkers et al., "This Affects Us All," flyer, April 1978, ephemera collection, Briggs file, Gay and Lesbian Schoolworkers folder, GLBTHS; BACABI, "Protect Your Rights," pamphlet, 1978, and BACABI, "Human Justice Rally—No on 6," flyer, November 1978, both Lichtenberg Papers, box 1, folder 12, GLBTHS; text of proposed law, in California Secretary of State, *California Voters Pamphlet*, CBPOD.

85. Rosa Perez quoted in BACABI, "San Francisco Says NO"; Gay Student Community et al., "Rally Against Prop. 6," flyer, November 1978, ephemera collection, Briggs file, Prop. 6 folder, both GLBTHS.

86. BACABI Labor Committee, "An Injury to One Is an Injury to All," 1978, Lichtenberg Papers, box 1, folder 12; BACABI, "San Francisco Says NO," both GLBTHS.

87. BACABI, "Human Justice Rally"; BACABI et al., "Workers Conference Against Briggs/Prop 6," flyer, 09-10 September 1978, ephemera collection, Briggs file, BACABI file; James Flynn quoted in BACABI, "San Francisco Says NO," all GLBTHS.

88. "La Proposición Seis" and Kuka, "Satélite," *Tiempo Latino*, October 1978, 2, 9.

89. "NO en 6, SI en U" cartoon and "Elecciones Cruciales el 7 de Noviembre," *ET*, November 1978, 2.

90. "Proposition 6 Complete Results" and Ivan Sharpe, "Gays Dancing in Streets—Briggs Vows to Fight On," *SFE*, 08 November 1978, 6; "Final Results by County" and Marshall Kilduff, "S.F. Maintains Its Liberal Reputation," *SFC*, 09 November 1978, 3C.

91. Ballot Simplification Committee, Analysis of Proposition U; Scott Weaver et al., Argument in Favor of Proposition U, both in SFRV, *SFVIP*, 07 November 1978, 101-2, SFBPD. On Proposition 13, see Self, *American Babylon*, 316-27.

92. Henry and Beverley Rutzik, Charlene Martinez, et al., Argument in Favor of Proposition U, SFRV, *SFVIP*, 101-2, SFBPD; "Elecciones Cruciales."

93. Hartman, *City for Sale*, 340-45.

94. MCO, "Policy and Resolutions Report," 1968, 7; MHDC, *Plan for the Inner Mission*, 16-17.

95. "BART enriches the rich"; "Rent Control Initiative," *ET*, 28 May 1975, 4.

96. Harvey Milk, "Housing Becomes a Major Problem," *BAR*, 16 March 1978, 11.

97. BAGL and LGA, "Speculators Get Out," GLBTHS; "Speculation Tax Ordinance," *San Francisco Progress*, 16 April 1978, 3.

98. San Francisco Board of Realtors, Argument Against Proposition U, in SFRV, *SFVIP*, 07 November 1978, 104, SFBPD; Coalition for Better Housing and San Franciscans Against Rent Control, "Vote No on U," paid advertisement, *BAR*, 26 October 1978, 11.

99. Marshall Kilduff, "Rent Rebate Is Defeated in S.F.," *SFC*, 08 November 1978, 1.

100. San Francisco Gay Liberation (SFGL), "Housing Problems and the Gay Community," flyer, 1979, Alfred Papers, box 4, GLBTHS; Randy Stallings, "Blacks Wrong on Who Speculates," *BAR*, 26 April 1979, 14.

101. San Franciscans for Affordable Housing (SFAH), "SFAH Comprehensive Housing Plan," plan overview, 1979; SFAH, "What Is San Franciscans for Affordable Housing?" flyer, ca. April 1979, both Meg Barnett Papers, box 1, LAPV notebook 2, GLBTHS; Hartman, *City for Sale*, 341.

102. Text of Proposed Initiative Ordinance—Proposition R, in SFRV, *SFVIP*, 06 November 1979, 122, SFBPD.

103. SFAH, "Take the Initiative," pamphlet, 1979; SFAH, "Caught in the Housing Squeeze?" ordinance summary, July 1979, both Barnett Papers, box 1, GLBTHS.

104. Rene Ramos quoted in "Yes. Rent Control," flyer, 1979, Alfred Papers, box 3, 1979 elections folder, GLBTHS; Clarissa Ward, Graciela Cashion, et al., Argument in Favor of Proposition R, in SFRV, *SFVIP*, 06 November 1979, 94, SFBPD.

105. SFAH, "SFAH Comprehensive Housing Plan," GLBTHS; Yori Wada et al., Argument in Favor of Proposition R, in SFRV, *SFVIP*, 92, SFBPD.

106. San Franciscans for Sensible Housing Policy (SFSHP), "Vote NO on R," pamphlet, 1979, Alfred Papers, box 3, 1979 elections folder, GLBTHS.

107. Dianne Feinstein, Argument Against Proposition R, SFRV, *SFVIP*, 06 November 1979, 96, SFBPD; SFSHP, "Vote NO on R," GLBTHS.

108. James Lazarus and Kathryn Pennypacker, "Regarding Summary of Residential Rent Stabilization and Arbitration Ordinance," memorandum to Clerk of the Board of Supervisors, 15 June 1979, 1–2, Barnett Papers, box 1, GLBTHS; Harry Britt and Carol Ruth Silver, Argument in Favor of Proposition R, SFRV, *SFVIP*, 94, SFBPD.

109. "How the City Voted," *SFC*, 07 November 1979, 1A.

110. Mark Blackburn, "Debate over Rent Control Has Spread to California," *NYT*, 28 October 1979, E5; Hartman, *City for Sale*, 343.

111. Juan Gonzales, "Pelando El Ojo," *ET*, December 1978, 2; San Francisco's Renters' Alliance, Argument in Favor of Proposition R, SFRV, *SFVIP*, 94, SFBPD.

112. Shoch, "Campaign to Elect Supervisors"; "Yes on T."

113. Issel and Cherny, *San Francisco*, 218; Wallace Turner, "San Francisco: 'NO' to the Old Liberalism," *NYT*, 11 November 1979, E4.

114. Betty Anello quoted in Oberweiser, "Housing in the Mission District."

115. Gonzales, "Pelando El Ojo."

116. Turner, "San Francisco: 'NO' to the Old Liberalism."

Epilogue

1. Mireya Navarro, "The New Wave of Salvadorans in the City," *SFE*, 24 March 1981, A1.

2. Steven P. Wallace, "The New Urban Latinos: Central Americans in a Mexican Immigrant Environment," *Urban Affairs Quarterly* 25, no. 2 (December 1989): 256, 259; Raquel Pinderhughes et al., *The LATSTAT Report: Poverty and Inequality in San Francisco: Focus on Latino Families and Children* (San Francisco: SFSU Urban Studies Program, 1996), 11–12; Cecilia Menjívar, "Immigrant Kinship Networks and the Impact of the Receiving Context: Salvadorans in San Francisco in the Early 1990s," *Social Problems* 44, no. 1 (1997): 104–23.

3. Pinderhughes et al., *LATSTAT Report*, 10; Cordova, *Heart of the Mission*, 8.

4. "Lively Times in Latino San Francisco," *Sunset*, October 1989, 32; Godfrey, *Neighborhoods in Transition*, 198–99; Cordova, *Heart of the Mission*, 166–68, 186–87; Juliana Delgado Lopera, "¡Cuéntamelo! A Queer History of Queer Latin Immigrants in San Francisco," *SF Weekly*, 26 June 2013, 10–17.

5. Dawn Garcia and L. A. Chung, "Many Hispanics Fear Mission District Is Losing Latin Flavor," *SFC*, 03 December 1990, A4; Martha Sanchez-Beswick, "Reaching Gangs," *Hispanic*, June 1995, 8; Godfrey, *Neighborhoods in Transition*, 199–200.

6. Latinos' annual per capita income stood at $9,766 in 1980 and $11,400 in 1990. The figures for whites were $18,558 in 1980 and $28,197 in 1990. See Pinderhughes et al., *LATSTAT Report*, 32, 36.

7. Joel Simon, "Mission Confronts Crisis of Change," *ET*, October/November 1986, 11; Garcia and Chung, "Many Hispanics Fear Mission Is Losing."

8. Pinderhughes et al., *LATSTAT Report*, 87; Wallace, "New Urban Latinos," 245–48.

9. Sue Hester quoted in Simon, "Mission Confronts Crisis." The assertion about subdued activism is based on a cursory review of media coverage and existing social science literature. Archival research is needed to offer a more conclusive assessment.

10. Wallace, "New Urban Latinos," 258–59; Menjívar, "Immigrant Kinship Networks," 111; Rodríguez, *Queer Latinidad*, 49, 76–77.

11. DeLeon, *Left Coast City*, 28; Ezquerro, interview; San Francisco Latino Democratic Club, club history, http://www.sflatinodemocrats.com/history, accessed 10 January 2018.

12. Justeen Hyde, Mindy Hochgesang, et al., *CAP Chronicles: A Retrospective Look at the Violence Prevention Initiative's Community Action Programs* (Los Angeles: California Wellness Foundation, 2003), http://www.calwellness.org/assets13/pdf_docs/cap.pdf; "Pax Christi Conference to Explore Peace Issue," *San Jose Mercury News*, 11 February 1995, 10F; Miriam J. Wells, "Unionization and Immigration Incorporation in San Francisco Hotels," *Social Problems* 47, no.2 (May 2000): 241–65.

13. Evelyn Nieves, "Mission District Fights Case of Dot-Com Fever," *NYT*, 05 November 2000, 27; Fernando Martí, Mission Anti-Displacement Coalition, "The Mission District: A History of Resistance," December 2006, 9–11, http://static1.1.sqspcdn.com/static/f/633596/9137878 /1288129554673/Mission+District+History.pdf?t, accessed 13 January 2018.

14. Rachel Gordon, "S.F. Supervisors Shift to Left," *SFC*, 14 December 2000, 1.

15. Allan Bérubé, "No Race-Baiting, Red-Baiting, or Queer-Baiting! The Marine Cooks and Stewards Union from the Depression to the Cold War," in Bérubé, *My Desire for History: Essays in Gay, Community, and Labor History*, ed. John D'Emilio and Estelle Freedman (Chapel Hill: University of North Carolina Press, 2011), 294–320.

16. Neil Smith, *The New Urban Frontier: Gentrification and the Revanchist City* (London: Routledge, 1996); Arlene Dávila, *Barrio Dreams: Puerto Ricans, Latinos, and the Neoliberal City* (Berkeley: University of California Press, 2004); Jane L. Collins, Micaela di Leonardo, and Brett Williams, eds., *New Landscapes of Inequality: Neoliberalism and the Erosion of Democracy in America* (Santa Fe, NM: School for Advanced Research Press, 2008).

17. Self, *All in the Family*, 327, 368; Nancy MacLean, "Southern Dominance in Borrowed Language: The Regional Origins of American Neoliberalism" in *New Landscapes of Inequality*, ed. Collins et al., 23–24.

18. John Geluardi, "The Class of 2000," *SF Weekly*, 29 October 2008, https://archives.sf weekly.com/sanfrancisco/the-class-of-2000/Content?oid=2169864, accessed 19 January 2018.

19. San Francisco Office of Labor Standards Enforcement, "Minimum Wage Ordinance News," https://sfgov.org/olse/minimum-wage-ordinance-mwo; SF Planning, "Eastern Neighborhoods Community Planning," 2008, 3, http://sf-planning.org/sites/default/files/FileCenter /Documents/1276-EN_brochure_8_2008.pdf, both accessed 20 January 2018.

20. Kerri Anne Renzulli, "10 Most Expensive Cities to Be a Renter," *Time*, 08 April 2016, http://time.com/money/4287132/most-expensive-cities-to-rent; Alan Berube, "All Cities Are Not Created Unequal," 20 February 2014, https://www.brookings.edu/research/all-cities-are-not -created-unequal, both accessed 20 January 2018.

21. Eve Bachrach and Jon Christensen, "What's the Matter with San Francisco?" *BOOM: The Journal of California* 4, no.2 (Summer 2014): 3–6; Gabriel Metcalf, "What's the Matter with San Francisco?" *CityLab*, 23 July 2015, https://www.citylab.com/equity/2015/07/whats-the-matter -with-san-francisco/399506; Jason Rhode, "What's the Matter with San Francisco: How Silicon Valley's Ideology Has Ruined a Great City," *Paste*, 23 May 2016, https://www.pastemagazine.com

/articles/2016/05/whats-the-matter-with-san-francisco-how-silicon-va.html, both accessed 20 January 2018.

22. Carol Pogash, "Gentrification Spreads an Upheaval in San Francisco's Mission District," *NYT*, 23 May 2015, A10.

23. Dan Kopf, "San Francisco's Numbers Are Looking More and More Like a Tech Company's," *Atlantic*, 09 May 2016, https://www.theatlantic.com/business/archive/2016/05/san-francisco -diversity-migration/481668/, accessed 21 January 2018; PolicyLink, *An Equity Profile of the San Francisco Bay Area Region* (Oakland: PolicyLink, 2015).

INDEX

ACKNOWLEDGMENTS

This book is the product of kindness—manifested in multiple forms, spread out across decades and geographies, and imparted by more people and institutions than I will remember here. It is with immense gratitude that I acknowledge them for their goodwill and support.

Historical actors, community leaders, and activists in the San Francisco Bay Area contributed to this project in many ways. They shared memories and personal archives, referred me to individuals for interviews, granted permission to reprint images, and encouraged me to keep probing. I am indebted to Ena Aguirre, Donna Amador, Ramón Barbieri, Adrian Bermudez, Charles Bolton, Al Borvice, Carmen Carrillo, Brian Cahill, Celinda Cantú, Sal Cordova, Anita Correa, Gwen Craig, Luis Alberto de la Garza, Larry Del Carlo, Esperanza Echavarri, Luisa Ezquerro, Francisco Flores, Herman Gallegos, Pete Gallegos, Bob Gonzales, Juan Gonzales, Roberto (Bob) Hernandez, Roberto Y. Hernandez, Manuel Lares, Andrew Lesser, Toby Levine, Spence Limbocker, Ruth Mahaney, Richard Marquez, Ben Martinez, Pilar Mejía, Mike Miller, Elba Montes Donnelly, Dorinda Moreno, Al Pacciorini, Albert and Dana Puccinelli, Jim Queen, Dhoryan Rizo, Gladys Sandlin, Concha Saucedo, Carol Ruth Silver, David Sánchez Jr., Eduardo Sandoval, Leandro Soto, Aaron Straus, Joanna Uribe, Judy Zalazar Drummond, and Alex Zermeño for their openness and helpfulness along the way.

Like most historians, I relied on the aid and know-how of archivists at numerous institutions, including the staffs of the Bancroft Library at the University of California (UC), Berkeley; the Special Collections and University Archives at Stanford University; the Special Collections at UC Davis; the Chicano Studies Research Center Library at UCLA; the Immigration History Research Center and the Social Welfare History Archives at the University of Minnesota; the Nettie Lee Benson Latin American Collection at the University of Texas, Austin; and the National Archives and Records Administration in Washington, D.C.; College Park, Maryland; and San Bruno, California. I am most appreciative for the assiduousness and assistance of Susan Goldstein, Christina Moretta, Tami Suzuki, and Tim Wilson at the San Francisco History Center, San Francisco Public Library; Deacon Jeffrey Burns and Chris Doan at the Archives of the Archdiocese of San Francisco; Kim Klausner and Rebekah Kim at the Gay, Lesbian, Bisexual, and Transgender Historical Society of Northern California; and Robin Walker at the International Longshore and Warehouse Union Library and Archives. Catherine Powell has backed this study since my first visit to the Labor Archives and Research Center at San Francisco State University; her expertise, advice, and dedication to labor studies enhanced the book's archival and interpretive dimensions. Catherine tirelessly identified manuscript collections, accommodated endless requests (in person and from afar), and frequently carved out time for illuminating conversations.

The middle sections of this book still contain morsels originally conceived while I was an apprentice at the University of Chicago. I thank the history department for taking a chance on me and the faculty who taught me and instilled a passion for historical inquiry, among them Kathleen Neils Conzen, Tom Holt, William Novak, and Amy Dru Stanley. Historical training under the guidance of George Chauncey and Mae Ngai was, simply put, extraordinary. Mae committed herself to my professional development early on, challenged me to think capaciously, and proffered ongoing wisdom. George saw scholarly potential in me long before I did. He engaged with my ideas sagaciously, believed in the research's merits, and counseled me in countless ways. I am honored to call George and Mae my mentors and friends.

Studying and socializing with Gabriela Arrendondo, Cathleen Cahill, Chad Heap, Clyde Long de Lugo, Theresa Mah, Dawne Moon, Andrew Sandoval-Strausz, Tiffany Trotter, and Mike Wakeford made my days in Hyde Park more meaningful, calmer, and less grey. Their solidarity and good cheer remain etched in my memory. While living in Chicago, I experienced the day-to-day wonders and tribulations of graduate school with Red Vaughan Tremmel. Red's brainpower, creativity, and love continue to impress and uplift me.

Over the years, many scholars have brainstormed with me, read fragments and drafts, served as conference commentators, sponsored fellowship applications, supplied professional advice, and fostered community over coffee, drinks, and meals. I am grateful for the insight, motivation, and generosity furnished by Luis Alvarez, Jyoti Argade, Eric Avila, Barbara Berglund, Nan Alamilla Boyd, Mark Brilliant, Kathy Brosnan, Al Camarillo, Margot Canaday,

Ernesto Chávez, Cary Cordova, Raúl Coronado, Arlene Dávila, John D'Emilio, Phil Ethington, Devin Fergus, Tom Foster, Marisa Fuentes, Matt Garcia, Christian Gonzales, Nicole Guidotti-Hernández, Ramón Gutiérrez, Christina Hanhardt, Mindy Hochgesang, Justeen Hyde, Mike Innis-Jiménez, Bill Issel, Ellen Iverson, E. Patrick Johnson, Regina Kunzel, Samantha Kwan, Aldo Lauria Santiago, Sophie Maríñez, Katynka Martínez, Patrick-André Mather, John Mckiernan-González, Martin Meeker, Joanne Meyerowitz, Magdalena Mieri, Lorena Muñoz, Michelle Nasser, Barry O'Connell, Colleen O'Neill, Monica Perales, Horacio N. Roque Ramírez, Raúl Ramos, Todd Romero, Vicki Ruiz, Margaret Salazar-Porzio, Guadalupe San Miguel, Alberto Sandoval-Sánchez, Myrna Santiago, Robert Self, Christina Sisk, Siobhan Somerville, Nicole Stanton, Steve Steinberg, Landon Storrs, Susan Stryker, Arlene Torres, Linda Veazey, Steve Velasquez, Richard Walker, Eric Walther, Carmen Whalen, Mark Wild, and Nancy Beck Young.

I have had the immense fortune to count on Lorrin Thomas, Steve Pitti, and Lilia Fernández as key interlocutors and allies. Lorrin read the entire manuscript judiciously and with zeal. She grappled rigorously with my interpretation, made superb recommendations for sharpening concepts and linkages, and urged more boldness with some assertions. Steve graciously spent time with an early version and flagged areas for improvement before peer review. He pressed me to clarify its stakes while commending my approach. Lilia has read many chapters, always dispensed constructive feedback, and mulled over my study's arguments and implications, in person and via telephone, on infinite occasions. She has regularly reminded me of its significance, cheered me on, and enriched my labors with optimism and friendship.

Encouragement and endorsement from colleagues at Hunter College buoyed me up as I wrote and revised. I thank Linda Martín Alcoff, Angelo Angelis, Rick Belsky, Anthony Browne, Sarah Chinn, Jennifer Gaboury, Pedro Juan Hernández, Ben Hett, Daniel Hurewitz, John Jones, Karen Kern, Edwin Melendez, Catherine Raissiguier, and Jonathan Rosenberg for their collegiality and well wishes. Words cannot fully encapsulate my gratitude to Donna Haverty-Stacke and Mary Roldán for their gravitas, leadership, compassion, and faith in me. Mary and Donna have staunchly championed my scholarship and career. I am delighted and privileged to count them as friends and colleagues.

To say that collaborating with Bob Lockhart at Penn Press has been rewarding is a sheer understatement. Bob is a phenomenal editor, and I remain awed by his acumen, ethic of care, patience, and enthusiasm for this project.

I also owe a great deal to the anonymous scholars who reviewed my work; they approached it with perspicacity, raised vital and probing questions, and offered invaluable suggestions to strengthen my analysis. Many folks at Penn Press, including Liz Hallgren, Lily Palladino, and Pat Wieland, labored energetically during the transition from manuscript to book; their talents and professionalism proved indispensable during the production stages. My sincere appreciation as well goes to Mike Webster at the San Francisco Planning Department for designing city maps, Sandra Spicher for her indexing services, and everyone who assisted in tracking down images.

Portions of Chapter 5 previously appeared in "Voice and Property: Latinos, White Conservatives, and Urban Renewal in 1960s San Francisco," *Western Historical Quarterly* 45, no. 3 (Autumn 2014): 253–276, and are reprinted here with permission from Oxford University Press.

Numerous grants and fellowships subsidized and sponsored my scholarship over the years. At Hunter, the Presidential Travel Award Program, the PSC-CUNY Research Award Program, and the Presidential Fund for Faculty Advancement provided monies for research, conference participation, and some publication costs. A semester-long visiting fellowship from the Center for Puerto Rican Studies afforded me precious time to write. Before settling in New York, a Chancellor's Postdoctoral Fellowship at UC Berkeley allowed me to conduct a year's worth of new research and to reconceptualize my framework. Funding for early work came from the Five College Fellowship for Minority Scholars, the Social Science Research Council Sexuality Research Program, the James C. Hormel Fellowship administered by the Lesbian and Gay Studies Project at the University of Chicago, and a Trustee Fellowship from the Social Sciences Division also at the University of Chicago. It is satisfying to credit them for investing in my education and development as a scholar.

Along with material support, dear friends, scholarly soulmates, and family have given me the gifts of camaraderie and emotional sustenance, which buttress me and feed my spirit. A heartfelt shout-out to Elida Bautista, Gloria Chacón, Manuel J. Contreras, Sandra Contreras, Francisco Dueñas, Eric Kessell, Simon Craddock Lee, Blanca Milloff, Nancy Raquel Mirabal, and Karen Orellana for nourishing me with joy, merriment, all kinds of advice, and boundless affection.

The words and actions of Edward Master in Chicago and Victor Rey Valdiviezo in San Francisco consistently concretize the meaning of unconditional friendship. Edward and Victor have stood by me since my graduate-school days, attended to my well-being from afar, doled out common sense, and always believed that the book would be perfect bound. I am immensely grateful for their magnanimity, thoughtfulness, loyalty, and good-natured spirit.

I am beyond lucky to benefit from Claudia Millian's brilliance, wit, and loving kindness on a regular basis. Claudia has been a scholarly and emotional anchor for decades. She has emboldened me to excel and take risks, nurtured me during trying times, and enlisted me as her copilot on many fantastic adventures.

This book, my vocation, and life as I know it simply would not be possible without the love, benevolence, and understanding of my mother, Amanda Contreras. Her trust, comfort, and steadfastness sustain me. *Mil gracias, mamá,* for facilitating and affirming my academic pursuits, curiosities, and explorations.